CRIME MOVIES

CARLOS CLARENS

CRIME MOVIES

From Griffith to the Godfather
and Beyond

W·W· NORTON & COMPANY· NEW YORK· LONDON

FIRST EDITION

This book is typeset in Linotype Caledonia, with display type in Foundry Bernhard Fashion and Comstock. Manufacturing is by the Maple-Vail Book Manufacturing Group. Book design is by Marjorie J. Flock.

Library of Congress Cataloging in Publication Data
Clarens, Carlos.
    Crime movies.
    Bibliography: p.
    Includes index.
    1. Gangster films—History and criticism. I. Title.
PN1995.9.G3C5   1979   791.43'0909'353   79-12313

ISBN 0–393–01262–X

1 2 3 4 5 6 7 8 9 0

CONTENTS

CRIME
MOVIES

INTRODUCTION

What we call Evil in this World, Moral as well as Natural, is the grand
Principle that makes us sociable Creatures, the solid Basis, the Life and Support of all Trades and Employments without Exception: That there we must
look for the true Original of all Arts and Sciences, and that the Moment Evil
ceases, the Society must be spoiled if not totally dissolved.

— Bernard Mandeville: *The Fable of the Bees,* 1714

NOT LONG AGO a critic or film historian could be laughed out of the field
for asserting one or more of the following propositions: that American
films reflected a sense of American history; that film art and the social
experience of filmmakers were inseparably bound together; that film genres
should be acknowledged as the one concept to take into consideration the
artist, the industry, and the society that encompasses them. Film theorists
may continue to debate the validity of the concept of genres in film study,
and even whether their existence should be admitted at all, but such problems have never particularly worried filmgoers, who, long before the controversy reached academic circles, had created their own genre categories:
"cops-and-robbers," "Westerns," "horror movies," "musicals." Genres, in fact,
were forged in the experience of movie-going: themes were reused, types
and situations became familiar, and a landscape more psychological than
physical was created. In other words, a "norm" was provided which the
great films would in time transcend. It is through the concept of genre that
an individual work like, say, John Ford's *The Searchers* (1956) assumes a
relation to a hundred lowly cowboy movies.

In the thirties and forties, critics here and abroad preferred to imagine
that Hollywood studios existed in a vacuum, inured against contemporary
reality by movie moguls attentive only to the demands of the film market.
To these critics, particularly Paul Rotha in England, Georges Sadoul in
France, and James Agee in this country, Americans went to the movies to
escape reality. They believed that the only "good" American films were the
ones that broke away from the industry's "conveyor belt" and turned their
backs on "mass appeal."

In the fifties, the *auteur* critics became the champions of individual film
artists. French critic Alexandre Astruc drafted the *auteur* theory around
the felicitous metaphor of the camera-as-fountain-pen (a film should be
read as a text); the cumbersome production hierarchy, which included the
screenwriter and the cinematographer, was subsumed into the director's
will for self-expression. Paradoxically, some of the directors most revered
by these critics were those who had toiled longest within the system, ful-
filling their obligations to the industry by turning out profitable products.

In the past decade, structuralism has availed itself of the notion of genre. A film is still to be considered as a text, but authorship is of minor consequence—one text reflects all texts. The primary aim is to isolate structures (filmic constructions) and to establish an organization at that level. But structural criticism in the cinema is too constricted an approach for a generation reared on the *auteur* theory. For instance, Colin McArthur's *Underworld USA* (Secker and Warburg, 1972), an otherwise lucid and valuable book, deviates from its generic approach to crime films to analyze the contribution of certain directors; yet McArthur's bias remains auteuristic and he ignores genre pillars such as Phil Karlson, Joseph H. Lewis, and Roger Corman.

The homespun quality of European films, retained by virtue of lesser industrialization, has often been extolled as an artistic alternative to Hollywood professionalism. But it is precisely in terms of their appeal and rate of consumption that American pictures are such unique artifacts for sociologists and historians. Many mass-produced films show artistic merit as well as a consistency of inspiration on the part of the director. In fact, it was genres that perpetuated structure and format in films. More significantly, genres enabled the industry to take into account fluctuations of public opinion. (It did not take long for film manufacturers to realize that "If at first you did succeed, try, try again"—mainly along the verified guidelines provided by genre. As early as 1904, Edwin S. Porter was remaking his most popular works, in addition to those of other directors, for the Edison Company.) The film / audience relationship also suggests another definition of genre: a series of films intended to arouse a specific response in the viewer. (Horror films, for instance, embrace a variety of themes, but can be grouped together in their intention to scare audiences.) Obviously, some adjustments in critical approach are in order.

The most recognizable film genre is the Western, providing (until recently) an energetic, epic vision of America during its years of expansion. The Western captured the European imagination in a way no other genre did, and to such a degree that it could safely be said that the American historical myth was essentially cinematic and violent. Whereas the Western deals with a fixed set of events in the past, crime films offer the reverse, critical view of the same myth of America based on more contemporary events. A sizable shelf of genre studies of the Western already exists, and there are quite a few works on the horror film, a genre better defined by intent that by content. But the crime film is more difficult to isolate, lacking as it does the readable iconography of the Western and the clarity of intent of the horror film. Cars and weaponry may function as identifiable signs, but what can be said to be the true intent of the crime film? To awaken in the viewer a civic conscience? To instill an awareness of a fallible society? To establish distance from a very real problem?

A close relative of the crime film is the psychological thriller (during the forties they seemed to substitute for the more traditional cops-and-robbers story). But in thrillers—be it *Laura* (1944), *Shadow of a Doubt* (1942), or even *Kiss Me Deadly* (1955)—the characters are much less emblematic than in crime films, and the viewpoint concerning criminals tends to be esoteric; society, since it is not directly involved, is absolved from responsibility for wrongdoing. The thriller deals with violence in the private sphere; at any moment, the detective's role can be usurped by another character, even the prospective victim. In a crime film the role of the lawman cannot be usurped. In a thriller, characters almost exclusively represent themselves; in crime films they must also represent the Criminal, the Law, and Society. (What might Clifton Webb represent, in *Laura* or *The Dark Corner* (1946), other than the Museum of Modern Art or his own exquisite demon?)

Since 1948 no serious film critic has failed to take into account Robert Warshow's famous essay, "The Gangster as Tragic Hero," which first appeared in *Partisan Review* (February, 1948). Indeed, most critics have allowed Warshow to do their homework for them. Looking back on gangster movies of the thirties after a hiatus of four years of war, Warshow saw the genre as a protest. "The gangster is the 'no' to that great American 'yes' which is stamped so large over our official culture" is probably the most overquoted observation pertaining to the genre. And it is dead right with respect to *Little Caesar* (1931) and *Scarface* (1932), the two films cited by Warshow in the essay from which it is taken ("The Westerner," *Partisan Review,* March-April, 1954). But Warshow stopped looking at gangster movies too soon. He had no regard for a contemporary film like *The Kiss of Death* (1947), simply because it failed to fit his thesis. Even if one allows for Warshow's historical moment, his essay fails to encompass such major crime-film variations as the grass-roots gangster of *High Sierra* (1940), the professional gunman who is above and beyond social advancement in *This Gun for Hire* (1942), or the nihilistic title character of *Dillinger* (1945). "The gangster is a man of the city," wrote Warshow. One wonders what he would have made of *Bonnie and Clyde* (1967) or *Bloody Mama* (1970). Would he have labeled the title characters "outlaws" and included them in "The Westerner"? Warshow categorized the gangster as being inescapably doomed. What would his reaction to *The Godfather* (1972) have been? Would he have qualified it as a dynastic chronicle in the line of, say *Cimarron* (1931)? Like most social commentators of the forties, Warshow limited genres to one dimension apiece, in order to suit his own, bruised, liberal sensibilities. The gangster in the iconography of the crime film has, however, emerged in as many variations as there have been costume changes.

Crime films (except at their most naive) often close on a note of temporary truce which subsequent crime films inevitably compromise. Even those thirties paeans to the G-man admitted that fighting crime was an unending struggle (as close as the FBI ever came to making an existential statement). There is no feeling of resolution, only of a society in flux, and of an industry within it. The great "yes" that Warshow saw in official American culture has been done away with by history and the programed shocks of the pop culture of the sixties. We are left to chart the historical patterns of the century with a thousand tales of mayhem.

It was inevitable that the Western would eventually disappear (temporarily, one hopes) from the American screen as soon as the response of the mass audience ceased to be predictable. To a large segment of the American public in the sixties and seventies, the Western suddenly stood for everything imperialistic and genocidal about America. The subtle ambiguities that made for the beauty of the genre largely went ignored; the sheer precision of Western types and situations worked as a factor in the genre's demise. The paradox is that the Western, at first regarded as the lowliest (that is, the most popular) of genres, is in fact the most stylized, the most intellectual, the genre most removed from the common experience of the viewer. Few spectators have actually felt the lure of the great open spaces; most have, however, experienced a suggestive *frisson* of recognition and anticipated violence at the sight of a car parked in a dark alley. The Western went thataway in the direction of television, and even there it barely survives.

But the crime film continues to thrive in its manifold mutations. By now the genre must surely have earned the right to be approached as neither a producer nor a controller of crime, but rather as the expression of America's changing attitudes toward crime. Crime films work in terms of transgression and retribution, just as horror movies tend to symbolize the normal and the monstrous in terms of what society may or may not tolerate. To expect crime films to take up the fight against crime in American cities is as naive (in terms of entertainment) and as antiquated (in terms of aesthetics) as to expect horror movies to banish nightmares from the collective unconscious. Like art, genre is more concerned with articulating facts than with manipulating them. Because they are so near in time to actual events, crime films provide a useful means to review a major strain of American violence along a dynamic continuum. They have taught us to look over our shoulders at night, and, as a result some of us are all the better off.

1. Characters in Search of a Genre

Much has been done, and is still being done, to wipe out this [gangster] evil which has long been a menace to the respectable citizen and this picture shows the situation as it is, and the extreme necessity for radical action on the part of the authorities.
— Blurb for *The Musketeers of Pig Alley* in the Biograph Catalogue, October 1912

NEW YORK'S OTHER SIDE: The Poor." This opening intertitle in D. W. Griffith's *The Musketeers of Pig Alley* established a geographic and social scene. It took the viewer slumming, away from uptown society, away from well-upholstered drama, into the seething topicality of Manhattan's Lower East Side—ghetto, melting pot, and red-light district, the fief of corrupt Tammany Hall politicians, the target of sociologists and reformers. In 1912, when the film was made, this turf was the setting for the most violent gang wars in the city's history.

Griffith's one-reeler—fifteen minutes at the projection speed of early silent pictures—was not an isolated phenomenon. Griffith himself had previously directed a number of slum melodramas: *A Child of the Ghetto* and *The Lily of the Tenements* in 1910, at least six others in 1911. And a number of contemporaneous productions with the word *gangster* in their titles are registered in the Catalogue of Copyright Entries of the Library of Congress; the notorious Black Hand secret society furnished the subject of a few more listed in the Film Index of the Museum of Modern Art in New York City. Unlike Griffith's work, however, most of these are either lost or unavailable, although their titles offer proof that poverty, corruption, crime, and social blight were familiar themes in early motion pictures.

The blurb in the catalogue released to exhibitors by the Biograph Company, Griffith's employers at the time, described *The Musketeers of Pig Alley* somewhat diffidently as "a depiction of the gangster evil" and went on to admit that the film "does not run very strong as to plot." *The Musketeers of Pig Alley*, for all that, rose above its faults. New narrative devices made it a key film not just within Griffith's own work but also in the context of the new genre.

The flacks at Biograph were right about the story. It was very slight, merely the thread of an anecdote on which Griffith hung a series of storytelling and representational innovations: A young couple moves into a tenement. To care for the wife's sick mother, the husband, a musician, takes a daytime job. The wife meets a brash young tough who later robs the husband of his wages. The mother dies alone in the parlor. At a dance hall, the tough prevents a pimp, member of a rival gang, from drugging the wife, a gesture that leads to a shootout in an alley between the two gangs. The tough survives, and the grateful wife rescues him from the law by lying on his behalf.

It is evident from the above that two seemingly incompatible sets of characters were brought into conflict in the story. The young couple pointed straight back to Dickensian bathos; for all the naturalism of their playing, The Little Lady (Lillian Gish) and The Musician (Walter Miller) were threatened innocents cut from Victorian cardboard; they would not be out of place in *Little Dorrit* or *The Old Curiosity Shop*. Dickens was to be a source of inspiration to Griffith throughout his career, even though *The Cricket on the Hearth* (1909) was the only direct adaptation from the novels. Obviously Griffith, like Dickens, felt very much at home in the cozy squalor of the lower classes. However, the second scene in *The Musketeers* introduced The Snapper Kid, Griffith's slum tough, who was closer to George M. Cohan than to Bill Sykes. As played by Elmer Booth—a professional stage actor unrelated to the celebrated theatrical family—Snapper came straight from the street life of 1912 to invade the Dickensian universe of the hero and heroine. With a cigarette dangling from his lips, wearing his hat at an aggressive angle, and tugging at his trousers with a boxer's behavioral reflex, he represented a new addition to the gallery of film types. His gangster was a rough, urban, back-alley Huckleberry Finn.

While The Little Lady and The Musician were capitalized conventions, The Snapper Kid was as idiosyncratic as his monicker. What made *The Musketeers,* despite the corny associations of its title, the most modern of Griffith's urban dramas was the absence of moralizing of any kind; the viewer entered a world presented as accomplished fact. The visuals no longer referred to previous pictorial influences such as the Millet images of *A Corner in Wheat,* but rather to the photographs of Jacob Riis, Arthur D. Chapman, and Alice Brower; a world of street arabs, hurdy-gurdy men, immigrants, and beggars; surly, secretive faces that never quite opened up to the viewer. The Lower East Side, location for the picture's all too brief street scenes, teems with life, a riot of races and types captured on the wing some sunny day by Griffith's cameraman, Billy Bitzer. The Little Lady walks along a crowded street that could be Delancey or Mott or Forsythe. (The scene was actually photographed on the much safer grounds of West 12th Street.) For an instant, reality overwhelms fiction. Two girls in the background of the shot stare openly at the camera, a man with a bowler hat and a forked beard sits in the sunshine—perhaps plumbing a Talmudic point. This is New York in the early part of the century, "a devil's dream, the most urbanized city in the world," as Michael Gold described it with a native son's affection and despair in *Jews Without Money*—the city that devours waves of immigrants and unwary small-towners, the symbol of American progress and American corruption.*

---

* The Lower East Side had, in fact, been used as a location since 1905, especially by the Edison Co., *vide* their *Desperate Encounter between Burglars and Police.*

All the interiors were shot at the Biograph studio, where the director attempted to preserve this big-city atmosphere. Griffith, who had perfected camera movement as early as 1909, notably in the lovely, airy panoramic sweeps at the beginning and end of *The Country Doctor,* now stressed the claustrophobic intimacy of the slum with static shots; in his Westerns and his rural stories, the camera often seemed to seek the open air, hungry for space; the city could not offer either. Instead, the film developed depth of field and diagonal movements of the characters across the frame. It defined the tensions of the disputed territory by having the rival gangs go through

Immigrants and toughs in "Bandit's Roost," photographed by Jacob A. Riis in 1895, the year movies were born. *Museum of the City of New York*

the same motions, the same entrances and exits; petty crooks on a treadmill fighting for each alley as if for a separate nation.

The highlight, a shot that has found its way into film courses and anthologies, shows The Snapper Kid and his sidekick (Harry Carey), a sallow-faced simpleton who vainly apes the Kid's insouciance, advancing toward the camera along a brick wall. Closer, closer they come until Snapper's face fills half of the screen and his companion hovers in medium close shot right behind. This motion forward was itself a negation of theatrical space, which the film upheld in those scenes laid in the heroine's parlor, with its uniform lighting, backdrop wall (bearing the American Biograph monogram as a bar to plagiarism or outright theft), and the sides of the screen standing for lateral partitions. Griffith, in fact, had devised the entire film in terms of the dialectical opposition of depth and flatness, street and home, space as milieu and space as limit. All of these are concerns of film theory to this day.

The Musketeers of Pig Alley also documented a change of sensibility in Griffith's films. This was no temperance lecture as were *What Drink Did* and *Brutality;* the approach to the various social problems was cool, matter-of-fact. The then-current specter of white slavery was raised in the dance-hall scene, when a man in a straw hat, later identified as a rival gang member, spikes the heroine's lemonade with some suspicious powders. (She should hardly be in such a place; but then, girls must dance.) Neighbors in a back alley mingle with prostitutes casually plying their trade. In one beautifully

Early film gangsters: The Snapper Kid (Elmer Booth) tries his charm on The Little Lady (Lillian Gish) as his less enterprising sidekick (Harry Carey) sulks. *The Musketeers of Pig Alley,* 1912. *Museum of Modern Art*

"The Gangster's Feudal War." *The Musketeers of Pig Alley. Library of Congress*

sustained shot, the gun battle in Pig Alley fills the frame with smoke as bodies contort and fall. The intertitles twice refer to higher echelons of crime and corruption, and toward the ending there occurs an inspired visualization of the film's theme: a crafty, smiling policeman indicates the saloon door to The Snapper Kid; a moment later, a hand appears through the half-open door and passes some bills to the cop, as the final intertitle in the picture announces, "Links in the Chain," and we retreat into the safety and moral comfort of a Victorian happy ending, The Musician embracing The Little Lady, one arm aloft in defiance at the city.

That disembodied hand was a bold Griffith touch that defined what could be filmed and what could not, a metonymy for the whole corrupt, graft-ridden system. Two weeks before the film's release in October 1912, "Big Jack" Zelig, a notorious gang leader with connections in Tammany Hall, was shot and killed by unknown gunmen on a 13th Street trolley car, just a few blocks from the Biograph studio at 11 East 14th Street. Three weeks before, while the picture was in production, New York had been shocked by the murder of gambler Herman Rosenthal, gunned down in front of witnesses at the Cafe Metropole, a hangout for Broadway lowlife on 43rd Street, by hired killers who obviously enjoyed immunity from the police. The killing had been ordered by Charles Becker, a lieutenant on the police force who got rich collecting graft from nearly every gambling, prostitution, and protection racket in Manhattan. The city was parceled out among the many gangs. The Lower East Side belonged almost exclusively to the Five Points Gang (named after the crossing of Broadway and the Bowery); the Eastman Gang controlled a territory that stretched from 14th Street to Monroe Street, and from the Bowery to the East River; Chinatown was split among numerous Tongs; Little Italy was disputed by the Black Hand and the Unione Siciliane. The skirmishes and wars that resulted from the infringement of each other's territory held New York in thrall that year.

For Griffith, as for many of his contemporaries, the city was the locus of crime and corruption. Griffith was a southerner, and the South had held to the Jeffersonian vision of a gracious, independent agrarian society. There was an effective ellipsis in an earlier film, *The Modern Prodigal* (1910): it opens with the country hero on the road to a city visible on the far horizon; the following shot, from exactly the same angle, shows the same man, now wearing convict stripes, running from the city. The city as moral pollutant was to exert a lasting hold on American beliefs, and, even though most of Griffith's literary models belonged to the older, genteel tradition of letters— Fenimore Cooper for the redskin stories, Bret Harte for the Westerns, and, of course, Dickens and Poe—he also adapted Frank Norris's *A Deal in Wheat* and must have been conversant with the work of Theodore Dreiser, both authors who used the city as a symbol of the frustrated American ideal in their break with nineteenth-century literature. Griffith's natural sympathies lay with the Horatio Alger innocents and hicks, but The Snapper Kid and the modernity he represented obviously fascinated him. From the lower left angle of Riis's photograph "Bandit's Roost" (1895), the real slum counterpart of The Snapper Kid gazes hermetically at the camera; in *The Musketeers of Pig Alley*, Griffith has captured him forever.

The underworld milieu reappeared in Griffith's epic *Intolerance* (1916), as background for the modern episode. This portion of *Intolerance* was later released in 1919 as an independent feature titled *The Mother and the Law*. Some of the notions and characters derived from *The Musketeers*, but the development was more complex; in the intervening four years Griffith had made *The Birth of a Nation*, and both he and the motion picture had taken a quantum leap forward. In *Intolerance*, the theme of the city as corrupting influence was woven into that of social injustice through the ages, the film's leitmotif.

Griffith based the modern episode of *Intolerance* on the bloody Colorado mining strikes of 1914. Violent reprisals following a strike force the main characters to leave their small town and seek their fortune in "the great city nearby." The Boy (Robert Harron) is recruited into a gang run by a hoodlum identified as The Musketeer of the Slums. According to one title card, "caught in the meshes of an environment too strong to escape," The Boy becomes "a barbarian of the streets." One girl (Miriam Cooper) becomes the gangster's mistress and, eventually, his murderer. Another young woman, The Dear One (Mae Marsh) is sustained by her Catholic principles and redeems The Boy from his life of petty crime after they marry. The gangster's death, however, is pinned on the young husband, and he is sentenced to hang. The wife, aided by a sympathetic policeman, manages to discover the identity of the murderer, and The Boy is snatched from the scaffold at the climax of one of Griffith's expertly constructed last-minute rescues. The three principal performers worked wonders with their rather sketchy characters, but Walter Long, as The Musketeer of the Slums, was a disappointment after Elmer Booth's Snapper Kid. (Booth, incidentally, had been killed in Los Angeles in a car crash in June 1915, just as *The Mother and the Law* was being readied. We can wistfully imagine the criminal allure he would have brought to the role.)

Griffith's achievement, for the most part preserved, has obscured that of lesser-known and thus less fortunate contemporaries and disciples. A 1915 film entitled *Regeneration* has recently resurfaced to add a much needed perspective on the period. It is the work of Raoul Walsh (then R. A. Walsh), who had played John Wilkes Booth in *Birth of a Nation* and assisted Griffith in its making. *Regeneration* was adapted from a popular play, Owen Kildare's *My Mamie Rose*, which was set in the Bowery and considered partly autobiographical. Owen, an orphan of the slums, runs away from brutish, drunken foster parents to find home and livelihood in the streets. He grows up to be a petty gangster (played by Rockliffe Fellowes), eventually redeemed through the influence of an aristocratic social worker (Anna Q. Nilsson) with whom he falls in love. The girl, however, is accidentally shot and killed by one of Owen's men; she reappears in a vision to prevent Owen from killing the culprit. One typical intertitle reads: "And then years pass and Owen still lives in a world where might is right—and where the prizes of existence go to the man who has the most daring in defying the law, the quickest fist in defending his own rights."

This was Walsh's first feature, and the camera setups in tenement halls and stairs inevitably recalled those of *The Musketeers of Pig Alley*. There were pictorial and symbolic effects, and occasional dips into bathos, that could be traced to Griffith as well. But the picture had its own tone and viewpoint. Walsh, a well-born New Yorker of Irish ancestry, was also sensitive to the promise of the city, not just its sordidness; he captured it in teeming, overhead panoramas that were more expansive than Griffith's street-level shots. And Walsh was attuned to the boisterous fun of street life, even to the good times to be enjoyed at Grogan's saloon, which would be anathema to the master. Whereas Griffith exhibited a Victorian moral view of poverty and crime—the deserving criminal issuing from the deserving poor—Walsh elaborated his own brand of Social Darwinism: "the most daring," "the quickest fist," assured the survival of the fittest in a competitive society. Ideologically at least, Walsh belonged to the next generation.

In January 1910, Griffith had fled New York in search of the sun; the slums and tenements in *Intolerance* are bathed in the southern California light and seem less crowded and squalid for it. Back East, most of the exterior photography had to be done early in the morning, while the light remained sharp and transparent. During the long winter months, sufficient outdoor light was not often available, and this slowed down production, even though the Biograph studio was equipped with Cooper-Hewitt mercury lamps for indoor shooting. Not wanting to be restricted by the weather, Griffith persuaded the Biograph front office to let him work in California in the wintertime. By the time he set a camera tripod on Los Angeles soil, other companies had been operating there for years. First to arrive was the Selig Company from Chicago, in 1907. As had Griffith's, Selig's move had to do with the vagaries and logistics of film production; the company came to photograph seascapes for its production of *The Count of Monte Cristo.*

But other companies had traveled to California for financial reasons. The choice of southern California as a production center was an effort by less prominent independent companies to flee the attacks and interference of a trust established in 1909 by the Patents Company, a coalition of the seven major domestic producers. Controlling film production through a monopoly of Thomas A. Edison patents, the trust could threaten to confiscate projection equipment or to cut off exhibitors' picture supply if they accepted films produced by other companies. Instead of crushing competition, however, the monopoly begat even more. So-called outlaw companies appeared overnight. They had no legal right to use the Trust's trump card, the much disputed Latham Loop (a device to control the flow of film from the large supply rolls and diminish jerky projection) and no legal access to the perforated film stock manufactured by George Eastman in Rochester, New York. Even so, ways were found to detour large shipments of film into the hands of the independents. And, whatever the hardships, the independents made up for any technical shortcomings by becoming more cinematically inventive and adventurous.

The trust countered with seizures and raids on outlaw studios in Manhattan, the Bronx, and New Jersey. The most powerful of the independents—the Mutual, Universal, and William Fox companies—answered the subpoenas and injunctions with a countersuit for unlawful conspiracy in restraint of trade. While the case dragged through the courts, both factions resorted to strong-arm tactics, to sabotage, and even to disrupting showings with stink bombs. Rallying, Fox and his independent associates found a powerful protector in the crooked bosses of Tammany Hall. It became common procedure to hire squads of goons with experience in strikebreaking or the "protection" racket to cajole, threaten, and intimidate the opposition. Professional gunmen infiltrated the extras during the shooting of an independent picture in Whitestone Landing, Long Island, and the resulting brawl, according to historian Terry Ramsaye, landed several actors in the hospital. Although financially less powerful than the licensed companies, the independents were too numerous to accept such a flimsy dictatorship. Fox won his first battle against the trust in 1912, forcing the Patents Company to supply films to his exchange, but guerrilla warfare continued for some time.

The upshot of it all was that the independents decided to abandon the New York, New Jersey, and Chicago production centers of the period. They first went to Florida, where the weather proved to be so hot that film stock rapidly deteriorated. They pushed south to Cuba, but a seasonal outbreak of yellow fever scared them back into the United States. San Francisco was too far from the Mexican border in case warrants were issued. The safest location was Los Angeles, only a short ride to Tijuana and Ensenada, where a filmmaker could comfortably sit out any legal storms. As tempers started to cool, other advantages became apparent. In southern California, the weather was sunny most of the year, and smog was a word yet to be coined. Mexican labor was cheap and abundant; union troubles were still fifteen years ahead. Within an hour's drive, the scenery provided spectacular changes, from the beaches of Santa Monica to the canyons of Topanga to the urban settings of Los Angeles itself. There were acres of semirural landscape and miles of wide avenues and unpaved dusty roads, the background of so many early comedy chases.

As late as 1913, California was still disputed territory. Enough of the wild and woolly West survived to lend a touch of romance and danger to filmmaking. In his autobiography, Cecil B. De Mille affectionately recalled how criminal hands had attempted to sabotage the negative of his first effort, *The Squaw Man*. The attempt succeeded, and the film survived only because De Mille had had the foresight to strike a second negative in anticipation of foul play. About the same time, De Mille was twice ambushed by a hidden sharpshooter. Like most of the independents, he would not be deterred. Business was booming and huge profits were being reaped by even the lowliest of quickie manufacturers.

When, in October 1915, after years of lobbying from both sides, Judge Oliver B. Dickinson ordered the trust dissolved as a violation of the Sherman Antitrust Law, Hollywood, along with Edendale, Chatsworth, and other suburban patches of Los Angeles, had been thoroughly colonized by the motion-picture community. The ramparts of Babylon were rising over Sunset Boulevard in preparation for *Intolerance*. Skeptics called it Griffith's Folly, which it turned out to be; but even then the place, so distant from the political and cultural centers of the nation, seemed to inspire moviemakers with the wildest fancies, and it would continue to do so for the next forty years. When the First World War placed the American film industry in the position of having to supply 80 percent of the world market, Hollywood was ready to meet the demand. The decline of the eastern studios began around this time, partly because of the passage of the Wheeler Tax Law in New York in 1917. But the keystone of the Hollywood style—that unique propensity to fantasize reality into something much larger than life—lay precisely in its remoteness from the events. The studios in the Bronx, Harlem, and Fort Lee, no matter how well equipped, were to remain earthbound by comparison. In time, the growth of radio and television, of communication and transport, shortened the distance, but in Hollywood's heyday, in the twenties and thirties, when writers, performers, and directors were recruited in New York or abroad, California seemed as distant as Cytherea, Barataria, or Graustark. From the Hollywood distance, Chicago was mythical too, as it was for Bertolt Brecht in Berlin; for both, Prohibition seemed an absurd continuation of the Gold Rush, and the bootlegger seemed heir to the American pioneer spirit.

The late teens to the mid-twenties were prolific years, although much material from the silent era remains lost or unrecovered. One can only try to surmise from contemporary reports, production stills, and the pictures that have survived what trends shaped public taste for a decade and a half, or for that matter, how public taste asserted itself on the screen in the period between the pre–World War era and the jazz age. The filmed depictions of crime in the American scene up to that time were in traditional modes such as the chapter play, the crook melodrama, the cautionary tale of big-city corruption, and an occasional sermon on the perils of drug addiction.

The chapter play or serial, which was a great commercial success just before and during the war, had been imported from France but took strong root in America. Every generation has its own bugaboos and obsessions, and the skeletons in the Victorian closet continued to rattle in the United States long after the good queen had gone to her rest. In France, the dominant theme of serials like *Fantomas* or *Les Vampires* was the secret society run by an archfiendish criminal, a fantastication of the anarchist movement then sweeping Europe. In America, however, the serial found anarchists to be of insufficient menace. A letter from Frank Leon Smith* in the November 1965 *Films in Review* notes that "Every serial ever made was a kidnap story. The conflict of heroes and villains has to be personalized and visualized, sooner or later, in girl-grabbed and girl-rescued episodes."

The kidnap motif that recurred in those early series can be read as a projection of the white-slave paranoia of 1910, when reports of prostitution rings, circulated and exaggerated by reformers and bluenoses, convinced Americans that the way to handle the problem was to pass the Mann Act against transporting women across state lines for illicit or immoral purposes. Setting the pattern for later national scares, Stanley W. Finch, the director of the Bureau of Investigation, then barely one year old and still without a definite mission in the life of the nation, fanned the fires of hysteria by stating that "unless a girl was actually confined in a room and guarded there was no girl, regardless of her station in life, who was altogether safe."

The Mann Act was received with mixed relief—it constituted in fact a legalized intrusion into private morality—and was accepted only after all of America had found titillation in dozens of newspaper exposures, stage plays, and dime novels that purported to show the predicament faced by every woman not already a forcible resident of Chinatown or the Tenderloin.

The white-slavery film traveled rapidly from admonition to exploitation before being censored from the better theaters. But at least one, *Traffic in Souls,* benefited from a Broadway opening in November 1913 and subse-

---

* Smith was staff scenarist at New York's Pathé studios and the author of *Bound and Gagged* (1919), *The Phantom Foe* (1920), and *The Green Archer* (1925), among other serials.

quently enjoyed a long run at Weber's Theater, a legitimate stage house. Advertised as based on the findings of the *Rockefeller White Slavery Report*—the published results of four years of investigations conducted by a grand jury headed by John D. Rockefeller—the picture was full of thrills already familiar to theatergoers. There was a heroine—decoyed and trapped by a prostitution ring—whose delivery is effected through the combined efforts of her sister and a police officer. And there was a respectable businessman, the sister's employer and the founder of the International Purity and Reform League no less, who is revealed to be "the man higher up," the mastermind for "they who traffic in souls." Euphemism ran rampant in the intertitles: a pimp observed in the exercise of his functions is identified as "the most infamous type of man: The Cadet"; and this evasiveness was continued into the brothel's decor, which exhibited nothing of the plush popular image of such places and rather more resembled a boarding house where girls were kept in rooms with barred windows. Out of doors, at the docks and railroad stations where the pimps prey on gullible immigrants and country girls, the image gained considerable authenticity by presenting the placid workaday sights of Manhattan.

Traffic in Souls was made without the approval of the Independent Motion Picture Company (also known as IMP and a forerunner of the large and still active Universal Pictures) by a director named George Loane Tucker, who had access to the company's facilities and contract players. The picture was saved from destruction by a cutter, Jack Cohn (a future vicepresident of Columbia Pictures). Cohn edited its best sequences in the parallel-action style already perfected by Griffith, thus generating a suspense patently missing from the pedestrian individual scenes. The last-minute rescue scene was almost worthy of the master himself—and, interestingly, *Traffic in Souls* antedated *The British of a Nation* by more than a year. As policemen close in on the traffickers by stealthily climbing up fire escapes and occupying the roof of what is obviously a real building on New York's Upper West Side, the captive sister is being forced to undress by a madam wielding a whip—an act of somewhat symbolic nature since no customer is in sight. The action cuts back and forth between the certified Puritanical fantasy and the unfaked athletics of the cops outside. The first stroke of the whip is intercut with a shot of the policeman hero blowing his whistle to signal the attack, and the aural correspondence between these separate actions is thrilling. Unsure of its achievements, the film reverted to cardboard and stasis for its moral coda: the villain slumped on the bed of his wife who died of shame and chagrin. By then, however, *Traffic in Souls* had resourcefully spanned the polarities of outmoded convention and bold new film techniques with which American audiences would live for the next fifteen years.

The success of *Traffic in Souls* inspired *The Inside of the White Slave Traffic,* which lived up to its lurid title and also became a valuable document by featuring scenes shot in New York's Tenderloin district and in the bordellos themselves. But a subject that had been approved of when discreetly clothed in Victorian convention was suddenly rejected as indecent and offensive to the public, and the film's exhibition was periodically stopped by censor raids and close-downs. Thereafter, sequels like *The Exposure of the White Slave Traffic* and *House of Bondage* were denied access to respectable screens. *The Moving Picture World,* a trade magazine that spoke for an industry too recently established to run any risks, lowered the boom on vice films: "They are intended to stimulate and exploit the morbid interest in the harrowing details of a sickening and revolting aberration of the human soul." As often happened, the social issue all but disappeared, leaving behind only a set of plot devices which the serial was to improve upon.

The first serials earned their name from the fact that weekly or bi-weekly chapters could be simultaneously seen on the screen and read in magazines and newspapers. *What Happened to Mary,* which launched the vogue in 1912, appeared in regular installments in *The Ladies' World. The Adventures of Kathleen,* which followed, was sponsored by the *Chicago Tribune.*

Most popular of all was *The Perils of Pauline,* which could be followed on the screen and in a number of Hearst papers through most of 1914. William Randolph Hearst personally supplied its title, and so unwittingly became responsible for the flood of alliteration that ensued with *The Exploits of Elaine, The Hazards of Helen, The Mysteries of Myra,* and *Dolly of the Dailies.* Hearst was also responsible for the fervor with which the serials pursued his policies of white supremacy, and—after war broke out in Europe—of preparedness.

Most of the serials, as their titles reveal, were concerned with women in jeopardy; and most of the villains, when they were not sinister hooded figures from the unconscious (often unmasked in the final chapter as a close relative of the heroine or some such father surrogate), were gypsies, wogs, redskins, or Orientals, racist stereotypes whose machinations were usually tinged with sexual threat. As America became inevitably drawn into the war, these villains were replaced by the Hun, a barbaric aggressor to be openly feared and covertly desired, the prime example being Erich von Stroheim's Prussian officer, who became popular as The Man You Love to Hate.

The serials began in the French style, that is, in episodes that were complete in themselves, although tenuously linked by the same characters and general plot.* They soon evolved into cliffhangers in which hero or heroine or both were left in a tight spot at the end of the episode, and the next segment resolved the elaborate problem. According to Frank Leon Smith, this extreme peril was referred to as a "blue jeans" situation—*Blue Jeans* was a turn-of-the-century stage melodrama in which the hero was found in the archetypal position of being bound to a log headed for the buzz-saw. The American serial makers refined the formula by having the hero change places with the heroine, and they also threw in all the ornate machinery of Victorian mystery stories. And yet, in a world of secret panels, trap doors, under-

---

* A French director, Louis Gasnier, who had assisted Louis Feuillade in Paris, was codirector of *The Perils of Pauline* and others. Feuillade was the great serial director responsible for *Fantomas* and *Judex* in prewar France.

ground tunnels, and hand clutching in the dark, the virginal splendor of Pearl White and her sister amazons never came undone. Trapped in a lair of Chinese devil worshipers in episode 13 of *The Exploits of Elaine*, Pearl is spared rape, a fate worse than death, in favor of ritual sacrifice to an Oriental demon who demands a bride "blond, beautiful and not of our race." White was forbidden by contract to appear in public without a blond wig; her fairness was emblematic of white womanhood. Like her contemporary Douglas Fairbanks, she was athletic and optimistic; as with Fairbanks, physical prowess banished sexual implications from the periodic bouts of bondage and discipline.

But the resonances were there all right. Serials eventually became expert at building suspense; the early ones seemed inept and stolid by comparison, although flashes of invention enlivened their rickety mechanics of danger and release. (In *Elaine*, the hero's wiretapping device was an authentic touch of science fiction: the room drenched in arsenic uncannily prefigured the accidental Roman poisoning of Ambassador Clare Luce in the fifties.) The influence of the serials upon national life was judged wide enough to prompt President Woodrow Wilson to take an active hand in curbing the racist excesses of *Patria* (1916), another Hearst serial, this time with Mrs. Irene Castle in the lead and Warner Oland as a villain who could alternately be identified as Japanese or Mexican. The American government was in dispute with Japan over some Pacific bases, and there had been no diplomatic relations with Mexico since the punitive Villa expedition; still, Wilson wasn't going to permit such warmongering at home after keeping America out of the war abroad. (Imagine Franklin D. Roosevelt taking time off from the New Deal to monitor the diplomatic policies of *Flash Gordon* or *Buck Rogers*.)

As heroes replaced heroines in the serials, escapism took over from timeliness in determining the subject matter of films. By the twenties, the white-slave scare was only good for a sophisticated giggle, and bordellos were casually cropping up in big-studio films like Metro's *Man, Woman and Sin* (1927). It remained for fringe productions, most made cheaply in old New York studios, to exploit vice for old-fashioned thrills. *A Little Girl in a Big City* (1925) contained some wild brothel scenes that could be removed at the will of local censors. *Is Your Daughter Safe?* (1927) attacked prostitution in the general apathy toward a grave social problem, bolstering its drive with documentary footage of child victims of venereal disease. These were "exploitation" films for the Middletown audience. Despite, or possibly because of, their lurid situations, they harked back to the more innocent days of the Yellow Nineties, when brothels were as much a social problem as a collective fantasy. The plight of the heroines in films such as *Fifth Avenue* (1925) and *The Road to Ruin* (1928) could find no sympathy from, as F. Scott Fitzgerald wrote, "a whole race going hedonistic, deciding on pleasure." In the former, an innocent girl from the provinces is forced to spend her first night in the city at a brothel, and she later finds herself being blackmailed for her lack of discernment. In the latter, a flapper (Helen Foster)

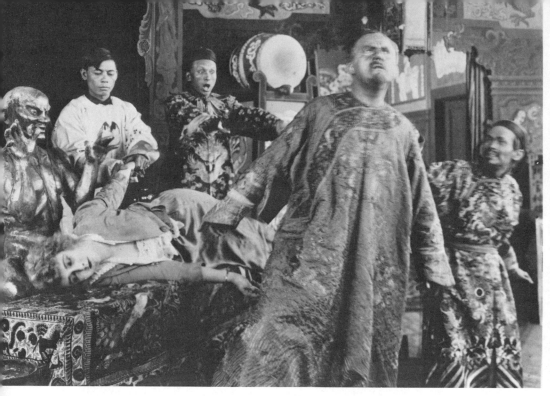

Girl trapped, girl rescued: the basic plot of the serial. Pearl White in the den of the Chinese devil-worshippers. *The Exploits of Elaine*, 1915. *Author's collection*

Milton Sills saves Irene Castle in *Patria*, 1916. *Author's collection*

A brothel without frills: John Gilbert, the unsophisticated hero of a highly sophisticated film of 1927, *Man, Woman and Sin. Metro-Goldwyn-Mayer*

sinks so low on the social scale that she must seek employment in a whore-house, where among her customers she discovers her own dissolute father. But these were isolated examples. By 1923, Hollywood and the movies joined the rest of the nation in celebration of the jazz age. According to Fitzgerald, they were four years late.

Drug addiction was frequently depicted on film in the teens, but in a curiously half-hearted manner that reflected the government's attitude to-ward the problem. Addiction was regarded as a character flaw in the indi-vidual or as the result of some tragic carelessness in prescription of narcotics, rather than as a major threat to society. In 1914, possession of heroin would get an American a mere nine months in prison, and it was not until the Harrison Narcotic Law was passed, on April 1, 1915, that the Treasury Department received official sanction to prosecute the legal manufacture and trade of opiates. (The choice of the Treasury Department, which seems unlikely today, was motivated by the fact that the antidrug bill imposed an occupational tax on prescriptions and patent medicines that contained narcotics or stimulants.) Almost overnight, many drug users found themselves penalized for their addiction. Victims were not only the habitual "hop-heads" or regular patrons of joss houses, but men and women who had unknowingly nurtured a dependence on paregoric or any number of patent elixirs containing opiates in fairly high quantities.

The limited urgency attached to warning people of the dangers of drug addiction, as compared to that of alcoholism, can be judged from the relatively small number of pictures that dealt with the former. Griffith, who made several one- and two-reelers at Biograph attacking the evils of the saloon (also the theme of his final feature, *The Struggle*, in 1931), approached but once the subject of drug addiction—in *For His Son*. In this 1911 one-reeler, an ambitious doctor (Charles Mailes) concocts and patents Dopo-Coke, a soft drink containing cocaine; it makes him a rich man, but his son (Charles West) dies in his arms, one of countless innocents who become addicted. The guilt was usually placed squarely on one individual with questionable motives, such as the satanic doctor in *The Devil's Assistant* (1917) who turns one of his patients (Margarita Fischer) to the needle in order to seduce her. With its red-tinted visions of hell, complete with Cerberus and Charon, this Mutual two-reeler qualified as early psychedelic. Other films dealing with drugs ranged from morality plays such as *The Dividend* (1916) to ordeals of trial and regeneration, *The Devil's Needle* (1916); from the casual inclusion of a dope addict among urban types in *The Penalty* (1920) to the resurgence in 1923 of antinarcotic feeling in *The Drug Demon* and *Human Wreckage*. The latter two appeared shortly after the death of actor Wallace Reid in a California institution where he was being treated for morphine addiction. Press and public absolved Reid of any guilt; it was disclosed that he had become addicted while being treated for a painful back injury sustained in an accident during the making of a film in 1919, and that he had shown great courage and resolve in trying to kick the habit. Reid's widow became active in national antinarcotic movements, making personal appearances in connection with *Human Wreckage*, in which she had played a role not too removed from her own experience as the wife of a famous addict. The picture was mostly sympathetic to users, especially to the character of a young mother (Bessie Love). A superimposed phantom hyena roams throughout the film, symbolizing the drug dealer, a small-scale (then) social evil, optimistically stamped out at picture's end. For a time Mrs. Reid became a free-wheeling crusader, appearing in an indictment of reckless driving titled *Broken Laws* (1924) and personally producing *The Red Kimono* (1925), an attack on prostitution that was infinitely less suggestive than its title. Even then, these pictures were regarded as curios; how could it be otherwise when small-town filmgoers were being tempted with

Patrons of the joss-house: Charles Ray and Ethel Ulman in *The Dividend*, 1916. *Author's collection*

the most lurid advertisements, promising "neckers, petters, white kisses, red kisses, pleasure-mad daughters, sensation-craving mothers, by an author who didn't dare sign his name." The film was *Flaming Youth* (1923), and its author was Samuel Hopkins Adams, a magazine writer and specialist in Americana, under the pseudonym of Warner Fabian. *Flaming Youth*, for the record, did not live up to its advance sales talk any more than *The Red Kimono* lived up to its lurid promise; it did, however, make a national figure of the "flapper," incarnated in the film by the young and fresh Colleen Moore, and the flapper thereupon practically put the streetwalker out of business, at least on screen, simply by making promiscuity fashionable.

Fifteen years elapsed between Griffith's "depiction of the gangster evil" and *Underworld* in 1927, unanimously regarded by cinema historians as the first gangster film with modern credentials. Indeed, *Underworld* seems to have sprung full-fledged from the head of its director Josef von Sternberg, if not from the typewriter of news reporter Ben Hecht.

According to Sternberg, *Underworld* was "an experiment in photographic violence and montage." But, apart from becoming a commercial success and the source of inspiration for many subsequent gangster films, *Underworld* meant different things to different people. "When I saw the first gangster films of von Sternberg," recalls the Argentinian writer Jorge Luis Borges in *Discussion*, "I remember that when there was anything epic about them—I mean Chicago gangsters dying bravely—well, I felt that my eyes were full of tears." And René Clair, the French filmmaker, wrote: "When the producers imposed on Sternberg the 'news-item' plot of *Underworld* ... they did not suspect that [it] would give birth to the poignant screen tragedies we know." Whatever it was, *Underworld* did not conform the scenarist Hecht's concept of gangster life and death in Chicago. Hecht had based his spare eighteen-page synopsis—full, by his own admission, of "moody Sandburgian sentences"—on a dozen years' experience on such Chicago dailies as *The Journal, The Daily News,* and *The Tribune and Herald-Examiner.* He had had a Broadway flop called *The Egotist* in 1923, but his credentials where crime was concerned were not to be disputed.

Hecht had never written a movie before, and he was relying on Arthur Rosson, a minor director with whom he had collaborated on the story, to preserve his vision on the screen. In Hollywood, Rosson was replaced by Sternberg, whose first film, *The Salvation Hunters,* had been extravagantly praised by Charles Chaplin, De Mille, and Griffith, among others, upon its release in 1925. The background of *The Salvation Hunters* was totally realistic, but the characters were wraithlike conceits that had little to do with reality, even as Hollywood understood it; which explains both the confusion and admiration the film garnered. *Underworld* was even less realistic—it was shot almost totally within the Paramount studio—as Hecht discovered much to his chagrin when the picture opened, without great hopes for success, in the summer of 1927. (Ironically, the film was a smash, and in 1928 Hecht won one of the first Academy Awards for his original story.)

In the pages of his autobiography, Hecht's Chicago—a construct of tabloid headings, hero worship, and sheer funk—doesn't seem all that real either. Sternberg's Chicago was simply "a great city in the dead of night," as the first title card proclaimed, recreated in the director's eye much the same way he would later recreate Morocco, China, or the Russia of the czarinas for his Marlene Dietrich films. Sternberg might just as well have started his picture with "Once upon a time in America, ..." as one might begin a saga or a fairy tale. Even before Sternberg introduced his characters, a montage set the style of the film somewhere between these two forms. In quick succession we are shown a clock tower, a waiting car, a drunk staggering along a sidewalk, an explosion inside a building which we instantly identify as a bank in the process of being robbed. None of this, however, is conveyed realistically. There follows an exchange via intertitle between the drunk, who is an unwilling witness, and the bankrobber Bull Weed, who storms out with his loot. Given the urgency of the situation, the dialogue is unlikely, to say the least:

DRUNK: The great Bull Weed closing another bank account.
BULL WEED (noticing the drunk is holding a bottle): That's what makes bums and
    squealers.
DRUNK: I might say, sir, that I'm a Rolls Royce for silence.

Bull drags the drunk, henceforth to be known as Rolls Royce, into the waiting car; it starts off, taking a corner at full speed, as a prone policeman shoots from the ground. Bull is subsequently revealed to be a kingpin of the underworld, a man at the top of his profession; Rolls Royce is identified as a disbarred lawyer at the bottom of the social ladder. The story is the graph of Bull's downfall and of Rolls's regeneration, the motivating forces being mutual respect and a moll known as Feathers McCoy.

Underworld may seem archaic when viewed in the light of current notions of gangsterism. Bootlegging was hardly mentioned, and Bull was presented as a simple gunman who robbed banks and jewelry stores. On the other hand, Metro had released *Twelve Miles Out*, adapted from a popular play, a full two months before *Underworld:* its hero, played by John Gilbert, was a rumrunner operating off the Long Island shore, at least nominally a more modern criminal than Bull Weed. The rumrunner's code of honor was tailored to the star's romantic looks however, and both suggested a gentleman thief or a soldier of fortune. Finally, it was Bull who projected the aura of the modern gangster.

The hearty handshake, the brutal bonhomie, the cunning cool in incriminating a rival while pulling a holdup—these became traits that stamped the actor George Bancroft as the embodiment of the gangster in silent pictures. Wired for sound, Bancroft's physicality somehow translated into mere bulk, but he had the right kind of crudeness for the self-made, first-generation hood.

Sternberg, rather than Hecht, elevated Bull Weed to heroic status by blemishing his pristine loutishness with the flaws of princes, lovers, and warriors: suspicion and doubt. It is safe to guess that the early Bull was mostly Hecht's creation and that the fall and moral redemption of the last reels belonged to Sternberg. To Hecht, as to Mark Hellinger and other twenties press prodigies, gangsters were not just good copy, but legitimate heirs to the robber barons of the nineties, to be cultivated and enjoyed and not too reluctantly admired. A gangster pal was both a badge of sophistication and a way of asserting that all successful Americans met at the top. In the early part of *Underworld*, Bull Weed and his exploits were full of a hearty humor that was not exactly Sternberg's brand. Bull Weed was a maverick in a world of criminal organizations, a bull loose in a series of china shops, dim enough to beam at a neon sign that promises him the city (actually an investment ad), illiterate enough to induce audience empathy. When Rolls Royce remarks with a tinge of irony: "Like Attila at the gates of Rome," Bull retorts with a guffaw: "Who's Attila? The leader of some wop gang?"

Unfortunately, Bull's two prize possessions—the shyster he rescued from skid row and the moll he has had elected queen of the yearly ball—are drawn to each other. Some of Rolls's class rubs off on Feathers, and soon Bull starts to feel pangs of jealousy. An inexorable chain of events, the need to assert his claim to Feathers, and his own sheer animal fury drive Bull to shoot Buck Mulligan, his lifelong rival in the underworld. Hecht, who based Mulligan on Dion O'Bannion, the only Chicago gangster ever to operate a legitimate flower shop, credited the inspiration for Mulligan's death scene to the experienced Hollywood screenwriter Herman J. Mankiewicz, who advised: "But you have to shoot [the villain] in the end. When he falls with a bullet in his forehead, it is advisable that he clutch at the Gobelin tapestry on the library wall and bring it down over his head like a symbolic shroud." As the scene concludes, Sternberg's gravity overcomes Hecht's flippancy, the cynical stage directions being played for stark light-and-shadow effect: Bull, haloed by streetlights in the dim backroom of a flower shop, shooting from inside his pocket, Buck laughing maniacally and clinging to a curtain that, ring by ring, gives way under his dead weight, grotesquely enfolding him. Sternberg then boldly cuts away to a judge passing the death sentence on Bull Weed for an act which, symbolically at least, stands for the killing of his own brutal self.

With Bull awaiting execution in the death house, the picture moved into a final, intricate weave of motives and loyalties. On the outside, Rolls and Feathers cannot help but consider their personal advantage in letting the law take its toll. "If we get Bull out, we're *his* again," says Feathers on the horns of her first moral dilemma; yet, rather than remaining just guilty lovers, they become involved in helping Bull escape. Their well-planned scheme fails, whereas Bull's impetuous dash for freedom succeeds. Reunited amid the dust and debris of a police raid on Bull's steel-plated hideout—the raw materials of the news item reworked by the director into a phantasmagoria of violence—the gangster realizes that, although Feathers and Rolls love each other, no betrayal has taken place. He gallantly allows them the chance to escape through a secret exit, himself staying behind to cover the flight. Ammunition soon runs out, and Bull is forced to surrender: he ties a white rag to the muzzle of his Tommy gun. Fondly caressing his weapon, he is a virtuoso bidding farewell to his instrument. His breakout has merely delayed the inevitable, a policeman reminds Bull, who smiles and says, "That hour was worth more to me than my whole life."

Underworld was a silent picture, so any attempt at realism was compromised beforehand. Bull inhabited a world of his own creation, limited by his actions and motives—the epic quality, in fact, that Borges detected in early Sternberg. The film's underworld partook of both the netherworld and a parody of society, never better defined than by the gangland annual ball— "a devil's carnival," announced an intertitle—during which the camera became a distorting mirror to render a montage of grotesque faces lost in a mass of paper streamers. The most defined citizens of this milieu, Bull and Buck, begin by behaving like rival politicos at a rally, then revert to brute force when Feathers becomes the disputed prize. Played by Evelyn Brent, Feathers was almost a mythical bird-woman; and time, which is to say film history, has left her exquisite vulgarity untouched, while more accurate or more realistic molls have dropped out of mind, as the power of the fable has proved to be more lasting than that of the news story.

In the last, doomed days of the silent era, *Underworld* launched a vogue

The bootlegger as hero: John Gilbert in *Twelve Miles Out*, 1927.
The girl is Joan Crawford. *Metro-Goldwyn-Mayer*

The gangster besieged and defined at last: Bull Weed (George Bancroft) fights it out with the police. His moll (Evelyn Brent) and best friend (Clive Brook) are allowed to escape. *Underworld*, 1927. *Paramount*

for gangster pictures. Many standard situations from the old "noble melo-dramas" were updated simply by alterations of the villain's wardrobe and weaponry and by introducing a certain glibness into the subtitles and lacing them with modern slang. (In the early years of the decade, Lon Chaney had played a proto-gangster hero in melodramas like *The Penalty* and *Out-side the Law:* a Gothic grotesque going about his shady business in a Lime-house of Hollywood's invention.) Following the release of *Underworld* by a few months, *The City Gone Wild* presented a reversal of standard hero and villain types. The film was written by Jules Furthman and his brother Charles, who had collaborated on the Sternberg picture. (The credits listed Charles Furthman as adaptor of Hecht's skimpy scenario, but his contribution was never regarded too seriously by either Hecht or Sternberg.) Lost for some years now, *The City Gone Wild* remains in the memory as marked by a definite striving for realism, but with visuals and direction (by James Cruze) on the prosaic side. The hero, a stalwart, incorruptible district at-torney, was played by Thomas Meigham; the gangster he tries to indict was played by Fred Kohler, Sternberg's memorable Buck Mulligan. About a year later, Meigham acted a variation of his D.A. role in *The Racket,* a film pro-duced by Howard Hughes, which may someday be rescued from the vaults. But Sternberg's own sequel of sorts, *The Drag Net,* again featuring George Bancroft and Evelyn Brent, this time around on opposite sides of the law, seems to be irretrievably lost.

Dressed to Kill (1928), however, has survived, and this film reveals a wit and a character of its own. It enlarged the lore and argot of the under-world and made points beyond Sternberg's concerns. It may have coined the image of the dapper, suave, humorous mobster who despises violence but is not above resorting to it. Mileaway Barry (Edmund Lowe) runs a speakeasy and a gang of hijackers, lives in tasteful surroundings, and seems to be leading a perfectly normal and happy criminal life when the picture introduces him—as if crime were just another symptom of economic over-growth, aggravated by an absurd legal experiment that had brought upper world and underworld closer together. Mileaway's career is brought to a violent and untimely end through his infatuation with Jeanne (Mary Astor), a girl posing as a thief and who is in reality trying to clear her boyfriend's name. Lowe and Astor rang variations of the tough-good-guy-on-the-make and the spunky-but-virginal-heroine, and their badinage was full of savory lines. Gangster: "Who's that petty-larceny Jane?" And to the girl: "What's your favorite name?" Later, in his digs: "You may be a good stall moll, but you can't stall me forever." And philosophically: "It only takes one dame to get nine [of] me in a mess." The background though, was quite authentic. There was a chilling suggestion of savagery now and then, as when a gun-man (Ben Bard) carefully shaves the tip of a bullet to make it "soft-headed," and more damaging to the victim. The gang's motto is "Everyone should be allowed to live, except stool pigeons." We see this put into practice when a police informer who works as a waiter is summoned to the office, and the hoods in their impeccable tuxedos close in on him; the man is offered a shot of whiskey: "Take a bracer, you're going to kiss the world goodbye," then a billow of smoke rises between the men, and there is a sudden cut to the orchestra playing fast and loud to drown the sound of the shot as couples crowd in on the dance floor. Two worlds coexisting in the harmony of supply and demand, with sudden death as the penalty for the one unforgivable crime of living in both.

Good as that silent pistol shot was in *Dressed to Kill*, it fell on deaf ears. Halfway through 1928, Warner Brothers released the first all-talking picture, *Lights of New York*. Combining the two current trends of the Broadway stage, the backstage musical and the gangster drama, this film was an attempt to cash in on the success of *Broadway*, the hit of the 1926 season, then in its second year in New York. *Broadway* had already been bought for the movies by Universal, and *Lights of New York* was a sort of trial run for all of Hollywood. It succeeded beyond expectations because of the novelty of sound. As a silent, it would have passed unnoticed, being static, flat, and crudely acted by actors in obeisance to some obviously concealed microphones. Audiences were treated to dialogue that was delivered in a rhythm that bore no resemblance to normal, or even theatrical, speech; no word could be uttered while the performer was in motion, and the pauses while the actors moved to and from the hidden microphones seemed an unearthly silence. Nonetheless, the impression created by those repetitive "Oh yeah?"s was enough to do away with a complete system of visual signs; not, however, before the silent movie had staged a final and extravagant display of what it could accomplish without words.

During this transitional period, there could be seen almost side by side such disparate representations of the criminal as those in *Forbidden Faces* and *Romance of the Underworld*, both made in 1928, the former a silent, the latter with sound effects but no dialogue. *Forbidden Faces* comprised a résumé of themes and techniques from thirty years of silence. Its most immediate reference was still *Underworld*, if only because the cast was made up of Sternberg regulars: Clive Brook, who played Rolls Royce, took the role of Heliotrope Harry, a character from the same timeless underworld that had spawned ethical jewel robbers like Arsène Lupin and Raffles, and William Powell, the gang boss in the lost *The Drag Net*, played his Apache sidekick. A tale of father love in a vaguely American contemporary milieu, the picture threw in a holdup, a prison riot, and an elaborate revenge scheme to pull off what amounted to a photographic tour de force. *Forbidden Faces* moved like a dream: after the obligatory intertitle to set the action in a nocturnal city, the camera soared giddily over a roulette table, then pulled back to reveal that a holdup was taking place; at the climax, the camera raced up four flights of stairs in pursuit of Harry's faithless wife (Olga Baclanova) and all but followed her down in her plunge to the street below.

Silence lent conviction to Heliotrope Harry. Even though the audience became familiar with Brooks's wellmodulated voice through his later work, it was well nigh impossible to imagine Harry's voice—one word would have

sufficed to frame him in a social context. Compared to Harry, the petty gangster played by Ben Bard in *Romance of the Underworld* badly needed
words. Instead of Brooks's expressive mime and the support of silence, the
role was fleshed out with behavioral bits (like the gangster's distasteful habit
of rubbing his shoe against his trouser leg) and a certain urban realism had
crept into the character to leave him stranded between two iconographies.
Romance of the Underworld was not as quaint as the title suggests. Originally a 1911 play and first filmed in 1918, this second film version bore no
relation to either of its precursors. Like *Forgotten Faces,* it was a tale of innocence threatened but ultimately preserved by fatherly intervention: A society wife and mother (Mary Astor) is blackmailed by a gangster whose
mistress she once was. She is saved by a middle-aged detective (Robert Elliott) who schemes to have the blackmailer shot by another crook and then
allows the killer to go scot-free for services rendered to the spirit of justice,
if not to the letter of the law. The values of that simple story seemed slightly
tarnished this time—as if during this intermediate stage, films were not simply wavering between silence and sound but also between fable and reportage and between the timeless verities they had long upheld and the acceptance of inevitable corruption.

Three events that left a permanent imprint on the American consciousness of the 1920s were Prohibition, the onset of the Depression, and the arrival of sound in the motion picture. These revolutionized American attitudes
in morality, economics, and esthetics, respectively. It is not an exaggeration
to view the third event as the one with the most lasting repercussions. Prohibition seems nowadays an absurd chapter in twentieth-century history, and
the Second World War eclipsed the pain and misery of the Depression while
allowing a romantic pentimento to emerge. But when pictures started to talk
and sing and make noises, they altered forever the way we perceive reality,
even the way we imagine ourselves to be. The beginnings of the talking
revolution are accurately annotated and can be discussed and analyzed; but
the final reverberations of those squeaky sounds are not yet anywhere within
ear range.

2. The Nights of Chicago

It's the new sensation of the films.

— Francis "Two Gun" Crowley, in his farewell note written
at the height of the Siege of West 90th Street, a gun battle
with the New York City police, 1931

THE MOMENT FILMS TALKED, the former continuum of silence was partitioned into syllables, words, lines, and dialogue; and, contrary to the expected, silence as a dramatic tool became more precious than ever. With sound, realism entered filmmaking, if only because cameras had to be cranked at a speed that would make gesture subservient to diction, the speed index at which images were recorded becoming that of the normal human voice. Even in the last summit silents, like *Underworld,* there was a jarring break between the fluidity of most of the scenes and the unnatural clumsiness of those demanding violent body movements. When the action became violent, it seemed like a technical mishap, as if the cameras had been cranked at some wicked speed. Sternberg's perfectly controlled actors turned into puppets whose grotesqueness had nothing to do with the stylization of the rest of the film.

The natural rhythm of sound regulates the speed of screen movement; otherwise we drift back into the spastic slapstick of the Keystone troupe or the balletic slow-motion of the great comedians at their most graceful. The sound film would find its middle range of realism, just as the silents had fitted an entire fabular content within their techniques; hence the much vaunted universality of silent cinema, which was expected to exact the same level of response as the other mute dramatic forms—ballet, pageant, and pantomime. No sooner had filmmakers learned to cope with sound, or technicians with the potential of recording equipment, than action in pictures became harmonious and lifelike. The fable was not totally destroyed. It was embedded in reality, overlaid with the factual, the anecdotal. That opening title in *Underworld* was all we needed to know: the city was a universal abstraction, sustained by silence. In the sound film, the city had to have a name, even if left unmentioned, and in due time, film not only identified its cities by name but transported the camera there to record the real buildings and streets. Even then, film was following in the steps of theater, which had also progressed (or regressed, according to value judgments) from the stylized to the realistic.

In France, *Underworld* was released as *Les Nuits de Chicago,* poetically a more apposite title and one that proved prophetic. The unnamed city was of course Chicago; at home and abroad the state of mind upon which Hollywood, safe and isolated, could spin a thousand violent fantasies. The French knew about Chicago from the tabloids, as did the majority of Americans. For Americans, Chicago was simply the most dynamic city in the union; by comparison, New York was tame and too sophisticated, Los Angeles a distant never-never land. Chicago was the city of Al Capone, where bootleggers shot it out in the streets, a semibarbarian outpost surviving the onslaught of corporate empires, technical innovations, and other signs of a premature American decadence.

In the twenties, Chicago was also the place in which journalism hardened into literature. A new school of writers found their inspiration, not, as had Norris and Dreiser, in America's loss of innocence, but in the vital interplay of violence, graft, and corruption that the city so generously provided. The movies had largely ignored this world while silence reigned, perhaps because facts were not that easy to arrange so that a moral conclusion could be drawn. Hecht had been betrayed, not by Sternberg as he thought, but by silence.

But from the moment that sound came, the great think-tanks that were the Hollywood studios watched Chicago closely, through the facts, figures, and fictions disseminated by a crime-happy national press.

Broadway had beaten the movies to the underworld. The 1927–28 season featured a spate of tough, fast-talking, liquor-and-crime melodramas including *The Racket, Nightstick, A Free Soul,* and a revival of the 1912 chestnut *Within the Law.* Most notable was *Four Walls,* in which the young Muni Weisenfreund (soon to become Paul Muni) played the leading role, that of Benny Horowitz, a Lower East Side gangster. Lee Strasberg and Sanford Meisner also appeared in it. All of these plays were bought for the films before they had finished their runs, except for *Within the Law,* which had already been filmed in 1917 and in 1923, and which would eventually resurface as *Paid,* a 1931 Joan Crawford vehicle.

The next Broadway season brought *Guns, Gang War,* and the archetypal newspaper comedy-drama, *The Front Page,* by Charles MacArthur and Ben Hecht (who had temporarily returned to his first love, the theater), as well as *Gentlemen of the Press,* the first of many copies. *The Criminal Code* appeared in 1929, inspired by recent prison riots in Canon City, Colorado, and Auburn, New York. The most successful and probably the most authentic of the crime dramas was *The Last Mile,* adapted by John Wexley from conversations set down by one Robert Blake, a prisoner awaiting execution for a murder committed in Texas. Blake had pathetically titled his memoir *The Law Takes Its Toll.* All the major studios vied for the right to this death-house drama, crude as the text may sound now. Both Spencer Tracy and Clark Gable made their marks playing a desperate tough named Killer Mears in different productions of *The Last Mile,* and both debuted in films as gangsters within the year. But it was Preston Foster who played the Mears role in the movie finally made in 1932, when crime films were dying the slowest death of any vogue in Hollywood. Most of these works improved on their passage to the screen, despite the bad recording and faulty delivery of the early talkies, simply because the swift, violent action they usually required could be more realistically staged on film.

One play that did not improve upon being filmed was *Broadway* (1929), mainly because Universal studios gambled one million dollars on the premise that audiences would rather hear the dialogue lifted almost intact from the original play, by George Abbott and Philip Dunning, than have it diluted by any filmic additions. A symbolic vignette enhanced the credits (a half-naked Satan sprinkling champagne over Broadway), but thereafter the action remained mostly confined to the Op Art vastness of a night club and to the few rooms backstage. A silent version was simultaneously made in consideration of the many theaters still unequipped for sound. It was full of elaborate camera movements and ran two reels shorter than the sound film—all the fast dialogue in fact slowed down the action. In the silent film, conversations were pared down to a couple of intertitles, and diametrically different impressions were obtained from watching the two versions.

As a play, *Broadway* had some modest pretentions to authenticity. The most sophisticated in the audience were familiar with the underworld's involvement in the night life and entertainment of New York; they could recognize in the play the likes of Larry Fay, who managed several night clubs for various mobsters, of Jack "Legs" Diamond, who owned The Hotsy-Totsy on Broadway and 44th Street, of Texas Guinan or Helen Morgan, both of whom rose from the speakeasies to pack the best clubs with the best people. The filmmakers, however, were faraway and foreign. Carl Laemmle, owner of Universal Pictures, was German; the man he inexplicably chose to direct the film version, Paul Fejos, was Hungarian. Together they conceived the night club of a hick's dream, or of a German intellectual's: the Paradise Club in the picture seemed to have been decorated by Kandinsky and was as high as a cathedral, possibly to accommodate the extravagant headgear of the chorus girls. The camera, mounted on a giant crane built expressly for the picture, rose, fell, gyrated 180 degrees, and zoomed through the stage curtain, coming to a stop only when the characters started to talk. Seen in its silent version, *Broadway* looked as if it had been made in Berlin in the twenties. But the sound version captured the confident mood of the period just before the money began to run out. The contemporaneity of the film was clear from the slang it employed: "I love you, little fellow, I love you. I'd do murder for you," says the gangster (Robert Ellis) to the chorus cutie (Merna Kennedy).

Broadway imposed its defects on the imitations that followed, although none of them had the same bizarre, hybrid look. (For a while, it seemed as if Universal was to take an exclusive option on the word *Broadway* to fend off instant rip-offs like First National's *Broadway Babies* and Columbia's *Broadway Daddies*.) Stereotypes of the bootlegger and the policeman, like those of the hoofer and the chorus girl, were to become prominent in many films for the next two years. Even pictures like Pathé's *The Racketeer* (1929), which didn't even have the excuse of being an adaptation from the stage, came to rely on the most banal dialogue while all violence was consummated off-screen, and the audience had to take the racketeer's word for it.

But no gangster picture from this early sound period took as many liberties with authenticity, or did so as consistently as did Josef von Sternberg's *Thunderbolt* (1929). The locale was once again the gangland of Sternberg's mind, and the characters were those that peopled his obsessions: the brutal yet vulnerable hero, the femme fatale in spite of herself, and the innocent youth who contests the hero's claim to the heroine. By this time everyone in Hollywood pretended to be an authority on the underworld,

The Paradise Night Club, as dreamt in far-off Hollywood by a German intellectual, for *Broadway*, 1929. The racketeer under fire is Robert Ellis, the chorus girl with the gat, Evelyn Brent. *Universal*

and here was Sternberg staging a third-degree scene as a solo number for the leading lady and orchestrating the convicts on the condemned row to supply an ironic musical counterpoint to the drama. In this, his first sound picture, Sternberg already illustrates the various uses of sound, keeping the camera fixed to a ringside table while a Harlem jazz-baby throbs out a rendition of "Daddy Won't You Please Come Home?" And moments later, when the police raid the club in search of the gangster hero, his soundtrack throbs again, this time with machine-gun fire, while the heroine (Fay Wray) sits alone at a table, shivering in her furs. The story (again by the brothers Furthman) fumbles strenuously to land Thunderbolt (George Bancroft) and Moran (Richard Arlen) in opposite cells on death row, both vying for the same furry creature, their feelings limned or mocked by a chorus of inmates who alternate "In the Summertime" with "Broken-

Dressed to kill: Jack Holt about to discuss business with Robert Ellis in *The Squealer*, an archetypal B-film of 1930. Flanking Holt and Ellis are Matthew Betz and Elmer Ballard. *Columbia.*

hearted." Sternberg deliberately turned his back on the facts and realities of crime. This is a fitting irony for the one director who could take credit for starting the gangster film genre yet responded instead to a code of ethics he found congenial, the primal force of a few desperate characters, and the play of light and shadow through prison bars. A decade after *Thunderbolt*, he returned to the genre, his career on the wane, to turn *Sergeant Madden* (1939), a sentimental melodrama of an Irish cop and his children, into a personal retelling of the Biblical tale of Adam and his sons.

Sternberg was not the only director whose personal vision would not be impaired by headlines and statistics. In 1930, when the Fox Company decided to film the best-selling novel *Louis Beretti* under the title *Born Reckless*, the project was assigned to John Ford, admittedly with his best work still ahead, but already a director capable of imprinting his personality on his films. If only Beretti had been an Irishman instead of an Italian, Ford would have felt more at home among these gangsters, who were no worse than sentimental roughnecks, certainly no more dangerous.

Since the film was set in 1917 and Louie was sent "over there" instead of up the river, Ford had a brief chance to show where his heart lay, which was nowhere near the Lower East Side. In *Born Reckless,* army life consisted mostly of card-playing, ball-playing, and fraternizing with the natives in relaxed comedy scenes that were reminiscent of *What Price Glory?* and other armed-forces dramas. The audience was also treated to war in all its terrible beauty and the caissons rolling over the camera. These scenes had a recognizable tension absent from the peacetime sequences, obviously because Ford found the underworld too petty and claustrophobic for his expansive brand of camaraderie, although he could not escape making clear the rapport between the soldier and the gunman.

In Ford's manual some men were more gifted for violence than others, and the Ford hero was usually a quiet man goaded into taking the most definitive action in defense of a group ideal. To Ford, the Irish—a clannish, defensive, male-dominated people—were among the great fighters of this world: In the first drill, the sergeant spots a drunken Irishman among the rookies and bellows: "Give him a gun!"

But in vain the film searched for the group spirit among the gangsters; the inevitable (by now) execution of a traitor was justified in Ford's eyes by making the victim a fop and a fool who, worst of all, adopted a British accent. Ford never quite explained why Beretti (Edmund Lowe) was a gangster in the first place, nor made clear why he and his lifetime buddy (Warren Hymer) should fall out, and the director was never more inconsistent than in an evasive ending that left Beretti dangling between life and death.

Some of the best Hollywood directors have found the gangster film less than inimical. Conversely, some of the best of these films, which is to say, some of America's best, have been the work of minor directors who found the gangster film the ideal genre. To make a gangster film work, John Ford had to make something else of it, for instance a comedy. Ford was to follow *Born Reckless* with *Up the River,* and original scenario by Maurine Watkins (who created the seemingly indestructible Roxie Hart in her play *Chicago*) which Ford changed into a sunny spoof of *The Big House,* the first major prison movie and then a current hit. The film was shot in three short weeks in mid-1930 to accommodate Spencer Tracy, who had been granted leave of absence from the Broadway production of *The Last Mile.* In his feature-film debut, Tracy exhibited more of a comic flair than the punchy, high-powered style that had made his New York reputation: his sly, dapper con man was full of cinematic twitches and throwaways. The ineffable Warren Hymer played Tracy's sidekick and sometime fall guy, a Cro-Magnon with the manners of a poet. The two were among Ford's most simpatico characters. Sent to Bensonatta, a midwestern penitentiary with all the comforts of a good, second-class resort, they quickly make themselves at home, reorganize the ball team, reminisce with the old-timers ("men with needles on their chests"), and in general enjoy the rituals and rewards of male society. If they eventually break out, it is merely to help a friend (the very youthful Humphrey Bogart) whose prison record is about to be disclosed by a blackmailer. A bit of scheming from Tracy gets the blackmailer liquidated by his own associates, upon which the two cons return to the big house and the big game for the prison pennant.

The picture was pure escapism, as if Ford could only see the resourcefulness, the humor, and team spirit of a fraternity closed to the straight world. The prison is inhabited by veterans of a small-scale urban war, each endowed with rank, nickname, and serial number. On the other side of the wall there is the women's section, and both communities have devised a foolproof communication system whereby messages are smuggled back and forth in the hemline of unsuspecting lady reformers. Ford celebrated such resourcefulness in the film's most elating comedy bit: a black woman prisoner (Mildred Vincent) stages a show of near-evangelical remorse in order to slip a note in the hem of a visitor's skirt, after which she straightens up and calmly informs her sisters in captivity, "Dat's two choc'late bars and one apple you owes me now."

The one grave note in this lark of a film is a passionate speech, a reference to *The Last Mile,* used by Tracy to persuade Bogart not to murder the blackmailer: "Did you ever see a guy die? I did. I spent eight months in that condemned cell. Believe me, kid, it's no picnic. Watching them go, one by one, and I wait day after day, week after week, month after month, wondering when will be my turn, listening to the drone of that lousy motor and watching those lights go dim." So untypical of Ford's film, this dark, claustrophobic admission of the fear of death doesn't quite fit Tracy's character. It may well have been included simply as a demonstration of Tracy's acting bravura.

The prison movie was nearly nonexistent. It was to gain currency after the summer of 1929, when the penal-reform issue was out in the open after the prison riots in Dannemora and Auburn. As usual at the time, the first reverberations were felt in the theater: *The Last Mile* and *The Criminal*

Code were quickly bought for the movies, but *The Big House* beat them to the nation's screens in June 1930. Produced by William Randolph Hearst at MGM studios, it was the first major Hollywood film to deal with such a timely subject. Frances Marion, a leading scenarist of the period, was given carte blanche to look into conditions at San Quentin, and Martin Flavin, who wrote the play *The Criminal Code* (bought by Columbia in March of that same year), was retained to furnish more of the same tough, authentic-sounding dialogue.

Marion based the picture's warden (Lewis Stone: stern, honest, paternalistic) on San Quentin's own James Holohan, and the viewpoint in *The Big House* was mostly his, taking for granted that "the prison system is cockeyed" but upholding the more comforting theory that "prison doesn't give a man a yellow streak, but if he has one it brings it out." Prison, in effect, was the test of a man's character, and the makers of *The Big House* were less concerned with reform than with performance under stress. The bad food, overcrowding, and casually brutalizing routine of prison life could be counted on to elicit the worst in any man—or the best, should the man be a Hollywood hero. Thus, put to the test, a weak but basically non-criminal type like The Kid (Robert Montgomery: manslaughter) will go to pieces and turn stool pigeon, but a delinquent with backbone like Morgan (Chester Morris: bank robbery) will live through it all and emerge a better man, a free man worthy of the happy ending. Their cellmate Butch (Wallace Beery: mass murder) is a lifer beyond recovery who will die leading a prison mutiny.

At times, in its flat photography and deployment of masses of people, the film was reminiscent of the German allegory of the twenties, *Metropolis*: leitmotifs of shuffling feet and geometrical patterns of robotlike humanity, great iron doors that opened and closed by remote control, one shattering surge of violence to disrupt a depersonalized, regimented world, and a final, unconvincing, evasive truce between masters and subjects. The scandals that triggered the project in the first place were subsumed into a narrative that exonerated everybody except one sadistic yard captain and one brutal desperado. The filmmakers were less concerned with social injustice than with recognizing an alternate society of men and admiring their resilience, their inventiveness, and especially their teamwork. (This last quality is the one common feature of *The Big House* and *Up the River*.) Isolation is the ultimate trial and punishment; a shot of an empty hall is sustained as prisoners in solitary confinement shout from cubicle to cubicle, attempting to make contact through iron walls. In contrast, the camera becomes fluid and complicitous as it follows a knife being passed under the dining table at the mess hall, or guns under the pews during chapel service; and as the revolt breaks out, the camera takes off in a liberating crane shot of the cellblock as it erupts into frenzied activity.

The Big House managed to stereotype a comparatively new roster of characters: the semihysterical weakling victimized by both guards and fellow prisoners, the informer, the ineffectual warden, the guard who deals out unnecessary punishment, and the strong-willed leader. They all reappeared half a year later, tightened and improved, in the film version of *The Criminal Code*. The picture rendered a significant change on the play by removing the tragic ending and, with it, the playwright's thesis that the prison system, as it existed, could turn a basically innocent man into a hardened killer. Originally, the young inmate serving time for an accidental killing

Knives passed in the mess hall: Matthew Betz, Wallace Beery, and Chester Morris in the first major prison movie, *The Big House*, 1930. *Metro-Goldwyn-Mayer*

was driven to stab the villainous guard, an act of desperation that doomed the warden's case for reform. The film spared the young man by having another convict, a minor character in the play, do the stabbing. The director, Howard Hawks, gave his reasons for the change in a much later interview: "I got together with ten convicts and said, 'How should this end?' and they told me in no uncertain terms. They had a great deal to do with the formation of many scenes because [the film] was built more or less on the convicts' code of not squealing."

Like Frances Marion before him, Hawks sought an authenticity that would validate his personal viewpoint. He was not concerned with exposing penal injustice but with exploring the relationships that can only be established in prison between keepers and prisoners, and among prisoners themselves. The Broadway-liberal line got short shrift in the movie, but this was hardly a case of California compromising, more that of a gifted filmmaker overlaying a bleakly pessimistic tract with his own themes.

Hawks's warden (Walter Huston) mingles with the inmates in the prison yard to earn their respect, and the picture is full of taut/comic encounters, as when the warden allows himself to be shaved by a cutthroat or adopts the guttural hollering of a yardful of rebellious cons. The hulking, taciturn Galloway (Boris Karloff) stalks through the film like an icon of retribution, and his climactic killing of the villainous guard is treated with near-ritualistic awe. For Hawks, prison could not possibly be the worst of all possible worlds if it still allowed for fierce commitments of fraternity and silence to be made within. There is no real feeling of wasted lives in Hawks's penitentiary, nor of real outrage. He was an Emersonian, a man-to-man idealist rather than a New Deal pragmatist: the reform of institutions took second place to the moral evolution of man himself.

But the reform zeal of the thirties would reach American films in less than a year. The spirit of the times began its infiltration of the industry upon the introduction of sound and the westward exodus of much of Broadway, and completed it with the shift of financial power from Hollywood to Wall Street after the fall of the stock market. The prevailing insecurity of the early thirties drew the attention of the executives to what was current and newsworthy.

By 1930, Darryl F. Zanuck was general production chief at Warner Brothers, a position comparable to that of Irving Thalberg at Metro-Goldwyn-Mayer in that, even though their names rarely appeared in the film credits, both were responsible for the policy of their respective studios. It had taken Zanuck six years to attain his position. Instrumental in bringing sound and dialogue to Warners, he had backed the production of *The Jazz Singer* with his own unit; he had lived through a merger with First National; and he had survived a Biblical disaster epic, *Noah's Ark,* which he had written and which turned out an epic disaster. He had entered the company as a twenty-two-year-old hack and had written two Rin-Tin-Tin movies. In later years, he sometimes referred to himself as "the greatest dog-script writer in history," but it did not take Zanuck long to graduate to people scripts. He turned them out in such effortless profusion that exhibitors wondered if he was the only writer on the Warners payroll. Without breaking his stride, Zanuck adopted various pseudonyms, such as Mark Canfield or Melville Crossman or Gregory Rogers; in little over a year he scored nineteen writing credits.

He was a fast, unsubtle writer, if we are to judge him (perhaps not too fairly) by the bits of dialogue in *The Dark Horse,* a 1932 political satire. His strength resided in story construction, which was all-important in the silent era. He became very conscious of the writer's role in the new talking pictures, and, unlike Thalberg, he avidly read novels and magazine stories. In 1929, an item in *The Reader's Digest* mentioning that four hundred and eighty-six gangsters had been killed in Chicago in one year sent him to the newspaper files to bone up on the underworld. Zanuck read through the current Chicago literature. A novel, *Little Caesar,* written by W. R. Burnett

"I got together with ten convicts and said, 'How should this end?' and they told me in no uncertain terms."—Howard Hawks. Galloway (Boris Karloff) stabs the sadistic yard captain (DeWitt Jennings) to save the boy's life and the warden's face. Phillips Holmes, Walter Huston in Hawks's *The Criminal Code*, 1931. *Columbia*

and syndicated in eighty-two American newspapers, stood out as the best. It was not quite literature, but it was a good deal more than journalism. Burnett, at his clipped, slangy best, rivaled the Hemingway of *Men Without Women*. Urged by Mervyn LeRoy, a house director at Warners who also believed in the project, Zanuck acquired the rights to the novel.*

Zanuck had discovered that there was a war raging in the two greatest cities in America right before everyone's eyes, only it seemed to belong primarily to the newspapers. Broadway had gingerly appropriated a few headlines, and many a Chicago newspaperman landed a play on the New York stage before heading west to pirate his own stuff. Once in Hollywood,

* Burnett had a long and impressive career, and many of his novels were adapted for the screen, among them *Iron Man* (1930), *Dark Hazard* (1933), *Dr. Socrates* (1935), *High Sierra* (1940), *Nobody Lives Forever* (1943), and *The Asphalt Jungle* (1942).

these journalists were set to work rewriting each other. One such writer was Bartlett Cormack, author of *The Racket,* who began his film career by adapting Ward Morehouse's play, *Gentlemen of the Press.*

Zanuck was more interested in journalists than in playwrights; he was not after canned theater like the movie version of *The Racket* or fancy stuff like that of *Broadway.* He was prepared to take a chance on properties that were not backed by Broadway prestige, and he began buying stories that seemed good movie material: *A Handful of Clouds,* an unproduced play by Rowland Brown, a screenwriter with one previous credit to his name (a Hoot Gibson Western titled *Points West*), which became *Doorway to Hell;* and *Beer and Blood* by John Bright, an unpublished collection of Chicago stories which became *The Public Enemy.*

Zanuck was allowed a small budget for the first of these, *Doorway to Hell,* despite Jack L. Warner's scant enthusiasm for the project. The film premiered in November 1930, at the Strand on Broadway, billed as "the picture gangdom dared Hollywood to make" and with the ads misrepresenting its subject as "the life story of Lou 'Legs' Ricarno"—obviously to cash in on the current notoriety of Legs Diamond, who had just survived five bullet wounds the month before. Any similarity, however, was due merely to this fluke in timing.* A runaway hit, *Doorway to Hell* was held over three weeks. A month later *Little Caesar* opened, and by then *The Public Enemy* had been rushed into production. Zanuck's gambit had paid off, the Warners motto proclaimed their pictures "Snatched from Today's Headlines," and the new vogue was auspiciously launched.

All three pictures told basically the same story, that of the rise and fall of a gangster. They shared the drab Warners look of the period, and many of their characters appeared interchangeable; yet a style was clearly taking form from picture to picture, almost independently of their directors. Archie Mayo, Mervyn LeRoy, and William A. Wellman were all contracted to the studio, but only Wellman had achieved some measure of success as the director of *Wings,* a World War I aviation epic made at Paramount studios three years before.

Being the first, and still uncertain of its conventions, *Doorway to Hell* was the weakest. The film was a romanticized version of the career of Johnny Torrio, the mobster who organized Chicago's South Side and who willed it to Al Capone before retiring in 1925. Seriously flawed by its screenplay—the work of George Rosener, a veteran scenarist and coauthor of a Broadway flop named *Speak Easy*—the dialogue seemed culled from silent-picture title cards. Cop to Hood: "You're going to treat yourself to a handful of clouds, I mean the kind that come out from the end of a .38 automatic." Hood to Cop: "I wouldn't mind the hot chair with you sitting on my lap."

Notwithstanding, *Doorway to Hell* minted a few clichés of its own. A mobster flips a coin; the running motors of an army of trucks drown the

---

* The film was timely in other respects as well. Creighton Peet in *Outlook* magazine wrote: "This is about the first real 'motion' picture the Warner Brothers have made this year, what with punk operettas and photographed stage plays."

sound of machine-gun fire; the gangster hero asks a plastic surgeon to make his dead brother look alive. Variations and refinements of these scenes, which must have seemed fresh and quirky when *Doorway to Hell* first appeared, have recurred in films like *Scarface, The Public Enemy,* and even as recently as in *The Godfather;* they were part and parcel of the genre-to-be. Furthermore, in its few flashes of violence, the film maintained a cool, casual savagery hitherto rare in underworld pictures. The opening sequence, for instance: a gunman (Dwight Frye) interrupts his pool game to collect a violin case, explaining in wide-eyed innocence, "I'm going to teach a guy a lesson." In a car, he efficiently assembles a Tommy gun prior to dispatching a suspected informer and fellow gang member on the steps of his tenement home, right under the eyes of a girlfriend—a neat camera setup from the inside of a stationary car. There was little additional violence, except for a body being hurled from a passing car, but the violence so expertly established at the outset tended to hover over the rest of the film.

The physical image of Lew Ayres (who played Ricarno) as much as the words he was made to say, undermined *Doorway to Hell.* To an audience of 1930, it was hard to believe that Ayres could be capable of mayhem and murder; to us, now, it is downright inconceivable. His presence conveyed no real menace, no resonance, no depth. In place of a gangland executive with a Napoleonic complex, there was a cute collegian, who, when he talked about a killing, sounded and looked like a frat brother describing an initiation. This removed the violence from the character, so that Ricarno emerged more victim than executioner, more patsy than mastermind. Betrayed by the moll he married and, less willingly, by his friend and henchman—a role in which James Cagney had but to snarl and clench his fist to make it work—he was left to mourn his kid brother in a shabby bed-sitter and, in the fade-out, to walk resignedly to an off-screen death at the hands of his former confederates. The end-card, with its sentimental valentine to the hero, placed the film in the silent-screen tradition:

The "Doorway to Hell" is a one-way door. There is no retribution—no plea for clemency. The little boy walked through it with his head up and a smile on his lips. They gave him a funeral, a swell funeral that stopped traffic, and then they forgot him before the roses had a chance to wilt.

Little Caesar was much less conventional. In the title role is a character who never begs for sympathy, one of the first legitimate antiheroes in the American cinema. Morose, dangerous, a loner, Cesare Rico Bandello is a small-town, small-time hoodlum who rises to near the top of the racket and stays there briefly before sinking back into obscurity and death. Rico's continuing fascination for us stems from the fact that what he did was done less for profit than for the acquisition of social status. As he states early in the film, "Money's all right, but it ain't everything. No, be somebody, know that a bunch of guys will do anything you tell 'em, have your own way or nothin'." Rico's more sophisticated urban colleagues find him at first uncouth and ridiculous, then a bad risk, for Rico is an efficient, remorseless machine who cares nothing for underworld diplomacy (he shoots the crime commissioner). They dub him "Little Caesar" because of his size, his name, and his pugnaciousness; Rico is nevertheless flattered. In a series of coups, he disposes of his employers and is finally entrusted with the North Side of an unnamed city (which is of course Chicago) by the Big Boy himself, a Capone idealized into an impeccably dressed man of the world.

Whatever humanity Rico displays is based on his friendship with Joe Massara (Douglas Fairbanks, Jr.), his accomplice in the early days. Massara goes straight and becomes a night-club dancer. (The character is based on George Raft, then making his first Hollywood films after years in vaudeville and a youthful association with Owney Madden, the man who organized

The film that launched the vogue: Lew Ayres, Robert Ellis, and James Cagney in *Doorway to Hell*, 1930. Ayres was miscast as a crime czar based on Johnny Torrio, who organized the Chicago underworld and willed it to Al Capone. *Warner Brothers*

the taxi racket in New York City and eventually became a millionaire beer runner.) This desertion is taken by Rico as a personal affront, he feels like a father betrayed in his ambitions for his child; but later, when Joe's dancing partner and mistress forces him to break with the gang, Rico's possessiveness of Joe takes the form of a nonerotic homosexual attachment ("Nobody ever quit me.").

At the center of *Little Caesar* was the performance of Edward G. Robinson. Any true distinction the film achieved was owed to the actor rather than to the direction (perfunctory but at least aware of the actor's potential) or to the screenplay, which, despite the additions of Francis Edward Faragoh and some anonymous contributors, derived its strong moments from the Burnett novel, even those famous last words, "Mother of God, is this the end of Rico?" (In half the release prints these were bowdlerized into "Mother of *mercy,* is this the end of Rico?" anticipating the objections of the United Council of Churches, one of the most powerful pressure groups in the country.)

Little Caesar was not the first film in which Robinson had played a gangster, and it certainly would not be the last. Born in Rumania and reared on New York's Lower East Side, he had played Shaw and Shakespeare as a member of the Theater Guild, created the role of Nick Scarsi in the original production of *The Racket,* and appeared in at least three underworld pictures before Hall B. Wallis, Zanuck's right-hand producer, approached him to play a minor gunman in *Little Caesar.* Although he considered himself a character actor—he was, after all, thirty-seven and far from the accepted image of the matinee idol—Robinson held out for the title role, until Wallis, with sensible foresight, gave in. Zanuck said "Every other underworld picture has had a thug with a little bit of good in him. He reforms before the fade-out. This guy is no good at all. It'll go over big."*

Rico Bandello had no family, no romantic attachments, and no religion, at least until the final incredulous outburst. Robinson, with his short stature and a glower that seemed embedded in his features, did not convey an ethnic background either. With very few psychological facts to go on, Robinson made his performance all gestures and animal physicality; he suggested, depending upon the scene, a bantam rooster, a bullfrog, a pug. Rico, in short, was as close to the *natural* gangster as Robinson could make him.

The ruthless energy with which Rico cut through the red tape and social pretensions of the underworld, along with his single-tracked ambition to be somebody, made him an attractive figure to the 1930 public. He was the hero as punk at a moment when American movies were launching a populist campaign to get the unemployed back into the theaters. Attendance had dropped 7 percent from 1929 and would continue to plunge through 1931; the theory that people went to the movies to forget about their problems seemed questionable for the first time. Rico was hardly a proletarian hero, but his well-remembered catch line, "Sam, you can dish it out, but you're getting so you can't take it any more," has a ring of resilience to

* Quoted by Alva Johnson in *The New Yorker,* November 10–17, 1934.

it, almost like the affirmative slogans the Roosevelt administration was to launch a year or two later. And Rico left no doubt that he could take it as well as dish it out: ambushed and wounded in the street, his instinctive reaction is to yell back at the aggressor, "Fine shot you are!" which suggests, along with a childish bravado, the professional's contempt for a bungled job.

In a genre as imbued with the protocol of death as the gangster film, it was the manner in which the gangster received his death that defined him as hero. Little Caesar, like Scarface later, is not doomed by the society he has plundered and outraged, but by a quirk or weakness in his nature. Except in those films where the gangster was a mere supporting player, as, for instance, Night Nurse (1931) or Love is a Racket (1932), the gangster's demise was rarely causal; causality robbed death of its grandeur, its tragic potential, scaled it down to a mere journalistic item. A violent, causal death (the gangster shot by the police or an adversary as a result of more or less complex plotting) reconciled the gangster with society in extremis, but the major genre heroes usually died, as they lived, in isolation from society, which is one of the characteristics of tragedy. In his autobiography, Edward G. Robinson claims to have recognized Rico's inherent tragic quality: "It was not, I told him [Wallis], merely a hokey-pokey cheap shot; it was rather like a Greek tragedy." In the end, Rico Bandello's uncontrollable pride forces him into a suicidal showdown with his traditional adversary, the police lieutenant; Rico would make the front page one last time rather than remain the underworld's forgotten man. He dies unrepentant and pathetically aware of the disparity between the blown-up image and the ignominious ending.

In January 1931, Zanuck was appointed chief executive in charge of all productions for the combined Warner Brothers and First National companies. He took personal credit as producer of The Public Enemy, and it can be deduced that he intended that project to be a reply to the objections raised against the new gangster-film vogue he had helped launch. Zanuck furnished his gunman hero with a complete case history, and he preceded and ended the film with a written card stating that "Tom Powers [the protagonist of The Public Enemy] and Rico Bandello are problems that we—the public—must solve." A series of sharp, short vignettes traces the early life of Tom Powers, sketching his Irish middle-class background, introducing his stern policeman father, his doting, ineffectual mother, and his straight brother. The film briefly documents Tom's graduation from petty thievery to small heists and the acquisition of his first revolver; he matures from a mischievous urchin in knickers and cap to a full-gown, vicious, minor hoodlum—the title could have been intended by Zanuck as ironic, apart from its come-on value. And around Tom and his fellow toughs the semi-rural, turn-of-the century American city grows and thrives and festers. When Prohibition comes to offer what Tom cannot resist—the chance to make some smart money—he is ready; he has been in training since childhood to be a lawbreaker, a bully, a killer.

A sociological alibi, no matter how perfunctory, lent the film a touch of

"Every other underworld picture has had a thug with a little bit of good in him. . . .
This guy is no good at all. It'll go over big."—Darryl F. Zanuck. Edward G. Robinson as
Cesare Rico Bandello in *Little Caesar*, 1931. His rise: Rico wears his first tuxedo,
hobnobs with The Big Boy (Sidney Blackmer), gets to the top. His fall: a nonerotic homo-
sexual attachment to Joe (Douglas Fairbanks, Jr.). "Nobody ever quit me." *Warner
Brothers*

respectability it badly needed, since there were some ugly spurts of violence
to justify. Today, however, *The Public Enemy* seems no more violent than
The Secret Six or *Bad Company*,* both released around the same time and
even more favorably received. Reviewing *The Public Enemy*, an anonymous
critic in *Photoplay* (May 1931) complained: ". . . the story's weak, so are

* Recently rediscovered, *Bad Company* (1931) may have been the first picture to feature the gangland
slaughter that took place in Chicago on St. Valentine's Day, February 14, 1929. (*Scarface* had run
into censorship problems that delayed its release.) There was as much violence in *Bad Company* as in

other things, so it's just another not-so-hot contribution to gang lore on the screen. Hasn't there been about enough?" By rough count, there were twenty-five gangster movies in 1931, not counting the Poverty Row rip-offs, and there were to be forty the next year. Most of these remained unseen for years while *The Public Enemy,* often revived, was on of the first films acquired for the collection of the Museum of Modern Art in New York, and it has moved into an enduring place in standard histories of the cinema.

At the last minute Zanuck switched directors for *The Public Enemy,* replacing the efficient but impersonal Archie Mayo with William Wellman, and it was Wellman's touch that made the film as tough, funny, and gripping as it was. Like so many other American directors—Ford and Hawks come immediately to mind—Wellman cultivated a career-long preoccupation with male groups, their rituals of belonging, codes of survival, and tests of endurance. Also, like Ford and Hawks, Wellman contributed to the genres that most obviously encompass these themes, the war film and the gangster film. But even in other types of movies he showed a marked penchant to feature pranksters, punks, and hustlers, the restless and rebellious in a nation that was grinding to an economic halt. In the first decade of sound pictures, Wellman was prolific but not very consistent; still one discerns strands of sympathy for certain asocial types, such as the hobo (in *Beggars of Life,* 1928), the migrant unemployed (in *Heroes for Sale,* 1933) and the juvenile delinquent spawned by the Depression (in *Wild Boys of the Road,* 1933). Like them, the gangster represented both the social mobility and the frustration typical of the period. For all of Wellman's firsthand war experience in the Lafayette Flying Corps, *Wings* is the most romantic of the flying sagas, much more so than Howard Hughes's *Hell's Angels* or Howard Hawks's *The Dawn Patrol.*

In peacetime, Wellman vested some leftover romanticism in the gangster. For a good part of *The Public Enemy,* the message appeared to be that it's a helluva lot of fun to bootleg, heist, enjoy the company of one's kind, and shoot it out with rival groups. Not only did the film perpetuate the theory that gangsters did not kill outsiders, just each other, but who else but "Wild Bill" Wellman would have thought of including the episode in which Tom Powers "rubs out" the horse that accidentally killed his pal Nails? Based on the death of Samuel "Nails" Morton and the subsequent revenge perpetrated on his horse by his friend Louis "Two Gun" Altieri, it was the right sort of anecdote to authenticate the fraternal, honor-among-thieves image of the gang.*

Like many other gangster pictures of the period, *The Public Enemy* suggested as much violence as it actually illustrated on screen, and the omission of certain graphic brutality was dictated as much by the new

The Public Enemy, not to mention the same graphic display of weaponry, but the protagonist in the former was a fantasy crime czar (Ricardo Cortez, adjusting awkwardly to the sophisticated psychology of the talkies after a career as a silent lover) who lusted after the dumb heroine (Helen Twelvetrees) when he should have been paying closer attention to her brother, a rival racketeer.
* Wellman's other gangster films include: *Ladies of the Mob* (1928), *Chinatown Nights* and *Woman Trap* (1929), *Star Witness* and *Night Nurse* (1931), *Love Is a Racket* and *The Hatchet Man* (1932), and *Midnight Mary* (1933).

possibilities offered by the soundtrack as by the peculiar situation created by the recently established Production Code. In the optional pre-Code *don'ts* and *be carefuls* that the film industry was expected, however loosely, to observe, there had been no provisions for the depiction of organized crime. The implied standards covered only two acknowledged criminal activities: drug addiction and white slavery (and, as we have noted, both were frequently featured throughout the silent era despite the warnings). When the Production Code was officially adopted by West Coast producers on March 31, 1930, at just about the time *Doorway to Hell* was ready to start shooting, organized crime was found, along with sex, among "the sins that often attract," as opposed to sins "which repel by their very nature" and which turned out to include murder (committed by individuals for private reasons, one surmises), theft, legal chicanery, "lying, hypocrisy, cruelty, etc." Within this esthetic reappraisal of sin, the censors recognized an appeal to the masses, especially, as the Code pointed out, to "the young and impressionable," and studios were entreated to exercise caution in portraying violence, so as not to lead the viewer into addiction or imitation.

Save for the machine-gunning in broad daylight of Tom's best friend and the unforgettable shock ending, wherein the rival gang delivers Tom's body wrapped in a grotesque, bloody parcel to his mother's doorstep, there was not that much violence in *The Public Enemy*. Where the film really went overboard was in its pervasive misogyny. The by-now anthological moment when Tom Powers shoves half a grapefruit into the face of his girlfriend (Mae Clarke) is preceded by some nasty verbal abuse ("I wish you were a wishing well so that I could tie a bucket to you and sink it"), and it seemed almost a fade-out, a casual footnote to the domestic life of the gangster. (This incident was a free reinterpretation of an actual episode involving the late Earl "Hymie" Weiss, some poor forgotten moll, and an omelet.) If today the scene does not quite seem "one of the cruelest and most startling acts ever committed on film," as Bosley Crowther once wrote, it is due to a hardening of our sensibilities as we submit to a frightening escalation in cinema violence. More significant seems the audience's reaction to the scene at the time of the picture's release. Not one reviewer failed to mention it, and it undoubtedly contributed to the film's success. This posits an identification of the sort that one would like to reject on moral principles, as if the baser instincts of a whole generation had been appealed to, unthinkingly, recklessly. In the context, however, of the early Depression morning-after, the act took on a different meaning. The girl became a nagging, simpering mate trying to restrain the man from taking to the road or to crime or some such alternative, any of which were vastly more attractive and romantic than sex-denying domesticity and a nine-to-five job. This was an appeal that men could identify with. The women who understood were in the majority that catapulted James Cagney to the top. They anxiously expected him to commit cinematic acts of mayhem against their own sex. They understood the weight of responsibility on their men and perhaps imagined that, were they in a similar situation, they would know better and act differently.

The intrinsic antiwoman attitudes of many American films were already at work in *Doorway to Hell*, and this is clear in the case of the leading lady. Dorothy Mathews (a nonprofessional) seems unnecessarily callous and unsympathetic in her calculated wooing of the hero's buddy and remorseless in her betrayal and duplicity. ("Have you got so much hoodlum in you that it won't come out?" demands the gangster hero in what sounds like role reversal). In *Little Caesar*, Joe's girl friend (Glenda Farrell) never recognizes the bond that exists between him and Rico Bandello; she pleads for Joe to betray Rico. Although Rico has refused to condone Joe's gangland execution and has even deflected a gunman's aim to save Joe's life, she finally takes it on herself to inform on Rico to the police. Another gang member (William Collier, Jr.) is a mother-dominated coward and potential informer. When Rico's fortunes decline, he is forced to hide at the home of a

A war raging in the big cities of America: *The Public Enemy*, 1931. Tom Powers (James Cagney) treats his women rough (in this case, Mia Marvin), but he would kill for his buddy, Matt Doyle (Edward Woods). *Warner Brothers*

grotesque harridan (Lucille Laverne) who supplies him with money in a parody of a mother-son relationship. These female characters gnawed at what was basically a male world.

With its ever-present antifemale pattern, the gangster film brought out the male chauvinist in many directors. Some women-oriented directors, such as George Cukor, John M. Stahl, and Gregory La Cava, instinctively steered away from the genre. Until *The Public Enemy*, Wellman had not seemed an especially misogynous director: *Wings*, after all, managed to be a war epic *and* a Clara Bow vehicle. Was it for the sake of authenticity then that he and the screenwriters lined up such a collection of cloying, ineffectual, predatory, clinging women? Since women are generally excluded from aggressive groups, like armies and gangs (though they may be nearby in the roles of whores or camp followers), the strength of the male bond supplies the real romanticism of war and ganster films.

Another last-minute substitution made *The Public Enemy* the hit it became in 1931 and accounts for most of the freshness and power it retains today. When the film went into production, James Cagney was scheduled to play a secondary role, as he had in *Doorway to Hell*, and he actually worked on the film for three days in the part of Matt Doyle, until Wellman had a chance to screen the rushes and recommend to Zanuck that Cagney exchange roles with Edward Woods, a pleasant but indistinct juvenile who was set to play the lead. Cagney's ferretlike energy paced the film, as it did most of his others, and, since his career turned out to be at least as consistent and coherent as Wellman's, a case can be made that the actor was the true author of his films, a view that Cagney himself appears to hold, realistically if not modestly.

Zanuck recognized Cagney's potential. He contracted with John Bright and Kubec Glasmon, Chicago druggists turned screenwriters, to write for Cagney in the way that songwriters work up special material for certain singers. With what attention they must have rerun Cagney's output of only five pictures, trying to determine what worked and why, and what had to be phased out from a persona that Cagney had minted overnight! Their problem was not to gild the Cagney style by laying on the charm; they had to preserve the hoofer alertness, the slightly bruised sensitivity that filtered through the aggressiveness, the hint that at any moment he could swing either right or wrong.* Such was Cagney's persuasiveness that his portrayal of an Irish gangster—admittedly not the first but certainly the most obvious— failed to raise any sort of protest from Irish-American groups. Hardly two years before, when Hollywood was even more reckless in its approach to minorities, *Chinatown Nights* had portrayed the Tong societies as a yellow-peril equivalent of the gangs, and *Wheel of Chance* had for its hero a Jewish racketeer by the name of Schmulka Turkeltaub (played by a very WASP-y Richard Barthelmess as one half of a dual role, the other being a twin

---

* A memo, either from Zanuck or Wallis, exists in the United Artists Collection of the State Historical Society, in Madison, Wisconsin. It reads: "Develop tough, hardboiled, cocksure Cagney—knows it all . . . gets start in gangster craze—women like him because of roughness—treats everybody as moll— he must start tough and rough . . ." (Quoted in *The Velvet Light Trap*, No. 7).

brother who prosecutes the racketeer). Both of these films had stirred their respective ethnic groups to threats of punitive action. Granted that the Irish were hardly a minority by 1931; still there were a hundred imponderables at work in *The Public Enemy* to ensure the empathy of the viewer if not an all-condoning leniency.

Cagney had attracted the most attention on Broadway as a mama's boy who drifted into bootlegging and murder in the play *Penny Arcade,* which, adapted to the screen as *Sinners Holiday,* became his film debut. There was another mother in *The Public Enemy,* who cuddled her vicious son and called him "my baby," and so Cagney continued to play the dutiful son / criminal to a succession of screen mothers, culminating in the mother-fixated, mad-dog killer of *White Heat* (1949). By then, dark psychological insights into the criminal mind had infiltrated film iconography, but in the breezy, sketchy, behavioral early thirties, Cagney was a boon.

In 1932, Lincoln Kirstein wrote in *Hound and Horn* magazine that: "Cagney has an inspired sense of timing, an arrogant style, a pride in the control of his body and a conviction and lack of self-consciousness that is unique in the deserts of the American screen. . . . No one expresses more clearly in terms of pictorial action the delights of violence, the overtones of a semiconscious sadism, the tendency toward destruction, toward anarchy, which is the base of American sex appeal." Kirstein was at the time mainly a dance critic (he went on to found The New York City Ballet with George Balanchine), and his appraisal was very much that of the balletomane, able to judge in terms of line, of balance and rhythm, of feeling translated into movement. Cagney's style displayed that most enviable American feature, the impression of spontaneous improvisation. On screen, Cagney must have composed his first real character the same way he had instinctively developed his own eccentric jack-in-the-box dancing style.

Cagney's background was lower-middle-class Irish-American. He was born in the notorious Gas House District around Tompkins Square, a Manhattan area that still maintains a melting-pot hypertension. He grew up in Yorkville, drifted into show business around 1919. His style seems the polar opposite of Edward G. Robinson's, within the American naturalistic tradition, of course. Robinson seemed to act by implosion, concentrating energy behind his precarious passivity, until the final, long-awaited burst. Cagney was all firecracker bounce; even in repose, he appeared to ricochet off the borders of the screen. At thirty-one (in *The Public Enemy*), he seemed an Our Gang kid gone wrong, which explained why some of his more violent outbursts, like spitting beer in the face of a cowed bartender or even the grapefruit episode, had an unpredictable, childish mischief about them. "I ain't so tough," mutters the wounded Tom to the audience, as he pathetically staggers out on the rainy, solitary street, having just wiped out half a dozen members of an enemy gang; it is an extraordinary admission to make, just how much of his tough act was precisely that, an act.

The inevitable teaming of Cagney and Robinson was, however, premature. *The Public Enemy* was barely completed when they were both rushed into *Smart Money,* a folkish tale of a small-time barber who becomes, through his unerring gambling instinct, a big-city big shot. His lucky streak, however, does not extend to women. Glasmon and Bright spiced up the Runyonesque yarn with black jokes, Jewish jokes, Greek jokes, and some relaxed (perhaps never so relaxed) camping around between Robinson and Cagney, who plays discreet support to the then more established Robinson. Cagney advises Robinson to stay away from blonds, in particular one who turns out to be a decoy from the district attorney's office and their eventual nemesis. "She'll be going away in a few days, then you can be my sweetheart again, dearie," retorts Robinson, touching ever so lightly on the ambiguities of a closed male world. Unpretentious and just as unmemorable, *Smart Money* launched a series of fringe, not-quite-criminal roles for Cagney and Robinson, in an attempt to enlarge their repertory without quite breaking the gangster mold.

The murder of Alfred "Jake" Lingle provided Warner Brothers with the criminal event of 1930. Lingle, a reporter for the *Chicago Tribune,* was shot in a crowded pedestrian tunnel at noon on June 9, the day before he was to meet with federal agents investigating Al Capone's finances. Lingle's killing was the last of eleven deaths attributed to the Chicago underworld in as many days. It was reported at first as an act of reprisal that seemed to shatter the tradition of immunity hitherto enjoyed by the Chicago press, but in fact Lingle did not even have a byline in the *Tribune,* although it soon became known that he enjoyed more than mere immunity from the underworld. He was on Capone's payroll to the tune of sixty thousand dollars a year, a sum that considerably supplemented the meager sixty-five dollars the *Tribune* paid him every week to gather information. Lingle was shot at close range by someone he knew and presumably trusted, obviously a Capone torpedo (who was never identified). The movies could not possibly ask for a better story, and Warner Brothers immediately set W. R. Burnett and John Monk Saunders to write a moral into a story that patently lacked one. A final screenplay by Robert Lord was before the cameras by year's end, under the direction of John Francis Dillon, and *The Finger Points* premiered in March 1931, unwittingly coincidental with Capone's indictment for income-tax evasion.

To evade possible legal action by Lingle's widow, Lingle was rechristened Breckenridge Lee and made into a Southern hick with ambitions of becoming an ace reporter in the big city. As a cub reporter for *The Press,* Lee listens to a morale-builder from his editor to the effect that "the press can't be bought, intimidated, or silenced." Inevitably, Lee's candor gets him in trouble with the mob; he is beaten up by a couple of thugs for exposing an illegal gambling casino, and, in order to pay the hospital bills, he accepts his first bribe from a personable gangster. Dropping his principles along with his drawl, Lee amasses a bundle of graft that he stashes away in a safety-deposit box, tipping off his benefactors to any imminent move from city hall while publicly attacking crime and corruption in his column. "This town is not for softies," he tells his remonstrating girlfriend. "Rome was a Quaker village compared to this town." In time, he becomes more of a liability than an asset to Number One, the fat-necked crime czar who, in this picture, is given the treatment usually reserved in the movies for presidents in office: an authoritarian bulk photographed from behind the chair of state. "I want to give you a little advice: Lay off," says Number One. "You're not talking to a chump, you're talking to a representative of the press. Quite a few people believe in it," replies Lee, suddenly repossessed by his calling.

Like the hero, *The Finger Points* was somewhat at a loss between denouncing the corruption of the big city and making a case for Lee / Lingle as a member of the press. It got very little support from Richard Barthelmess in the leading role, other than the fact that the Barthelmess reserve had been filed away in the collective memory of a generation as emblematic of Griffithian innocence and idealism. As a performer, Barthelmess linked with the movies' past; in the small role of the gangster who is instrumental in his

Al Capone, given the treatment reserved in the movies for presidents in office, tells a reporter to lay off. Richard Barthelmess, as a newspaperman inspired by Jake Lingle, in *The Finger Points*, 1931. *Warner Brothers*

corruption, Clark Gable forecasted the decade that was just beginning. Gable's was the charm of compromise, an urban Mephisto working his crooked spell on the last American innocent. Lee's corruption was made visual by having his measurements taken for an expensive wardrobe, the movie's modest paraphrase of the passage from Fitzgerald's *The Great Gatsby* concerning Jay Gatsby's shirts.

The Finger Points did not measure up to the best from Warners; it was a rush job in which lines were fluffed and action was sparse. It came to vivid life in the sequence of Lee's death: the camera shadowing him through the early morning semideserted streets, a priest entering unexpectedly from the left of the frame as a hint of retribution, a milkman who casually fingers the victim for some unseen gunman in a second-story window; then, a spray of machine-gun bullets that blast Lee against a housefront, his arms spread open to suggest, however furtively, his martyrdom. It is always exciting to watch sudden death on the screen, as it is to read about it on the printed page; but Lee's demise awakened no deep emotional response comparable to that of Little Caesar's.

Any social criticism that may have been implicit in *Little Caesar* or *The Public Enemy* found articulate, if discreet, expression in Rowland Brown's *Quick Millions* (1931). A pugnacious leftist, Brown had written a few slanted speeches in the play upon which *Doorway to Hell* was based, but when the film version reached the screen, the single line that could be construed as critical of the social system was a fleeting nostalgic reference to the slum childhood of its gangster hero and the typhoid epidemic that decimated his family. Deleted passages were more outspoken:

Gangsters are really the invention of capitalists. My first job was breaking a strike at twenty bucks a day. . . . I was over on one strike in Pennsylvania and saw a lot of my countrymen working there, and living like animals, so I decided I was on the wrong side of the fence, and became a labor leader, and later an underworld power. . . .*

Such critical self-definition was nowhere to be found in the finished film but, within a year, Brown was directing his first film, *Quick Millions*, for Fox and being penalized, not for his politics (which could always be tempered in the final cut) but for his temper which, as rumor had it, had moved him to take a poke at a studio executive. Even if one suspects the original screenplay was toned down by coscreenwriter Courtney Terrett (late of *The New York World*) and dialogue writer John Wray (coauthor of *Nightstick*), the picture is quirky and personal. For the first time, it features a working-class hero, a truck driver named Bugs Raymond (Spencer Tracy in his second film role) who sets up a protection racket for garage owners, builds up a fleet of trucks, and moves in on the city's construction business. Bugs's dream, however, is to become legitimate:

I'm just a guy with a one-ton brain who's too nervous to steal and too lazy to work. I do other people's thinking for them and make them like it. I realize that human

---

* Quoted in *The Velvet Light Trap*, #16, p. 3: Gerald Peary, *Doorway to Hell*.

beings have their weaknesses and all the man-made laws in this country were made to protect honest people. And how many people will admit that they're honest? Racketeering is just getting what the other guy's got in a nice way.

Bugs was an unusually lucid and articulate film figure in a period that consistently depicted gangsters as driven by societal forces beyond their comprehension.

Brown gave his picture to the look and feel of an inside job, justifying the Fox claims for his familiarity with the milieu: "Through his varied experience he had frequent contact with gangster types and concededly knows more about them than any other person in motion pictures." What best attested to the film's veracity—which was only of relative importance, after all—was the relaxed bonhomie that presided over scenes of gangsters

Gangsters among themselves: one can almost smell the expensive aftershave and choke on the cigar smoke. George Raft and Spencer Tracy in *Quick Millions*, 1931. *Twentieth Century-Fox*

among themselves; one could almost smell the expensive aftershave and choke on the cigar smoke. At a gangland party, George Raft, who plays Bugs's bodyguard and deadly factotum as if to the manner born, breaks into an impromptu, graceful solo to a boozy arrangement of "St. Louis Blues" that the camera seems to catch almost on the sly, while Bugs goes among guests and cohorts looking for cash to buy his girlfriend an expensive diamond; Bugs finally collects twelve thousand dollars from the hood who is cooking spaghetti in the kitchen. Brown's humor was laconic and occupational: at his own testimonial dinner, Bugs has the guests held up, to collect evidence on corrupt city officials; one guest hides a ring in his mouth but is forced to comply when a deadpan hood orders him, "Spit diamonds." Dressing for the opera, Raft fastidiously selects the rod that will best match his tails.

Bugs's obsession with respectability proves to be his undoing. He declines to take part in an unpopular milk racket, and his refusal triggers a gang war that outrages the citizenry into action. Bugs has fallen for a luscious society girl (Marguerite Churchill) who enjoys putting him down: "My grandfather used to drive a team of mules," she taunts him, "I'm afraid he'd think you a parasite." When she coolly announces her decision to marry someone from her own set, Bugs makes up his mind to abduct her from her wedding. "Bad business but a swell idea," says a gang member, and the already jeopardized underworld realizes that Bugs will simply have to go. Bugs does not quite make it to the church, but his tophat does, rolling on the carpeted path as a symbol of his toppled social ambitions.

Throughout the film, Brown sacrificed violent action to irony. There was one graphic shooting—when Raft, who has become a liability, is liquidated on Bugs's orders—which proved that Brown could have easily indulged his audience had he wanted to. As it was, Quick Millions was too offbeat to achieve the larger popularity of its competitors. Brown's career as a director was limited to two other films in the early thirties, although his writing credits extend into the fifties with Kansas City Confidential. His second film, Hell's Highway (1932), produced by David O. Selznick at RKO, was an exposé of convict camps that managed to be released ahead of the better-publicized, more ambitious I Am a Fugitive from a Chain Gang. Hollywood hokum has been known to succeed where its more pretentious efforts have failed, but Hell's Highway was a hopeless compromise that managed to gulp down its own message, offering as a curtain line, "Prison is a pleasure," from a murderous bigamist (Charles Middleton) faced with the prospect of release. Brown's third and last, Blood Money (1933), produced by Zanuck's newly formed Twentieth Century Pictures, was set on the busy, shady periphery of gangland, among shysters, stoolies, club owners, and bail-bond officers; and, like Dashiell Hammett, Brown excelled in recreating little ceremonies of trust and betrayal within a picaresque society soon to be hopelessly sanitized by Damon Runyon. Brown's attention to the kinky behavior of the ruling class furnished the one consistent social comment in all three of his films. The sadistic warden (C. Henry

Gordon) in *Hell's Highway* who likes to play his fiddle after hours, the perverse debutante in *Quick Millions* (whom Fitzgerald would not disown), the nymphomaniacal society girl (Frances Dee) in *Blood Money* with a hysterical hankering for rough trade—all of them served as strategic opposition to the healthy appetites of Brown's heroes and hoods.

The Public Enemy, with its credentials of articulate intention, moralistic ending, and case-history structure that appeared to compensate for the reasonable amount of violence it contained, was nonetheless to arouse disseminate, termitelike civic groups into coordinated protest and threats of action. The gangster-film genre suddenly crystallized, and *The Public Enemy*, as the archetype, was open to attack. The pressure groups, for the record, included such disparate organizations as the World War Veterans of Shenandoah Valley, the Exchange Club of Elizabeth, New Jersey, and the Federal Council of Churches of Christ in America. Like most cases in which censorship is invoked, these groups merely sought some token reassurance that the community was still properly policed. The Patrolmen's Benevolent Association was the most vociferous of the groups—understandably so, since its members stood to suffer the most from audience identification, or lack thereof.

The self-appointed moral forces of the nation—civic organizations as well as the more militant factions of the Catholic and Protestant churches—were kept at bay by one much maligned man with the skills and temperament of a country lawyer, an evangelist, and a professional lobbyist. Will H. Hays was no stranger to corruption. He had acted as middleman between the Republican Party (which he had served as national chairman) and Harry F. Sinclair, one of the oil financiers who constituted the notorious Ohio Gang and were ultimately exposed in the Teapot Dome scandal. Hays had accepted two hundred sixty thousand dollars in Liberty Bonds on behalf of the party, plus a personal gift of eighty-five thousand dollars. But by 1928, when he was being denounced within the GOP for selling advantageous oil leases "to the willful despoilers of the nation," Hays had already resigned his job as paymaster general under the Harding administration in order to direct the new, self-censoring organ of the film industry, the Motion Picture Producers and Directors Association (commonly abbreviated MPAA). He had assumed the job in 1922, and he was expected to do for the movies what Judge Landis had done for baseball, that is, to keep it clean for the masses. (The Fatty Arbuckle scandal in 1921 had aroused as much public indignation as had Arnold Rothstein's fixing of the 1919 World Series.)

In 1927, the first code of self-regulation had been formulated, and, by 1931, it was under attack from most sides. "All the Hays *dont's* could be condensed into one commandment," wrote Alva Johnson in a *New Yorker* profile in 1933, "don't hit anybody that can hit back." Legally most gangsters couldn't, and whether they would have is open to doubt, considering that the movies conferred upon them a certain acceptability.

A number of recent reports,* mostly British and mostly concerned with mass response to television, offer convincing proof that, at least where children are concerned, identification with violent characters is more likely to occur when violence is perpetrated by a "positive" rather than a "negative" figure. Another point to emerge from these reports is that audience identification cannot take place when bland, egoless figures are involved. One can retroactively apply these findings to the early days of sound movies and their comparatively naïve audiences. Dialogue and song had brought stasis to a medium that, almost ontologically, was related to motion; and violence had a liberating effect on the viewer. Spoken dialogue, usually of a moralizing nature, reinforced by cautionary titles, were feeble compensation for violent action.

Passivity does not invite empathy, especially in a pragmatic nation, haunted by frontier spirits old and new, where conflict is unfailingly resolved in physical terms. An essentially passive hero, likely to be found in foreign films (for instance in Eric Rohmer's "moral tales"), has yet to appear in America, where desire is ideally translated into action without any mediating reflection or ideology. And criminal activity is in general sharply individuated. On the screen, a character is sharply defined by his activity, and if this activity requires concentration, steady nerves, and a certain dexterity, it cannot fail to communicate to the viewer the bracing awareness of the physical action itself. A "heist" or "caper," from inception through execution, has the power to ensnare us in total commitment independent of ideology.

In the early thirties, the best that Hollywood could offer were cautionary father-figures like Lewis Stone's warden in *The Big House*, and all the sensible admonitions in that film were obliterated by the vivid impression of Wallace Beery clutching a Tommy gun. Even in the iconography of the American silent film, the image of W. S. Hart wielding his six-shooters rivals that of Chaplin's Tramp. American films specialize in violence to this day, and it was not until the social and political changes wrought by the Roosevelt administration and the reorganization of the FBI in the mid-thirties that the conventions of the crime genre were reworked in favor of the lawman. This reversal followed closely on the decision to grant the G-men, hitherto unarmed federal lawyers, special powers to carry firearms. The man with the gun was still the center of attention, but now he wore a badge.

It is curious to come across an editorial in the form of a film review in *Outlook*, a critical weekly of rather liberal views for 1931:

Furthermore, *Doorway to Hell, Little Caesar, The Secret Six, Quick Millions* and now *The Public Enemy* are too alive, too exciting and too important a part of the economic and political life of the American community to be suppressed, even to protect a few half-witted imitative morons. Perhaps if we see enough of them some of us will get enough energy to do something about gang rule.

* Among them: Hilde Himmelweit and others, *Television and the Child*, BBC Audience Research Department, 1971; *Violence on Television: Programming Content and Viewer Perception*, BBC Audience Research Department, 1971; André Glucksman: *Violence on the Screen: a Report on Research into the Effects on Young People of Scenes of Violence in Films and Television*, British Film Institute, 1972.

Outlook was in fact espousing the official Hays line—indeed, some of the defenses invoked on behalf of *Scarface* less than a year later were drawn almost verbatim from the above quote. The gangster film, ideally, was expected to mobilize the viewer into taking action against the outrages depicted on the screen. This was also the moral excuse used by the press, except that gangsters usually made such good copy and were rendered in such lively, believable terms that a mimetic response was almost certain.

A righteous image had to be found and opposed to that of the law-breaker. The obvious choice would have been that of the policeman. But 1931 saw the publication of the findings of the Wickersham Committee on Law Observance and Enforcement (headed by former Attorney General George W. Wickersham), which included the well-publicized Fourteenth Report exposing police corruption and brutality. The image of graft-taking police officials was barely tolerated in comedies like *The Front Page*, yet scenes of brutal third-degree methods had been accepted rather casually as standard police procedure—even though the "sweating out" of a suspect constituted a glaring violation of civil liberties.

A film such as *Alibi* (1929), like the stage play *Nightstick* (1927) that inspired it, seems now to exist solely to support two vivid and rather repellent third-degree sequences. In one of these, a hood suspected of driving a getaway car is terrorized: a window is opened, fingerprints are erased from a gun; a detective dons a pair of gloves while informing the suspect that he's to be shot "while trying to escape," shoots the gun at the floor, then presses it against the victim's head; the room literally swirls around in multiple exposure. The scene backfires and becomes an indictment, not of the cringing "cowardly" hood, but of the nominal heroes—the upright detective and the police inspector. *Alibi* was too crude a piece of filmmaking to draw any sweeping conclusion, even allowing that it was one of the earliest sound films that dealt with gangsterism and also possibly the first in which the dread rattle of the submachine gun was recorded simultaneously with its shattering visual effect. Nevertheless, the film surely must have tarnished the official image of the fair and humane police force. The third degree continued to appear in films—in *The Vice Squad, Paid, The Secret Six, Beast of the City, Penthouse*, to mention a few—until Section 9 of the Production Code of 1933 specifically laid down the law, calling for "discretion and restraint" and the depiction of such methods "within the careful limits of good taste." But nowhere in this belated attempt to whitewash the image of the law enforcer was a disclaimer or condemnation of the third degree to be found.

This frustrating state of affairs inspired a series of films, such as *The Secret Six* and *Star Witness* (both 1931) and *Beast of the City* (1932), which culminated in Cecil B. De Mille's misguided *This Day and Age* (1933). All of these gratified the viewer's suppressed longing for justice, privately and ruthlessly administered, without the bother of legal niceties and compromises. These films promoted wish fulfillment rather than civic consciousness; they were nostalgic for a simpler, pragmatic America where good and violent citizens took the law into their own hands in defense of

Sweating out prisoners and suspects: Convict Richard Dix plays into the hands of the wardens to save his kid brother (Tom Brown) from the "sweat box" in *Hell's Highway,* 1932. *RKO-Radio*

Ritual terrorizing of a hood (Elmer Ballard) in *Alibi,* 1929. *United Artists*

the community. Although California has always been prone to extreme forms of politicization, no amount of research could turn up evidence of a right-wing conspiracy at work through these pictures. Never mind that William Randolph Hearst bankrolled both *The Secret Six* and *Beast of the City* (and paranoiacs may even draw sinister conclusions from the Marion Davies comedies), still the monumental misalliance of Hearst, the pro-Roosevelt anti-Semite, and Louis B. Mayer, the kosher Republican, guaranteed that the message, *any* message, would be lost.

The early thirties were closer to the Wild West than to Watergate, the Minute Man and the town marshal were (and may still be, for Middle Americans) powerful mythical figures. Add to this the mood of exasperated outrage that followed one of the most heinous incidents in gangland, the 1931 street battle in East Harlem in which a child was killed and several people wounded, and you get a crop of vigilante fantasies transposing the conventions of the Western to the current crisis, often more explicitly violent than any gangster film. The power of the posse was made to seem a desperate but necessary solution.

The Secret Six was that rarity, an underworld story conceived and written by a woman, Frances Marion, who also scripted *The Big House,* and both films were directed by her then husband, George Hill. In its attempts to demystify the image of the criminal, *The Secret Six* was tough and unsentimental in a way that male-scripted films seldom were. There was little romantic distortion, and one can gather Marion's attitude from the scene in which a young and brittle Jean Harlow calmly munches on an apple as the remains of a gangster are taken out in a coffin. Marion certainly wasted no sympathy on hoods. Scorpio (Wallace Beery) is a butcher in the stockyards, a proletarian brute who rises in the ranks of the underworld, propelled by a seedy, unemotional shyster, Newton (Lewis Stone). Scorpio disposes of the competition mostly by shooting them in the back—so much for honor among gangsters. He comes to dominate Centro (a pseudonymous city that represents Cicero, the Capone stronghold) while his political candidate, Nick the Gouger (Paul Hurst in a wicked cartoon of Chicago's former mayor "Big Bill" Thompson), is elected mayor. Like Capone, Scorpio sleeps in silk pajamas and ornate beds; he employs a mincing male secretary who rewrites his correspondence in impeccable business form. "Don't say 'rotten,'" advises the secretary. "All right, say 'stinking,'" counters Scorpio, "none of that sissy stuff for me."

Marion's underworld was an assortment of misfits, mental defectives, stoolies, the vermin of society; and she let them have it. *The Secret Six* included the usual police interrogation and a scene, lit by flashes of machine-gun fire, in which a smiling, moronic young hoodlum is mowed down in a darkened speakeasy, bullets ripping through a player piano. The fade-out was suitably unheroic, with Scorpio walking to the chair, dim and unrepentant to the last; even so, it bowdlerized Marion's original ending in which Scorpio was trampled to death under the hooves of stampeding cattle, in the stockyards whence he rose.

The Secret Six set a precedent of sorts, in that it was the first crime picture to pass Chicago's censorship board without cuts. Hearst had paved the
way by having the plot serialized in two of his papers there, the *Herald-
Examiner* and the *Evening-American,* and Hizzoner Bill Thompson had already been replaced by Anton Cermak as mayor. *The Secret Six,* for all its
positive intentions, did not come up with a sympathetic, credible law-and-
order image. The Secret Six of the title was inspired by Elliot Ness and his
team of undercover agents, who gathered enough evidence to get Capone
convicted on a tax-evasion charge. Recruited by the chief of police after
his peremptory dismissal by the new puppet mayor, the Secret Six is made
up of executives from the Treasury Department, the Internal Revenue
Service, and the Department of Immigration. They wear hoods like Klans-
men and keep somewhat sinister assignations as they wage war on Scorpio
and his organization. When legal action fails, thanks to Newton's shrewd
courtroom tactics plus a bit of intimidation and/or bribery exerted on the
jury, the Secret Six settles for a commando raid on mob headquarters that
shatters Scorpio's grip on the city.

The Ness operation, which thirty years later would inspire one of
television's longest-lasting series, "The Untouchables," had been a model of
legal strategy. But Hollywood's impulses tugged traditionally toward the
violent solution, never more than in the early thirties, instead of the tedious
democratic process. Popular pulp magazines, along with the comic strips
and radio serials, made acceptable the notion of a domestic death squad:
Doc Savage, The Shadow, and other interim heroes before the advent of
the fully credited G-man carried an implication that private action had to
compensate for the ineffectuality of the law. The figure of the masked
avenger was obviously an American creation missing, at least until recent
times, in European pulp literature.*

An unpopular film nonetheless, *The Secret Six* was noticeable mainly as
a steppingstone in the careers of Jean Harlow and Clark Gable, here playing formula juvenile roles, contrasting with the established villainy of
Beery and Stone. For its time, the film was cast against the grain. Neither
Beery nor Stone would again be allowed to lapse into unsympathetic roles.
Harlow was rushed into a companion piece, *Beast of the City.* As a sensu-
ously ironical gang-girl, she is the one who grabs at our sympathies today,
with her contemporary resilience not unlike that of Gloria Grahame in the
fifties, when she essayed similar parts. (When asked by a young cop if she
likes to get hurt, Harlow replies: "Oh, I dunno, it can be fun if it's done in
the right spirit." Oceans of profundity in the unimaginative blacks and
whites of *Beast of the City!*)

The new picture took its cue from a written prologue, signed by Herbert Hoover, to the effect that "instead of the glorification of the gangster we

---

* In his *Theory of Film Practice* (Praeger, 1973), Noel Burch touches on the differences between the
sensibilities of American and European children: ". . . the violence inherent in American life gives children in that country a sophisticated awareness that prepares them for these [horror] films. . . . The European child living in a society where daily violence is rare, is far more sheltered, and therefore more
vulnerable than his American counterpart." Daily life in Europe has grown increasingly violent in the
recent past with a corresponding escalation of violence in comic strips, pulp literature, and movies.

need the glorification of the policemen, who do their duty and give their lives for the safety of society." As portrayed in this and other crusading films, society was hardly worth defending. Images of social and moral decay recurred throughout *Beast of the City:* patrons in a speakeasy boo a raiding police squad, the mayor and the police commissioner are studies in corruption in high places, witnesses are bribed, the usual shyster role is filled, and so on. Against this evidence of graft, venality, apathy, and the failure of established law, the resolve to rescue society from itself is almost inevitable.

Swarthy gangsters and a blond decoy: Jean Hersholt, Wallace Ford, Jean Harlow, and J. Carrol Naish in *Beast of the City*, 1931. *Metro-Goldwyn-Mayer*

The one just man in this modern city of the plain is a police captain, played by Walter Huston, a paragon of civic rectitude and domestic virtue who speaks in vivid Biblical tones: "This town is as rotten as an open grave," or "If a guy hasn't got the strength to go straight, he turns yellow inside." Corruption has even touched the captain's younger brother (Wallace Ford), a detective inducted into the gang through a liaison with the moll played by Harlow. The captain offers him a chance to make amends: the greaseball gang boss (Jean Hersholt) must be provoked into personally shooting the brother, so that a posse will be justified for breaking into the speakeasy stronghold. In a climactic gunfight, the gang is wiped out by a staunch vigilante group, and the brothers die hand in hand, united in violence for all eternity, the censor having made obvious allowances in view of the film's moral purpose. Nothing in either *Little Caesar* or *The Public Enemy* could match in violence a shot of a wounded, dying J. Carrol Naish drooling blood. Despite the hue-and-cry about violence on the screen, these two earlier films were virtually blood-free.

The original story of *Beast of the City* is credited to W. R. Burnett, but it was not so much an original as an updating of his own Western novel, *Saint Johnson* (1930), which was filmed at the same time at Universal studios, this time preserving the original's Old West period and locale. The two versions can be profitably compared. The anecdotal material was structurally the same—a man of action enforces the law in his community—and Walter Huston played the lead in both versions, in *Law and Order* (as *Saint Johnson* was retitled) a romanticized version of the historical Wyatt Earp. The makers of *Beast of the City* (Charles Brabin directed, John Lee Mahin adapted from Burnett's book) were naïve enough to believe that transferring Tombstone to the usual large, unnamed American city and making Earp into a cop would automatically comply with the requirements of a morale-builder. There is a sequence in *Law and Order* that deals with the hanging of a pathetic, simple-minded, and likable rancher who has irresponsibly killed a man. The justice or validity of such an act was not questioned in a Western context, at least not in 1932. The force behind Wyatt Earp was not merely society, which the Western as genre invariably establishes as fluid and yet to develop. It was instead civilization itself which granted the marshal the special powers of his demimythical office, first and foremost the license to kill. Behind the policeman hero of *Beast of the City* there was only an urgent social problem which the picture attempted to solve with a modern reenactment of the gunfight at the O.K. Corral.

A simplistic longing for the allegiances of frontier life is a reflex reaction in times of crisis; but the Western might not be, after all, the perfectly viable form that André Bazin imagined. It takes time to hone conventions and build rationales. It is not by accident that the gangster heroes in *all* the films previously discussed (and in *Scarface* and others soon to be of concern) are put to death either by their own kind or by the police serving as a faceless, impersonal instrument of society. At this point, the audience was not quite ready to grant the modern lawman a license to kill; that license belonged only to the law.

In May 1931, Jack L. Warner had announced that his studio would stop producing gangster pictures; that, as a matter of fact, he had not allowed his fifteen-year-old son to watch any of them. Behind this sudden policy reversal, one divines Zanuck about to get the jump on the other studios by launching the next vogue—the social-consciousness film. To corroborate Warner's claim of going straight, William Wellman began shooting *Star Witness* a month later, and the picture, a sort of rebuttal to *The Public Enemy,* was released by August.

The story (by Lucien Hubbard, a Zanuck-appointed studio supervisor) brings the threat of violence into the lives of a middle-class American family which has witnessed an underworld slaying. The family might identify the culprit as mobster Maxie Campo (Ralph Ince), but all are intimidated into silence, with the exception of visiting Grandfather Summerville (Charles Sale, a vaudeville monologuist who specialized in Americana), a veteran of the Civil War. At a symbolic level, Grandpa stood for an older, idealistic America, unswerving in the performance of its duty, simple and courageous and wise. His demiurgical qualities are suggested, for instance, when he locates his abducted grandchild (Dickie Moore) through the poetic expedient of playing "Yankee Doodle Dandy" on his tin whistle during a citywide quest. The lovable old codger also delivers a speech or two about the loss of the old Union spirit and the perils of allowing foreigners to run the country. *Star Witness* vividly came to terms with its "America for Americans" theme; there was a montage of scenes showing the police raiding premises and breaking down doors to round up suspects, a purge of what looks like the

The American family threatened: Maxie Campo (Ralph Ince) towers over the fallen Grandpa (Charles Sale) and intimidates the Summervilles into silence, in *Star Witness*, 1931. *Warner Brothers*

Lower East Side. Grandpa's testimony sends Campo to the chair in the most economical of denouements: as Grandpa takes the oath in court, there is a cut to a headline announcing the execution. His civic mission accomplished, Grandpa returns to the old-folks home. Driving in an open wagon alongside a Civil War cemetery, he muses that soon he should be joining his fallen comrades as part of the inviolate American past. The viewer is left to wonder what is to become of the nation when men like Grandpa are no more.

"It was to call attention to the evil of racketeering, and to point to the uncontaminated idealism of American youth, that I made ... *This Day and Age* in the spring of 1933," reminisced Cecil B. De Mille in his autobiography. It was a strange statement to make; by this time, Roosevelt was in the White House, Prohibition had ended, the gangster film had filled the screens for almost six years, and the Production Code, reinforced by the Catholic Church, was about to muzzle Hollywood for the next twenty. *This Day and Age* was a diagram of mob violence that, in our day and age, suggests such disparate forces and events as Mussolini's *squadristi*, the Nazi book burnings, the Columbia University sit-ins, and the May 1968 student riots in Paris. The vortex of the violence is a redneck gangster (played by Charles Bickford) who runs the protection racket in a college town. He

A gangster tried in a kangaroo court of college students: Edward Nugent, Charles Bickford, and Richard Cromwell in *This Day and Age*, 1933. *Paramount*

murders a kindly Jewish tailor (Harry Green) and is acquitted on a legal technicality in an atmosphere of adult apathy and/or cynicism. Thereupon the outraged college students plan and execute the kidnapping of the gangster, try him in a kangaroo court, and obtain a signed confession from him by lowering him into an abandoned mine shaft full of rats, after which he is turned over to the police.

In his *King of Kings*, De Mille had conceived a Christ figure that would be equally acceptable to Jews, Catholics, and Protestants; in *This Day and Age*, he aimed at dramatizing a lynching without alienating either southern conservatives or liberals anywhere. He cunningly hedged his bet by including Jewish and black stereotypes among the gangster's victims and judges. He took up more than half the film's running time to set up our most vindictive responses; then, all scruples duly removed, he allowed us the release of a justified lynching (bloodless as well), playing upon our basic ambivalence to violence and, incidentally, delivering one of the more vivid crowd scenes in his long and specialized career. He managed this by hitting upon the gangster figure as a sort of universal scapegoat on which to discharge our guilt.

In retrospect, 1931 looms as the peak year of the gangster film; and yet, of some four hundred pictures produced in Hollywood and in the eastern studios that year—eight new releases a week, a staggering amount by today's diminished standards—a mere forty could be considered members of the genre. The year literally started off with a bang as *Little Caesar* went into general release; it was followed by a distinguished array of violence that included *The Criminal Code, The Finger Points, The Public Enemy, Quick Millions, City Streets, The Secret Six,* and *Smart Money*. All of these were far from being blockbusters as we understand the term today, yet they were seen, talked about, and written about to such an extent that a mere 10 percent of the yearly output suddenly came to represent the dominant trend, outgrossing and outclassing war films, Westerns, musicals, and society dramas.

If in 1931 the moviegoer sought a respite from the headlines and the breadlines, the upper world had definitely lost out to the underworld: Norma Shearer and Joan Crawford were smart enough to desert their Art Deco penthouses to go slumming in *A Free Soul* and *Dance Fools Dance,* a move that netted them better-than-average vehicles. If the world was seeking escapism, then the musical—being the most removed from reality—should have been the most favored genre of all. And yet, 1931 was a disastrous year for musicals. That violence on film could provide an escape, especially in a period of acute economic crisis, was a possibility voiced by some and ignored by an ever growing number of reform-minded groups. Hollywood crime films of the early thirties dealt with gut reactions, with street life, with recognizable locales like slums and speakeasies, and they came as close to making a social comment on their period as any genre ever has. Pressure groups apart, they were not considered subversive, at least not by the ever watchful Will H. Hays. In fact, Hays was capable of arguing the case for crime films in the open, and when, in 1931, a group of New Jersey civic leaders intensified the drive against them, following the death of Winslow Eliot, a twelve-year-old boy who was shot by a friend in a playroom that the victim had decorated as a speakeasy, Hays fought back from the pages of *The New York Times*.

In his memoirs, Hays wrote: "The gangster cycle was a natural because the gangster cult had been a main theme of journalism for a decade. But there was no tendency in these crime stories to say to the audience, 'Go thou and do likewise.' On the whole, penologists acquitted the industry of any incitement to crime and sometimes even praised it as a deterrent to crime." In Hays's opinion, drinking and fornicating were the urgent issues, the hip flask inevitably leading to the one-night stand and the subsequent dissolution of American family life. The moviegoer of 1931, economically insecure and conscious of his low social status, could be more easily incited to drink and debauchery than to actual crime; there was altogether too much sex on the screen for Hays's taste, and drinking was treated much too casually. To begin with, the Puritan ethic made guilt inseparable from sex to most Americans, and since 1920 the Volstead Act had made white-collar criminals out of thousands of drinking adults throughout the country. Hays insisted that the screen remind audiences of their guilt, moral as much as technical, and the industry complied with a few half-hearted pictures like Leo McCarey's *Wild Company,* so sanctimonious and outmoded that one senses some sort of subversion operating under cover of moralizing.

When the crime wave flooded movie theaters in the Depression, Hays attempted to establish an etiquette of violence. He took pains that blood did not show on the screen or that the gun and the victim did not appear in the same frame. Place a still photo from the most violent gangster picture next to a UPI shot of the real Saint Valentine's Day Massacre, an untidy, blood-spattered obscene tableau of death, and one will realize the cosmetic skill of camera angle, arrangement, and lighting that went into making movies more brutal than was supposedly permissible. From the artistic point of view, Hays's influence was infinitely beneficial; not because it deterred some moviegoers from imitation but because it forced filmmakers to use subterfuge, ellipsis, and stylization, and to convey much of the forbidden through a system of visual hints. Ironically, Hays himself was godfather to the gangster hero that the films borrowed from the tabloids.

That the criminal image could function as a projection of collective resentment does not seem to have bothered Hays much; if it did, he probably dismissed it as cathartic. There was evidence on the screen itself that the gangster was the romantic male figure of the period. When audiences respond with massive identification, the result is instant celebrity for the performer on display, and the three revelations of 1931 were Gable, Cagney, and Robinson. Spencer Tracy and Humphrey Bogart would eventually follow the same route, but it took them longer to reach stardom. Neither was lucky enough to play a killer in his early career, the vicious type that Robinson and Cagney had created in their best films, or that Gable had

The end of a bandit chase, New York City.

The untidy, blood-spattered tableau of real death: a news shot from a documentary, *The Cry of the World*, 1933. *Twentieth Century-Fox*

in four of his releases that year; and so, their film personalities lacked the charisma endowed by crime. Upon achieving star status, these performers would be recast in sympathetic/romantic roles that, however, did not totally erase the original image. They remained tough and aggressive and, in some cases, more than merely misogynous, but the traits were put to work in another context. The latent antisocial image could be made to surface whenever their careers showed signs of flagging, and Robinson, Cagney, and Bogart made spectacular comebacks in the forties and fifties by recycling their original hood characters to suit the changing times.

The film that was to jolt the already uneasy truce between filmmakers and civic groups was *Scarface*. Late in 1930, Hollywood learned with a certain trepidation that Howard Hughes was about to produce a gangster epic to surpass all others in cost, scope, authenticity, and, needless to say, violence. In the film world, Hughes was considered a maverick. He was a multimillionaire eccentric who resembled Lindbergh in looks and reserve, and his main interests (and vast holdings) resided in aeronautics and oil drilling. He dabbled now and then in film production, thinking very little of shelving a completed film, *Hell's Angels,* to have it remade with sound and dialogue at a cost of an extra million dollars. (Twenty years later, Hughes was to spend so long editing another aviation picture, *Jet Pilot*—seven years—that by the time of its final release the jets looked as obsolete as the Fokkers and Spads of *Hell's Angels;* whereupon the picture was re-called and new aerial sequences shot at great expense.) Time and money meant little to Hughes, who was a compulsive tinkerer with his movies; they meant just about everything to the rest of the industry. And therein lay the source of Hollywood's worries. Would Hughes abide by the Production Code of Ethics, like all the major studios, or was he about to challenge what was at best a shaky gentleman's agreement?

Hughes decided to base his film on the life and times of Alfonso Capone, the Scarface Al of the tabloids, the most powerful underworld figure of the twenties, and one of America's icons. As a matter of fact, Capone's own film debut had been announced around the same time by his theatrical agent, William C. Grill. Capone's film was to be produced in New York City, and his two-hundred-thousand-dollar salary was to be turned over to an unemployment fund. Capone could well afford to be that generous: his gross weekly income was estimated by *The New York Times* as two million dollars. But the project never took shape. The Hays Office laid down the law: the motion picture, it said, could not be used as a medium for charity or for personal promotion of any kind. And so the real Capone's film appearances were confined to the newsreels, where he was often seen going in and out of courtrooms, flanked by his lawyers, invariably beating the rap. His fan mail at the time was staggering.

One can imagine what attracted Hughes to Capone: a feeling perhaps that his own influence was a match for the gangster's, a certain admiration for the self-made man, the sheer fascination that Capone held for his entire generation. (Capone received more media coverage than President Hoover.) The first Hughes press releases refrained from mentioning the gangster by name, but it was soon made public that Caddo, the Hughes film outfit, had acquired the screen rights to *Scarface,* a 1930 novel by Armitage Trail (pseudonym for Maurice Coons) in which the hero bore a biographical re-semblance to Capone, and that Fred Pasley, a reporter from *The New York Daily News* and an authority on Capone, had been retained as technical adviser.

Hughes brought in Howard Hawks as coproducer and director. Hughes had greatly admired Hawks's *The Dawn Patrol,* a much tauter and more dramatic aviation picture than his own *Hell's Angels.* In fact, he had tried to stop the release of *The Dawn Patrol,* claiming that it was an infringement on his picture; when this failed, he enlisted its director. In all his film ventures, Hughes never made a wiser decision than hiring Hawks. Lewis Milestone, the rather lugubrious director of *All Quiet on the Western Front,* was the house director at Caddo, the man responsible for *The Racket* and the then unreleased *The Front Page,* and whose forte was montage rather than repartee. At this point Hawks had yet to make a talkie comedy; he was eventually to remake *The Front Page* as *His Girl Friday* in 1940, hitting on the idea that it would be twice as funny to make the star reporter a woman, and he was right. Hawks began the Hughes project by having all the research cross-filed, then he added some inside information bought directly from the underworld. For the final screenplay he went after Ben Hecht himself, overcoming Hecht's well-publicized contempt for crime films, all of which, since the *Underworld* experience, and next to real front-page stuff, seemed to him revoltingly gutless compromises.

Hecht and Hawks got along fine, having worked in harmony during the preproduction of *Underworld* four years before. It was an association that was to endure for six more projects. Hawks was tall and wiry, like a cowboy sportsman, a type that could not but appeal to an easterner like Hecht. The directors that earned Hecht's esteem did so less by their achievements than by their boozing, gambling, and wenching. Hawks was master of all of these, but he was a self-effacing director besides—most of the contemporary publicity attributed *Scarface* to Hughes instead of Hawks—and he seemed to Hecht the very antithesis of Josef von Sternberg, who was quiet and intellectual off the set but extremely imperious at work, and who Hecht regarded as the despicable embodiment of the artistic director.

Hecht, who liked to flaunt his cultural credentials when he wasn't being rough, rowdy, irreverent, or profane, was intrigued by Hawks's proposal that the Capone family be portrayed as if they were the Borgias set down in Chicago. This meant primarily a suggestion of incest between Capone and his sister. The same suggestion appears, understated, in the original Trail novel, in which the hero's downfall is brought about by his impulsive killing of a gunman who has seduced his kid sister. In the novel, this is made doubly ironic by the fact that she does not know she is the hero's sister and that the Capone character ignores the fact that she and the gunman have married.

Hecht's interest was aroused for exactly eleven days, in January 1931, at the end of which Hawks had a working script and most of the dialogue for *Scarface.* John Lee Mahin, Seton I. Miller, and W. R. Burnett received screen credit for continuity and dialogue, but Hawks credited Hecht almost exclusively. At his own request, Hecht was paid one thousand dollars a day, a good rate for the period but still quite below the twenty thousand allocated to the scenarist in the generous budget. Later, he could boast of winning the difference from Hawks while playing backgammon aboard the Twentieth Century Limited from New York to Chicago, but, what was more important to Hecht, his reputation as one of the shrewdest, fastest writers in the business was consolidated.

The Borgia angle was barely visible in the film as released, but it was still clear that both Hecht and Hawks were aiming at something more ambitious than the usual. "These were violent times," said Hawks, "and violence made the story." There were at least fifteen killings in the script, a statistic that made the Hays people sit up and take notice. The most infamous deeds of the past decade were lovingly woven into the narrative. In addition to the Saint Valentine's Day Massacre, which furnished a brief episode, the opening sequence was a reenactment of the death in a telephone booth of "Big Jim" Colosimo in 1920, shot by Capone under Johnny Torrio's orders, and a hospital killing in the film was derived from an episode in the career of Legs Diamond. Several scenes had already figured in Hecht's original treatment for *Underworld*, such as the killing of Dion O'Bannion in his North Side flower shop and the siege of the gangster's bunker. The latter found factual confirmation in the capture in April 1931, of Francis "Two Gun" Crowley after the famous Siege of West 90th Street.

Both writer and director contended to be on speaking terms with the Capone mob, but who did not in those days? Capone disclaimed any personal knowledge of writers like Edward Dean Sullivan, whose *Rattling the Cup* and *Chicago Surrenders* were regarded as inside jobs, and, in an interview with *Variety*, he mocked the authenticity of gangster films. But Hecht counted as one of his cherished memories a visit by two of Capone's henchmen, who wanted to make sure that the picture contained nothing derogatory about the Big Boy. Hawks says that Capone himself was shown some of the rushes and marveled at the accuracy of some of the scenes. Anything for an imprimatur from the man himself!

When *Scarface* finally faced its audience, Capone was serving time in a federal prison in Atlanta for income-tax evasion. Still, he could have sued for libel had he wanted to. There was nothing in *Scarface* that could have possibly harmed his legend. The screenplay exercised license of the most poetic sort. As in the original novel, the hero's name was Tony Camonte, and his rise in the underworld followed broadly that of Capone's under the tutelage of Colosimo and Johnny Torrio, but these characters had their names changed respectively to "Big Louie" Costillo and Johnny Lovo. In the final reel Camonte died, while in real life Capone had a few years to go, most of them in prison, until his nonviolent death in 1947. A number of Capone's personal traits, however, were incorporated in the Camonte character: a taste for Italian opera, cultural aspirations, a facial scar. The funniest sequence in a film that is often darkly humorous has Camonte attending a performance of *Rain* with what looks like an orchestraful of bodyguards. "I like to see some shows like that. Serious." Called away at intermission to rub out a rival mobster, he leaves behind a moronic underling who later reports on the fate of Sadie Thompson: "She climbed back in the hay with the Army." Replies Camonte with a wink, "That's-a fine, she's-a smart girl." Capone must have chuckled if he ever saw the scene.

Paul Muni, who played Tony Camonte, did not physically resemble Capone, who was squat and round faced. (Rod Steiger, Neville Brand, and Ben Gazzara, who played the role later, and without benefit of pseudonyms, were closer to the mark, especially Gazzara, whose Italian mannerisms seem unforced in comparison to Steiger's.) Muni mercifully refrained from mannerisms; he acted like an immigrant all right, though not quite Italian.

Of Austrian Jewish parentage, Muni had emigrated to the Lower East Side at the age of four, and, by the time *Scarface* was made, he had been an actor for twenty-four years, first with the prestigious Yiddish Art Theater and then on Broadway. Brought to Hollywood by the Fox Company in 1929, he had seen all the good roles go to the Studio contract players: Louis Beretti (in *Born Reckless*) to Edmund Lowe, Liliom (in the film from Ferenc Molnar's play) to Charles Farrell. After two minor pictures he returned East, disillusioned with the talkies; a few months later, he tested for *Scarface* and won the part. Muni, a man whose screen image was never quite fixed, was a rarity in a generation of great behavioral actors like Cagney, Robinson, and Tracy. His European stage training showed: he relied too much on dialect, on make-up, on a forced body language that was not natural to him. It is not surprising that Fox once considered grooming him as a new Lon Chaney; in his second film he played seven different roles, including that of a black boxer. Muni was never wholly believable as Zola, Pasteur, Juarez, or the Chinese peasant of *The Good Earth;* he was too laboriously playing at being these characters so foreign to his nature. When he did not resort to makeup or theatrical mannerisms, as in *I Am a Fugitive from a Chain Gang* or *Hi Nellie,* he was earnest but gray. Arguably the most proletarian performer until the advent of John Garfield, Muni easily projected an engaging loser quality.

In *Scarface,* Muni's mugging showed, especially in contrast to the minimal emotion displayed by George Raft, who played Rinaldo, Camonte's buddy, bodyguard, and unwitting nemesis. Nonetheless, Hawks found a way to manipulate Muni and bring out the essential childishness which is Camonte's most winning quality. There is something exhilarating about Muni handling his first Tommy gun in the film, like a kid with a new toy: "I'm goin' to write my name all over this town in big letters. Outta my way, I'm spittin'."

During production, the violent aura surrounding *Scarface* was played up by the gossip columns and fan magazines, with special attention paid to the Gaylord Lloyd episode. On a visit to the Westwood studios, one of three sound stages that Hughes had rented for the film, Harold Lloyd's brother had lost an eye when a percussion cap exploded prematurely. The company was cleared of any responsibility—Lloyd had carelessly shifted position to get a better view of the action—but the papers magnified the incident. As it turned out, it also had artistic repercussions. For the most violent scene in the film, a daylight raid on Camonte's restaurant hangout, Hawks had the set cleared so as not to endanger the extras, then had it cribbed with machine-gun fire. Later, the actors reenacted the scene in front of a screen on which the shooting was back-projected. Muni, Raft, and other cast members and extras cowered beneath the tables as the room seemed to explode and splinter into debris above and around them, a larger-than-life effect that is almost surreal and that would have been impossible to achieve in any other manner.

"Get outta my way, I'm spittin'." Paul Muni, as Tony Camonte in *Scarface,* 1932, gets his first Tommy gun. Vince Barnett and Karen Morley at his side. *United Artists*

After viewing a rough-cut of the picture, there followed a list of recommendations from the Hays Office that not even Hughes could afford to disregard, under penalty of being refused the MPAA seal of approval. A scene with Tony and his sister Cesca (Ann Dvorak) in each other's arms, after he has slapped her and torn the bodice of her dress, allowed the incest theme to surface and was ordered deleted. With a touch of regret, Muni was to declare later: "The character had to be made harder, less sympathetic, to satisfy the censor," and the censor had probably grasped that most of Tony's humanity resided in his attachment to his sister. The wages of crime were not to be displayed: a sequence aboard the gangster's yacht was removed.

But other demands seem picayune, for instance, a short scene in which Camonte buys a lamp for one thousand dollars as a gift to his mother also had to be cut. Furthermore, the Hays Office called for erasures and voice-overs in the soundtrack and advised the reshooting of several scenes. The outcome of these recommendations was a new finale as well as the inclusion of a carefully written prologue that denounced gangster rule in America, "the callous indifference of the government," and asked the audience, "What are *you* going to do about it?"

Hecht and Hawks had meant *Scarface* to be a violent tragicomedy, not an indictment. Hawks remembers what first attracted him to the Capone legend: an anecdote about a testimonial dinner for a mobster at which Capone was to deliver the eulogy. Halfway through his speech, Capone's mood grew darker, until he finished by beating up the guest of honor with a baseball bat. It is a scene that does not appear in *Scarface* (but turns up intact in Nicholas Ray's *Party Girl* twenty-seven years later), yet one deduces that Hawks's viewpoint must have been affected by the absurdly violent situation: Capone's professional ego breaking through the thin veneer of gangland sociability.

Disgusted, Hawks refused to comply with many of the Hays requests; he agreed, however, to shoot a new ending, one in which Camonte dies an ignoble death on the gallows. By then, Muni was back on Broadway appearing in the hit play *Counsellor-at-Law*, and Hawks managed the ending mostly through suggestion: a tracking shot of stockinged feet half-dragged along a prison corridor, a group of newsmen attending the execution, a hand that pulls a lever, a trapdoor that opens. His assistant, Richard Rosson, took over the direction of an additional scene in which a group of reform-minded city officials band together to crack down on rampant gangsterism; a child's death is mentioned at one point, obviously to profit from the public outrage that followed such an incident in New York City, the one accidental killing that earned Vincent Coll the nickname "Mad Dog." All spoken reference to the city of Chicago was struck from the soundtrack, and furthermore, *Scarface* was retitled *The Menace* to dispel whatever doubts were left in the public mind. It was under the new title that the picture was scheduled for release in January 1932, but Hughes contested the title change, threatening to release it without the Hays sanction. It took another four months of haggling before the film opened in New York on May 20, under a compromise title, *Scarface, Shame of the Nation*.

Many a reviewer forsook the film's Rialto opening to catch it in Newark, across the Hudson River, where the original ending, showing Camonte being shot down by the police on the sidewalk outside his hideout, had been retained. Each state had its own board of censors, and Colonel James Wingate, who controlled the board of New York, had been known to censor a movie simply for its depiction of a graft-taking cop or city official. Wingate, who was shortly to join Hays in the formulation of a revised and much stricter Production Code, probably regarded the altered *Scarface* as safely defused, as did the reviewer, of the *World-Telegram*, who praised it as "a

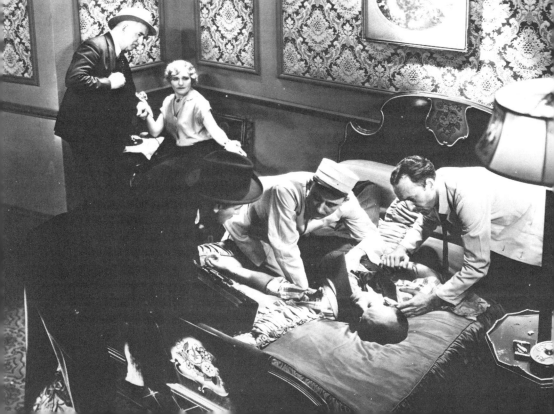

The censor's cuts: too many killings and a suggestion of incest. Two shots missing from the release print, and a scene between Tony and his sister Cesca (Ann Dvorak) that had to be toned down. *Scarface. United Artists*

richly philosophical crime-does-not-pay story." *Scarface* became an instant hit, despite (or because of) the tampering of its attendant publicity and the fact that the film was denounced by one of the most powerful pressure groups in the East, the Order of Sons of Italy in America, as a discredit to the Italian community. The movie went on to become perhaps the most famous crime film of its time in the United States,* though it is not often seen nowadays, all legal prints in this country having been recalled by the late Howard Hughes.

All the additions and corrections hardly made a dent in *Scarface*. To satisfy the censors, an entirely different film would have been necessary. The one that Hecht and Hawks had conceived could not be expurgated that easily; it was too permeated with both of their personalities. Hecht was too gaudy a cynic and too much of a sophisticate to editorialize or descend to sob-sister sentiment. His cops were hard-bitten heavies who never removed their hats, a touch that helped to distinguish them from the hoods, whom they otherwise resembled in speech and ruthlessness. The police lieutenant

* Due to its banning in certain states, it took some time for *Scarface* to recoup its costs of $712,000. Chicago, for instance, would not see the film until more than a year after its release. Foreign sales were limited, and Nazi Germany prohibited the showing of the film, outright and permanently.

The Capone episode that inspired *Scarface* was missing from that film but turned up intact in *Party Girl*, 1959. Lee J. Cobb is the Capone character, John Ireland, his righthand killer. *Metro-Goldwyn-Mayer*

who went after Camonte was not moved by a lofty concern for the public welfare but by personal hate; criminals were "lice" and his ambition was to see Camonte die a coward's death in the gutter, "where a horse has been standing and where you belong." Neither did Hecht entertain any illusions about the crusading fervor of the press, although he liked to boast that journalists manipulated public opinion and were willing to take on the making or breaking of an underworld reputation. Early in *Scarface*, the scene shifts to a city room where an editor (Tully Marshall), wise to the underworld, as was the famous Walter Howie of the Hearst papers, weighs the repercussions of the film's initial killing: "Do you know what the death of Big Louie means? The town's up for grabs. There's a new crew coming out." In the best Hearst tradition, he stirs up the imminent conflict with a war-type headline.

Hecht's florid journalese found visual expression in Hawks's style—rapid-fire, eye-level, gripping. While *Little Caesar* and *The Public Enemy* stuck to their flat realistic *grisaille* and loose, unadventurous framing, in *Scarface* Hawks went for violent chiaroscuro, tight grouping within the frame, and fluid, stalking camera movement. *Scarface* was Hawks's most expressionistic film. It was just as stylized as *Underworld* but much more ferocious: darkened rooms, bodies silhouetted against drawn blinds, pools of light that seem hardly reassuring. The imminence of death that attends every gangster film was made visual here by an X motif hovering over each impending victim. The suprarealistic approach turned out to be perfectly fitting, for the gangster hero of *Scarface* was not done in by the law, like Rico Bandello, or by a rival mob, like Tom Powers, but by his own demons. The film clearly drifted from journalistic chronical and sociological statement into the classic inevitability of tragedy.

Hawks's dramatic films usually dealt with various forms of male society, professionals of one type or another, bound together by a shared sense of purpose; it is useless to search for moral concern at any other level than that of this recurrent theme. In his *The Dawn Patrol* there were no patriotic speeches, and if war was damned at all it was merely as a great absurd event that required that young men fly their rickety airplanes and confront an identical, impersonal adversary. The dogfights take place in the air, far above menial considerations of cultures and boundaries. The picture was about teamwork, male bonding, group loyalty, and most important, about acquiring and perfecting a certain deadly skill. As the underworld power play of *Scarface* unfolds, and "straight" society remains in the background, apathetic or intimidated, it takes very little effort to read the same motifs into this film, especially in the gun battles and car chases which were treated as pure kinetic spectacle.

Camonte's irresistible rise, like that of his two film predecessors, was a violent variation of the American success story. As Camonte becomes more professional, more efficient in his job, he grows progressively more human, that is, more American. At first, he is only a shadow materializing out of the night to put an end to the career of his former employer, Big Louie Costillo. The shadow whistles the theme of the sextet from *Lucia di Lammermoor;* in a film as carefully worked out as *Scarface* even this small detail had its special significance, for the lyrics translate as: "What restrains me in such a moment?" and the same music recurs at key moments of violence. When Camonte emerges from under a towel at a barbership for the audience's first look at him, he turns out to be a simian, pomaded immigrant with an ugly gash on his cheekbone and a vaudeville Italian accent. The Americanization of Camonte can be gauged by the gradual loss of that accent, which corresponds to an evolving wardrobe style, loud, striped shirts and checkered jackets giving way to tie pins and silk robes of expensive bad taste; so that at picture's end Camonte is almost accent-free and tuxedo-sharp—even his hairline seems to have receded from the Neanderthal brow.

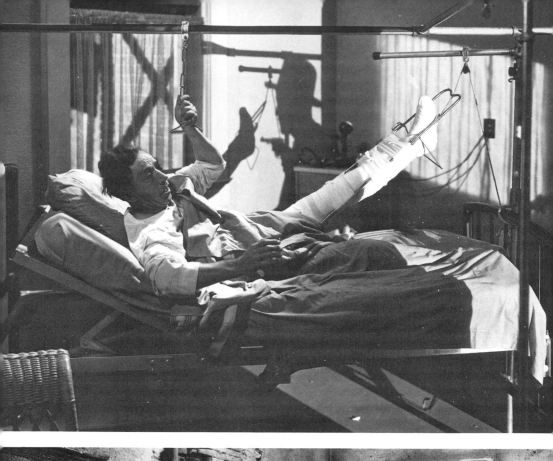

X marks the spot: a visual leitmotif carried out through the killings. Boris Karloff (center photo) as Camonte's doomed rival, Gaffney. *Scarface*. *United Artists*

Along the way, he has collected a social secretary (Vince Barnett) and a girlfriend (Karen Morley), the former a tiny, stupid hood who can't write and who dies without ever mastering the telephone, the latter the hard, blond mistress of his former employer, in her own right as much of a status symbol as the big cars and fancy duds. From punk to czar, Camonte lives by his motto, "Do it first, do it yourself, and keep on doin' it." Initiative, the personal touch, perseverance, will take a man to the top of the heap in America.

Outside the steel-shuttered windows of his living room, a Cook's Tours sign whets Camonte's megalomania by flashing "The World Is Yours." In the five years since *Underworld* had been filmed there had occurred an escalation in ambition; the big, nameless city was no longer enough. Tony Camonte launches a bold series of raids, bombings, and killings. The X-marks-the-spot device becomes the film's running metaphor. The street sign of an undertaker throws a crosslike shadow over a body lying on the sidewalk; the mock-modest camera averts its eye from the bloodbath on Saint Valentine's Day to pick up a crisscross trellis above the victims; a new height in ingenuity is attained in the bowling-alley murder of Gaffney

A quick glimpse of the St. Valentine's Day Massacre that managed to pass the censor. *Scarface. United Artists*

Woman as prize: Camonte has his eye on the boss's mistress. Karen Morley, Osgood Perkins. *Scarface. United Artists*

Cesca works her wiles on Rinaldi (George Raft). *Scarface. United Artists*

The siege of Camonte's apartment, and a sign that promised him the world. *Scarface.*
United Artists

(Boris Karloff), a North Side rival who crosses out his scorecard before
scoring his best and last strike.

With every potential rival disposed of, Camonte's downfall can only
come from within, from that part of himself unaffected by success: his
Italian ethic of family honor. This ethic shows itself mostly in his possessive relationship with Cesca, his jazz-baby sister who has gone even
further than Tony in shaking off Old World restrictions. Out to seduce the
saturnine Rinaldo, Cesca performs a sensuous dance at the infamous Paradise No. 2 Club, and, when Tony leaves town for a while, she leaves home
to move in with Rinaldo. On his return, Tony shoots Rinaldo in a fit of
jealousy, a fratricidal killing that becomes the first crack in Tony's armor.
From a hysterical Cesca he learns that she and Rinaldo had married, but
by then it is too late, for he is already being sought by the police for the one
careless, unprofessional crime in his career.

Donizetti furnished Tony with a leitmotif, the finale will be grandly
operatic. Like desperate, guilty lovers, the Camonte siblings reunite to
repel a massive police attack against Tony's house. Cesca has come to
avenge Rinaldo; she becomes instead her brother's moll: "Sure I'll load

Liebestod: **Tony and Cesca reunited as the police close in.** *Scarface. United Artists*

them. I'm not afraid. I'm like you, Tony." Laughing maniacally, Tony shoots back at the assailants. The exhilarating romanticism of the siege, a *Liebestod* of searchlights and gunfire, is bluntly cut short when a ricocheting bullet hits Cesca; her death leaves Tony alone and lost. Tear gas forces him out into the staircase, where he is overpowered. Taunted and manacled, he makes an irrational dash for the street and is coolly shot down by an anonymous policeman with a Tommy gun. The camera tilts upward from the sprawling body, Tony's own final X, to the luminous Cook's sign promising the world, the precise distance between the gutter and the dream.

3. The Morning After

THE DEATH OF Tony Camonte, most flamboyant of the "gutter endings," marked the peak and the passing of the crime film in its first sound phase. After twelve dry years it had become obvious to Americans that drinking was as natural as sin. When Franklin D. Roosevelt won the Democratic nomination on July 1, 1932, his bread-and-wine platform rested on the twin issues of unemployment and repeal, the order of importance dictated by the statistical fact that there were eleven million jobless Americans against half a million convictions for offenses against the Volstead Act. By then, President Hoover was about as popular as the Hoovervilles, the shanty towns that bore his name and mushroomed on the outskirts of every major city. The Republican motto "Sit Tight" seemed constipated and defeatist next to Roosevelt's campaign song, "Happy Days Are Here Again," which came from a 1930 movie musical, *Chasing Rainbows*.

The Hoover administration had indeed sat tight through graft and gangsterism. Only the very naive would believe that the racketeers who had made enormous profits from bootlegging would disappear once that activity was no longer illegal. But it seemed certain that the underworld was about to change its image along with its main source of revenue. Drugs, gambling, prostitution, the labor and loan-shark rackets would fill the void left by repeal. The bootlegger alone was about to become extinct, and with his absence the underworld was to lose much of its glamour.

The studio directors decided to wait, all the while keeping one eye on the headlines for signs of a new social climate, and the other eye on the theater, then a medium much quicker than the cinema to grasp what was timely and to offer it to the paying customer. With Prohibition in the balance, Hollywood, with its usual uncertainty where morals and mores were concerned, felt insecure about portraying leading characters as either wet or dry; and Hays was still barely preventing the pressure groups from storming the industry.

In that uncertain 1932, one of the more curious pictures—certainly one of the more reactionary—was *The Wet Parade*. Adapted by John Lee Mahin from the Upton Sinclair novel of the year before, this film was little more than a temperance tract. Metro-Goldwyn-Mayer had stood behind Hoover's dry platform; later in 1932, the president was reverentially depicted in

Washington Masquerade. It took some resolve, mostly of the wrong kind, tempered with caution, to come up in an election year with a film that was as old-fashioned and unpopular as D. W. Griffith's last film, *The Struggle.* There was also some doublethink at work, for *The Wet Parade* was entrusted to the director Victor Fleming, one of Ben Hecht's great boozing companions.

The Wet Parade was crudely polemical, a catalogue of the evils and ravages of alcohol: in the days before Prohibition, an alcoholic Southern aristocrat (Lewis Stone) slashes his throat in a pigpen; comes the Volstead Act and his son (Neil Hamilton) is permanently blinded from drinking defective liquor; a New York hotel owner (Walter Huston) clubs his wife to death in a drunken rage; and a Prohibition agent (Jimmy Durante) is murdered by mobsters. The bluenose heroine (Dorothy Jordan) smashes the bottles in her dead father's study and turns on his friends: "Friends of my papa's, were you? And now you're going to celebrate his dying with whiskey! It was your whiskey, wine and bourbon that killed him. Get out of here and take your filthy whiskey with you! I never want to smell it on anybody's breath ever again. I only hope I'll live to see the day that every drink that was ever made is poured into a cesspool where it belongs!"

To counteract this tirade, *The Wet Parade* offered a nostalgic tintype of June 29, 1919, the day before Prohibition went into effect: lines outside the liquor shops, the frantic stocking up, a barbershop quartet wearing black armbands, traversing packed saloons and night clubs, "Auld Lang Syne" at midnight. Then, one lurid murder sequence in a cellar lit by the fires of hell, actually coming from a furnace, where Huston, acting like a composite of John Barrymore and W. C. Fields, develops the DT's. Before Huston is sentenced to life, a defense lawyer sums up his case: "This man was used to alcohol all his life. They made a law, took it away from him and gave him poison instead." The one really frightening moment in *The Wet Parade* was a documentary on the brewing and bottling of bootleg liquor, showing the best labels affixed to homemade alcohol of dubious quality. Even that image was compromised by a subsequent jab at the government for adding a chemical to grain alcohols in order to make them undrinkable. According to *The Wet Parade*, the Noble Experiment failed in part because careless bootleggers sometimes neglected to redistill the alcohol in order to remove the poison. In the film's very uncertain ending, one member of an abstemious couple who have just become parents says: "He's being born into an awful mess, but they'll have it all figured out by the time he grows up."

A trend seldom vanishes overnight. The gangster made sporadic appearances in the early thirties in films like *Night Court, Three on a Match, Me and My Gal, Afraid to Talk,* and *Night World,* but he had been demoted to the supporting cast, a mere plot contrivance rather than a genuine dramatic character. It was nevertheless impossible to eradicate all traces of the gangster from the movies' dramatis personae. Instead, his best attributes—his brashness, resourcefulness, and disregard for convention—were usurped by the hero, with a concomitant improvement in his chances for success. If the hero thereby lost moral stature, it was all part of the wising up of America in a period that valued, above all, casual self-assurance and a perfect grasp of the moment. The new breed of protagonists included borderline characters such as the journalist (*Night Court, The Crusader*), the gossip columnist (*Scandal for Sale, Love Is a Racket, Blessed Event*), the gossip newscaster (*Okay America*), the shrewd, morally flexible lawyer (*Lawyer Man, The Mouthpiece, State's Attorney, For the Defense*). Lastly came the law enforcer (*Radio Patrol, Undercover Man, Me and My Gal*), who had yet to recoup the prestige he had enjoyed in the days before the microphone began to pick up moral ambiguities along with dialogue.

Despite Hays's loyal, if not entirely objective, claims to the contrary, Hollywood stood accused of irresponsibility, of glorifying the underworld, of lulling its vast audience into acquiescence rather than stirring its civic conscience. But, by 1932, Capone was a model prisoner in Atlanta, cutting out overalls in the prison workshop and reputedly sleeping in his customary silk pajamas. The infamous New York gambler, Arnold Rothstein, had been dead for four years, yet his legend had gleaned only a minor work, *Street of Chance* (1930).* Legs Diamond had been shot dead in 1931 on the same day that he had been acquitted of a kidnapping charge. To the public this was a somewhat reassuring sign that the underworld had a more expeditious sense of justice than did the courts. Upon Diamond's death, organized crime seemed to condemn the personality cult and·opt for an efficient, faceless corporate image.

With the underworld deprived of its celebrities, the motion-picture industry looked elsewhere. Having accustomed the public to the lingo, the behavior, and the complex caste system of the underworld, filmdom directed its attention to social issues such as journalistic ethics, archaic penology, racial bigotry, collective violence, and unemployment. The exposé film was merely a rechanneling of the energy generated by the gangster film. It borrowed the typology and the cool descriptive style of reportage, and it exploited the public's familiarity with legal procedure—unmistakable proof that the gangster film had served *some* social purpose. (In *Scarface,* a shyster springing Camonte redefined habeas corpus for the last row of the balcony: "Ya gotta produce da body.")

Hollywood often hedged its bet too carefully; in some cases it skirted the real issue while preserving a token indignation. Yet the exposé films, despite all their compromises and timidities, managed now and then to touch a raw nerve. This was confirmed by the string of libel suits they engendered. The gangster film had boasted that its events were drawn from life and that its characters were real. Now the film companies had to take cover behind the disclaimer that "the events and characters depicted in

* *Street of Chance* featured William Powell as a gentile gambler named "Natural" Davis who nobly laid down his life for the sake of his kid brother. The Rothstein saga was resurrected in the mid-thirties, when Fox released *Now I'll Tell,* purportedly based on the memoirs of Mrs. Rothstein. The film didn't live up to its title. Rothstein was rechristened Murray Golden and played by Spencer Tracy as a compulsive gambler rather than as a Manhattan mastermind of crime, and, this time around, he died to leave his wife well provided for by his insurance policy.

this photoplay are fictional, and any resemblance to persons, living or dead, is purely coincidental." This safety clause legally removed these films from the arena of the factual, and, ironically, it also guaranteed their reformist fervor.

Evidence of the new trend can be traced to *Five Star Final* in 1931, a picture that lingers in memory as a gangster drama even though no gangsters appeared in it. However, it featured Edward G. Robinson, still fresh in the public's mind as Little Caesar, this time playing the managing editor of a muckracking newspaper, a man all angles and know-how in the Hecht-MacArthur mold. But the tone was different, sober rather than comic: Robinson resigns from his job after his circulation-boosting methods result in scandal and a double suicide. The film also seemed to take for granted that the American public, or the segment thereof that read the tabloids, got their kicks from the sensational exposure of scandal and corruption without ever taking a positive stand on the issues involved. *Five Star Final* was the product of Zanuck and Hal Wallis at Warner Brothers, a studio thereafter identified with pictures as sparse, agile, timely, and cynical in outlook as the Hays Office would pass without choking. Compared to the Warners films, Metro pictures of the same period were staid and overstuffed, Paramount's too stylized and foreign.

The resilience and speed of the Warners films came straight from Broadway, as did most of the performers. Only a cut is faster than a blackout, and the films improved upon the stage plays from which they were adapted. The Warner roster consisted of performers expert in portraying big-city types, masters and mistresses of double-talk and survival: Cagney, Robinson, Warren William, Joan Blondell, Glenda Farrell, and, on a nonexclusive basis, Bette Davis, Spencer Tracy, and Lee Tracy. Zanuck had specific ideas about actors, and he did not hesitate to outbid, or steal from, the rival studios. The rise of Lee Tracy, as much as that of Cagney or Robinson, reflects a radical turnabout in the public's taste. From the viewpoint of the seventies, Tracy seems an outrageous triumph of mind over matter, or rather, articulate cynicism over strong and silent idealism. Tracy had seven pictures in release during 1932, and another seven in 1933. His popularity was out of proportion to his range, but he could deliver dialogue faster than anyone in the business, and somehow this torrential patter distracted from the fact that he was just an older Cagney, with less bounce and sex appeal. (Cagney had once been Tracy's understudy during part of the New York run of *Broadway*.) Like Pig Latin, Tracy became a fad, spinning out variations on Walter Winchell, the *New York Mirror* columnist and broadcaster, in *Blessed Event* (1932), *Clear All Wires* (1933), and *I'll Tell the World* (1934). The first of these adapted from a play by Manuel Seff and Forrest Wilson and directed at top speed by Roy del Ruth, highlighted a speech in which Tracy, relishing his own bravura and every grisly detail, describes an electrocution to a threatening but impressionable gangster (Allen Jenkins); the implication was that a fast-talking reporter was more than a match for a killer and could figuratively get away with murder. All along, the film preserved the breezy irreverence of the stage original, poking fun at motherhood, blacks, Jews, homosexuals, police methods, the radio industry, crooners, and, inevitably, Walter Winchell himself.

A fast-talking reporter is more than a match for a dumb gangster: Lee Tracy and Allen Jenkins in *Blessed Event*, 1932. *Warner Brothers*

This was the heyday of the gossip columnist. In 1932, Winchell was also impersonated by Lew Ayres in *Okay America* and by Douglas Fairbanks, Jr., in *Love is a Racket*, in which Lee Tracy was miscast as Winchell's legman. It was also open season on gangsters, part of the phasing-out of a character that seemed suddenly undesirable. The gang chief (Lyle Talbot) in William Wellman's *Love is a Racket* rubs elbows with the Broadway elite at Sardi's but lacks the social graces, however crude and superficial, of a Tony Camonte. The chief is shot dead in his Atlantic City penthouse by a veteran gold digger (Cecil Cunningham), and the Winchell-type hero covers up the crime by destroying all evidence and hurling the body over the parapet to the street below. The visual epitaph: a shoe lying in the gutter, a couple casually strolling by, a scream from the girl. The murderess goes scot-free, and the poor dead slob doesn't even get a fancy funeral.

The action in *Okay America* was faster and more furious than all the talk in *Blessed Event*. A prime example of Hollywood at its most hysterical and reckless, it told of a Manhattan columnist (say, Walter Winchell), who becomes the reluctant envoy of a crime czar (say, Al Capone) to negotiate the release of a kidnap victim (say, the Lindbergh child) in exchange for a promise of immunity from the president of the United States (say, Herbert Hoover). The columnist succeeds, or at least appears to succeed; in fact, the president has refused to compromise. The gangster has the hostage released, whereupon the columnist murders the gangster to save the government any possible embarrassment. The columnist is subsequently gunned down in mid-broadcast, his on-the-air signature furnishing his dying words and still another message of reassurance to the millions out there.

Such a heroic flight of fancy could be construed as another proof of the movies' irrational imaginings, were it not that *Okay America* reflected—even if in a distorting mirror—the uneasy summer of 1932, when a Bonus Army of war veterans encamped in Washington, putting the White House under moral siege and prompting the intervention of federal troops under Douglas MacArthur.The picture, scheduled for a September release, only a week after that of *Blessed Event,* was in production throughout June and July, and some of the effects of a crisis showed in a few controversial notions that found their way into the characters. The gangster (Edward Arnold) seems a projection of the ruthless capitalist, a man of taste and also of boundless ambition: "Ten years from now I won't have to ask [the president] any favors. I'll tell him," he exults. For all his youthful charm, the columnist (Lew Ayres) comes across as slogan-spouting opportunist, dispensing justice through his gossip column, with a passive nation of readers and listeners to back him up. *Okay America* was bracingly physical, as only an *echt*-Hollywood director like Tay Garnett could make it: a comic strip in which a demagogue reporter vied with a capitalistic gangster for a nation up for grabs.

Walter Winchell and William J. Fallon, Arnold Rothstein's personal lawyer (popularized by the tabloids as "the attorney of the damned"), loomed as the counterculture heroes of this period, characteristically at ease on both sides of the law. Within months of each other in 1932, Warren William and John Barrymore appeared on the screen as lightly disguised versions of Fallon in *The Mouthpiece* and *State's Attorney* respectively. Implicit in both films was a view of the law as a set of flexible rules rather than as a rigid moral code, and Fallon was depicted as a man who could stretch the law to the limit with his brilliant oratory and courtroom shock tactics. No one seemed to mind except Fallon's son, who brought suit against Warner Brothers charging that *The Mouthpiece* libeled his late father. The suit was shortly dropped, presumably when Warners settled out of court, and the picture played out its bookings and was twice remade, first as *The Man Who Talked Too Much* (1940), with George Brent, then as *Illegal* (1955), with Edward G. Robinson. By the time of the remakes, Fallon seemed to belong to the ages, like the notorious hoods he had represented.

Released to coincide with the Roosevelt inauguration in March 1933, *Gabriel Over the White House,* on the other hand, was a political cartoon with disturbing social implications. Any potential satire, however, shriveled

from a lack of humor. In a moment of aberrant crisis politics, a party pol-
itician (Walter Huston) is elected president. A car accident knocks some
wild notions into his head, and he suddenly becomes a man of steel, cutting
through constitutional red tape to put through a sensational reform program.
Some of the presidential policies involve the suspension of civil rights, a
foreclosure on all European loans, and the detention and mass execution
of criminals on Ellis Island (within view of the Statue of Liberty).

Originally a novel written by Thomas F. Tweed, an Englishman who
had once served as secretary to Lloyd George, and who had never set foot
in America, *Gabriel Over the White House* was produced by Walter Wanger
with the backing of William Randolph Hearst. At the time, Hearst was
supporting Roosevelt—during the Roosevelt campaign, he was an occasional
speechwriter—and seeing this freak of a movie it is quite revealing to note
the effort to invest the presidential hero with some of the attributes of the
strong men of Europe. In this respect, fortunately, the picture turned out to
be less prophetic than in others. Huston, for example, addresses the nation
by radio in the manner of Roosevelt's later "fireside chats," the president's
personal secretary (Karen Morley) is explicitly identified as his mistress,
there are far-sighted predictions of war in the air and of a Washington
Covenant which seems like a first rough draft of the United Nations Charter.
Huston, who had played Lincoln for Griffith three years before, retained
some of the mannerisms of the previous role, and he was backed by dramatic lighting and inspirational music.

The president's main antagonist in the entire Union is Nick Diamond
(C. Henry Gordon), another Capone impersonation, an oily, scarred, arrogant bogey whose function in the film was to provide sufficient provocation to justify its hard line. In this case, he has the secretary machine-
gunned within the hallowed precincts of the White House. That Capone
was a key fantasy figure of the period is demonstrated by the following
dialogue (by Carey Wilson), which takes place in the president's study:

PRESIDENT: You're a menace to this country, Mr. Diamond, and the most inexpen-
sive way to get rid of you would be to eliminate yourself, return to your
country.
DIAMOND: Why? I'm what I am today by public approval. The people wants something, I give it to them.
PRESIDENT: We're in the same boat. I, too, exist only by the will of the people.

Gabriel Over the White House came even closer to making an overt
fascistic statement in an ugly trial scene in which Diamond and his gang
are court-martialed and sentenced to summary execution. Here, sets and
camera placement exhibited the austere geometry of a New Order, a chilling God-is-with-us fanaticism. But it is improbable that all of the film's
tendencies can be blamed exclusively on Hearst. There was, after all, the
mediating influence of Louis B. Mayer at Metro, where the film was made;
that of Walter Wanger; even that of Gregory La Cava, one of Hollywood's
best-humored directors, although here untypically restrained. Like the

vigilante pictures that preceded it, *Gabriel Over the White House* gave shape to a national longing for reform in domestic politics and an end to crime, even if it misdirected this longing and fell for the deadly delusion that civil rights are but a small price to pay for trains running on time.

The president's mistress gunned down by gangsters within the walls of the White House: Karen Morley and Walter Huston in *Gabriel Over the White House*, 1933. *Metro-Goldwyn-Mayer*

The classic example of social protest on film remains *I Am a Fugitive from a Chain Gang* (1932), which provided Paul Muni with an effective about-face after *Scarface* and supplied Zanuck with the prototype for a new trend. The film was based on an explosive memoir written by Robert Elliott Burns, first serialized in *True Detective Mysteries* and then published by Vanguard Press. Burns had worked on a chain gang for months, then had escaped to live an honorable life for seven years. He founded *The Greater Chicago Magazine* and rose to acquire an annual income of twenty thousand dollars. Betrayed by his estranged wife, he voluntarily returned to Georgia with the assurance of a full pardon in a short time. The state, however, declined to keep its promise: Burns served a full year on a chain gang in LaGrange, was made a trusty, and one day simply walked away. He headed north and wrote of his experiences. In 1932, he was living in hiding in New Jersey when Zanuck acquired the film rights to his book and approached him to serve as technical adviser for the adaptation. Burns went to Hollywood under the protection of Zanuck and Warner Brothers to work on the screen-play with Sheridan Gibney, Brown Homes, and Howard J. Green; Hal Wallis was assigned to produce and Mervyn LeRoy to direct.

For the most part, the resulting picture stuck to the facts, and Paul Muni made Burns—rechristened James Allen in the script—the archetypal thirties fall guy, an innocent victim of circumstances. A restless World War I veteran, Allen wanders from job to job, until one evening he is forced by a fellow vagrant to rob a cash register of five dollars. They are caught *in flagrante delicto,* the tramp is killed by the police, and Allen, his un-willing accomplice, is sentenced to hard labor. The judge's gavel dissolves into a blacksmith's hammer as leg irons are fastened on Allen. As an exposé, the story would have been more effective had the filmmakers taken fewer pains to certify the hero's innocence. To document the cruelties and humilia-tions inflicted on the inmates of Southern prisons of the time, no such gloss was necessary. It was as if inhumanity were less on trial than injustice; the specific disappeared into the general. As a result, our outrage was displaced: we were shocked that such an experience could befall an innocent man when we should have been shocked that it could befall anyone at all.

But whatever its shortcomings, filmic and otherwise, the picture stirred up controversy in circles other than critical ones. It was released November 11, 1932, and three weeks later Burns was arrested in New Jersey as a fugitive from Georgia justice. While extradition was pending, Governor A. Harry Moore of New Jersey was flooded with appeals for leniency, and finally, on December 22, Moore officially refused to extradite Burns. The following day, *I Am a Fugitive from a Chain Gang* was voted Best Picture of the Year by the National Board of Review, which amounted to an en-dorsement from the establishment. This hardly impressed the South. A Georgia newspaper carried the headline, YANKEE LIES, and two prison wardens, J. H. Hardy and P. Philips, sued Warner Brothers and its affiliate, the Vitaphone Corporation, for alleged attacks upon them in the film. Warners had been prepared for such suits all along; in fact, the film's pre-miere had been so delayed while every legal aspect was being cleared that another chain-gang picture, *Hell's Highway,* was rushed through production at R.K.O. Radio and released a full two months ahead of its competitor. In *I Am a Fugitive,* there was no mention or depiction of the state of Georgia, no southern accents, and, were it not for the high percentage of blacks in the chain gang, the story might have been located anywhere in the United States. Backed by public opinion in the North, the filmmakers stood their ground; and liberals in the South soon organized a committee to look into conditions at state prison institutions. Reform was slow in coming, and the chain-gang system was not abolished until 1937. Burns could nevertheless take much credit for its dissolution. Despite minor scrapes with the law, most of them dismissed, Burns remained free until his death from cancer in 1955.

Time and history have left *I Am a Fugitive from a Chain Gang* en-crusted with a power and a pathos it might not originally have had. LeRoy's

terse, economical style worked best in short, jabbing scenes: Allen, down
and out, tries to pawn his Belgian Croix de Guerre only to be shown a
drawer full of dozens such decorations; when he learns that his pardon has
been refused, Allen clenches his fists, twitches, and falls back on his bunk
like a man with the bends. LeRoy conveyed a strap beating through its
psychological effect on the inmates (who thereby became surrogates for the
audience) rather than by its physical effect on the victim; a scene that,
despite the ellipsis, seemed unbearable at the time. Only now, after the
experience of extermination camps, are we left as receptive to the will to
survive as to moral indignation. A shadow on the wall, a track shot along
the bunks, a fade-out, these were merciful yet evasive. There is little doubt
that LeRoy, for all his distance and impersonal approach, knew what his
audience would stand for. The film worked fine when it sketched the touching kinships that develop amid brutality and despair, a Depression commitment to the fringe people: a black titan of a convict (Everett Brown)
loosens Allen's shackles with unerring blows of his hammer; a sweet, tough
moll (Noel Francis) wanders into a shabby rented room to offer herself to
the fugitive. The final scene, a furtive nocturnal exchange between Allen
and his girl (Helen Vinson), was subtle and disturbing.

ALLEN: No friends, no rest, no peace. . . . Keep moving, that's all that's left for me.
SHE: Can't you tell me where you're going? Do you need any money? How do you
    live?
ALLEN (in a whisper and already swallowed by the night): I steal.*

The social-crusading films, whether dealing with inhuman (or unfair)
treatment of the individual in corrective institutions (as did *I Am a Fugitive,
Hell's Highway, Road Gang*) or trying to come to grips with lynching as a
social symptom (for instance *Fury* and *They Won't Forget*), offered the
scarcely reassuring image of an utterly fallible society. The implications
were that a man could be so hopelessly misjudged by society as to justify a
subsequent life of crime, or that circumstantial evidence could be misread
in such a way as to convict the innocent. The ultimate, self-destructive
stage of the socially conscious films made in Hollywood in the mid- to late
thirties dealt with men and women as the innocent pawns of a vindictive
fate that used society as its instrument (*You Only Live Once, Let Us Live*).
The black, despairing lesson of the latter films, not incidentally the work of
foreign directors nurtured on expressionism, was that man need not be
strong or upright or courageous, but only lucky.

The last significant gangster to appear on the screen before 1933, when
the reorganized Hays Office launched its campaign to suppress the breezy

* During the Second World War, a Selective Service official asked Sam Giancana, a reputed leader in
the Chicago crime syndicate, what he did for a living. Giancana replied, "I steal." The draft board
labeled Giancana "a constitutional psychopath with inadequate personality manifested by strong antisocial trends." He was classified 4-F and sent back to the rackets. In the seventies, Giancana was
linked to an alleged CIA plot to murder Fidel Castro; he himself was murdered in his Chicago home
in 1975. Was Giancana simply exercising the right of the film buff to quote from his favorite film? Had
he consciously carried this particular image in his mind all those years?

A blow from the hammer of a black convict (Everett Brown) delivers James Allen (Paul Muni) from the chain gang in *I Am a Fugitive from a Chain Gang*, 1932. *Warner Brothers*

"No friends, no rest, no peace. . . . Keep moving, that's all that's left for me." Allen's final meeting with his girl friend (Helen Vinson), in *I Am a Fugitive from a Chain Gang*. *Warner Brothers*

amorality that pervaded the movies, was inspired not by the headlines, but was drawn from a *bona fide* literary work. In a moment of recklessness, Paramount had bought the film rights to William Faulkner's *Sanctuary* shortly after its publication in 1930. The novel was subsequently denounced as obscene and degrading, and *The London Times* deemed its characters "devoid of interest except to the neurologist and the criminologist." Paramount hoped against hope that some kind of compromise could eventually be worked out with the censor. Three years and several adaptations later, the picture went before the cameras in February 1933, as the trade papers and conservative press issued a campaign of intimidation. The ruling on *Sanctuary* from the Hays Office informed Paramount that neither the film nor the credits would be allowed to mention the name of the book. Benjamin Glazer, the foolhardy producer of *Sanctuary*, complied by changing the title to *The Story of Temple Drake*—perhaps in the hope that some remnants of the scandal would at least be attached to the heroine's name— and by crediting "a novel by William Faulkner" as source material. Some pressure was applied to force Paramount to abandon the project. The leading man initially chosen, George Raft, declined to perform; he had no intention of hurting his screen image by playing a sadistic gangster who raped the heroine with a corncob and was impotent to boot. Raft was replaced by a rising young actor named Jack La Rue, whose career was ultimately scuttled by this big break.

The Story of Temple Drake was released in May. The hero was no longer nicknamed Popeye, he was no longer impotent, and he didn't carry, along with his gun, the symbolic load of American decadence that he had carried in the novel. He had become a city punk named Trigger, loose in the Mississippi hill country, and the much anticipated and dreaded rape scene was, *pace* the Hays Office, conveyed by filmic means such as a flicker from Trigger's cigarette, a scream from Temple Drake, and a fade-out into darkness that suggested everything Hays objected to. A curious piece of Southern Gothic, all brooding light effects, the film succeeded in creating its own run-down world of oversexed heroines, demon lovers, half-wits, prostitutes, and poor-white moonshiners.

Despite all the elisions and evasions demanded by the Code, the story stuck closely to that of *Sanctuary*. A *film noir* before its time, the film did not quite fit into any of the Hollywood categories of the period. The adaptation (by Oliver H. P. Garrett) and direction (by Stephen Roberts) leaned whenever possible toward the side of bawdiness: Temple's black mammy (Hattie McDaniel) reads the events of the previous wild evening in her young mistress's panties, a scene which may delight us today with its comic punch but which at the time was tantamount to waving Temple's panties under the noses of the bluenoses. And some touches were undeniably strong: when Temple breaks the sexual and psychological spell that keeps her in bondage to the gangster, a scene nowhere to be found in the novel, she shoots him with his own gun. His dead fingers close on her hat, and she must pry them open to retrieve the incriminating evidence. In the trial

The gangster as damned soul: Jack La Rue as Trigger in *The Story of Temple Drake*, 1933, as William Faulkner's controversial novel *Sanctuary* was retitled for the screen. Not even the novel's gangster hero, Popeye, was allowed to retain his name. *Paramount*

that closes the film, Temple is made to realize and reject the extent of her moral downfall. This was, of course, a pure Hays touch, and it managed to obliterate any power the film may have previously generated.

Trigger, with his existential impassiveness, minimal gestures, and self-depiction as gangster-object, prefigured the theatrical / literary gangsters of *The Petrified Forest* and *Winterset*. He was the killer as damned soul, quite a ways from the snapping turtle of a Rico Bandello or the red-blooded, fancy-free brute of a Tom Powers. With Trigger's demise, the gangster vanished, for all relevant purposes, from the screen for a couple of years.

There were ripples of discrimination against *The Story of Temple Drake* in Boston, where Hays was taken to task for allowing "degeneracy" to creep into films. Many films—including *Convention City*, Mae West's *I'm No Angel*, and even a tear-jerker like *Mary Stevens, M.D.*—might take credit for ending the relatively benign period of Hays rule. These and other films flagrantly violated the Code and today seem like lively bursts of carnality in a constricted world. But in his autobiography, Hays cited as the last straw a review for *Baby Face* that appeared in *Liberty* magazine and was entitled "Three Cheers for Sin!"

In the summer of 1933, the Catholic bishops of North America considered a boycott of Hollywood films in order to call the industry to moral order. Such a boycott would have meant a fearsome loss of 30 percent of the population as potential customers. To add to the confusion, the Irish Free State had refused to exhibit *The Public Enemy*. After all, the Irish-American image had to be upheld abroad—although with Europe in turmoil and a crisis at home, this concern with propriety was like trying to salvage an umbrella in a shipwreck.

This was also the year of the National Recovery Act, and not one but a massive set of codes were being established to control every facet of American industry. The one pertaining to motion pictures was the longest and most detailed of some six hundred, and it included provisions on labor, trade, and exhibition. Hays saw a chance to strengthen his strictures and sharpen the old Code, presenting his authority as an alternative to Washington control. Every film company, since they all depended upon interstate trade, was liable to be brought under federal jurisdiction, and the MPAA was aware of the not too remote possibility that the government would seize the industry.

In this tense period, an alarming book appeared. Titled *Our Movie Made Children*, it was written by one H. M. Forman under the aegis of a research firm, the Payne Fund. One of the speculations the book presented as fact was that *Little Caesar* had directly inspired three murders, the most widely known of which was the 1931 shooting of Winslow Eliot. Hays could have refuted the book's charges against the film industry; he had inside information that the interviewees in the book had been led and that such all-important factors as social environment and family criminality had been ignored. (The book had gone on sale before the Payne Fund's polling techniques were validated.) But the opportunity to assert his power was too perfect for Hays to waste.

Threatened with massive boycotts and walk-outs, the members of the MPAA had to choose: would their moral arbiter be some faceless bureaucrat in an impersonal agency in far-off Washington, or would it be Hays himself, friend and defender of the industry, a public-relations man who, in his spare time, had consolidated the producers' hold on the nation's movie houses? He alone could quell public hostility by enforcing a strengthened version of the original Code.

The Code recommendations that had formerly been accepted or rejected by producers as a matter of protocol or of good or bad taste now became a matter of law. The chastened MPAA voted for home rule, and producers agreed to withhold distribution of any film lacking a seal of approval from Hays's man in Los Angeles, Joseph I. Breen, who thereupon assumed the sonorous title of Production Code Authority.

Formerly a Washington newspaperman and at one time a labor mediator, wearing for life a scarred cheek won in a mining dispute, Breen had the Code revised, accepted, and signed by all of the majors and most of the independents. The studios herded into production adaptations from the classics, family pictures, and other films with uncontroversial themes. Over a year later, faced with the revival of the gangster cycle (triggered by the success of a gangster comedy, *The Whole Town's Talking*), Breen resorted to a complete about-face on the crime picture. It was perfectly acceptable as long as it endorsed the inspiring, if overrated, feats of J. Edgar Hoover's G-men.

4. The First Crusade

Never before, on any level of government, have the American people been
subjected to such brainwashing on behalf of any agency.
— Fred J. Cook, *The FBI Nobody Knows*, Macmillan, 1964

THE GANGSTER CULT in the twenties and early thirties had grown naturally and spontaneously from the everyday realities of Prohibition,
nourished by factual accounts of life and death in the underworld
and eventually being reshaped into the topical fiction of Hemingway, Burnett, Hammett, and others. The violence extant in society had infiltrated the
stage and screen despite the disapproval of law enforcers, the constant
watch of the censor, the threats of patriotic groups, even despite the
reticence of the criminals involved, who soon found themselves to be mere
exploitable items. Coming so suddenly to an end in the midst of the Depression, the Capone era was bound to leave an emotional void in the minds of
most Americans.

Encouraged by the national impact of the Lindbergh kidnap case in
1932, Homer Cummings, attorney general under Herbert Hoover, was
moved to scare the wits out of the Daughters of the American Revolution
in a speech that stated: "We are now engaged in a war that threatens the
safety of our country, a war with the organized forces of crime." Cummings's
appraisal seems somewhat extreme and hysterical in the context of a social
climate that had scarcely changed since the year before, but his speech
was deeply influenced by the emotional charge of the case. Lindbergh then
rated as America's Hero, and the crime was of a particularly hateful sort,
so much so that even the imprisoned Capone had offered to help locate the
perpetrators. Still, the Lindbergh kidnapping was but one of 285 that took
place in 1932; a good number of these went unpublicized and, one assumes,
unsolved. The major consequence of "America's crime of the century," as
the tabloids dubbed the Lindbergh kidnapping, was stronger, more active
participation of federal agencies in crime control.

The original Bureau of Investigation had been created as a secret
agency of the Department of Justice by Theodore Roosevelt in 1908.
J. Edgar Hoover had been appointed acting director in 1924. Until 1933,
when the Lindbergh Law, one of the first bills passed by the Roosevelt
Administration, enlarged the list of federal crimes, the Bureau of Investigation had been empowered only to deal with violations of the Dyer Act, in
which interstate transportation of stolen cars was deemed a federal offense.

Agents of the bureau had been unable to carry arms or make arrests; this privilege and duty belonged only to local police forces or marshals, which explains why the bureau remained an obscure agency throughout Prohibition. But the Lindbergh Law made it a federal offense to send ransom notes through the mail and to cross state lines in kidnap cases. A year later, the following crimes also came under the bureau's jurisdiction: national-bank robbery, racketeering in interstate trade, crossing state lines in order to avoid prosecution or giving testimony, interstate transportation of stolen goods, and resisting arrest by a federal officer.

Along with the new powers and responsibilities came a new image for the bureau. The unassuming title of Bureau of Investigation was expanded into the more impressive, but certainly misleading, Federal Bureau of Investigation, which suggested that it was the one and only federal agency of its kind. Although the bureau took almost exclusive credit for solving the Lindbergh case, it was, in fact, the Treasury Department investigators who had insisted, despite Lindbergh's promise to the kidnappers, upon marking the ransom money and who, more than two and a half years after the abduction and subsequent death of the Lindbergh baby, had traced some of the bills to Bruno Richard Hauptmann in the Bronx. Hoover also grabbed credit for his agents for the Robinson kidnap case in Pasadena, and for the capture of bank robber Harry Brunette, in which the FBI had jumped the gun on both the New Jersey and New York police.

To build up the image of the FBI as an elite outfit, the agency's official propaganda often stressed vividness over authenticity. The kidnapping of Charles Urschel in Oklahoma City in July 1933 provided the bureau with some good copy. The very night of the kidnapping Hoover was on a direct line to Mrs. Urschel; the final capture of the culprit, a rather minor and unviolent hood ironically dubbed "Machine Gun" Kelly, was a master stroke of legend-making. According to the FBI, Kelly had screamed "Don't shoot, G-men!" before surrendering, and the hitherto faceless and nameless special agents, sometimes referred to vaguely as "feds," stood nicknamed for posterity. (G-man, the FBI promptly explained, was an underworld abbreviation for "government man.") An alternate version of the same incident offered by FBI detractors and backed by the testimony of Memphis Police Sergeant W. J. Raney, who actually made the arrest, was infinitely more prosaic but also more in keeping with Kelly's character. Ordered to drop his gun, the kidnapper acquiesced, stating, "I've been waiting all night for you." Kelly lived the rest of his life in prison and died in 1954. Perhaps apocryphal, his line was a semantic necessity, corresponding to that other momentous change in the popular parlance of the twenties, when malefactors ceased to be "crooks" and became "gangsters."

The image that Hoover and his publicist, Louis B. Nichols, created for the FBI agent was that of a dedicated, clean-cut crusader, a courageous fighter who was also an expert in the most advanced techniques of crime detection; but above all, the G-man was incorruptible, a trait that was especially appreciated after the bribery scandals of the preceding decade.

Albert Bates and Harvey Bailey, kidnappers in the Urschel case, 1933, and Clyde Barrow, Public Enemy No. 4, 1934: vividness stressed over authenticity in reporting crimes and captures. *Universal*

Building up the image of an elite outfit: pulp-magazine cover, circa 1935. *Author's collection*

Hoover added some shrewd touches to his campaign. The Public Enemy Number One accolade vested on a succession of criminals was timed to precede either their capture or death; and further to convince the nation of the necessity of his tactics, Hoover had statistics compiled that soon became the yardstick by which the ills of American society were to be gauged for the next forty years.

The bureau's Crime Records Division fed stories of case after successful case to newspapers, magazines, and pulps, where they often appeared under the Hoover byline. Some were adapted into radio plays for the *Gangbusters* serial or into comic strips such as *War on Crime*. The best known cases came from the Midwest, whence sprang the new figure of the Depression desperado. This character, of almost pure American stock, was to displace the flashy, foreign, urban mobster from the front pages and to establish an affective rapport with the gunfighters of the Old West. His ambitions seemed engagingly modest when compared to those of such empire builders as Al Capone or Arnold Rothstein. Years later, Alvin Karpis, a member of the new breed, summed up his desires in his memoirs, written during a thirty-three-year stretch in prison: "What I wanted was big automobiles like rich people had and everything like that. I didn't see how I was going to get them by making a fool of myself and working all my life. So I decided to take what I wanted."

To the reading and listening public, the Depression desperadoes seemed like just-folks who had also felt the pinch and improvised a life of crime— types much closer to home than the Chicago mobsters of old. And the desperadoes were colorful characters who had no wish to remain anonymous. Many wrote letters to the local papers and police, and Bonnie Parker left sentimental poetry scattered in the wake of her escapades that unfailingly found its way into the news.

These criminals became prize trophies for the new FBI. "Pretty Boy" Floyd, who had taken part in the Kansas City Massacre of June 17, 1933, in which he had reputedly machine-gunned to death a special agent, three policemen, and the convicted mail robber they were escorting to prison, was shot down by G-men in 1934. "Baby Face" Nelson was killed in 1934. Kate "Ma" Barker and her son Fred were besieged and mowed down by the FBI at an obscure Florida resort in January 1935. Alvin Karpis, once of the Barker gang, was arrested by Hoover himself, to quell criticism that the FBI director never risked his own neck although his name was officially mentioned in accounts of every capture and every action.

Not one of these characters was claimed by the movies at the time— not even John Dillinger, who was without doubt the most charismatic criminal of the decade, a midwestern legend in his own brief lifetime, and Hoover's personal obsession. Dapper, athletic, theatrical, Dillinger started his crime career in earnest after his parole in May 1933 from an Indiana state prison, where he had served four years for felony and assault. Upon his release, he pulled a series of daring bank robberies and managed two highly dramatic jailbreaks. His exploits were built up by the local press with the connivance of the police, who thereby expected to reap a larger amount of credit for his eventual capture.

After his second jailbreak, Dillinger drove his getaway car from Indiana into Illinois, a federal offense and just what Hoover was waiting for. On April 30, 1934, however, Dillinger and four of his gang members, including Baby Face Nelson, succeeded in escaping from an FBI siege at the Little Bohemia Lodge, a Wisconsin roadhouse. The bureau's failure to capture the gang was due to its sheer mismanagement of the operation. Dillinger was subsequently proclaimed Public Enemy Number One, although it has not been proved to this day that he ever killed anyone. On September 22, 1934, three months after his escape, he was ambushed and killed by the FBI as he was leaving the Biograph movie theater in Chicago accompanied by two women, one of whom was Anna Sage, thereon elevated to notoriety in the tabloids as "the Woman in Red." In fact, Sage was a Roumanian-born brothel keeper who fingered Dillinger for the FBI in exchange for a possible stay of deportation. The stay was not granted. There was, and still is, reasonable doubt about the identity of the man who was shot that night. The FBI claimed that the criminal had undergone plastic surgery in Chicago shortly before his death, and that his fingerprints had been erased by acid, which made absolute identification impossible. Whether the victim was really Dillinger, his legend continues undiminished.

In spite of his renown, Dillinger remained off-limits for the movies during the next eleven years. The archives of the MPAA contain a telegram sent by Hays to Breen shortly after Dillinger's death:

No motion picture on the life or exploits of John Dillinger will be produced, distributed or exhibited by any member [of the MPAA]. . . . This decision is based on the belief that the production, distribution or exhibition of such a picture could be detrimental to the best public interest. Advise all studio heads accordingly.

But other forces were at work to prevent the Dillinger story from reaching the screen. Hoover cherished the case as the exclusive property of the bureau, despite public knowledge that most of the credit for Dillinger's demise belonged to Agent Melvin Purvis, who resigned from the FBI a year later and wrote of his experiences in a book titled *American Agent*. Hoover, who never tolerated any personality cult other than his own within the agency, was outraged by Purvis's arrogance in setting himself above the bureau. Purvis was mentioned neither in the official history of the bureau, Don Whitehead's *The F.B.I. Story*, nor in *Persons in Hiding*, which was published under Hoover's name in 1938 but was actually ghost-written by Courtley Riley Cooper, an experienced reporter. In both of these books, credit for the Dillinger operation was shifted to the Chicago bureau chief, who was nowhere near the Biograph that memorable night. But in the mid-thirties, the names of Dillinger and Purvis were so closely entangled that Hoover added his weight to the Hays Office interdiction. A few salient facts of the case were freely borrowed by Hollywood in the spate of G-men films that followed, but Dillinger's name was never mentioned, and neither, much to Hoover's relief, was Purvis's.

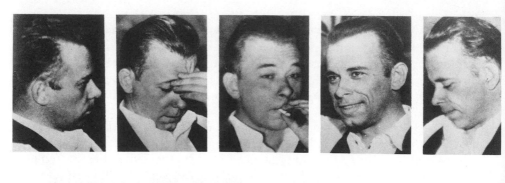

John Dillinger, the most charismatic criminal of the decade. *Universal*

Is it perverse to wonder what Dillinger must have thought of the movie he had sat through at the Biograph that last evening in Chicago? It was Metro's *Manhattan Melodrama,* glossy gangster stuff, and Dillinger must have derived some mild amusement from watching Clark Gable impersonate a racketeer and gambler who is a softie at heart and who not only loses his girlfriend (Myrna Loy) to his lifelong pal, the district attorney (William Powell), but also goes to the electric chair like a gangland Sidney Carton doing a far far better thing, in order to preserve the new couple's happiness and the D.A.'s political career. Virile friendship is carried to sentimental extremes in the film: the Cain and Abel motif of so many other gangster stories, also known as the "There but for the Grace of God" syndrome, here made still another appearance.

In *Manhattan Melodrama,* racketeer and district attorney share the same Lower East Side boyhood, both lose their parents in a fire aboard a Hudson River excursion boat, both are adopted by the same kindly Jew (George Sidney), whose death in a Union Square riot—clubbed by a policeman as he is heckling a Trotskyite and succeedingly trampled by the stampeding mob—will speed the boys along their divergent paths. Young Blackie (Mickey Rooney about to grow into Gable) hurls a tearful challenge to a society that shows no more regard for a patriotic Jew than for a foreign agitator: "Someday I'll get even with the rotten cops!" Cut to the film's visual leitmotif of hands spinning on a clock that bears the inscription,

"Young man, observe the time and fly from evil." Dissolve to 1920 and to the grown-up leading men encased in their social and antisocial roles.

The story forced Gable to kill twice: first a rival gambler, acted by Noel Madison, whose slick jet-black hair and sullen expression leave no doubt as to his rotten character and expendability; then Powell's secretary, who threatens to disclose to the voters Loy's premarital fling with Gable, a revelation which would surely prevent Powell from being elected governor of New York State. Both killings are performed with grim resignation; it is obviously not in Gable's nature to kill anyone, not even a crooked cop, or indeed to do anything more dishonest than running a gambling joint or betting on the Dempsey-Firpo fight. Just as revealing of the new Hays policies was the suppression of the sexuality that Gable had projected in films such as *A Free Soul* and *Night Nurse*. Alone in his king-size bed at dawn, Gable turns down the girls when they telephone to offer him some company.

In the new reign of film censorship, uplift and manly sentiment were to stand in for the previous violence and sexuality. When Powell prosecutes Gable for the second murder, an act he is vaguely aware Gable performed on his behalf, the friends indulge in mutual courtroom adoration. Gable is

The last film Dillinger saw: *Manhattan Melodrama*, 1934, starring Clark Gable, whom Dillinger was said to resemble. On the left: Leo Carrillo, William Powell. *Metro-Goldwyn-Mayer*

given to muttering, "Class ... it's written all over him," and writing a humorous caption for a cartoon of himself sitting on the electric chair, "Okay, kid, I can take it, but can you dish it out!" (Would Rico Bandello have turned in his unmarked grave?) The outcome of the trial sends Powell to Albany and Gable to the death house. As the time of execution draws close, Gable sends a Hattie Carnegie nightie to a former moll as a last token gesture of his machismo, and he looks lovingly at Powell from behind bars. Powell starts to break down, which greatly embarrasses Gable. He admits to the first killing to ease Powell's conscience; *that*, at least, had no redeeming reasons behind it. And anyway, prison is no place for a red-blooded gambler to spend a lifetime. Cheerfully, Gable goes to the chair, accompanied on the last mile by his old friend and parish priest (Leo Carrillo) who has himself come up in the world to become prison chaplain of Sing Sing.

At this time Hoover still distrusted the movies. As did most law enforcers, he blamed Hollywood for glorifying crime. He had declined to cooperate with requests for access to FBI files, and film producers knew that it was almost impossible to get around the Hays Code without some sort of endorsement from the bureau. The films were then running far behind other media which, as Jack Alexander wrote in his 1937 *New Yorker* profile of Hoover, "bloomed with sagas of aggressive federal purity." Jack L. Warner, a good friend of Hoover's, finally convinced him that the Bureau of Investigation should be represented on screen. It was poetic justice that the studio which had most glorified the image of the criminal should now attempt to raise Hoover's boys to the same popular status.

In most existing prints of *G-Men* (1935) the Department of Justice seal immediately follows the Warner Brothers logo. Hoover granted this seal of approval for a 1949 reissue of the film, to mark the occasion of the FBI's twenty-fifth anniversary. A filmed prologue, also added in 1949, refers to *G-Men* as "the grand-daddy of all G-Men pictures," but there was evidence on the screen that it came to be a model in a rather haphazard fashion. *G-Men* certainly did not start out as anything more institutional than a good action film—the producer, Lou Edelman, was distinctly second-string compared to Zanuck, Wallis, or, later, Jerry Wald—but as the plot unfolded, it became an exciting indoctrination course.

There does not seem to have been any direct production supervision from the bureau, as there was in the television series of the sixties; although Hoover, according to studio press releases, supplied a few technical advisors and passed approval on the leading man.*

To inaugurate the official image of the FBI agent, James Cagney was the logical choice for the lead, even though the picture had to work overtime

---

* In light of the bureau's traditional distrust of most things Jewish and all things intellectual, it is unlikely that either Paul Muni or Edward G. Robinson, both under contract to Warner at the time, were considered for the lead. Robinson, however, played a G-man in *Confessions of a Nazi Spy* in 1939, at the outset of a wartime truce with the Communists. Nevertheless, both he and Muni were blacklisted during the cold-war period.

to dispel old resonances—mostly the echo of a hundred gunshots—every time he held a submachine gun. Purity did not come as naturally to Cagney as aggressiveness. At his most familiar ease, moving in and out of the precincts of the underworld, one knew that Cagney could easily infiltrate any mob; he made the G-man the gangster's Doppelgänger, his Other. This duality became explicit in a number of later films dealing with the bureau, notably *The Street with No Name* (1948), directed by William Keighley (who also directed G-Men), and *I Was a Communist for the FBI* (1951), in which audiences were treated to a timely switch of adversaries.

The story of *G-Men* was adapted by Gregory Rogers from "Public Enemy No. 1," one of several news stories that had cashed in on the Dillinger-Purvis popularity, but the film mentioned neither man by name. ("All characters and events depicted in this photoplay...") The screenplay, by Seton I. Miller, who had also worked on *Scarface*, changed the emphasis from the unmaking of a criminal to the making of a G-man, and, in doing so, it borrowed a few clichés from "service" movies: the trainee is submitted to some routine hazing by his counselors, who at first resent or misinterpret his punk mannerisms, his credentials (Cagney's Brick Davis is supposed to be a Phi Beta Kappa from the slums), and the fact that he was put through law school by a retired bootlegger. From this period of trial, Brick emerges a fully appointed G-man; fully armed as well, since the historical congressional bill is passed halfway through the picture. Brick then puts his knowledge of the criminal world to splendid use, tracing a gardenia found in a getaway car to a gangster he knew in his prebureau days and who was involved in the murder of a college friend. A hunch is worth hours of dreary detection, and the FBI gets its man.

The film bides its time until the revenge motif is firmly established; then the screen explodes with the kind of violence missing since the days of *Scarface*—sufficient, incidentally, to get the picture banned in Chicago. The big, expert set piece is based on the siege of the Little Bohemia Lodge, but whereas that particular incident proved to be a fiasco for the bureau, the fictional counterpart is a thrilling battle that ends in the near extermination of the gang. The scene also illustrates the cutting of Brick's ties to the underworld, for he is forced to shoot his erstwhile benefactor (William Harrigan), who is being held hostage by the brutish, hulking Dillinger distortion (Barton MacLane) and used as a shield to effect his getaway. The fatherly bootlegger dies in Brick's arms, but not before absolving him of any Oedipal guilt: "You're okay."

The final section of *G-Men* deals with a kidnapping, a crime so distasteful to the Hays Office that it had been barred from the screen since early in 1934, when Paramount had tried to cash in on the Lindbergh case with *Miss Fane's Baby Is Stolen*. The Crime Section of the Production Code stated that "the kidnapping or illegal abduction of children are acceptable... only when (1) the subject is handled with restraint and discretion... and (2) the child is returned unharmed." To comply with the second proviso, *Miss Fane's Baby* sacrificed the restraint and discretion

prescribed by the first to a nickelodeon car chase that returns the abducted child (Baby Leroy) to his movie-star mother (Dorothea Wieck). The screenplay was written by Adela Rogers St. John, who had covered the Lindbergh case; the film's happy ending seems all the more obscene in the light of the actual events. The perpetrators of the Lindbergh crime were still at large when the film was released, but in the picture, the kidnappers are arrested, indicted, convicted, and sentenced in a mere eight hours. With this wishful outcome, Hollywood was pleading for a revision of the California kidnap laws.*

In *G-Men*, the kidnap victim was not a child but a woman: a starched sexless nurse (Margaret Lindsay) whom the picture promoted as heroine, while it bypassed the wistful chorus girl (Ann Dvorak), typed from the start as not-quite-right for a future G-man and married thereon to the villain. Shot while passing on information about the abduction, the chorus girl dies in Brick's arms, begging him to kiss her, just this once, and he complies. The gangster film saw women mainly as predators, but the law-enforcement film exploited them as victims, a tactic guaranteed to outrage and alarm the general public again, as it had during the white-slavery hysteria of the early 1900s.

Hoover aimed at instilling in audiences a feeling that society was threatened and that only his small but growing force of elite crusaders stood between the safety of American women and children and all the assorted mobsters, mad-dog killers, and other public enemies. It is probably to Hoover's credit that the G-man films never attained the rabid excesses of the vigilante movies. Although the typecasting was loaded—those prim, dedicated young WASPs pitted against the flashy Latin hoods—the FBI's objective was certainly not to encourage citizens to become law enforcers, but to train them to recognize the symptoms of crime and relay them to the agency.

G-Men made a fairly effective recruiting poster for adherence to FBI theories, but a second stab at filming the Dillinger case revealed the danger of polarizing cops and robbers. In *Let 'em Have It*, released shortly after *G-Men*, the crime busters (Richard Arlen and Eric Linden among them) were as colorful as collar-ad types, with none of the idiosyncratic tics that

---

* The Hays Office theory on kidnapping seems in retrospect more plausible than that espoused by the FBI at about the same time. While the bureau maintained that kidnapping would become a standard revenue source for the underworld after repeal, the Hays people adhered to the unofficial line that kidnapping was a one-shot crime, the work of loners, amateurs, crackpots, and sex perverts. Although it was likely that these types could be influenced by even so trivial an experience as a movie, it was clearly impossible to control their unpredictable behavior.

G-man James Cagney and gangsters Russell Hopton, Edward Pawley, and Barton MacLane in *G-Men*, 1935. Can you tell them apart? *Warner Brothers*

Sadism and revelry at the Little Bohemia Lodge: the audience must feel outraged to justify the violence. The gangsters are Barton MacLane, Russell Hopton, Noel Madison. Their molls: Gertrude Short, Frances Morris, Florence Dudley. The victim is William Harrigan. *G-Men. Warner Brothers*

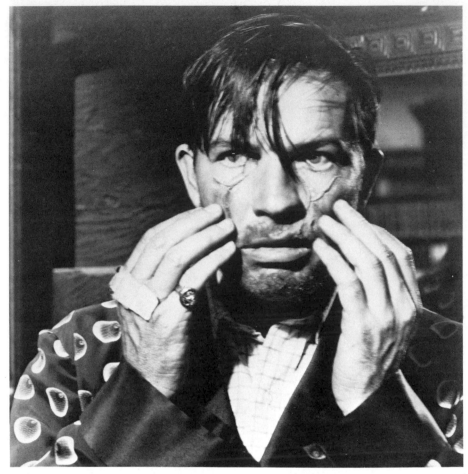

Literally a marked man: Bruce Cabot as a killer who has undergone plastic surgery discovers his initials carved on his new face. *Let 'em Have It,* 1935. *United Artists*

Cagney got away with in a similar role. On the other hand, the gangster was magnified with camera setups and lighting in the expressionistic style of horror movies of the same vintage. The new film covered some of the same territory as the first, including scenes of the Wisconsin hideout and the death of a young friend which galvanizes the hero into action. But it drew on an unauthenticated fact of Dillinger's career for its spectacular climax. Joe Keefer (Bruce Cabot) undergoes plastic surgery to escape recognition and has the reluctant surgeon killed after the operation; after days of agony, the bandages are removed to expose the gangster's own initials engraved on his features, the mobster as monster, literally a marked man.

Apart from a few specific locales and props such as laboratories, charts, and detection paraphernalia, the crime-buster film lacked an imagery of its own. This is clear even in two stills from two James Cagney films of such different orientation as *G-Men* and *The Roaring Twenties:* the labeling may vary but it hardly affected the costuming, the weaponry, or the physical details of the character. Both Cagneys were defined as men of action; in fact, the detective had been mobsterized. If, as the bureau advocates contended, kids all over the country were now playing at being G-men instead of gangsters, it was partly because the exciting theatrics of violence were available to both.*

With *G-Men,* Warner also revived its flagging tradition of punchy subjects drawn from current headlines. Darryl Zanuck, the man who started it all with *Doorway to Hell* five years before, had left in 1933 to form his own Twentieth Century Films, which merged soon thereafter with the moribund Fox Company to create one of Hollywood's lasting major studios, Twentieth Century-Fox. For one of his first projects there, Zanuck was inspired by a recent kidnapping, that of the Weyerhauser boy in Tacoma, Washington, a case cracked by the FBI in May 1935. By July, *Snatched* was ready for release, but the picture was hardly a hack job. Coscripted by Kubec Glasmon (who also worked on *The Public Enemy*), the story was informed with all sorts of topical tensions. The original title was vetoed by the Hays organization, and the film reached the public with a release title that had the ring of one of Hoover's own slogans: *Show Them No Mercy.* The film preached cooperation in the fight against crime, and it also amounted to a crash course in marked-bill spotting. It suggested that no citizen however uninvolved, no bystander however innocent, was exempt from danger. Glasmon put a chilling line in the mouth of the "government man from the Bureau of Investigation": "They [kidnappers] may be encouraged by success, and kidnapping will become a daily occurrence." And an even more chilling one in the mouth of a kidnapper: "Innocent people have the best memories."

Show Them No Mercy is about an American family, made archetypal by the presence of a child and a dog, held prisoner by a gang of kidnappers hiding out in an abandoned farmhouse. The criminals are so well characterized—the dapper, reasonable Cesar Romero; the unspeakably brutal Bruce Cabot; Warren Hymer, retarded and kind; Edward Brophy, the pitiful butt of Cabot's sadistic jokes—that the picture ends up creating as much suspense in their behalf as in that of the young couple, Rochelle Hudson and Edward Norris, who are appealingly helpless at first. But as menace piles up on humiliation, the couple grow aware of the need to fight for their baby's life, that is, for the future. After the rest of the gang has been decimated by G-men, the wife graphically machine-guns the Cabot character. Her

---

* It is not surprising to find an editorial in *The New York Times* of May 5, 1936, expounding on the differences, none too obvious, between gangster and G-men stories:

Once upon a time they were called gangster films, and they aroused much concern among parents and educators. Now they are called G-man films, and they seem to enjoy wide approval. Where the essential difference comes in is hard to see. It is still a picture of crime and violence. The amount of gun-play is heavier than ever, with consequent results on young nerves. No higher moral is perceptible.

The old gangster stories paid formal tribute to virtue by showing that crime does not pay, and that is all the new G-men fables can boast for a lesson. Under the old dispensation, the newspapers would have stories of small boys playing bandits and doing themselves serious harm. Under new conditions small boys will incur serious accidents playing Federal Secret Service agents.

J. Edgar Hoover deploys his forces, realizes the power of the movies, and supervises his sharpshooters: *You Can't Get Away with It*, 1936. *Universal*

action was a call to arms to America's wives and mothers that so impressed the Hays censor that he lifted the ban on blood and visible wounds for this film.

Responding to the outcry at this recurrence of violence on the screen, the FBI acted quickly to emphasize the patient detection work rather than the marksmanship of its G-men. *You Can't Get Away with It* (1936), a three-real featurette, used newsreel shots of despoiled banks and bullet-torn cars to illustrate the pursuit, capture, and extermination of the likes of Dillinger and Baby Face Nelson. Intercut with this footage were documentary scenes of ballistics tests, microscopic analysis, the workings of the massive Central Fingerprint Bureau—scientific detective work of which the FBI could be justly proud. In one scene, Hoover was even coaxed into making a rare screen appearance.

The short film proved to be the ideal format for presenting the law-and-order crusade and regimenting any excessive violence. With *Buried Loot* in 1935, Metro launched a series of one- and two-reelers, the *Crime Does Not Pay* series, and the studio released these films regularly for more than a

The *Crime Does Not Pay* series: the short as ideal format of the law-and-order crusade. In the first of the series, *Buried Loot*, 1935, Robert Taylor effects his getaway in priestly garb. *The Perfect Set-Up*, 1936, dealt with the notorious Millen Brothers case (which

also inspired *Let Us Live*, its liberal counterpart). The baby-barter racket was exposed in *Women in Hiding*, 1940. In *While America Sleeps*, 1939, spies and saboteurs were added to the rogues' gallery. *Metro-Goldwyn-Mayer*

decade afterward. They were meant to stimulate public trust in the several branches of the law. Aimed at a youthful audience, the shorts often preceded the main feature. Though their messages were frequently at odds with those of the features, they were intended to fulfill the industry's civic obligations. The greater part of their content was codified, from the visual leitmotif of the series—the opening shots of a badge, a gun firing directly at the viewer, and a car chase—to the schematization of locale ("a large Midwestern city") and character ("for obvious reasons names have been changed"). The subjects included all sorts of felonies and misdemeanors, from loansharking (*Money to Loan*, 1939) to shoplifting (*Think First,* 1939) to illegal adoption (*Women in Hiding*, 1940). But except in *Jack Pot* (1940), an exposé of the nationwide slot-machine racket, any reference to the Mafia, the syndicate, Murder Inc.—the decade's underworld empires whose existence the FBI persisted in ignoring or denying—was conspicuously missing from the series. And if at any time the attentive moviegoer became conscious of the alarming variety of delinquents that proliferated during the Depression, the formula invariably dramatized for reassurance, implying that such individuals were ordinarily rank amateurs.

Initially produced by Jack Chertok, the *Crime Does Not Pay* series reached a high level of concision and skill, benefiting from the largess of Metro-Goldwyn-Mayer. MGM permitted the use of standing sets and stock footage from its more expensive projects and the casting of young contract players such as Robert Taylor, Van Johnson, Laraine Day, and Cameron Mitchell. Directors Fred Zinnemann, Jacques Tourneur, David Miller, and Joseph Losey found the series a useful, if necessarily limited, training ground; being forced to make every shot count was a good opportunity to introduce a little *mise en scène*—although generally the series emphasized montage. At least one short broke away from the series and became a feature, Tourneur's *They All Come Out* (1939). This expanded seven-reel version of the original two-reeler was commissioned by the Justice Department as a documentary on federal prisons, and it dealt more sympathetically than the original possibly could with the plight of ex-convicts attempting to rehabilitate themselves. Another two-reeler, Losey's *A Gun in His Hand* (1945) contained the core of a story later developed in his feature, *The Prowler* (1950).

In many episodes of *Crime Does Not Pay*, an actor identified as "your MGM Crime Reporter" introduced an official—a judge or police captain or FBI agent—who delivered a lecture straight to the audience. This seems at best redundant, since what made the series such effectve propaganda was its ideological transparency, which never permitted anything extraneous, whether motivation or ambiguity, to muddle the blacks and whites of the message. Naturally, the series served with the same efficiency during World War Two, when spies, saboteurs, alien smugglers, and black-market operators were added to its rogues' gallery.

The *Crime Does Not Pay* series was phased out shortly after the war, even as a certain complexity of motives began to creep into story and characterization. In *A Gun in His Hand*, the protagonist was a corrupt policeman, something unheard of in movies of five years before. The hero of the closing episode, *Luckiest Guy in the World* (1947), was no professional criminal, just an irresponsible husband (Barry Nelson) who accidentally kills his wife in an argument over money. A subsequent, premeditated murder to cover up his wife's death turns this bungling amateur into the perfect criminal. And the husband collects all sorts of benefits until one evening when, as an innocent bystander in a street gunfight, he is hit by a stray bullet. His dying words, "I almost got away with murder," could serve as a proper epitaph for the series, which, in the majority of its forty-eight installments, had managed to refuse the intervention of fate as much as the fallibility of the law.

In their heyday, the mid- and late thirties, the shorts were judged so effective in the curbing of crime that Metro could boast not only of endorsements from Hoover and the attorney general, but of two Academy Awards (for *The Public Pays* in 1936 and *Torture Money* in 1937). Hollywood continued to pay its dues to the law throughout the late thirties, but mostly in the shape of dozens of B-films. Even though Hoover was the purported author of a book titled *Persons in Hiding* and was reported to be joining the film industry in an executive capacity in March 1939, the movies drawn from the case histories in the book never quite made it as A-productions. They were relegated by Paramount, which acquired the rights, to the lower half of double bills where they could be seen promoting law, order, and the bureau, often at loggerheads with the main attraction—the big, spectacular gangster pictures that had backlashed into fashion by the late thirties. A photograph of Hoover was used to publicize the films as a token endorsement, but it was not until almost a decade later that the FBI began to take an actual part in movie production. When *Persons in Hiding* was made, Hoover apparently lacked the time, power, or inclination to supervise the series personally. Instead he relied on the Hays Office to impose the inevitable load of retribution.

The Hoover stories were not just "a mine of second-rate material," as a *New York Times* critic wrote at the time; in fact they were quite the opposite. The first of the series' four dramatizations, likewise titled *Persons in Hiding* (1939), dealt with Bonnie and Clyde, charismatic as ever, though admittedly much less mythologized four years after their death than they were to be in 1967, when they effected a grandiose filmic comeback. After the disproportionate build-up in the Hearst papers came the foreseeable Hoover debunking: Bonnie and Clyde were just a couple of petty criminals, one a silly girl who hankered for expensive dresses and perfume, and the other a gritty ex-con who inveigled her into a series of holdups. Nevertheless, this little B-film, with its B-film ambitions and a meager shooting schedule of eighteen days, could not quite suppress the romantic aspect of an outlaw couple meeting by the roadside or hiding out in shabby rented rooms. As it stands, the picture came out so soon after the actual event that it cannot help but fascinate us today: this was surely the way Americans

Bonnie and Clyde: a girl who hankered for dresses and perfume and a gritty ex-con who inveigles her into a series of holdups. Patricia Morison and J. Carrol Naish in *Persons in Hiding*, 1939, first of four B-films adapted from a book supposedly written by J. Edgar Hoover. *Paramount*

thought about Bonnie and Clyde in the thirties—as picturesque but unglamorous second-raters. Trapped by its B-format, the film vacillated between abhorring the criminal, as did the *Crime Does Not Pay* series, and viewing him sympathetically, as would any full-bodied fiction along the lines of *Angels with Dirty Faces*. The real intelligence was in the script, coauthored by William R. Lipman and Horace McCoy, the latter the author of *They Shoot Horses Don't They?* and a novelist of some prestige. Additionally, the acting of Patricia Morison and J. Carrol Naish had the thumbnail readability of character actors in thirties movies; given more screen time, Morison and Naish might have nicely filled out the roles with detail and shading.

Second and third in the series were *Undercover Doctor* (1939) and *Parole Fixer* (1940). Fourth and last was *Queen of the Mob* (1940), which watered down and distorted the career of Ma Barker and her homegrown gang; a career made unforgettable by its overtones of violent momism—the American family gone extraordinarily wrong. The family name in the picture was changed to Webster and, curiously, the reviews did not once mention the Barkers. While still only a program filler, *Queen of the Mob* featured a legitimate stage tragedienne, Blanche Yurka, as the ferocious heroine. She brought a preacher-woman austerity to the part, and touches of contradiction were written in to nicely round out the character. For instance, Ma Webster liked to celebrate Christmas with her boys, buy presents for her grandchildren, keep the family together, unto death. The tabloid ending was tidied up, no bullet-riddled corpses side by side, still

"All right, G-man, you win!" Blanche Yurka as the ferocious Ma Webster (read Barker) in the last of the *Persons in Hiding* series, *Queen of the Mob*, 1940. *Paramount*

holding on to their Tommy guns. Instead, Ma Webster was allowed to out-
live her sons—the last of whom lay dead at her feet, beside the Christmas
tree, still wearing his Santa breeches and boots—only to surrender to the
law with an "All right, G-man, you win."

By 1940, the attention of the FBI was monopolized by the threat of
foreign agents on American soil. The *Persons in Hiding* series obviously
belonged to the past. Even then, Hollywood had realized that the stories of
Bonnie and Clyde, of the Barkers and their ilk, were better told from the
criminals' angle than from the viewpoint of the law. The mechanism of
crime and retribution had been the prime mover of law-enforcement films—
after all, there was all that violence to justify—but it did not take long to
see that legality alone would never capture the public's imagination. Stay
close to a character, whether in print or on the screen, and that character
ran the risk of turning into a protagonist. The fresh-faced juveniles who
usually played G-men, the character actors who played their bureau chiefs
(like Lynne Overman in *Persons in Hiding*) came into the picture after the
crimes had been set up dramatically (so that retribution would be effective), but by then a bond had already been established between criminal and
spectator. The sequence of cause and effect invariably elicited audience
identification. And then, as now, identification was Hollywood's ultimate
concern.

5. A New Deal for the Gangster

Criminals do not die by the hands of the law. They die by the hands of other men.
— George Bernard Shaw, *Man and Superman*

THE GANGSTER FILM staged a comeback in the guise of comedy, just at the period of maximum vigilance that followed Joe Breen's appointment to office in 1933. It was clear even then that the Production Code Authority applied Breen's interdictions less rigorously in the case of comedies and cartoons. Yet it should have been obvious from the recent example of the Mae West pictures, as from the sexual and scatological content of many matinee shorts, that comedy per se did not confer acceptability. Breen, however, continued to regard comedies rather benignly throughout the decade until 1941, when he was called on the carpet—by none other than Cardinal Spellman of New York—and reprimanded for approving the Garbo comedy *Two-Faced Woman*. (In the fifties, *The Moon Is Blue*, another comedy, finally delivered a deadly blow to censorship.) The comedy of manners, of lack thereof, flourished throughout the New Deal, from *The Three-Cornered Moon* to *The Awful Truth*, and this genre illustrated the social shifts of the period much better than did any straight drama.

The Hays Office tolerance of gangster comedies derived from an appreciation of the funny and edifying spectacle of a gangster striving—ridiculously, unsuccessfully—to crash post-Prohibition society. In *Little Caesar*, Rico was at his most ingratiatingly vulnerable when he paraded in his new elegance—the loud Art Deco robe or the white tie and tails rendered incongruous by his five-o'clock shadow—for the benefit of an admiring sidekick. Rico was so appealing because he was a natural, the racketeer as social arriviste. At the palatial home of the Big Boy, Rico thanks the butler for taking his hat and coat, and is duly impressed when told that a painting is worth fifteen grand, a sum that he logically ascribed to the gilt frame.

To find his place in the New Deal, the movie gangster went legitimate, a reform undertaken as a survival tactic, and one with a refreshing lack of moral impulse. "It's all over, we're washed up, our racket can't last much longer. I'm getting out, and if you're smart you'll all get out. From now on, no organization," proclaims Bugs Aherne at the outset of *Little Giant*, on hearing of Roosevelt's election-night victory on the radio. This 1933 parody of *Little Caesar* starred Edward G. Robinson as a reformed bootlegger who becomes the fall guy for a bunch of upper-class swindlers and snobs, and almost marries a predatory society woman. Bugs is taken in by his new social circle, but the uncouth parvenu proves no match for the sophisticates, at least until he reverts to his old ways, whereupon a little of the old Chicago expediency manages to set matters right. A bit more world-wise, Bugs keeps his resolve to stay out of the gutter: he marries a democratic blueblood (Mary Astor) who serves as his social secretary, and the gang settles down to play polo on the front lawn in images redolent of suburban serenity.

In *Little Giant*, although the gangster had not yet been sentimentalized, he was already subject to some of the optimistic fantasizing of the Frank Capra Depression comedies. The first of these Capra films was a sort of gangster comedy, based on Damon Runyon's short story *Madame La Gimp* and featuring a Broadway fauna of news vendors, pimps, touts, gamblers, peddlers, and night people, all derived from the tabloid via the fairy tale: warmth and togetherness on the fringe of the underworld. Dave the Dude (Warren William), the gangster figure, is a bon vivant with the best interests of his turf at heart, a picaresque godfather when it comes to preserving a child's illusions or an idealized image of motherhood. Retitled *Lady for a Day*, Capra's brew of slang, sentiment, and corn took Radio City Music Hall by storm, and, in an attempt to cash in on the windfall, the gangster comedy subsequently reached maudlin highs and lows in such Runyonesque pictures as *Little Miss Marker, The Lemon Drop Kid,* and *Little Miss Glory*.

When Bruno Hauptmann died in the electric chair as the convicted kidnapper of the Lindbergh child, Runyon exulted in his column: "The wolfman is dead!" But elsewhere, his comic creations functioned to clean up the underworld's image in the years of Charles "Lucky" Luciano. In 1935, Runyon collaborated with the playwright Howard Lindsay on a Broadway comedy, *A Slight Case of Murder,* that turned out to be a rip-off of *Little Giant,* with updated one-liners. The play was bought by Warner Brothers for another Robinson vehicle and filmed in 1937. Through the movie ran a streak of bad taste that was strictly post-Code. While the violence in *Little Giant* was mostly verbal (culminating in an inspired threat: "Be quiet or I'll stuff my foot in your mouth," directed by the hero at a scheming dowager), the characters in the new movie played hide-and-seek with a bunch of corpses left as incriminating evidence at Robinson's country home, and most of the jokes dealt with disposing of "the parties." One dead hood, with the Runyonesque name of "No-nose" Cohen, is left propped against a neighbor's front door in homage to *The Public Enemy,* and much sleight-of-body takes place while Robinson, a retired bootlegger, copes with his socially conscious wife (Ruth Donnelly), a juvenile delinquent by the name of Douglas Fairbanks Rosenbloom (Bobby Jordan), and a state trooper (Willard Parker) who wants to marry Robinson's daughter; all while a boozy, grotesquely sentimental party goes on. It takes a lot of strained vaudeville to get the trooper to shoot a gang of already dead racketeers. While Robinson glowers his consent to the marriage, his wife explains Robinson's phobia of the law to the prospective son-in-law: "He doesn't like uniforms, he's a pacifist."

Robinson also starred in *The Whole Town's Talking* (made in 1934, released early in 1935), which drew raves from the critics and literally brought the gangster back with a bang. It was a comedy, and a very funny one, written by Jo Swerling from a story by W. R. Burnett and directed by John Ford at Columbia, a Poverty Row studio then rapidly rising in the industry through a series of successful pictures directed by Frank Capra. *The Whole Town's Talking* seems to have been written with Capra in mind, but in Ford's hands the whimsy and warmth of Swerling's "little people" were played down in favor of cranky humor. The film is about two men of diametrically opposed temperament who share the same face (that of Edward G. Robinson). Jones is an office accountant who dreams of the pert secretary (Jean Arthur) a few desks down but is too shy to confide in anyone but his pet canary; "Killer" Bannion is Public Enemy Number One. Jones is mistaken for his double so often that the police decide to supply him with an identity card, and Bannion intrudes into Jones's otherwise uneventful life in search of the card, which virtually assures him carte blanche to operate right under the eyes of the law. The gangster is in fact borrowing the meager identity the clerk enjoys, an official piece of paper certifying his anonymity. In exchange, the clerk learns a thing or two about the charisma of fame and the power of intimidation from the gangster.

Swerling and Ford could afford to have Killer Bannion played straight because their film was founded on the opposition of anomie and notoriety. Bannion is well aware of his news value, scanning the papers for inaccurate reports of his exploits while Jones and the secretary, who is mistaken for his moll, enjoy the sudden glare of attention; especially the girl, who plays the part to the comic hilt while being given the third degree at headquarters, cigarette dangling from one corner of her mouth, muttering with ferocious intensity, "Bannion . . . Bannion? . . ." Jones faints after a final act of courage, having behaved for an instant like Bannion, the man of action, whereupon one assumes he will settle down to a safe workaday life.

Joe Breen and his seven staff members did go to work on the straight portions of the script, deleting a kidnap scene and rendering through suggestion a gripping murder within prison walls. But the real point of *The Whole Town's Talking*, that in every milquetoast there beats the secret heart of a mobster, resided mostly in the comic opposition of the two Robinsons. To explain the disproportionate popularity of this basically unassuming comedy one could do worse than elaborate on the gangster as the release mechanism for a million frustrated moviegoers. (A Chicago poll in 1931 disclosed that Hollywood stars and Chicago mobsters topped the list of best-known personalities on the American scene; as a life choice, stardom and grand-scale crime loomed equally out of reach for the average man, as if stars and public enemies existed on a different plane of achievement, creatures of a separate fate.)

The first inevitable clash between Breen and the industry came in the wake of the success of *The Whole Town's Talking*. For some time the studios had looked wistfully at the headlines, and the Hays Office had managed to keep them in line, partly by dangling the ever-present threat of a boycott

and partly by pointing to the more obvious improvements brought about by
the Breen regime, such as the higher quality of scriptwriting. But in February 1935, *The New York Times* reported that five majors had admitted
scheduling projects based on the careers of Dillinger or Baby Face Nelson.
Censorship could no longer stand in the way of profit; one crime picture
had paid off and others were being sped along to cash in. The best Breen
could do was to insist that the focus be shifted to the federal crime fighter
and that the stories reiterate the crime-does-not-pay moral. And so, Dillinger—this time with his name intact—entered the screen not as the hero
of his own story but as a semifictional target for the G-men. By 1937, the
second gangster-film cycle was in full force, replete with elaborate exer-
cises in violence that drew upon the archetypal crudities of the first. The
look and character of American movies changed markedly, and so indeed
had the rackets, when the gangster reappeared to convey some timely notions about, and for, Americans.

Broadway's contribution to this second cycle was the existential gangster, a lonely, passive figure who took on the pathos of a threatened species.
The movies needed some time to appropriate this pretentious, high-flown
concept and render it in terms of, say, *High Sierra*. Within the space of two
seasons in the mid-thirties, New York theatergoers were treated to *Small
Miracle, Winterset, The Petrified Forest,* and *Dead End.* Except for the first,
a modest thriller in the mold of *Grand Hotel* or *Dinner at Eight,* these plays
were loaded with ambition and sociopoetic significance, and one of them,
Winterset, was even afflicted with blank verse. But all of them featured a
gangster at the end of his rope.

The original text of Robert E. Sherwood's *The Petrified Forest* (play,
1934; film, 1936) described the looks of the fugitive mass murderer, Duke
Mantee: "well-built but stoop-shouldered, with a vaguely thoughtful, saturnine face. He is ... unmistakably condemned." Adapted for the screen by
Charles Kenyon and Delmer Daves, the text retained much of the play's
artificiality; fortunately the gangster's dialogue consisted mostly of mono-
syllables, and even more luckily, Humphrey Bogart was allowed to repeat
his stage role. Sherwood brought a vagrant poet (Leslie Howard) face to
face with Mantee in an isolated luncheonette in the Arizona desert so that
he could sum up the significance of the old-time gangster: "You're obsolete,
Duke, like me." The social growth of America had done away with types
like the poet and the gangster. To the poet, Mantee is "the last great apostle
of rugged individualism"; to an old-timer, he is the very essence of America:
"He ain't a gangster, he's a real old-time desperado. Gangsters is foreign.
He's an American."

Reorganized crime left a maverick like Duke Mantee stranded behind
the times while the poet was being rendered obsolete by the advent of a
prosaic new world. Both had returned to the old frontier to die. With in-
sufferable conceit, the poet asks to be put out of his misery: "Will you do
it, Duke?" And the gunman drawls back: "Sure I'll do it. Let me know when
you want to be killed." In the end, as Duke makes his getaway, he keeps

his word and guns down the poet without passion or animosity; then he takes his leave: "I'll be seeing you soon." Tired and taciturn, Mantee sits out the film, a gun in his lap, indifferently picking his teeth. To him every man is "pal," every woman is "sister"; he is respectful of old men and society women, and, despite his record and impending extinction, he comes across as just another member of the proletariat.

Humphrey Bogart as Duke Mantee in *The Petrified Forest*, 1936, described by author Robert E. Sherwood as: "well-built but stoop-shouldered, with a vaguely thoughtful, saturnine face. He is . . . unmistakably condemned." Adrian Morris and Joseph Sawyer are the two other gunmen. *Warner Brothers*

Most of the Broadway gangster plays toyed with the idea of brotherhood between the gangster and the man in the street. In his play, *Small Miracle*, Norman Krasna paraded a cross section of types whose social status dictated the viewer's response. In 1935, a hatcheck boy or an usherette was bound to fare infinitely better than a society lady or her gigolo. In the picture version, adapted by Krasna and retitled *Four Hours to Kill*, the greatest bid for sympathy was made for the gangster Tony Mako (Richard Barthelmess), handcuffed to a detective (Charles C. Wilson) portrayed as a paragon of humanity. Tony is being taken back to the pen to be executed; the anger and resentment that led him into crime have long deserted him—he is already as good as dead. Rather improbably detoured in Manhattan between trains and treated by his kind keeper to a Broadway show, Tony is galvanized into one final act of violence by the chance to

exact revenge on the stool pigeon who informed on him. After Tony kills
the stoolie, he thankfully allows himself to be shot by the detective, a variation on the mercy killing of the poet in *The Petrified Forest*.

Sympathy for the gangster: Tony Mako (Richard Barthelmess) handcuffed to a detective
(Charles C. Wilson) is as good as dead. *Four Hours to Kill*, 1935. *Paramount*

Blank verse in the mouth of a gangster probably seemed a bold and
intriguing idea in 1935, but Maxwell Anderson's *Winterset* can now be seen
as a thirties curio that mixed together the liberal obsession with the Sacco
and Vanzetti case and murkily Shakespearean characters in a romantic Depression setting. Two gunmen amble through the play, like damned ghosts.
"They soaked me once too often in that vat of poisoned hell they keep up-
state to soak men in, and I'm rotten inside," announces Trock Estrella to
his henchman, Shadow. His days numbered, Trock revisits a poetic never-
neighborhood under the arches of the Brooklyn Bridge to seek out the son
of an anarchist executed years before for a crime he and Shadow had committed. The film drawn from the play was heavily edited from the original
text by Anthony Veiller and directed by Alfred Santell; it represented Hollywood's most serious attempt at the elusive form of poetic realism. Trock
(Eduardo Ciannelli) and Shadow (Stanley Ridges) have left all reality behind; in the end, they seem more exorcised than destroyed, but Ciannelli's
aging basilisk, fleshed out with more conventional characterization and dia-

logue, was to enhance many a later Hollywood crime film.

A new group of stage actors—Ciannelli, Bogart, Joseph Spurin-Calleia (who played Tony Mako on Broadway and soon after shortened his surname to Calleia for Hollywood)—represented the second-generation gangster as quite a different breed from the sharp, grasping, healthy hoods of Robinson, et al. They were low-key and moody loners who carried with them an aura rather than a milieu; thinking man's gangsters. Duke Mantee summed it up: "I spent most of my time since I grew up in jail, the rest of the time I felt as if I were dead." Duke, Trock, and Tony were waiting for the forties, when they would move to center stage.

The thinking man's gangster: Eduardo Ciannelli as Trock Estrella in *Winterset*, 1936— quite a different breed from the healthy hoods of Robinson and Cagney. *RKO-Radio*

Meanwhile, one reads a deep kind of comradeship, typical of Depression literature, between the criminal and other losers in a faulty social system in *The Petrified Forest, Dead End,* and *Small Miracle*. In *Dead End*, Sidney Kingsley made equals of the gangster "Baby Face" Martin and Drina, the jobless, embittered waif who bears the mark of a policeman's club on her forehead. And the writer stressed the similarities between these two and a gang of street kids growing up by the waterfront, under the penthouses of Sutton Place. Like them, Baby Face retains a primal innocence which somehow resists the corruption of poverty; he has fled the tenements to seek out a career in crime and, after many years, he returns to the old block. His mother, a toil-worn harridan, slaps his face and moans, "Stay away, leave us alone to die, but leave us alone." Even more painful is Baby Face's en-

Baby Face Martin (Humphrey Bogart) returns to East 53rd Street to give a lesson
in crime to the neighborhood kids, Leo Gorcey, Bobby Jordan, Bernard Punsley (fore-
ground), Gabriel Dell, Huntz Hall, Billy Halop (above). *Dead End*, 1937. *Samuel
Goldwyn / United Artists*

counter with his boyhood sweetheart who has taken to streetwalking. "Why
didn't you starve first?" he berates her. "Why didn't you?" she replies. The
scene deteriorates into a tawdry transaction of twenty dollars.

When this scene appears on the screen, Bogart, playing Baby Face,
wipes his face with one hand, as if disgustedly wiping away a memory; it is
a gesture that portends the later Bogart. The film version of *Dead End*,
adapted by Lillian Hellman and directed by William Wyler, bore the mark
of a prestige production: where the play had attempted realism the filmmakers substituted metaphor. It opens with a panoramic view of a studio-
made skyline, then the camera descends past the terraces of the rich and
into the tenements, as if seeking out the lower depths of the city, the waterfront where the street kids play and are gradually bred into criminals. The

crushing effect of the city is emphasized in the opening shot—which is reversed at film's end as the camera leaves the scene of the crime—and this theme is occasionally restated through stagy, well-lighted vignettes of squalor, and by using low-angle shots of the characters (especially Bogart and his henchman) silhouetted against the oppressive towers. Yet Bogart himself moves and acts within the vast constricting decor as impervious to social comment as to the far-fetched artiness of *The Petrified Forest*. At this stage in his career he could still play a mean character, but it was a meanness that lacked the metaphysical resonance of, say, Ciannelli's Trock in *Winterset*. The hopefulness, the reformism of the New Deal first had to fade before Bogart could come into his own as a major popular hero; the world of the private eye—in which he would find his most natural habitat—had to be beyond improvement or repair. The hero of *Casablanca* had survived the hard times and doomed crusades of the thirties, and he could humorously caution the Nazis against invading a New York turf like that of *Dead End* where he had served time. In the mid- and late thirties, the promise of social reform was still being bought with the death of a gangster.

In the same period the psychiatrist and the priest appeared at the gangster's side, respectively offering diagnosis and absolution. The analyst was still imprecise when not actually disturbing, but the priest quickly became a stock character, which was all right by the Breen line and flattering to the Catholic church, the most vocal of the religious organizations. Two priests that captured the attention of the mass audience furnished the models. Father Coughlin, the "radio priest," pleaded for direct intervention of the church in affairs of state; in his visionary but transient fervor he saw the Archangel Gabriel, and not Satan, hovering over Roosevelt's White House. During the 1936 reelection campaign, however, he branded the president a traitor and a communist; he also intimidated—at any rate, impressed—Will Hays. Father Flanagan, founder of Nebraska's Boys Town, was nearly canonized in two pictures starring Spencer Tracy, and Flanagan's tough, pragmatic brand of religion informed the slum-bred padres of *Angels with Dirty Faces*, *Mutiny in the Big House*, and other films.

But all attempts to explain the criminal as a neurotic were bound to be tentative, half-hearted affairs. *The Amazing Dr. Clitterhouse* (1938), based on an English play by Barré Lyndon, was adapted to the American scene by John Huston and John Wexley, the locale transferred from St. John's Wood to Park Avenue. The eponymous hero (played by the indispensable Edward G. Robinson, now eons away from Rico Bandello) is a Manhattan doctor whose clientele includes judges, socialites, and the chief of police, but whose real vocation is criminal psychology. Clitterhouse is working on a book which he hopes will be a valuable contribution to science, and he intends the book to be a first-hand study of the criminal psyche, not behind bars but at large, still reeling from the excitement of crime. In the name of field research, he becomes an amateur burglar.

As the leader of a gang of burglars, Clitterhouse plans and executes several jobs which leave the police baffled. He tests the crooks' reactions after each *coup* and, insidiously, the champagnelike exhilaration of crime

A combination of Father Flanagan and Father Coughlin, the slum-bred padre brings tough, pragmatic religion to the big house: Barton MacLane and Charles Bickford in *Mutiny in the Big House*, 1939. *Monogram*

Glenn Ford, John Litel, and Barton MacLane in *Men without Souls*, 1940. *Columbia*

starts to rub off on him. The scientist is driven to premeditated murder when a gang member penetrates his incognito and attempts to blackmail him; but Clitterhouse flunks the perfect crime when a phone number in a matchbook links him to the dead man, and he is arrested and tried for murder. The defense presents Clitterhouse as a monomaniac. If he were found insane, Clitterhouse would be legally irresponsible, but a decision of insanity would also invalidate his life's work. Trapped by this paradox, Clitterhouse argues so vehemently for his sanity—contending that the work of a madman could still make perfect sense and be of immense usefulness to society—that he is pronounced insane by the jury. Clitterhouse is last seen on the witness chair, calm amid pandemonium, muttering to himself, "Amazing . . . really amazing."

Society doctor becomes gang leader: in *The Amazing Dr. Clitterhouse,* 1938, Edward G. Robinson as a psychologist in the underworld. Maxie Rosenbloom as the loyal-moronic gangster type, Claire Trevor as the gang's fence, Humphrey Bogart as "a magnificent specimen of pure viciousness." *Warner Brothers*

The by-now obligatory social comment was put in the mouth of the gang's fence (Claire Trevor) who launches into a tirade about stock promoters and slum landlords as the real criminals of society. But otherwise, the picture was curiously elitist, constantly emphasizing the superiority of the cool scientific mind. Criminals were explained, not in terms of neurosis or as victims of mental disorder, but as "types." "Rocks is a magnificent specimen of pure viciousness" is the doctor's Lombrosian description of the one crook who refuses to submit to his leadership (Bogart, in an honestly sleazy performance), while the rest of the gang falls into the categories of loyal moronic or just plain moronic. The director of *The Amazing Dr. Clitterhouse* was a Russian emigré, Anatole Litvak, who had also worked in Berlin, and there was a heavy-handed stylization to his underworld that at times brought Bertolt Brecht to mind; except Litvak did not quite know how to handle his ironies.

Another European director, the Hungarian Charles Vidor, more attuned to the analyst-gangster relationship, fared better with *Blind Alley* (1939). The motion-picture adaptation (by Philip MacDonald, Michael Blankfort, and Albert Duffy) is more complex than the 1935 play by James Warwick; there is real rapport between the psychiatrist (Ralph Bellamy) and the gangster (Chester Morris) who invades his home and keeps him, together with family and guests, as hostages before effecting his getaway. The doctor

The analyst (Ralph Bellamy) reconstructs a childhood trauma for the gunman (Chester Morris) who then finds himself incapable of asserting his virility. Ann Dvorak is the moll, and the film is *Blind Alley,* 1939. In his recurrent dream, the gangster seeks shelter from a rain of blood, a scene shown in negative film stock in both versions, the latter starring William Holden and retitled *The Dark Past,* 1949. *Columbia*

is allowed to move freely around the house, in case the police should drop in, and quietly, expertly, he sets out to disarm his captor by exposing the gangster to the meaning of a recurring nightmare. The gunman dreams of rain turning to blood, of an umbrella that provides no shelter. Probing into his past, the doctor discovers a classical Oedipal situation: as a young boy, the gangster had betrayed his brutal father to the police to remove the rival for his mother's affection. He had watched from under a table as the father was gunned down, and blood had dripped down on him from the tabletop. (The dream is shown in negative film stock, an adroit device.) The analyst reconstructs the traumatic experience for the gunman, who thereon finds himself incapable of asserting his virility: he cannot use his gun in unconscious imitation of the father he abhorred. The gangster finally allows himself to be shot down by the police. Apart from the novelty of its psychiatric jargon, Vidor's film was noteworthy because it largely ignored considerations of right and wrong: the criminal was exonerated as the possessor of a disordered mind who had no choice but to act out his compulsion and the psychiatrist functioned as an objective doctor/detective.

In the late thirties, gangster pictures were updated with shrewd additions of violence and moral message, the latter compensating for the former in the Hays book of rules. *Angels with Dirty Faces* (1938) could be considered as the New Deal remake of *The Public Enemy, Each Dawn I Die* (1939) as that of *The Big House:* both surpassed their archetypes in violence, and both were relentlessly redemptive. They starred James Cagney and, largely dispensing with the excess baggage of sweetheart and mother, partnered him with a strong male antagonist; from the play of revolt and authority a dialectic of salvation was established. *Each Dawn I Die* seems the more aberrant of the two—it reversed roles and deprived Cagney of the violent outbursts expected of him—but the end result was the same. Cagney is an investigating reporter railroaded into prison on a fake charge of drunken driving and manslaughter because of his attempts to expose the connections between politics and the underworld in a big American city. On the train taking them both to the pen, he meets a big-shot racketeer, George Raft, whose opening words to Cagney are: "How tough are you, babe?" The film favors Raft's racketeer over Cagney's crusader. Even though innocent of any crime, Cagney must still harden himself to be admitted into the tough-guy elite presided over by Raft. A decade before, this evolution would have required a process of corruption, as with the Kid in *The Big House*. But in *Each Dawn I Die*, Raft remains the absolute authority figure, the man who knows all the ropes and takes an active hand in clearing Cagney. William Keighley, the director, completed the transformation initiated in *G-Men* by developing the softer, more vulnerable traits of the Cagney character (Cagney breaks down before the parole board) and by

New Deal revisionism: *The Big House* becomes *Each Dawn I Die*, 1939, with a softer Cagney and a narcissistic Raft. John Wray remains sadistic as ever. *Angels with Dirty Faces*, 1938, made Cagney walk the last mile and turn yellow as a favor to priest Pat O'Brien. *Warner Brothers*

emphasizing Raft's narcissistic superiority: the tentative courting gestures, the betrayal fantasies, and the final sacrifice are structured much like a heterosexual romance. Keighley released tension with expert thrusts of violent action: In a scene all the more impressive for being so brief, a stool pigeon is knifed during the prison screening of an aviation epic, the whirr and putter of the soundtrack drowning out the victim's dying gasps.

Angels with Dirty Faces combined the various strands of the New Deal cycle, knotting them together in an emotional death-house confrontation that made it the most popular gangster picture of the period. Cagney plays Rocky, a slum tough returning home to the Lower East Side after a prison stretch to find himself being eased out of the racket, none too gently, by his former partners, Bogart and Bancroft, to whom Rocky seems an embarrassing anachronism. Pat O'Brien plays Jerry, Rocky's childhood friend, now grown into a priest who combines the more distinctive features of Father Flanagan (a concern for the underprivileged young) and Father Coughlin (a demagogic radio voice). As youthful partners in petty crime, Rocky had once saved Jerry's life; twenty years later, Jerry is determined to save Rocky's soul.

Spiritual redemption was a relatively new concern in gangster films. In the early part of the decade their major preoccupation was whether the gangster hero would die game or turn yellow before the end. Tom Powers, we were left to imagine, died game; so did little Rico, despite his wondering if his death was worthy of his stature. But by 1938, social concerns pulled for the gangster's immortal soul, and *Angels with Dirty Faces* and *The Roaring Twenties*, which followed in 1939, ended with both a bang and a prayer. John Wexley and Warren Duff are up there in the credits but, according to Pat O'Brien, it was Rowland Brown who contributed most of the script ideas for *Angels with Dirty Faces*. The ending can in fact be found in an excised scene from the Brown screenplay for *Doorway to Hell* in which Louie Ricarno recalled the legendary hoods of his youth: "We kids kind of worshiped Lefty Louie, Gyp the Blood, and Dago Frank. . . . Why, we even sent them a letter telling them that we hoped that they would die game."[*]

The climax of *Angels with Dirty Faces* is no longer the brilliant action sequence in which Rocky shoots it out with his rivals but instead a scene in which the priest comes to death row to ask Rocky to destroy his own popular hero image by dying like a coward: "This is a different kind of courage, the kind that only you and I and God know about. I want you to let them down. They've got to despise your memory." The shadows grow longer and more expressionistic as Cagney and O'Brien walk the last mile together, and melodrama gives way to mystery play. Cagney finally complies with the destruction of his romantic image and has to be dragged screaming and sobbing to the electric chair. "I don't think anybody knew, even Cagney, whether Rocky was actually afraid or if he was doing a courageous gesture for a pal," reminisced Pat O'Brien in *The Velvet Light Trap* thirty-seven years later; but the film itself is less ambiguous than memory would

[*] Quoted in *The Velvet Light Trap*, No. 16

have it. When the Dead End Kids ask if Rocky really died "like a yellow rat," Father Jerry resorts to a Jesuitical loophole: "He died like they say," and he then leads the boys into prayer "for a boy who couldn't run as fast as I could."

Rocky was arguably Cagney's best role. (The psycho gunman in *White Heat* did not quite belong to the same actor; his body, for one thing, lacked much of the taut expressiveness it had in the earlier pictures.) Cagney worked some personal observations into his portrayal: a catch phrase ("What do you hear? What do you say?") that rat-tat-tats on the soundtrack, and also possibly a residual Catholic piety that Cagney put into effect when, uncomfortable in church, the gangster betrays the lapsed Irish choirboy within by unwittingly mouthing the words to "Hosannah in Excelsis." As the referee, Cagney turns a basketball game with the Dead End Kids into a choreography of dirty tricks. The direction of Michael Curtiz, a specialist in swashbuckling Errol Flynn romances, backed Cagney all the way, emphasizing the moral chasm between a gangster with his roots in the gutter and an operator with a gun in his drawer. Cagney was surrounded with teeming street life while Bogart and Bancroft were strictly indoor characters, and Bogart dies appropriately clutching the phone in his spectacular fall over a barstool.

Barely six years after repeal, the mood of *The Roaring Twenties* (1939) was one of romantic revisionism. The screenplay by Jerry Wald, Richard Macauley, and Robert Rossen was an elaboration on an idea of Mark Hellinger's. Soon to become the producer of much grittier, tougher films than *The Roaring Twenties,* Hellinger was another of Broadway's sentimental romancers, a man who considered himself a connoisseur of the underworld and to whom, according to his biographer, Jim Bishop, "practically all bad men were really good men who were forced by circumstance to work outside the law." Hellinger's feelings were out front in the film's written prologue, which muses that, "bitter or sweet, most memories become precious as the years move on. This film is a memory." A narrator's voice (John Deering's) describes in fake news-commentator tones the coming of Prohibition and the birth of the bootlegger, "a modern crusader who deals in bottles instead of battles." And against an historical background of newsreel clips and headlines the audience follows Cagney's progress from doughboy in the trenches to Manhattan's top purveyor of bootleg liquor, then his precipitious decline after the crash wipes him out, the girl he loves runs off with a buddy, and repeal sends him back to cab driving. The film finished up with his redemption and death.

Although *The Roaring Twenties* dealt with the passing of an American way of life—that of the twenties gangster—its tone was more expansive than fatalistic, more one of elegy than relief. The fiction that the film inserted between harsh facts and dates tended to make gangsterism as integral a part of the American experience as the World War. The breathless pace of Raoul Walsh's directing style, cramming twenty years into ninety minutes, could well afford to retain only the most significant detail, and the picture became a distillation of a hundred other gangster movies, including Walsh's own handful since *Regeneration.* Social significance seems irrelevant when a work is conceived as an epic poem of sorts, and the key scenes in *The Roaring Twenties* bore a capitalized stylization that only Walsh was capable of achieving. The Mythic Meeting, for instance, has Cagney and Bogart coming face to face aboard a rumrunning boat, under cover of night and fog, to renew an association that began years before in the trenches. The Inevitable Confrontation comes years after, when a down-and-out Cagney stakes his life in behalf of a third wartime buddy, now the assistant D.A., and the climax is a superbly staged gunfight in which Bogart is pinned to the wall of his fancy bedroom by the sheer impact of lead. The Redemption of the Good Gangster has Cagney staggering out into the snow to die on the church steps. The epitaph, really a reiteration of the film's message, is delivered by the ever faithful aging chanteuse (Gladys George) over Cagney's dead body: "He used to be a big shot."

The year 1939 proved to be a watershed, and indeed the genre could not be taken any further in the direction of nostalgia than *The Roaring Twenties.* (Walsh himself, after an interlude of two superior nongangster films, shifted the focus from spiritual redemption to personal alienation in *High Sierra.*) In the gray, muffled mood of the thirties, the twenties were revived as vivid, if slightly tarnished, Americana—an era in which a bootlegger, hijacker, and gunman like Cagney's Eddie Bartlett could die in the gutter and still wake up with the angels. *The Roaring Twenties* exaggerated the transience of the period. "Eddie, the days of the racket are over," says the speakeasy hostess stranded in an achingly unglamorous Depression saloon; and Cagney enforces a suicidal pact of sorts on Bogart, the sharp operator who survived the coming of the New Deal: "It's a new kind of setup, you and I don't belong."

If Hollywood appeared to prefer the misty moralities of *The Roaring Twenties* to the drab depiction of criminal realities as represented by *Marked Woman* (1937) it was because the past was safer than the present when accusations of civic corruption were to be portrayed. If the public of the period preferred the nostalgic good-gangster-versus-bad-gangster fantasy to the actual exposé, it was possibly because of the higher dramatic definition of the former. Although the mid- and late thirties saw the heyday of Lucky Luciano, Frank Costello, Vito Genovese, Meyer Lansky, and other top executives of the various crime syndicates, none of these men enjoyed the show-off flair of the Chicago mobsters; their *modus operandi* belonged in court records and income-tax reports rather than in screaming headlines and tabloid prose. They may have killed the same old way, perhaps more efficiently than before, but the hoopla was reserved for courtroom theatrics. Betting, extortion, prostitution, narcotics, and labor racketeering (all of which Hollywood had experienced firsthand, especially the last) were not so much ignored as shunted into dozens of bread-and-butter program pictures, with types and situations carried over from the bootleg era.*

---

* To the star-conscious public, these films dispensed moderate doses of Edward G. Robinson (*Bullets or Ballots, I Am the Law,* which dealt with civic corruption), Bette Davis (*Bureau of Missing Persons, The Big Shakedown, Fog Over Frisco, Special Agent,* all of which applied the same formula to a wide range of felonies), and Humphrey Bogart (*Racket Busters,* on mob control of the unions).

One event to provide a fresh set of circumstances for the genre was the conviction on June 7, 1936, of Lucky Luciano on sixty-one specific charges of compulsory prostitution. The verdict was a legal (if somewhat unorthodox) victory for Special Prosecutor Thomas E. Dewey. Luciano claimed under oath, and again in his memoirs, that he never concerned himself directly with prostitution, yet Dewey produced a convicted felon named Joe Bendix who linked Luciano's name to the prostitution racket on the East Coast. Finally, it was the testimony of key witnesses Florence Brown, Nancy Dresser, and Mildred Balitzer, prostitutes all, that won the case for the politically ambitious Dewey and sent Luciano to the state prison in Dannemora with a thirty-five-year sentence. Florence Brown's drug addiction had earned her the *nom de métier* of "Cokey Flo," but, according to Luciano's memoirs, on the stand she sounded "like Dewey'd rehearsed her in the leadin' part of *Bertha The Sewin' Machine Girl*." Two years later in Paris, Brown and the others recanted their testimony, signing affidavits to the effect that they had perjured themselves in exchange for protection, immunity, and financial gain. Nonetheless, the story of the whores who put the crime czar behind bars was too good to pass up, and between Luciano's conviction and Brown's recantation, Hal Wallis of Warner Brothers stepped in and bought and produced it as a movie that starred Bette Davis and featured Humphrey Bogart and Eduardo Ciannelli as the counterparts of "Cokey Flo," Dewey, and Luciano.

In adopting the heroine's viewpoint, instead of that of the investigator or that of the mobster, *Marked Woman* took a feminist stance that was rare for the period and even rarer for the genre. The tight, tough screenplay by Robert Rossen and Abem Finkel rechristened the heroine Mary Dwight, removed her drug addiction, and placed her profession somewhere between the verbal euphemism and the discreet fade-out: Mary shares a brownstone apartment with four other hostesses working in a luxury clip joint operated by Johnny Vanning (the Luciano character). Exploited by the underworld, looked down on by the law, the girls resolutely stick together, at first because their livelihood depends on it, then their lives as well. Mary has reached a working compromise with the all-pervading corruption of the big city. She is hard and cynical, and, this being the Depression, she has no false illusions about good honest work: "We've all tried this twelve-and-a-half-a-week stuff. It's no good living in furnished rooms, walking to work, going hungry a couple of days a week so you can have some clothes to put on your back. I've had enough of that for the rest of my life, and so have you."

Unlike her real-life model, Mary turns against Vanning not for mercenary or opportunistic reasons but, as in Jacobean drama and indeed as in most Hollywood action pictures, for revenge. Mary's kid sister, fresh out of college and naïve enough to fall for the lure of Vanning's penthouse crowd despite Mary's warning, becomes a reluctant party girl and ends up in the morgue. "I'll get even if I have to crawl back from the grave," threatens Mary, and Vanning has her beaten up and her cheek slashed. The other hostesses rally around Mary's hospital bed, take the stand under threat of death, and get Vanning convicted. In the fade-out, the five women link arms and march out into the foggy, anonymous night while the less sympathetic, because hopelessly moralistic, district attorney gets all the credit.

Had *Marked Women* been written or directed by a woman instead of by Lloyd Bacon, Warner's all-purpose director, the theme might have extended from the exploitation of women by the underworld to that by society at large. Nonetheless a real feeling for women crept in between the frames of this gangster film, which also happened to be a Bette Davis vehicle. (There is one breathless escape scene done in three shots, the second of which is an overhead view of the fugitive girl, Isabel Jewell, finding sudden protection in an elevator cage and hysterically pushing buttons.)

Cokey Flo stands up to Lucky Luciano in *Marked Woman*, 1937. Bette Davis and Eduardo Ciannelli as their fictional counterparts in this *film à clef* in which Bogart played an idealized Thomas E. Dewey. *Warner Brothers*

The film's mood of suspended threat derived from Ciannelli's dapper, hedonistic gangster, a Trock without fatuous lines, in contrast to the hard-boiled dames and henchmen in his employ. A scene that recurred in other crime pictures of the period, like *Racket Busters* and *Counsel for Crime*, shows Vanning getting a rubdown while transacting business, a self-indulgent luxury that almost amounts to a social provocation. The picture operated at this sophisticated level of tension and dispensed with overt violence: the pivotal disfiguring of the heroine is shown in long shot as the other girls wait helplessly in the parlor, and an off-screen thud followed by a scream conveys the effect of ruthless routine and is all the more shocking for it.

The darker, more pessimistic films of the thirties, such as *Fury, You Only Live Once,* and *Let Us Live,* were not the work of American directors but of German expatriates newly arrived in California in flight from Nazism. These brooding, disenchanted, doom-laden pictures ususally ended on a note of ineffective hope that was expected to redeem the prevailing, un-American mood of despair. The vision of America in these films was both personal, that is, aware of the quirks, seeming incongruities, and contradictions of democracy, and darkly metaphysical, for what they were in effect saying was that fate is the destroyer, and that man might struggle against it but ultimate defeat was inevitable. The subversive common denominator of these films was their acceptance of the utter unreliability of any social system. Armchair Freudians would have it that their director-analysands suffered from exile symptoms and nightmarish memories of aberration on a national scale.

Fritz Lang's first American movie was *Fury* (1936), the story of a lynching that featured memorable scenes of mob hysteria and that toyed with the theme of collective guilt. John Brahm's first important work in this country was *Let Us Live,* about an innocent man mistakenly identified as a murderer and almost executed. Both pictures found their bases in fact: there was such a lynching in San Jose, California, a few years before; there was such a murder case in Lynn, Massachusetts, in 1934. But neither Lang nor Brahm were out to fictionalize these miscarriages of justice. To already devastating fact they simply added selected dark touches from their cultural experience.

The city in *Fury* is a sprawling, empty landscape of elevated trains, dejected lampposts, and rain, scored by melancholy jazz reminiscent of the music of Kurt Weill. It is "a world of war and crime, strikes and taxes," as gleaned from a newspaper by the man-of-the-people, Joe Wheeler (Spencer Tracy). Details add up to entrap Wheeler in a kidnap charge: little things like peanut shells in the envelope containing the ransom letter, and marked bills that are inexplicably found on Joe. Arrested in a midwestern town that Lang had fashioned into a petty hell of idle storekeepers and vicious rednecks, gossip distorts Joe's case and turns it into an inflammatory cause that soon has the townsfolk exploding into a lynch mob. Miraculously (but not quite), Joe escapes unseen, returns to the city, and remains in hiding while twenty-two rioters are indicted for his murder. He ultimately relents and appears in the courtroom to deliver one last statement full of misanthropic irony: "They're murderers. I know the Law says they're not because I'm alive."

Fury was made at Metro-Goldwyn-Mayer during a period of labor unrest in which Hollywood shied away more than ever from depicting riots, strikes, and lynchings, which makes it all the more improbable that this most conservative of studios would produce such an outspoken attack on mob rule. Although as early as 1933 Roosevelt had condemned lynching as collective murder, no federal antilynching bill had yet been introduced by 1936, for fear of alienating the southern Democrats on the eve of reelection. This was also the year when strikes swept the production industries, and Louis B. Mayer was dead set against allowing union organizers into his personal fief. The screenwriter John Howard Lawson, eventually one of the Hollywood Ten, ascribed a more sinister motive to the making of *Fury* at MGM, albeit one more plausible than the sudden liberalization of L.B., who had had all blacks cut from the film, even from the smallest role. In *The Film in the Battle of Ideas,* which Lawson published in 1953 while the blacklist was in force, he wrote:

Hollywood made a contribution to the campaign against FDR and against the labor movement by showing a mob setting fire to a jail in order to kill an innocent man. *Fury* taught a lesson in the perils of collective action, which tied it with newspaper propaganda against the trade unions. Since the labor movement and its allies were strong at the time, *Fury* shows group insanity divorced from social issues, and ends with the hero forgiving the leaders of the mob and pleading for tolerance.

Such underhanded motivation, which could also be applied to the filming of Dickens's *A Tale of Two Cities* at the same studio the year before, escaped the critics at the time, who praised Lang's picture for its social courage.* (It had once escaped Lawson as well: he ignored all political significance when extolling *Fury* in an earlier book on screenwriting.) Today, with *Fury* placed in the context of Lang's work as the transition between his German films, symbolic and tending toward the abstract, and his budding American career, tending toward hyperrealism and much more topical in subject matter, we can recognize a bleakness and an ambiguity in his view of social issues that betray as much concern for John Doe as contempt for the society that begat him. In the picture's second half, when hysteria has subsided into guilt and resentment, Middle America is shown huddled around its radios, a group portrait of inert, vicarious thrill-seekers.

Fury failed at the box office except in New York City, but its glowing reviews established Lang's career in California. He was offered another story along the same lines, *Death in the Deep South* by Ward Greene, a novel based on the Leo Frank case, in which an Atlanta Jew, charged with the murder of a fourteen-year-old girl, was lynched in 1915. But Lang turned it down, and the film was directed by Mervyn LeRoy at Warners as *They Won't Forget;* it was effective social protest even though it lacked the powerful subtext of Lang's films.

On his own, Lang went on to make *You Only Live Once* (1937, often remembered as inspired by the careers of Bonnie and Clyde), a down-

---

* A minor independent 1950 picture, *The Sound and the Fury,* almost equaled Lang's sense of outrage without hedging its bet or missing out on the facts of basic social injustice: two kidnappers, one a killer and the other an unwilling accomplice, are lynched by an angered mob. Although the victims are guilty, the viewer nevertheless cringes at the rush and rage attending their summary execution.

beat drama that spun an inescapable web of circumstantial evidence around a three-time loser trying to go straight in a hostile society that has tagged him as beyond reform. Eddie Taylor (Henry Fonda) and his bride (Sylvia Sidney) suffer all kinds of hassles, taunts, and indignities before Lang and his scenarists (Gene Towne and Graham Baker) bring in the decisive intervention of fate: a hat left at the scene of an armored-car robbery incriminates Eddie. By the time he is exonerated—the real culprit having been found at the bottom of a marsh, drowned in the car that still holds the loot—Eddie has been tried and sentenced to death, broken out of death row, and is shooting his way out of prison, killing both the prison doctor and the chaplain in the process. Pursued, the Taylors escape into the backwoods and keep running until they are finally gunned down by a state trooper as they attempt to cross the border into Canada.

With a brilliance touching on the perverse, Lang assailed the legal tenet that holds that a man is innocent until proven guilty. But innocence can deceive the eye of the spectator and evidence is too often misleading. The armored-car robbery is carried out by a man in a gas mask who might just be Eddie Taylor; in the scene that follows the getaway, Eddie enters Joan's kitchen, hatless, rain-soaked, gun in hand, an image of furtive guilt that leads us into doubt and momentarily places the viewer in the same camp as all of Eddie's persecutors. Eddie becomes what his accusers always said he was at the very moment he is proven innocent: his escape from death row is a practical demonstration of another, more hopeful counter-fate at work. Eddie slashes his wrists with a tin cup to force his removal to the prison hospital, and there he feigns hysteria so that he will be transferred to the isolation ward, where a gun has been stashed under a mattress. This hairbreadth chain of events, a demonstration of cunning and courage, will prove futile, a mere stay of execution.

The lovers are predestined to die together; they are star-crossed from the moment Eddie takes Joan up to the bridal suite to the accompaniment of an ominous chorus of frogs croaking in a nearby pond. (Frogs, Eddie tells Joan, cannot survive the loss of a mate.) About to poison herself as Eddie goes to the chair, Joan is reprieved by a nick-of-time phone call that informs her that Eddie has escaped. As Joan and Eddie drive through the night into the highway heartland of America, they attain the status of legend. "They're being blamed for every crime committed in the country," bemoans Joan's sympathetic sister (Jean Dixon). The persecuted couple manage to retain their innocence in the face of hardship as they become the scapegoats for a nationwide network of pettiness and prejudice. (The Taylors must obtain gas for their car at gunpoint, but after their departure the gas-station attendants loot the cash register.) It is a flight that leads them from nativity—Joan has her baby in an abandoned shack, assisted only by Eddie, who later brings her wildflowers—to crucifixion in the cross hairs of a telescopic rifle.

Not by accident Lang gave the most transcendental lines to the sympathetic chaplain (William Gargan), who nevertheless comes to doubt Eddie's

"They're being blamed for every crime committed in the country." Joan and Eddie
Taylor (Sylvia Sidney and Henry Fonda) attain the status of legend. *You Only Live
Once*, 1937. *Walter Wanger | United Artists*

innocence: "Every man is at birth endowed with the nobility of a king—the
state of the world makes him forget his birthright." As the world relentlessly
closes in on the Taylors, Father Dolan delivers absolution: "You're free,
Eddie, the gates are open!" The wretched of this earth may inherit the king-
dom of heaven, but they don't stand a ghost of a chance in this world of
ours. Lang introduces the priest as the umpire in a prison baseball game
(shades of Father Flanagan) and loses him in a portentous fog enveloping
Eddie's escape; like the Taylors, the priest has progressed from the prosaic
to the symbolic. Never popular with the public—if the hard print of box-
office returns is to be trusted—*You Only Live Once* was perhaps too grim
a fairytale for the thirties' taste, but in retrospect it seems as representative
of the period as another, equally stylized picture, *The Grapes of Wrath*.
The European gloom of the former, the loaded naturalism of the latter,
were philosophical positions rather than topical sociology.

The Towne-Baker screenplay of *You Only Live Once* (preserved in the Film Department of the Museum of Modern Art) was a fairly realistic affair that could have served Wellman or LeRoy or any other Hollywood director who had some insight into the American social experience. On screen, it is hard to believe that the crucial armored-car robbery was suggested by one of Dillinger's most daring exploits: it has become a hellish vision of smoke, rain, and carnage. The condemned man's cell may have been researched in San Quentin and Alcatraz, but when Lang finished with it it resembled an abstract cage radiating shadows like a spider's web. And the same control was applied to the performers. German actors were more adept than Americans at contorting and twisting their bodies into expressive signs; but in *You Only Live Once*, Henry Fonda, hitherto a lanky, awkward leading man with a somewhat undefined presence, hunched his shoulders and clamped his wrists together as if born to wear handcuffs. For years after, Fonda's face would never look so much at home as it had behind bars, where his deadpan suddenly embodied all the injustice of modern society. Destined to play the same basic role of a spunky, downtrodden heroine in Lang's first three American films (*You and Me* being next), Sylvia Sidney became that Hollywood rarity, an actress who could play a working-class girl without glamorizing her beyond recognition (as had Ginger Rogers in her proletarian comedies) or making her into a hard-boiled dame (as Joan Blondell and Glenda Farrell did at Warners). Sidney managed to be recognizably attractive and reasonably committed to the class struggle, and she came as close to an agit-prop pinup as the period and the system permitted.

Perhaps to erase the European gloom that infused his early work in Hollywood, Lang reprised many scenes from his first two American films in his third, giving them a comic or hopeful twist and almost managing to keep the threat of despair off-screen. Made at Paramount in 1938, *You and Me* was Lang's *Threepenny Opera*. It was both his one and only comedy and a didactic musical dedicated to the proposition that crime does not pay—at least not petty crime and certainly not at the then-going rates of small time professional thievery. The spirit of Bertolt Brecht, whose plays Lang had admired in Berlin days, hovered over the action, and Kurt Weill, Brecht's usual collaborator, wrote two songs which Lang illustrated with montages of diffuse romantic clichés. The songs were titled "You Can't Get Something for Nothing" and "My Good-for-Nothing Man," and somewhere between those two themes the film made a case for just treatment of ex-convicts and parolees, who were at the time denied their civil rights and therefore forbidden to marry.

Most of the action in *You and Me* is set in a large department store where the rapport between personnel and public at first seems peculiar. A toy salesman tough-talks a tot into buying a goose rocker she does not like, another scares a customer with his safecracker lingo, a shoplifter is caught red-handed but allowed by a sympathetic clerk (Sylvia Sidney) to go unpunished. It transpires that most of the salespeople, hired by a benign store owner (Harry Carey), are either ex-cons or on parole and that a clandestine romance is in progress between Sidney and George Raft, a sporting-goods salesman with a convincing line ("There isn't a racket I haven't tried."). On their wedding night, a wicked-witch landlady is suddenly transformed into a good fairy: "Tonight you can make all the noise you want." Lang was here perhaps making amends for sending Eddie and Joan to their doom without a proper honeymoon.

But whenever possible, *You and Me* takes off on fanciful tangents, most strikingly during a Christmas reunion dinner for jailbirds, who start reliving the good old days in stir, at first wistfully, then rhythmically, and finally in the *sprecht*-singing style associated with Brecht and Weill (even though this piece of music was composed by Boris Morros). A mousy ex-convict (George E. Stone) looks at the bars in the window and sighs, "Come to think of it, it was kinda cozy in that cell." Dissolve to endless corridors in the prison where Number One arrives to serve time; and the convicts launch into an obsessive patter-song:

> *Do you hear us? Do you hear us?*
> *Stick with the mob! Stick with the mob!*
> *Hey buddy, hey buddy, hey chief!*
> *Stick with the mob!*

This transposes into musical terms one of Lang's weightier themes from Germany: the nearly mystical communion between underworld members, a spiritual bond forged by criminality and which, if threatened, could result in group operations on a larger and more efficient scale than those of the police. In *M*, Lang's best-known German picture, the beggars, pickpockets, prostitutes, safecrackers, and gunmen of a large city organize to ferret out, entrap, and dispose of a child murderer. When, in *You and Me,* Raft discovers that he has married an ex-convict like himself and leaves Sylvia Sidney, she loses herself in the city, whereupon Raft engages the help of his fellow parolees to retrieve her.

German humor, however, seemed less palatable to Americans than did Teutonic transcendence, which was a special province of the exiles. John Brahm was a fellow expatriate of Lang's, and his direction was very much in the Lang style. His first American A-picture, *Let Us Live* (1939), was full of glowingly photographed prison walls, and it is obvious that Brahm's writers had closely studied Lang's films: there was even a Langian "miracle" —a bullet lodged in an apple—to send an upright police detective (Ralph Bellamy) in search of the real culprit. The film was all the more derivative for the typecasting of Henry Fonda as one of two cabdrivers wrongly accused of murder—Fonda, alone in Hollywood, seemed capable of convincingly delivering lines like "We haven't a chance, us little people" and "The law can't admit being wrong."

The last line might explain why *Let Us Live* was ultimately trimmed and released as a B-picture. The script (by Anthony Veiller and Allen Rivkin) was adapted from a magazine story, "Murder in Massachusetts,"

"Stick with the mob!" The nearly mystical communion of underworld members in *You and Me*, 1938. Left to right: Adrian Morris, Jack Pennick, Roger Gray, Kit Guard, Roscoe Karns, Robert Cummings, Barton MacLane. *Paramount*

written by Joseph Dinneen and published in *Harper's* in March 1936. Dinneen's story was too true to be good for the legal image of Massachusetts. Two years earlier, two Boston taxi drivers had been identified by seven of eight witnesses as participants in a theater holdup in which a bill poster had been killed. The two men were indicted for murder and were heading for a certain conviction when, in the third week of their trial, two notorious gangsters, Irving and Murton Millen, were arrested in New York and admitted to the robbery among other crimes. The cabbies were exonerated, and the Millen brothers and an accomplice were executed in 1935.

Dinneen suggested that the police had acted irresponsibly and that the district attorney had pressured witnesses in order to secure a quick conviction. By the time Samuel Goldwyn acquired the screen rights to the story for a project starring James Cagney, the governor of Massachusetts, James M. Curley, was suing both the author and *Harper's* for libel as a result of an even less flattering follow-up article titled "Kingfish of Massachusetts." With such a controversial property in his hands, Goldwyn decided to sell it to Columbia. (The fact that Cagney had returned to Warners after a brief free-lancing period may have been instrumental in Goldwyn's decision; or perhaps the producer had his hands full with the legal entanglements surrounding the filming of Lillian Hellman's play, *The Children's Hour,* and had decided that one controversy was enough.)

The state of Massachusetts advised Harry Cohn's lawyers at Columbia that the studio refrain from suggesting that these events, although a matter of public record, had taken place in a specific community. The state further advised that it would bring legal action against Columbia if the studio implied that the Boston police had acted rashly or that the courts had been inefficient. Among studio heads, Cohn had the most reason to avoid a legal fight, which would have brought certain dealings into the open. *Let Us Live* was not shelved, but it became a B-picture overnight. Ironically, the Dinneen story, shorn of any accusation of rashness of unfairness, had already found a slot in the *Crime Does Not Pay* series, as *The Perfect Set-Up* (1936).

In August 1939, Hollywood's crusading fervor was about to be cooled by a scandal that exposed corruption at the highest level of the industry and had lasting repercussions. That year columnist Westbrook Pegler revealed in the *New York Journal-American* that Willie Bioff, the West Coast representative of the powerful stagehands' union—officially known as International Alliance of Theatrical Stage Employees (IATSE)—had been charged, back in 1922, with operating a house of prostitution in Chicago and had been convicted of pandering and sentenced to six months in prison. Bioff had served only twenty-four days, but this long-forgotten conviction was opportunely played up by the Scripps-Howard newspapers in the middle of the actors-versus-stagehands dispute. Robert Montgomery, a Metro contract actor and a prominent member of the Screen Actors Guild, offered to fund an investigation out of his own pocket. Subsequent probing of the policies and methods favored by Bioff and his mentor, George E. Browne, vice-president of IATSE, exposed a long and dismal record of intimidation and compromise that showed how major film companies, under threats of fomenting strikes, had paid off Bioff and Browne, and through them the Chicago syndicate.

A federal investigation got under way in August. IATSE was charged with labor racketeering, Joseph M. Schenck, president of the MPAA, who had acted as middleman in the payoff, was charged with income-tax evasion and perjury. It was revealed that Metro, Fox, Warner Brothers, and Paramount had together paid half a million dollars for protection. According to Nicholas M. Schenck, president of Loew's, Inc., the parent company of MGM, Bioff's original asking price had been a whopping two million dollars, and he had actually threatened the life of Louis B. Mayer. Metro had agreed to pay fifty thousand dollars a year, an expenditure that would be as hard to justify to the New York front office as to the IRS—it was charged off to production items down the line. Warner Brothers (the studio that had been saluted by *Life* as "the least chickenhearted of the Hollywood companies" in recognition of its civic courage) had also paid up, and so had the two other majors. Much of the money was delivered in cash by Joe Schenck himself, but one personal check for one hundred thousand dollars became incriminating evidence. Bioff and Browne were convicted in 1941, and IATSE, ordered to pay trial costs, disowned the two men. Schenck was also convicted, served one year and one day, and upon his release was accepted back into the film industry, although his influential days were over.

Columbia Pictures was conspicuously missing from the list of victimized film companies, since Harry Cohn, as it soon became well known, had a direct line to the Chicago syndicate in the person of one John Rosselli. Cohn never paid tribute, which partially explains the studio's reticence to deal with controversial subjects. Most of Columbia's crime pictures were B-productions, and some of them were notable for a restraint missing from those of other studios. Cohn, it seems, favored trial scenes as the climax rather than the more expeditious shoot-outs with police or G-men. Another possible explanation was Cohn's notorious penny-pinching; sets built for more expensive films had to earn back their cost by doing duty in the smaller ones. (One such décor was the beautiful courtroom in *Mr. Deeds Goes to Town*, which turned up again in *Criminal Lawyer*, *I Promise to Pay*, and others.)

In prison, Bioff and Browne decided to talk to federal investigators about the infiltration of Hollywood unions by the Chicago mob. This cooperation earned their release in December 1944 and landed John Rosselli and six Chicago underworld figures in prison. (A seventh, Frank Nitti, committed suicide rather than serve a second prison term.) Rosselli's life story was improbable and flamboyant enough for a dozen crime pictures. Throughout his career, he held many different positions with the Mafia and the film industry. At one point he even worked for the Hays Office, where he struck up a lifelong friendship with the leading censor himself, Joe Breen. After serving his sentence in the extortion case as a result of Bioff's and Browne's testimony, he made a comeback as an independent producer, and, with Breen as partner, he was responsible for three crime pictures, *He Walked by Night*, *T-Men*, and *Canon City*. Rosselli fronted for the Chicago syndicate in Las Vegas in the fifties, and, after a period of relative discretion, he was again in the headlines as one of two Mafia leaders—the other being Sam Giancana—linked to CIA plots to assassinate Fidel Castro in the early days of the Cuban revolution.

Rosselli, as well as Bioff and Giancana, died in the violent tradition of gangsterism. The various ways in which they were executed had been rendered familiar to moviegoers through the years; at least Hollywood cannot be faulted with inaccuracy in that respect. One morning in 1955, Bioff, living under an assumed name in Phoenix, Arizona, was blown to pieces by a bomb placed in his pickup truck. Giancana, who had lost prestige in the syndicate, was shot by a hit man who somehow gained entrance to his well-

guarded suburban Chicago home in 1975. The details of Rosselli's demise—
he was asphixiated aboard a yacht, then his legs were sawed off so his body
would fit inside an oil drum that was found floating near Miami in 1975—
furnished one of the most gruesome stories to appear in the usually reserved
pages of *The New York Times*. The killers in all three cases remain unidentified.

Infiltration by the syndicate was hardly news to Hollywood insiders.
But the industry took pains not to have it spread beyond the inside pages
of the major newspapers: there is no mention of Bioff or Browne in the fan
magazines of the period, and the mass audience knew of the movies only
through the fan magazines. As a diversion, Hollywood kept putting its most
entertaining gossip on the line. The union scandals nevertheless wrecked
any project that had even remotely to do with such issues as corruption,
union troubles, or actual, thriving gangsterism. Critics of the industry could
now point a suspicious finger and tell Hollywood to clean its own house
before presuming to denounce similar ills elsewhere.

The most memorable of the twilight-of-the-gangster pictures came appropriately at the very end of the cycle, with darkness at hand and the
optimism of the New Deal in sharp perspective. Technically, *High Sierra*
(made in 1940, released in January 1941) was the story of a heist that went
haywire (and as such it pioneered a trend that would flourish after the
war), but the film was mainly a farewell to grassroots America, as epito-
mized by the independent farmer and the midwestern bank robber. Roy
Earle (Humphrey Bogart) embodied both: a wayward farmboy who joined
up with the Dillinger gang, spent years in prison, and upon his release
found himself, part relic and part legend, in a world of "twerps, soda jerkers,
and jitterbugs," as doomed as the migrant farmworker he met on the road
to California. The younger folks in the movie were mostly portrayed as
inept and spineless (the raw punks under Earle's orders disastrously botch
their first big job, a resort holdup) or as silly and opportunistic (a crippled
farm-girl restored to health through the gangster's help spurns him for a city
slicker). Only one character proved worthy of Roy: Marie Garson (Ida
Lupino), bruised, resilient, also from a disappearing breed, that of the taxi
dancer.

The plot of *High Sierra*, as well as its tough, melancholy dialogue, came
straight from the novel by W. R. Burnett. It was adapted by John Huston
with Burnett himself so that the muddy red of the original came across as
forlorn gray on the screen. Burnett's Roy Earle had a vision of things
changing for the worse: "Folks used to a free existence didn't take to living
off people or being handed charity." It goes without saying that the gangster's big speech in the novel ("In this country nobody's straight..."),
which Burnett tinged with the leftist fervor of the period, is nowhere to be
heard in the film, and so much the better. Had Roy Earle been played by
Muni or Robinson, a political awareness—however vague or inarticulate—
would have seemed natural, if only because character and performer belonged so irrevocably to the thirties. But *High Sierra* was poised between

decades and already pointed toward the forties, a time of angst and dis-
illusionment. Bogart took over the central role from George Raft—the
original but by now unimaginable casting choice—after Raft failed to grasp
the dramatic necessity for a tragic ending in a story that relentlessly propelled its hero to his doom. The essence of Bogart's Roy Earle was precisely
an edgy, weary intimation of mortality that was totally apolitical; Earle
knows that there is no hope for himself and very little for the rest of us; he
could hardly be a security risk in a nation heading for war and welfare.

Bogart and Raoul Walsh, who directed *High Sierra*, may well have
taken their cues from another passage in the novel, which was reproduced
almost verbatim in the film. "Remember what Johnny Dillinger used to say
about guys like you and him?" reminisces an old-timer, "that you were
rushing toward death, that's it, rushing toward death." In Walsh's world,
people once used to a free existence could never be satisfied with promises
of social improvement, from either right or left. Freedom's only coordinate
was death. There were no options for Roy Earle, dramatically speaking;
and when Walsh, more than thirty years later, expressed his regret that the
gangster was not allowed to escape with the loot and the girl, he was
forgetting that the hero's fate was predetermined, less by the censor than
by the opening sequence in which Earle, who has just been released from
prison, takes time off to walk in the park and feel the grass growing under
his feet. Earle was a blunt, effective image of the grassroots gangster, and
he also presaged that character's extinction as modern America hardened
into concrete and asphalt.

The national decline is charted by Roy Earle's drive to the West, where
he is to organize a major "caper." Revisiting his home country in Indiana,
he is at first mistaken for "someone from the bank" by a mortgage-ridden
sharecropper. There are Okies on the dusty road, and in California, once
the last frontier, the oases have been polluted. A garish, overripe resort has
sprouted in the middle of the desert. It is patronized by the rich and the
ugly, waiting to be fleeced. With his prison haircut and his austere dark
suit, Bogart moves against the prevailing grays of the film as a man done
in by time and history, in mourning for himself. One look at the rich,
hedonistic couple who accidentally stumble on the scene of the holdup,
and we root fervently for Earle to succeed in this, his last crime. The utter
loneliness of the gangster, his longing for a vanished freedom, finds beautiful expression in his recurrent dream of "crashing out," and also in his
poetic-hayseed theory that "the earth is like a little ball turning in the night,
with us hanging on to it." The world has grown too civilized and too corrupt. Only in the open space of the sierra can Earle find a refuge. In the
end, nature does not offer redemption, only death—but at least it is a clean
death—far from the gutters of the city.

Inside *High Sierra* there was a Western waiting to be born, and, in
1949, Walsh himself directed the same story set in the Old West and titled
Colorado Territory. A third, updated version was directed by Stuart Heisler
and released in 1955 as *I Died a Thousand Times*. The last lacked any im-
mediacy or resonance, unlike the westernized version, which improved on

High Sierra in certain respects. Walsh was one of Hollywood's major landscape artists, and inevitably the story gained in spaciousness by being set
back sixty years. In its way, *High Sierra* was an outdoor picture, a novelty
among gangster films: its most haunting image might very well be that of
Roy Earle shivering in the dawn air, his Tommy gun at his side and
mountains all around, as if to highlight the pathetic insignificance of the
hunted man. A corresponding shot in *Colorado Territory* removed the
image of the pursued hero from the problematical "now" to relocate it in
the safe historical framework of the Old West. The original version was
mythmaking in progress—it replayed themes that had recurred in American
literature since Fenimore Cooper: to wit, that social change in America was
particularly abrupt and ruthless; that lawlessness was tolerated, even encouraged, as long as it pushed the frontier farther into the wilderness; and
that self-reliant, violent, natural societies had to be periodically destroyed
by the demands of history. *High Sierra,* equating the thirties gangster with
the frontier badman and the doomed man of the soil, was a turning point
that left behind the last innocents and opened the way to the great neurotics
of modern cinema.

Two disappearing breeds from the thirties: Roy Earle, the grassroots gangster, and
Marie Garson, the taxi dancer. Humphrey Bogart and Ida Lupino in *High Sierra,* 1941.
A clean death for Roy, far from the gutters of the city. *Warner Brothers*

6.   All Quiet on the Home Front

We may be rats, crooks and murderers, but we're Americans.
— *Seven Miles from Alcatraz*, screenplay
by Joseph Krumgold, 1943

PROMOTING DOMESTIC SECURITY and manipulating patriotism are two of the main concerns of wartime propaganda. Even before Pearl Harbor, the film industry revised its priorities to further the notion that the United States had succeeded in stamping out prewar crime along with poverty, that union troubles had never existed, and that every resource of the new prosperity should be devoted to the war effort. (There were still six million unemployed in 1941; but rearmament would soon turn the propagandists' premature fiction into reality.) As if the unspeakable crime of foreign aggression had eradicated domestic delinquency, the gangster figure virtually disappeared from the screen between 1941 and 1945, and he was replaced by a recycled version of the Abominable Hun or a new and improved Yellow Peril. In a few opportunistic films, the gangster was allowed to act as a last, incongruous bulwark of Americanism (*All Through the Night, Seven Miles from Alcatraz, Lucky Jordan*). But by and large, the movies supplied the public with an image of a seamless democratic society, free of dissent. From the Hollywood output of the war years, one might deduce that all major crime perpetrated in the nation was the work of foreign spies and saboteurs; that, in fact, these were the only barbarians within.

The anti-Nazi campaign was launched by Warner Brothers with its production of *Confessions of a Nazi Spy*. The film was not quite as timely as it purported to be—two years had elapsed since the columnist Heywood Broun first denounced the subversive activities of the German-American Bund—but it had taken months to overcome the traditional timidity of the New York film executives. The catalyst was the closing of the Warner Brothers exchange in Berlin, following the stomping and death of its manager in a riot. When the picture finally went into production, the studio took all kinds of precautions. The relative boldness of the enterprise must have been greatly relished by Jack L. Warner, who, in his memoirs, claimed that making *Confessions of a Nazi Spy* placed him on Hitler's personal death list; and by Edward G. Robinson, starred as an FBI agent, who was compelled by anonymous threats to place his family and himself under surveillance for a time. The screenplay was adapted by Milton Krims and John Wexley from Leon G. Turrou's book, *The Nazi Spy Conspiracy in America,* which told of German subversion in the United States, including the arrest and conviction of four agents who received prison sentences ranging from two to eight years in December 1938. Tourrou, the FBI agent who had directed the operation, subsequently resigned to write the book and aid in the production of the film.

Warners had made hate-group exposés earlier in the thirties, films such as *Black Legion* (1936), which attacked a fascist secret society operating in the industrial centers of the Midwest, and the studio tackled the Bund in the same manner.* Like the Black Legion, the Bund had attacked FDR, often viciously, and this was provocation enough for Jack Warner, an ardent partisan of the New Deal who appended the NRA logo to Warner picture credits. But certain issues were evaded altogether in the film. There was, for instance, no mention of anti-Semitism.

The importance of the Bund was blown somewhat out of proportion to its real threat—following a disappointing show of force at a Madison Square Garden rally in February 1939, it had been officially disowned by Germany. Fritz Kuhn, the Bund director, nevertheless sued Warner Brothers, Turrou, and the screenwriters for five million dollars for suggesting "a connection with the world-wide espionage system launched by the German government." But Warners stood its ground and filed a strong countersuit to the libel charge. By then, it was September 1939—the film had been released in April and rendered obsolete by European events, despite consecutive additions of newsreel footage and newspaper headlines.

Confessions of a Nazi Spy was useful in acquainting the filmgoer with the policies and methods of the Nazi regime. The film deployed a spectrum that ranged from the ruthless, intellectual Goebbels (Martin Kosleck)— who admits that Americans are "a liberty-loving people" as he orders a flood of propaganda to stir racial and labor tension—to a Bronx bumbler of a spy (Francis Lederer), who is flattered and maneuvered by the wily FBI agent into disclosing the identities of his accomplices. Nazis, as a rule, can be recognized by their Teutonic features, their heavy topcoats, and their willingness to beat up loyal German-Americans. The film's *cri de coeur* was improbably placed in the mouth of an American Legionnaire (Ward Bond) as he is being forcibly evicted from a Bund rally: "You guys are worse than gangsters!"

Robinson supplied a calm omniscience to his role that further ingrained the image of the G-man as the man who knew best, reassuring the viewer that the nation was in good hands and that a flawlessly humane system was operating. Like Inspector Maigret, Robinson carries a pipe instead of a pistol, never indulges in shooting matches; at times he just sits out the conspiracy, but he turns up at the right moment aboard the German ship *Bismarck* to remind a starchy, arrogant, female agent (Dorothy Tree) that "New York harbor is still very much part of the United States." Even today that assertion seems a shameless bid for applause. Like every effective father figure, Robinson's FBI agent knows both when to coddle and when to

* A film denouncing the more rabid and powerful Ku Klux Klan was never too seriously considered at the studio, for to do so would have meant taking a stand on the truly controversial issue of civil rights, which would have lost Warners part of the southern audience.

punish: "There's no third degree with the Federal Bureau of Investigation," he tells the cringing, overemotional Lederer, who then responds to fair play by spilling everything he knows. "In this country we don't spread sawdust on the floor of our prison yards," confirms the judge who later passes sentence on the four agents. And the epilogue sends the audience home comforted and proud, as good propaganda should: the G-man overhears a soda jerk deliver a bellicose speech to his customers that ends with "We'll show them." "The voice of the people, thank God," mutters Robinson.*

"You guys are worse than gangsters!" Lionel Royce and Henry Victor, Nazi henchmen in *Confessions of a Nazi Spy*, 1939. *Warner Brothers*

Two and a half years before war was officially declared on Nazi Germany, Hollywood all but abandoned its isolationist position and found for itself a perfect all-purpose villain. In the unstable days between Munich and Pearl Harbor, Nazi conspiracies flourished on the American screen more often than in American soil. By war's end, passion and hysteria spent, the Federal Bureau of Investigation felt it safe and encouraging to disclose that a mere twenty-seven foreigners had been convicted of espionage from 1938 to 1945, as against sixty-four American traitors, and that not one single

---

* In 1947, *Confessions of a Nazi Spy* was scanned for communist propaganda. Ostensibly the House Un-American Activities Committee wanted to know why Hollywood had not devoted itself to exposing communists with equal energy. Robinson and screenwriter Wexley landed on the blacklist, but Richard M. Nixon, the California representative, thought that Warners had done "a fine job." By then, Jack Warner and the FBI would have preferred that the film be forgotten.

instance of enemy-induced sabotage had been proven. The facts bore witness to J. Edgar Hoover's efficiency as well as to Hollywood's paranoia, which did not always run on parallel tracks.

They Came to Blow Up America, a B-film produced by Twentieth Century-Fox in 1943, carried a pointed foreword to the effect that the facts depicted were not authenticated by the bureau, for reasons that will become obvious. In the summer of 1942, two four-man saboteur groups had been put ashore by submarines off Long Island and Florida; fourteen days later, all eight were in the hands of the FBI. Tried in military court, they were convicted of espionage and six were electrocuted. The FBI, however, had

Fateful meeting in Amagansett: George Sanders as the FBI agent based on William Sebold, tries not to betray his cover when a coastguardsman spots a Nazi saboteur (Ralph Byrd) just landed on Long Island. From *They Came to Blow Up America,* 1943. *Twentieth Century-Fox*

little cause for pride in the whole operation: the Germans had acted in a most unprofessional manner from the start, offering a bribe to a coastguardsman who had caught them in the act of debarking in Amagansett. After that, the mission seemed doomed to two of the saboteurs, who thereupon betrayed their comrades to the FBI. The bureau acted promptly upon their phone call and rounded up the rest of the party. The sentences of Peter Burger and George Dasch were commuted to life imprisonment due to their assistance; later, during the Truman administration, they were deported to Germany, where Dasch subsequently published an embellished version of his change of heart and the ignominious failure of the mission.

But Hollywood beat Dasch to his own story by at least twenty-five years. *They Came to Blow Up America* offered its version of the sabotage mission and the reasons it had failed and two of its members had been spared the electric chair. The movie welded the facts of the Dasch expedition with others borrowed from the case of William Sebold, a German-born American who had acted as a double agent for the Gestapo and the FBI and who had been responsible for uncovering the largest spy ring operating in prewar America. The hero of the film, rechristened Carl Steelman and played by George Sanders, then a specialist in Nazi roles, becomes an FBI agent who poses as a Bund member in order to be recruited by the Gestapo and trained at a sabotage school in Berlin. Steelman obtains a list of secret agents operating in the United States and leads his own sabotage group into the hands of the waiting G-men. Clearly, there was little glory for either side in the actual facts of the case. However, since most of the details were in the public domain, the film could be, and was, made with neither Hoover's consent nor authorized access to the bureau files.*

If, even without Hoover's full consent, the G-man found himself a wartime hero in the movies, the gangster became *persona non grata* for the duration. When Pearl Harbor was bombed, *Johnny Eager* was ready for release, *The Big Shot* was well into production, and *This Gun for Hire* was at a point in its shooting schedule that made it possible to incorporate an anti-Japanese message. But other films in earlier stages were indefinitely postponed until the day when social criticism, even at the established level of the gangster film, could safely return to theaters without raising doubts about Hollywood's patriotism. It is all the more ironic that, when the House Un-American Activities Committee investigations began in the late forties, proof of communist infiltration would be detected in the semiofficial propaganda movies—*Mission to Moscow, The North Star, Song of Russia, Days of Glory, Counterattack*—in which the industry, as part of the war effort, had joined other ultraconservative entities like *The Reader's Digest* in overselling Russia as America's soul mate, and Ivan as John Doe in a droshky.

"One gangster running down half a dozen men was pale stuff when Hitler was acting out scripts more brutal and obscene than anything dreamed of by Chicago's North Siders or the Warner Brothers," wrote Alistair Cooke in *Garbo and the Night Watchman*. Yet *Johnny Eager,* which was a box-office success in the first year of the war, proved that this last batch of underworld films had been undertaken at a moment when war, if not exactly remote, seemed at least irrelevant to their subjects. *Johnny Eager,* moving in a glossy forties world that often flattened its characters as in an expensive *photo-roman,* nevertheless set its story in the present. Johnny Eager (Robert Taylor) is a paroled racketeer who appears to drive a taxi for an honest living, but in reality masterminds New York's gambling syndicate. Eager is also capable of doing his own killing should the need

* *They Came to Blow Up America* was not the first film to capitalize on the Sebold case. In 1941, Monogram, the poorest movie company on Poverty Row, produced *The Deadly Game,* in which an FBI agent (Charles Farrell) impersonated a Nazi.

arise, and he is a genius at working up alibis: he pretends to be napping in the next room during an all-night poker session when in fact he is disposing of a treacherous upstart. But another airtight alibi backfires: Johnny impresses a society girl (Lana Turner) into believing she shot and killed a gunman in his defense, an elaborate hoax that Johnny uses to blackmail her stepfather, the D.A., into submission. The only hitch is that the girl nearly goes insane with remorse, and Johnny is not heartless enough to let her. The effect of the finale is somewhere between soap opera and grand opera: Johnny walks the wet, gleaming streets under the elevated subway, shoots it out with his former accomplices, and is gunned down by a cop whom Johnny has had transferred to a quiet precinct as a favor to the cop's wife, once Johnny's mistress. "Just another hood, I guess," reports the policeman on the phone while an alcoholic poet—Van Heflin (Academy Award for Best Male Supporting Performance), who throughout the film has displayed an excessive, maudlin affection for Johnny that the Hays Office dared not name in 1941—cradles the dead gangster in his arms and offers a counter-obituary: "This guy could have climbed the highest mountain in the world."

Mervy LeRoy directed *Johnny Eager* from a screenplay by John Lee Mahin and James Edward Grant. A more willful director than LeRoy, with a stronger personal grasp of the material, would probably have remained

Love story: dead gangster and alcoholic poet, Robert Taylor and Van Heflin in *Johnny Eager*, 1942, one of the last gangster pictures for the duration of the war. *Metro-Goldwyn-Mayer*

impervious to changes in the national mood, but LeRoy's pictures were like litmus paper, affected even by the individual house styles as he went from Warner Brothers, a studio with Democratic Party ties, to MGM, a Republican bulwark. Warner pictures were usually abrasive and egalitarian; they seldom failed to place the hero within a larger social context. At Metro, the tendency was more aristocratic; the hero was most often a dramatic entity with only vague social references. From Little Caesar to Johnny Eager, the gangster completed the romantic transformation from frog to prince.

But even at Warner the gangster was wallowing in fatigue, irony, and self-pity: *The Big Shot* was a calculated but inferior remake of *High Sierra,* a long-winded obit for a gangster (once again played by Bogart), as he told his story in a flashback from his deathbed in a prison hospital. More enterprising, although by no means a perfectly realized film, was *This Gun for Hire,* a modest B-plus Paramount thriller adapted from Graham Greene's novel about a London gunman hired by an industrialist to murder a socialist minister. The locale was transferred from rainy Britain to sunny California, but a few hints of Greene's "vast desolation" remained in the psychological landscape of the characters, even though the religious preoccupations he had imposed on them were dropped for the film. The picture carefully preserved Greene's "usual left-wing scenery" (as George Orwell once called it), and it added a wicked American twist by making the capitalist villain (Tully Marshall) a decrepit double for Henry Ford. This was perhaps not all that surprising, due to the politics of one of the scenarists, Albert Maltz, who eventually became one of the Hollywood Ten. The other adaptor was W. R. Burnett, whose style Greene had evoked in his novel. The changes Maltz and Burnett wrought on the hero were a revaluation in American terms. In the original, Raven was a harelipped virgin of a man, loquacious and bigoted, haunted by one specific murder in his career, that of the minister's secretary who fought for her elderly life with a passion that left its mark on the hardened killer. The picture substituted a monosyllabic gunsel in a raincoat—the first emblematic use of the garment—and removed the harelip. In the film Raven is obsessed by a recurring dream in which he reenacts the stabbing of an aunt who beat him as a child and who once branded him with a red-hot iron. Metaphysical anguish had been displaced by psychic disturbance. The effect was roughly the same: Raven is as sexless as the angel of death.

In the opening of *This Gun for Hire,* a man lies in bed, dressed except for his coat, awake and indifferent to the afternoon sounds of children and a piano outside his rented room. An alarm clock goes off. Raven sits up and unhurriedly makes ready for a job, checking his gun and the coordinates of the intended victim. He pours milk for a kitten. In the hall, he passes a sexy slattern on her way to make up the room. A moment later, he catches her mistreating the cat; Raven spins the girl around and tears her dress. "Go on, beat it." No exclamation point, no emotion. Later, about to shoot the shady lawyer who is his unsuspecting victim, Raven is momentarily fazed by the presence of the man's mistress in the apartment. "Don't worry—my

The daily solitude of the urban psychopath: Alan Ladd, as Raven in *This Gun for Hire*, 1942, prepares for his job in a scene that would inspire many imitations, here and abroad. *Paramount*

secretary," explains the lawyer, sealing her fate along with his. With the faintest smile, Raven readjusts his plan, takes out his gun, and first plugs the man, then shoots the woman through the bedroom door. In the hallway outside, a crippled child asks him to retrieve her ball. Raven's reflexive gesture is to reach for his gun and suppress a potential witness; yet he does not. A child is not a woman—soiled, adulterous, full of deceit. Children and animals are the last vehicles of grace and the killer can thus respond with grace only to them.*

The middleman in Raven's assignment is a fat, fastidious executive named Gates (Laird Cregar), whose impeccable bulk makes Raven all the

* The opening of *This Gun for Hire* echoes through similar sequences in a number of films that dealt with the daily solitude of the urban psychopath: *He Walked by Night* (1948), *The Sniper* (1952), and *Taxi Driver* (1976). In *Le Samourai* (1968), the French director Jean-Pierre Melville elaborated a funeral elegy on this scene, which had been simply a behavioral note in *This Gun for Hire*

punier and seedier as well as more noble. Raven kills man to man, almost
as an extension of the daily struggle, while Gates, ruthless and unscrupulous
as he is, becomes nauseated by the ugly details ("I can't stand violence.").
He has, however, the esthete's curiosity about the man of action: "How do
you feel when you're doing . . . this?" "I feel fine," answers Raven, cutting
short any further morbid interest about his job. This was Hollywood's laic
version of Greene's religious alienation: a joyless, efficient assassin whose
profits were almost negligible, whose acts only perpetuated a monotonous,
squalid existence. He was almost a new criminal type. No wonder Greene
as film critic admired *Four Hours to Kill* as much as he saw through the
contrived poeticism of *The Petrified Forest:* the reviews for both films bear
the same date, 1936, as Greene's novel.

Greene's leftist wavelength in *This Gun for Hire* is occasionally dis-
rupted by dumb patriotic plugs from the heroine (Veronica Lake), a waif-
like stage magician whom Raven picks up as a coverup or possibly as a
hostage on the night train to Los Angeles. The gunman has been paid in
marked bills and Gates has set the police on his tracks, so Raven trails the
murder plot all the way up to the capitalist who instigated it; in the sanctum of big business, an old man sits in a wheelchair dreaming of power and
ready to sell out to the Japs. Here, a populist brotherhood is asserted when
the tycoon's valet turns on his master, and delivers him into Raven's hands:
"Fifteen years dressing you, nursing you, cleaning you, listening to your
dirty deals. . . . Give it to him!" Raven wipes out the traitors who double-
crossed him, and the nation profits from his private vendetta. He dies, shot
by the police, a little-boy smile on his face, asking the girl with his last
breath: "Did I do all right by you?"

The film did not live up to the best in the script: Frank Tuttle's direction seldom connected with the theme, and the running time of seventy-five
minutes, standard B length, was too compressed. Its strengths resided in
the efficient villains and in Alan Ladd, who played Raven in his first major
role. Usually a wooden actor, with a smile that never quite jelled and no
particular ability to deliver dialogue, Ladd projected here a laconic pessimism construed by the mass audience as romantic appeal. But gangster
pictures went off the agenda for the next few years, so Ladd never had a
second chance to elaborate his gangster persona. Quickly rushed into a remake of Hammett's *The Glass Key,* he played the tough but upstanding
hero, and he was next cast as the title character in *Lucky Jordan,* a racketeer
drafted into the army and molded into a model patriot who turned against
his underworld relations.

A real difference existed between the pasted-on patriotics in *This Gun
for Hire* and the simplistic antagonism of good gangster versus wicked Nazi.
Even by Hollywood standards, the war brought a comparative loss of realism in films; when death became a day-to-day probability for a large percentage of Americans, the film studios set about to manipulate violence or
simply spirit it away. This was hardly the case with either *This Gun for
Hire* or with the psychological thrillers, mostly B-films, that portrayed crime

almost as a matter of personal initiative. These films currently stand up so much better than the rest that they have come to misrepresent the period. Their private, modest violence indicated a discreet refusal to accept the patriotic paeans that were official A-film fodder.

By comparison with period headlines, the exploits of Roger Touhy appeared quite mild. Touhy, a second-rate underworld figure of the thirties, had been convicted of kidnapping in 1936 and was serving a ninety-nine-year sentence at the Stateville Prison in Joliet, Illinois, when, on October 9, 1942, he and some other convicts effected an exciting daylight jailbreak by stealing a truck, scaling the walls, and escaping by car, leaving behind two wounded guards. In the ensuing two months, Touhy was the object of a nationwide dragnet, the most intensive of the war years. On December 29, the police closed in on his Chicago hideout. Two members of the reorganized Touhy gang were killed by submachine guns; the rest, including Touhy, surrendered to the police.

During the time he was a fugitive, Touhy managed to displace more than one historical event from the popular consciousness. To the tabloids his exploits meant a welcome return to the prewar days of Dillinger and Karpis. Even before he was recaptured, a film project, based on his notorious over-the-wall escape, was under consideration at Twentieth Century-Fox. The even better publicized capture changed the original concept. The assigned producer, Lee Marcus, dispatched the director Robert Florey and a camera crew to Chicago in January 1943, just a few days after the events, to photograph the actual locations. (In a period when every new headline seemed to cancel even the most immediate past, the haste with which Marcus acted may have been due to a suspicion that the public would soon forget Touhy.) It was the first time that such a thorough location shooting had taken place. "The shooting at 1254–56 Leland Avenue had taken place just a few days before, and the place was a mess," recalls Florey. "For a week at Joliet, the warden allowed us to shoot many scenes and 'plates' inside and in the courtyard, using trusties as doubles and reproducing the escape in long shots." Florey received all the official help he required from the mayor and the chief of police of Chicago, and the Stateville warden allowed him to interview Touhy and the members of his gang who were still at Joliet.

The film was completed in a tight thirty-three days at the studio, then ran into all sorts of interference. The script, by Crane Wilbur and Jerry Cady, refrained from using any real names other than those of Touhy and his lieutenant, Basil Banghart—yet Fox was threatened with a suit by Jake "The Barber" Factor, the kidnap victim and a one-time Touhy associate. The general antipathy of the project was obvious in the cut demanded by the Hays Office: one complete reel, on the grounds of extreme violence ("Bad for the general public," according to Florey). Even though the FBI received a good share of credit for the capture in the film, the bureau insisted on a disclaimer to warn the public that the portrayal of agents in a

movie did not constitute an endorsement from the FBI and should not be
construed as a seal of approval on the material. Hemmed in on all sides,
Fox considered shelving the picture but finally resolved to release it more
than a year later, when the case was almost forgotten. Even then, a cautious
statement from the producer in the pressbook instructed exhibitors that "we
wouldn't be justified in making a picture about Touhy except that he is representative of an era—and thank goodness, a passing era at that." *The New
York Times,* reviewing the release version, which bore the title *Roger Touhy,
Gangster!,* contributed another wreath: "Gang rule and gang murder seem
half a century out of date in view of the present international goings-on."

It is ironic that *Touhy,* disowned by the bureau, pioneered the quasi-
documentary techniques that two years later would become the trademark

"We wouldn't be justified in making a picture about Touhy except that he is representa-
tive of an era—and thank goodness, a passing era at that!"—Pressbook for *Roger Touhy,
Gangster!,* 1944. Left to right: Anthony Quinn, George McGrill, Frank Jenks, George E.
Stone, Victor McLaglen, unidentified bit player, Preston Foster, Horace McMahon.
Twentieth Century-Fox

of the semifactual exposés endorsed by the FBI, such as location photography, precise identification of characters and locale, and a concluding on-camera speech by an official (in this case, the Stateville warden). In the film's mutilated form, Touhy (played by Preston Foster) was neither hero nor victim, and he definitely lacked the appeal of his fictional forerunners. The script attempted to define him mainly through his quirky interest in astrology: Touhy is a Scorpio and his forecast for the month of October 1942 reads: "A new door opens for you. The future is assured." Except for a mild Napoleonic complex—"I won't let them forget me," muses Touhy in jail—he is the sort of boorish gangster usually confined to play the heavy in thirties movies. His calculated meanness further robbed the character of any sympathetic qualities, and in this respect the film was faithful for once to the criminal it depicted, a two-bit, ugly, brutal punk. The prison break— the film's *pièce de résistance*—is cool and distanced, as if shot by a newsreel crew. But curiously, for a picture that portrayed Prohibition and its repeal as events from another century, there was hardly any feeling for a period that was then just a decade away. Film memory, mostly in the line-up of familiar faces (George E. Stone from *Little Caesar*, Foster himself from *The Last Mile*), had come to replace firsthand knowledge of the period.

Not surprisingly, Roger Touhy was mentioned in neither Don Whitehead's *The F.B.I. Story* nor Fred J. Cook's demystifying *The FBI Nobody Knows*, one obvious reason being that Touhy's capture conferred minimal prestige on the bureau. Until the end of his life, Touhy continued to provide embarrassment to the law. Ten years after Florey's film was released, the Touhy case came under revision, and the original sentence was modified in the light of new evidence that revealed that one important witness had perjured himself and favorable evidence had been withheld by the state. Touhy was finally released in 1959, having served a total of twenty-three years, and some three weeks later he was gunned down, presumably by a diehard Capone executioner.

In a way, Hoover's reticence was justified. Little more than a B-film, *They Came to Blow Up America* had ventured into his private preserve, when all the while he was considering an A-film tribute along the lines of a documentary. Hoover was waiting for the right filmmaker and the right moment to fling open the bureau files. At the end of 1944, the war was going well for the Allies, and the FBI had every reason to boast of its wartime record. There was such a congratulatory mood in the air that Hoover had no misgivings about disclosing for the first time the wiretapping and surveillance techniques that had served the FBI so well in obtaining evidence against suspects and foes.

Hoover therefore pledged his cooperation to Louis De Rochemont, who had the financial backing of Darryl F. Zanuck, then production chief at Twentieth Century-Fox. De Rochemont had been the producer of *The March of Time*, a documentary series sponsored by *Time-Life* in the late thirties and early forties, so he was used to working with factual footage, and he had recently organized masses of Navy combat film into an entertaining and commercial documentary feature, *The Fighting Lady*. It was understood from the start that his deal with the FBI would include the use of bureau film, as well as permission to shoot scenes within the department. The new picture, however, was not to be a documentary in the strictest sense, but a fictional amalgam of cases drawn from the files, which were open as wide as security permitted and placed at the disposal of the screenwriter.

Initially known as *Now It Can Be Told,* the project called for extensive location shooting in New York and Long Island with cameras hidden in specially designed cars and trucks provided by the bureau. Since the film was not a newsreel, clearances had to be obtained from passers-by under the New York right-of-privacy laws. Every professional actor and technician had to be investigated by the bureau beforehand, in part because they would come in close contact with classified material. The clearance of cast and personnel must have been done exclusively on a political basis, for one major role was actually played by a homosexual. Hoover's vigilance had yet to reach the paranoid peak of later years, when he would have whole sequences of *The FBI Story* reshot because he disapproved of the politics, sexual and other, of a couple of extras in the background.

Lloyd Nolan, who had appeared in *G-Men* as an athletic instructor and had played many a gangster and convict in his early career, was chosen to play a seasoned FBI inspector, a role that carried over into a subsequent picture, *The Street with No Name*. Both Nolan and William Eythe, who played an undercover agent, went through a two-week indoctrination course at the bureau training school. Nolan made a rock-solid anchorman for Eythe, younger and less familiar to filmgoers; the interplay of fatherly experience and youthful daring was perpetuated in countless service films and gradually replaced the love interest once considered indispensable. It is easy to imagine that Hoover was relieved and even flattered to have his own celibacy adopted by Hollywood's G-men; it seemed almost an assertion that service to the nation exacted a crusader's total commitment and left no time for romantic entanglements. (In the old *Persons in Hiding* series, whenever the vows of celibacy were broken, it was a sure sign that the agent with a wife and kids would not live to the end of the picture. In *Parole Fixer,* the killing of Jack Carson furnished a pretext for having Hoover comfort the grieving widow on the telephone.)

De Rochemont and his chosen director, Henry Hathaway, exercised the greatest care in the choice of the variegated middle-European types who made up the lower echelons of the film's spy ring. Except for Signe Hasso, a Swedish actress, and Leo G. Carroll, the English character actor, the roles of spies and traitors were undertaken by unknown players. It was not easy to determine on sight the subversive strain of the foreign conspirators in *The House on 92nd Street,* as *Now It Can Be Told* was finally titled. In retrospect, it seems that the real target of the film was less the nearly vanquished Nazi of World War Two than the communist infiltrator of the cold war. With no new scenes, *The House on 92nd Street* could easily have been made to work against the Russians simply by altering a few words in the soundtrack.

With a few changes on the soundtrack, the Nazi spies could have passed for Communists. William Eythe, another version of William Sebold, in *The House on 92nd Street*, 1945, the semidocumentary that finally met with Hoover's approval. *Twentieth Century-Fox*

Through years of alliance with Russia, Hoover remained distrustful, actively and successfully lobbying to prevent a Soviet study force inspecting American security methods. *The House on 92nd Street* revealed the paraphernalia of counterespionage: the two-way mirrors, hidden cameras and microphones, the camouflaged vehicles, the microphotography detection process. The most impressive memory bank in the world, the Fingerprint Collection, was displayed in all its awesome efficiency. During the war, the bureau had intensified its drive to fingerprint every adult American in the name of national security, an Orwellian ambition of Hoover's that raised many a liberal eyebrow and was regarded by some as a significant step toward a police state. Basking in the first summer of peace in four years—the film premiered in Washington in September 1945, four weeks after the end of the war—Americans were ready to grant that such extreme security methods were necessary, even desirable.

The House on 92 Street was marketed as a true story drawn from the

MAX BLANK

MAX BLANK AND PAUL FEHSE

MAX BLANK

MAX BLANK AND PAUL FEHSE

EVERETT ROEDER

HEINRICH STADE AND PAUL FEHSE

Various members of the Duquesne spy ring in authentic photographs taken by FBI agents. And the same hidden camera technique re-created for *The House on 92nd Street* to catch the master spy (Leo G. Carroll) primping before a two-way mirror. *Twentieth Century-Fox* files of the FBI and reenacted before the cameras with the permission of J. Edgar Hoover, but the facts were not unassailably authentic. The case of William Sebold, the double agent who had already been featured in *They Came to Blow Up America*, was used as a starting point for the first screenplay by Barré Lyndon and Charles Boothe. Additional material was culled from the FBI files by John Monks, Jr., prewar coscenarist of films like *Brother Rat* and *Strike Up the Band* and recently discharged from the Marines. Monks also embroidered into the script the case of the enigmatic "Joe K.," code name for Kurt Frederick Ludwig, a German agent spotted at a Manhattan traffic accident when he grabbed a briefcase from an injured man, another spy who subsequently died in St. Vincent's Hospital. Monks dipped into the file of "The Doll Woman" which dealt with microphotographic information on convoy routes; and details and data were borrowed from half a dozen other cases to spin a semifictional web of espionage around the ultra-secret Project 97, which the picture offered as a euphemism for the real, and ultra-ultra-secret, Manhattan Project, a code name for the atom bomb. *The House on 92nd Street* was already in the can when the first A-bombs were dropped on Nagasaki and Hiroshima. De Rochemont

had not counted on that much timeliness, and the film's narration was re-recorded at the last minute to clarify the true nature of Project 97.

History dramatized what in the *post facto* film was basically a contest of technologies between the brisk, fanatical Nazis and the no less fanatic but much more relaxed federal agents: Bill Dietrich (Eythe) graduates from the Pension Klomstock, the famous Hamburg school for saboteurs and spies, then returns to the United States with orders to set up a secret radio station in an isolated coastal spot in Long Island. He is, we learn from the start, a loyal American of German ancestry and an FBI agent with a conduit to Inspector Briggs (Nolan). Henry Hathaway's direction kept the story taut, although most of the violence was muted and covert. (There was nothing, however, about the drudgery of espionage, as exploited much later by John le Carré.) And there was a final fictional flourish: When the federal agents close in on the house on 92nd Street, a boutique that serves as a front for the spy ring, the modiste is revealed to be the mysterious "Mr. Christopher," whom we have hitherto glimpsed in expertly faked "official footage," and identified as the mastermind-cum-executioner of the spy ring. In the decades since, however, the more devious strategies in the film have spectacularly backfired. Now, when the effete, middle-aged traitor (Leo G. Carroll) primps before a two-way mirror, we are mostly conscious of an invasion of privacy. When Mr. Christopher removes her wig and reveals

"Mr. Christopher," the bizarre androgyne (Signe Hasso) who is the mastermind-executioner of the spy ring. *The House on 92nd Street. Twentieth Century-Fox*

herself as a bizarre androgyne, the film seems to be hinting that perverse sexuality lurks behind all un-American activities. Now, since the tables have been turned on the FBI in the interim, any kinky trait seems preferable—not merely in the dramatic sense—to the homogenized purity of data collectors.

The Second World War had brought about years of patriotic machine-gunning by the likes of Bogart, Alan Ladd, and Robert Taylor, and the absence of the gangster from the screen went practically unnoticed. But in March 1945, two months before V-E Day, a small-budget, drab-looking picture about John Dillinger was released without the slightest squawk from the Breen office. Just as important, *Dillinger* surprised the industry by breaking records and making a tidy profit for the King brothers, who had previously operated on the fringe of the industry. Frank and Maurice King had started out as bootleggers, gone into vending-machine concessions after repeal, and finally entered independent film production in the late thirties. Having secured the rights to the stock footage that constituted one-third of *Dillinger*—car chases and Tommy-gun battles culled from half a dozen thirties films, plus the armored-car heist from *You Only Live Once,* which turned up with circuitous logic in a film about the real Dillinger—the King brothers took a chance on a crime picture that risked being refused the seal of approval. They commissioned a loosely factual screenplay from Philip

A man gifted for violence at a particular moment in history: Lawrence Tierney in *Dillinger*, 1945. *Monogram*

Yordan, then an obscure scenario writer who had surprised Broadway with a hit play, *Anna Lucasta,* and then they hired Max Nosseck, a Polish-born director who resisted temptations to glorify or embellish material that had already felled some natives. Dillinger was played by Lawrence Tierney, a hulking young actor, as a dour, unemotional psychopath, even though news shots of the original had shown a personable man with a lopsided grin not unlike Gable's.

There was no mention in *Dillinger* of Melvin Purvis, or for that matter, of anyone other than Dillinger who had certifiably existed; and a tabloid natural like the Woman in Red was reduced to a blond moll (Anne Jeffreys) who betrays Dillinger to the feds to avenge the death of another lover, done in by the possessive Dillinger *with an ax.* Any factual basis of the film was overwhelmed by the violence of the stock footage. When *Dillinger* was released the reviewer for *P.M.* magazine noted that "there seems to be not a sequence in which somebody hasn't a rod in his hand and scarcely a setting which is not a plundered bank, a jail, a gangland hideout or a scorching highway chase." Even a knockabout Disney cartoon turns up that fateful evening at the Biograph.

From sheer corner-cutting, the genre had been distilled to its essence: *Dillinger* may have been the first conceptual gangster epic, and not until Roger Corman's *The Saint Valentine's Day Massacre* (1967) were we to witness a comparable detachment. After dozens of pictures for or against the gangster, here was at last a picture that took no sides, that withheld sympathy and rationale, and that simply showed the hero as a man gifted for violence in a particularly violent moment in history; skill divorced from heroics, mayhem without a cause.

7. Shades of Noir

I cannot get over the idea that the [House Un-American Activities] Committee attacked Hollywood for a reason. I think it had three reasons: (1) to destroy trade unions; (b) to paralyze anti-fascist political action; and (c) to remove progressive content from films. There *must* have been *some* progressive content, *some* results of progressive action in Hollywood, or Jack [Howard Lawson] would not write: "There was to be no more talk of human aspirations and national social objectives." What *was* this talk of "human aspirations and national social objectives"?

— Letter from Dalton Trumbo to Sam Sillen, 1953

IN 1946 HOLLYWOOD released four hundred and six features and accrued the highest annual grosses up to that time. The film companies, sensing that peace would bring an end to the ban on strikes, were prepared with a backlog of unreleased films, and the public had yet to lapse into postwar apathy. The war was over, the foreign markets were reopening to American films, and, although the British were already making inroads in the domestic market, a foreign-film invasion was not the threat it would later become. Hollywood's worst headache in 1946 was a long, debilitating, and occasionally violent dispute over jurisdictional rights between two craft unions—the monopolistic IATSE and the dissident splinter group known as the Conference of Studio Unions. The chief issue was the hiring of painters and carpenters by the studios. There was violence in 1945 when the CSU called a strike, and again in July 1946, with pickets and bloody clashes at the gates of Metro and Warner Brothers.

The guild bulletins and trade papers bristled with charges and counter-charges. Screenwriter Dalton Trumbo attacked Roy Brewer, the head of IATSE, deeming him a fit heir to the racketeer reign of Bioff and Browne—even though the union had done considerable housecleaning since their forced departure. Brewer riposted with accusations that the Communist Party was attempting to take hold of the film industry, and that the CIO had a direct line to the CSU. In retrospect, none of these allegations appears legitimate, except that Herbert Sorrell, leader of the CSU, was indeed taken for a ride in classic Chicago-mob style the following year and severely beaten, and the Screen Writers Guild, which supported the CSU, did count a fair number of Communists among its members. Late in the winter of 1947, a small item in the trades announced that the House Un-American Activities Committee would conduct an investigation of possible Communist influence on the film industry. To Hollywood, which had just reeled in $125 million in profits, this was but distant thunder.

In this state of financial security and political tension, a series of gradual steps—any bold break with tradition would obviously have been thwarted by the Code—was taken in the direction of portraying a more complex moral system, allowing for ambiguity in the spectrum from Right to Wrong, and moreover for a tinge of despair to neutralize the rather monotonous Hollywood optimism. Even conservative directors like Frank Capra and William Wyler publicized their views that, now that the war was over, American films should reach their belated maturity. The change, however, was already under way. When American pictures began to be released in France after the war, the change was so apparent that the term *film noir* was coined by alert critics and applied (more judiciously then than now) to the tawdry-glamorous, big-city, low-life thrillers which would continue to thrive into the mid-fifties. *Life* magazine, then a bulwark of middle-class, middle-brow opinion, tagged the trend as "Hollywood's profound postwar affection for morbid drama." Stylistically, these films constitute one of the richest periods in American cinema.

At first, *film noir* meant just the adaptations from the *série noire,* a paperback series so known because of its standard black covers. These offered American detective and gangster fiction in translation, most of it written in the thirties and refined from pulp magazines like *Black Mask.* As such, *film noir* had its roots in prewar literature and eschewed the realities of postwar crime. Historians and sociologists will find little or no rapport between the underworld depicted in the *film noir*—not exactly a class, a group, or a milieu—and the events that marked American crime from the legal execution of Lepke Buchalter in 1944 to the mob assassination of Bugsy Siegel in 1947.

No real-life criminals were portrayed in American films from *Dillinger* in 1945 until *Baby Face Nelson* in 1957, roughly the heyday of the *film noir.* In 1947, the Breen Office refused the Code seal to a screenplay based on Westbrook Pegler's biography of Al Capone (the gangster had died in January of that year). In December, while public attention was focused on the Hollywood Ten, who had refused to testify before the House Un-American Activities Committee, a thirteenth section was added to the existing twelve in the MPAA Code in order to make Breen's decision official. It read:

No picture shall be approved dealing with the life of a notorious criminal of current or recent times which uses the name, nickname or alias of such notorious criminal in the film, nor shall a picture be approved if based on the life of such notorious criminal unless the character shown in the film be punished for crimes shown in the film committed by him.

The measure was clearly directed against the Capone project, but it was also to preclude reissues of films like *Scarface,* and, following the adoption of the amendment, studios were ordered to drop a number of projects whose titles had been registered with the MPAA. These included *He Trapped Capone, Killer for Hire, Assassin for Hire, Killers All, Baby-faced Killer, The Gangster's Moll, Gangster's Glory, Professional Killer,* and *The Killer.*

Obviously, the major companies, always ready to jump on the bandwagon, had attentively followed the negotiations between the Breen Office and Jack Pegler, an independent producer who had the rights to the Capone book.

The logical alternative to the masculine, violent gangster film was the psychological thriller, usually with a vicious heroine at its center. The latter sort of film became a trend that boomed in the postwar period and furnished the *film noir* with its titles. Some foreign observers, like Ado Kyrou, read into this fresh burst of misogyny an expression of resentment toward women, a reaction to four years of wartime idealization, during which women had only two permissible roles, the waiting wife or the bachelor girl who did her bit for the war effort: faithful Penelope and Rosie the Riveter. But there was more. The war and its psychological aftermath contributed to the popularization of Freudian theory and jargon. A growing interest in psychoanalysis supplied filmmakers with a new approach to everything the Code deemed objectionable.

To deal with forbidden matters, the best recourse was to deflect sexual behavior toward criminal behavior, which was easier to justify in the eyes of the Breen Office. (In turn, the censor was supposed to uphold the consensus in sexual mores.) According to Breen logic, a criminal going to his doom could indulge in illicit sex, since he was doomed anyway, and punishment for a criminal act implied punishment for unacceptable sex. Take, for example, a minor but typical *film noir*, *Born to Kill* (1947), in which motivation was centered around the frustrated lust of the heroine for a murderer, and in which supporting characters furnished a chorus of depravity. An objective correlative had been found for behavioral attitudes that could not be tolerated in normal film characters.

In the long run, this repression had a strong effect on the style of *film noir*. In prewar Europe, the sexual content was manifest in a handful of thrillers that prefigured *film noir*, films that left little unsaid, like *La Tête d'un Homme* (1932), from the novel by Georges Simenon, *Le Puritain* (1937) from a screenplay by Liam O'Flaherty, or *Le Dernier Tournant* (1939), the first screen adaptation of James M. Cain's *The Postman Always Rings Twice*. In Hollywood, such material had to be structured in more subtle and stylized ways in order to slip past the watch of the censor.

Among the first recognizable *films noirs* were John Huston's *The Maltese Falcon* (1941) and Frank Tuttle's *The Glass Key* (1942). These two Dashiell Hammett novels had been filmed before, yet the early versions lack for the most part the defining qualities of the remakes. The climax of *The Maltese Falcon*, in which detective Sam Spade consigns Ruth Wonderly, the murderess, to the police—tantamount to delivering her to the hangman—was played for laughs in 1931 and 1936. In his remake, Huston staged the scene with such lyricism (a feeling missing in the novel—Hammett was more deadpan than Huston) that it became a summation of the duties and dilemmas of the private eye. Likewise, the second features derived from Raymond Chandler's *Farewell, My Lovely* and *The High Win-*

dow—which became *The Falcon Takes Over* and *Time to Kill,* both 1942—discarded everything but the zippy action. Yet the same sources yielded archetypal *films noirs* three or four years later. From watching various versions of the same thriller, it becomes obvious that *noir* is more likely to be in the eye of the director than on the printed page—and even likelier to be in the eye of a cinematographer like Nicholas Musuraca or John Alton.

Film academics have employed the term *film noir* as a blanket definition for any movie without a happy ending, from *King Kong* to *Citizen Kane:* quite a large piece of fabric, and full of holes. In American films, any pessimistic implication was usually more than tempered with exhilarating physical action and uplifting strings on the soundtrack. True metaphysical anguish was likewise outside the range of Hammett, Chandler, Cain, and David Goodis, and beyond their concern. Even at its bleakest, the *film noir* can be comfortably assigned to the middle ground of the crime story, and only the naïve or the insecure would rank Céline and Sartre among *série noire* authors—although quite possibly a *film noir* or two might be whittled down from their works.

It was through the work of émigrés like Fritz Lang, Otto Preminger, Robert Siodmak, Billy Wilder, John Brahm, and Curtis Bernhardt—not forgetting Alfred Hitchcock, who served his apprenticeship in Berlin studios—that Hollywood evolved from the objective certainties of the thirties to the private ambiguities of the postwar period, never skipping a beat or losing sight of entertainment values. In exchange, the new environment stimulated these transplanted Europeans: style was made to conform to the accepted Hollywood notion that the well-made film must never show its seams or flaunt its technique; nonetheless, films became more personal. One could read the director's signature through the house style of the various companies, and, as the films became less uniform in their presentation of *one* social and moral system, Hollywood entered its postclassical period—like the novel, in search of reality.

For the sake of realism, crews were dispatched to locations "where the events took place," but reality, as the novel also discovered in time, turned out to be an elusive, relative matter. Labor troubles contributed to this on-location policy to a certain degree, but as soon as they subsided, the fresh and exciting look of city streets, moldy hotel rooms, and flyspecked dives was brought home to the sound stages. Whether in the studio or on location, the visuals of the *film noir* were unmistakable: the fake and the real were unified by lighting, and all drabness was banished from the frame. Screen space grew darker and deeper. As a rule, when a character entered a room and switched on the lights, the shadows remained as threatening as before. Even before the war, a cultivated look of menace had begun to appear through the use of fast-emulsion film stock and depth-of-field lenses. The success of a *film noir* can often be gauged by the degree of contrast on the screen. A studio as house-proud as Metro preferred to sacrifice mood to opulence, and their version of *The Postman Always Rings Twice* (1946) was more like a *film gris.*

A more modest studio like RKO-Radio was willing to experiment with dark areas to conceal the limits of a cramped set or disguise its familiarity. *Film noir* came more naturally to RKO, and the first cohesive *noir* visuals were evident in early B-films such as *Stranger on the Third Floor* (1940), *Cat People* (1942), and *The Seventh Victim* (1943), whose unifying theme happens to be fear and obsession.

The fully realized *noir* look first appears in *Murder, My Sweet* (1944), an *echt*-forties thriller which rarely gets its due because of the relative unpopularity of its director, Edward Dmytryk, and the miscalculation of casting Dick Powell as Philip Marlowe, a crooner playing a private eye, his dimples showing through the stubble.*

Murder, My Sweet was an adaptation of Chandler's *Farewell, My Lovely,* and the Marlowe character was portrayed in it for the first time under his rightful name. (His adventures had formerly been appropriated for The Falcon and Michael Shayne, second-feature heroes.) The novel was expurgated with taste and imagination by John Paxton, but enough remained to allow a glimpse of Chandler's bleak vision of Southern California, what W. H. Auden called the Great Wrong Place.† Marlowe was a relatively fresh character in pictures: a Los Angeles private investigator with a dingy downtown office, a gun permit, and the best philosophical line in his shady profession. First-person off-screen narration was soon done to death.

"You're a stupid little man in a dirty little world," the fake psychiatrist (Otto Kruger) tells Marlowe in words that elicit no rebuttal from the hero. Marlowe's world is dirty all right, littered with empty bottles and dead bodies; yet, as Chandler himself said of his turf, "certain writers with tough minds and a cool sense of detachment can make very interesting patterns out of it." Most of these patterns were basic to the *film noir*. They could be arranged along the lines of a detective story that, in its course, exposed a brutal and corrupt society that did not always coincide with the straight world's idea of itself. Even in the safer context of the detective film, the mere depiction of evil in places higher than the underworld conferred an awareness of the seamy side that other genres never provided.

Both Adrian Scott and Edward Dmytryk, who respectively produced and directed *Murder, My Sweet,* turned up three years later among the Hollywood Ten. Many left-oriented screenwriters and directors were logically drawn to the *film noir*—among them, Ben Maddow, Ring Lardner, Jr., Carl Foreman, Albert Maltz, Dalton Trumbo, Jules Dassin, John Berry, Abraham Polonsky, and Joseph Losey. Compared to the more prestigious social dramas—like *The Best Years of Our Lives*—the *film noir* positively

---

* Powell was still a notch or two above Robert Montgomery, George Montgomery, James Garner, and Elliott Gould, all of whom would have a crack at the role in years to come. But, unfortunately for Powell and *Murder, My Sweet,* Humphrey Bogart came along a year later in *The Big Sleep* to make the Marlowe role his own for good. More recently, Robert Mitchum, thirty years too old for the part, nevertheless brought to it a pleasant forties resonance.

† Chandler researched the Los Angeles underworld for his original screenplay, *The Blue Dahlia,* filmed in 1945. Even though reality had supplied Hollywood with a juicy murder case right in its own backyard, the murder and dismemberment of a callgirl nicknamed by the tabloids "The Black Dahlia," the only connection with the Chandler script is in the title. Chandler's main source of inspiration was the genre itself, rather than actual events.

reeked of the facts of life. It was easier to instill a feeling that all was not
perfect in American society by way of the ambiguities of *film noir* than to
take on the system and risk the cooptation of any subversive message.

The underworld was much more than a backdrop in *The Killers* (1946),
a film suggested by Ernest Hemingway's short story which, since its publication in 1927, had affected the way gangsters spoke on the screen. (By
1928, a silent picture called *Walking Back* had already pirated the story's
tough, rhythmic patter (for its intertitles.) For the first time Hemingway
had reason to endorse a film adaptation of his work. With a respect due only

The cultivated look of menace in *film noir:* frame enlargements from *Murder My Sweet,*
1944, reveal screen space growing deeper and darker. Dick Powell as the dislocated
hero, Philip Marlowe, is threatened successively by Ralf Harolde, Claire Trevor, Mike
Mazurki, and (out of frame) Miles Mander. *RKO-Radio*

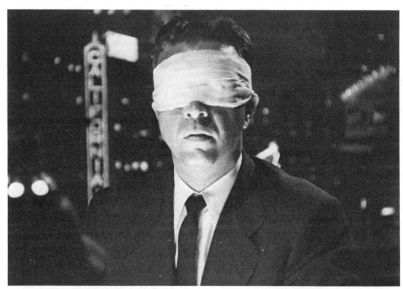

to Shakespeare and Holy Writ, the tight first reel of *The Killers* reproduced much of the story's original dialogue:

—Talk to me, bright boy, what do you think's going to happen? I'll tell you.
    We're going to kill a Swede. Do you know a big Swede named Ole Andreson?
—We're killing him for a friend, just to oblige a friend, bright boy.

The film begins with a long subjective shot from a moving car: two hired gunmen (William Conrad and Charles McGraw) are driving into a small town. The opening location shots (California doubling for New Jersey) set up a realistic tone that is swiftly overcome. As the gunmen sit at the counter in a roadside diner, intimidating employees and customers to obtain information about the Swede, the harsh overhead lighting makes them omi-

"We're going to kill him for a friend, just to oblige a friend, big boy." Two hired gunmen (Charles McGraw and William Conrad) taunt the proprietor (Harry Hayden) of a small-town diner in the opening sequence of *The Killers*, 1946, which retained Hemingway's original dialogue. *Universal*

nous hulks and stimulates a lingering memory of Gestapo interrogators. As such, they are etched in the viewer's mind: they will reappear only at the very end to communicate a fear disproportionate to their basically realistic character.

Among those interrogated at the diner is Nick Adams (Phil Brown), the sempiternal Hemingway narrator, here reduced to a minor character; Nick attempts to warn the Swede of the impending arrival of the killers, but the Swede (Burt Lancaster) refuses to save himself. The killers fulfill their mission and return to the city, leaving Nick, the reader, and the movie-goer wondering about the Swede's last words—"Once I did something wrong"—and his lost will to live.

After this opening, *The Killers* became a caper story about a meticu-lously planned holdup—closer in fact to W. R. Burnett than to Heming-way, although not surprising, since John Huston had written the scenario. Originally set to direct as well, Huston withdrew after a disagreement with the producer, Mark Hellinger, and the film credits Anthony Veiller, Hus-ton's collaborator, as sole author. Since *High Sierra,* Huston's work had borne the acknowledged influence of Burnett and would continue through the forties to deal with the failed efforts of mismatched adventurers (in *Treasure of Sierra Madre*) and revolutionaries (*We Were Strangers*). In 1950, Huston would return to the source by directing another caper story, *The Asphalt Jungle,* from a Burnett novel published the year before.

Something in the immediate postwar mood encouraged the prolifer-ation of caper stories, possibly because of an inherently noble theme—men working together toward a goal that, though neither patriotic nor uplifting, stressed teamwork and drew from each participant a performance of skill and courage. The caper was a peacetime refinement of the war story, pre-serving the dynamics, but substituting crime for flag-waving and rhetoric: a terrain as propitious to Hemingway as to Burnett. And, after four years of combat, hardship, and all sorts of foul play more or less sanctioned by war, crime must have seemed less forbidding and remote. War had made obvious the relative ease with which moral barriers could be crossed. In crime movies, as in the real war, civilians were expendable. In *The Asphalt Jungle,* Huston and Burnett would define crime as "a left-handed form of human endeavor."

The Killers employed several narrators to piece together the past, the same structure used in Orson Welles's *Citizen Kane.* One such flashback exists merely as a cinematic flourish: a junkie (Jeff Corey) is badgered at at his deathbed for his piece of the puzzle, which is then lucidly visualized, even though the narrator has been pronounced "dead except he's breath-ing." Collecting the stories, the insurance investigator (Edmond O'Brien) reconstructs a web of betrayal and deceit: how the Swede, an ex-prizefighter, was inveigled into a payroll robbery through his infatuation with a gang-ster's moll (Ava Gardner); how he was made to appear a traitor after the robbery was successfully accomplished, while the moll and her lover (Al-bert Dekker) absconded with the loot; how, years later, to cover up forever, the lovers had the Swede murdered by contract.

The screenplay, with its deft borrowings from Hammett and Burnett, pleased Hemingway (and its deadly heroine, straight from Cain, may well have gratified his misogynous side). Yet the film's prevailing mood of wasted passion and elating violence can only be credited to Robert Siodmak, the director who took over from Huston. After creditable work in Berlin and Paris before the war, Siodmak made his Hollywood reputation in 1944 with *Phantom Lady,* a mystery thriller from a William Irish novel; so hyperbolic was Siodmak's style that the film was almost surreal. Between 1946 and 1949, Siodmak made three gangster movies which were even better: *The Killers, Cry of the City,* and *Criss Cross.* The Siodmak touch was a mutation of European realism which combined authentic-looking studio work with real locations shot in a most artificial manner. A good example is the famous payroll robbery in *The Killers,* a sequence photographed on location in a single dolly-and-track shot as daring as the heist itself, while an off-screen narrator tells us that five men were involved and a quarter of a million dollars stolen. The Olympian viewpoint of the camera seemed to disdain the hard facts of the crime.

Like his European colleagues, Siodmak conceived of crime, in any form, as a *crime passionnel*—although women were excluded from the male group, they supplied the incentive for the hero and were the cause, even unwittingly, of the ultimate failure of the enterprise. *Criss Cross* (1949) arguably Siodmak's best film, was a rarity, a caper movie that also stood up as the story of an *amour fou.* Typical of both *The Killers* and *Criss Cross* was a scene showing the gang clustering around a table, tensely breaking down the caper into individual assignments, a brief moment of truce when rivalries and differences were set aside—then Siodmak cut away to the women (Gardner in *The Killers,* Yvonne DeCarlo in *Criss Cross*) smoldering on the fringe of the group, as they guided the hero's involvement. These women were the real stakes in the game.

It did not matter that the heroes were losers anyway, duped by women into crime; while the men schemed and strove for their less than admirable goals, our allegiance never faltered. Would either Hitchcock or Lang, to whom Siodmak was compared, ever have featured a hero without will power or a heroine without brains, as Siodmak did in *Criss Cross,* and moreover have made them riveting objects of identification? Siodmak conveyed better than his fellow expatriates a Teutonic taste for the subtleties of sexual enslavement; he shared this quality with American directors like Joseph H. Lewis and Nicholas Ray, whose crime movies were as lyrical as his own.

Although a caper movie, *Criss Cross* never strayed far from its doomed couple. In the astonishing opening scene, the camera swoops down on a parking lot, isolating Steve and Anna as their embrace is exposed by the glare of headlights. The bold, intricate screenplay by Daniel Fuchs, starts the night before the heist, then flashes back to the events leading up to it as Steve drives an armored truck to the prearranged spot where it will be held up. Much of the film is seen through Steve's eyes and interpreted through his narration.

It is the point of view of a disaffected young man, obsessively drawn to his divorced wife. After Anna marries a small-time racketeer named Slim Dundee (Dan Duryea), Steve makes her his mistress. "It was in the cards, and there was no way of stopping it," muses Steve resignedly. Others try to separate them. His mother warns him against Anna because "in some ways [Anna] knows more than Einstein," and a police-detective friend threatens her with prison. The mother and the detective fail, of course, and since *Criss Cross* is nothing less than a gangland version of Tristan and Isolde— as an occasional string crescendo from Miklos Rozsa's score reminds us—the lovers are fated to die in pain, terror, and each other's arms.

Yvonne DeCarlo, as Anna, smoldering on the fringes of the male group as they plot a caper, in *Criss Cross*, 1949: a story of an *amour fou* on the edge of misogyny.
Universal

Caught in flagrant adultery one afternoon, Steve gets himself out of a tight spot by offering to join Dundee's gang as the inside man in an armored-car robbery. It would seem at first that Steve has improvised the heist to divert Dundee's attention from his liaison with Anna, but the film soon makes clear—by little twists of character peculiar to *film noir*—that Steve is not quick-witted enough to make up such a plot on the spur of the moment and that the crime has been in his mind for some time as the means to escape with Anna to an easy life beyond Dundee's reach.

As in *The Killers*, the heist is the culmination of a group effort and also
the point where cross-purposes clash. Realizing that he is being set up by
Dundee, Steve turns against his accomplices and decimates the gang before
collapsing with a broken collarbone. He regains consciousness in a hospital,
a hero wounded in the line of duty, fearfully aware that sooner or later
Dundee will come after him. Immobilized in a plaster cast, he keeps a night
vigil on the corridor reflected in a mirror in his room. A mild-mannered
salesman (Robert Osterloh), ostensibly waiting for news of his wife's condition after a car accident, suddenly appears at Steve's bedside, metamorphosed into a grim messenger of death. Cutting the wires that keep Steve's
arm in traction—pain has rarely been as excruciatingly conveyed as with
the twang of those wires being cut—he spirits Steve away to a last rendezvous with Anna in a seaside house that patently could only exist as a matte
painting.

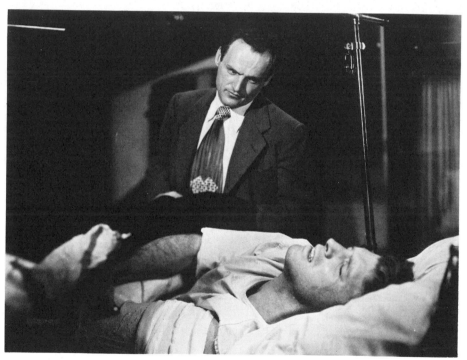

**Death, in the form of a mild-mannered salesman (Robert Osterloh) will spirit Steve
(Burt Lancaster) away to a final rendezvous with Anna, in *Criss Cross*. *Universal***

Criss Cross progressed steadily from the topographic realism of its
opening shot, an aerial view of downtown Los Angeles, to the subjective
delirium of a final image that blurs and fades out as if to convey Steve's
agony and death. In retrospect, Siodmak came closer to Sternberg's fancies
than to Hecht's facts. It took Huston's caper picture, *The Asphalt Jungle*
(which he adapted with Ben Maddow from Burnett) to restore the under-

world to an American dimension. Here the narrative was linear, the tone realistic rather than esthetic; as a whole, the film was less exhilarating than either *The Killers* or *Criss Cross*. *The Asphalt Jungle* is a man's movie: Huston defined his criminals neither by their police records nor their psychological case histories, but by their professional standing within the underworld.

The crime is the brainchild of Doc Reidenschneider (Sam Jaffe), who has had seven years in prison to perfect the plan. The big heist—a million dollars in diamonds locked in a jeweler's safe—is prepared in businesslike fashion, and, like any sound commercial proposition, it requires financial backing and careful screening of technicians. In partnership with a bookie (Marc Lawrence) and a well-heeled attorney (Louis Calhern) who will act as fence, three specialists are hired and paid off, in Doc's words, "like housepainters": a "boxman" or safecracker (Anthony Caruso), a top driver (James Whitmore), and a "hooligan" or gunman (Sterling Hayden) to complete the crew. Take for instance the scene in which the boxman tries out for the job:

—What boxes have you opened?
—Cannonball, double-door, even a few Firechest, all of them.

The Asphalt Jungle holds its breath during the robbery, filmed, according to Huston, with the advice of safecracking experts to ensure maximum authenticity. But almost immediately the caper turns into a tragic failure. The boxman is mortally wounded while trying to get away, the lawyer attempts to double-cross the gang, the bookie loses his nerve and confesses to the police. The diamonds are suddenly valueless, and all Doc can do is to accept some of the ante money from the hooligan and try to escape. His predilection for nymphets—a character trait that Huston handled here with finesse and sympathy years before *Lolita*—makes Doc linger too long at a soda parlor, and he is arrested. The hooligan, shot by the lawyer's bodyguard in the scuffle over the loot, will live just long enough to return to his beloved bluegrass country to die among the horses.

Although MGM did not tamper with it, *The Asphalt Jungle* was criticized for its liberal attitude toward the underworld. In Huston's words: "My defense ... was that unless we understand the criminal ... there's no way of coping with him." This is a proposition that Huston conveyed, at its simplest, by having the straights misconstrue the hoods, their dark-mirror images. "When I think of all those awful people you come in contact with, downright criminals, I get scared," says the lawyer's crippled wife (Dorothy Tree); to which her husband replies: "There's nothing so different about them." In full close-up, this statement carries the conviction of truth.

Some of the characters are sketchily drawn, like Whitmore's hunchback driver whose affection for the hooligan is never clearly defined; others, like the boxman, are sentimentalized into worried family men. But Doc, the bookie, and Emmerich, the lawyer, are vividly, painstakingly written and performed. Huston excelled at showing the subtle shifts of calculation and

respect that take place between them: the way that the bookie defers to Doc, and the exquisite *politesse* exhibited by the older men, one an amateur criminal in a society of professionals, the other a wise man of the underworld, both familiar with human nature and resigned to the basic flaws of the social system. Only the lower order could still dream of prestige and status: for their superiors, success means escape and nubile girls. When Emmerich commits suicide rather than face exposure and disgrace, Doc is dismayed by such poor judgment: "How could he be so foolish? He would have got two years at most." Offered a gun as a parting precaution, Doc politely declines: "Thank you, I haven't carried a gun since my twenties. You carry a gun, you shoot a cop. Bad rap, hard to beat. You don't carry a gun, you give up when they hold up on you."

As a writer-director, Huston denied himself the editing flourishes and heady camera work of the Siodmak pictures, relying instead on a nigh-perfect ear for dialogue—his forte at this point in his career, as *The Maltese Falcon* led us to expect—and an eye for subtle shifts of character. Jaffe and Calhern owed Huston the performances of a lifetime (and Marilyn Monroe, in the minor role of Emmerich's mistress, owed him her best bid for stardom). There was a gravity in particular to Jaffe's acting, with a mischievous glint illuminating the face of a patriarchal monkey, that inevitably captured audience support. Just as rotten apples and traitors are liable to be found in both camps, Doc has an equivalent figure of authority in the stern police commissioner (John McIntire) who delivers the lawman's homily: "... Suppose we had no police force, good or bad. The jungle wins, the predatory beast takes over." Doc's philosophical acceptance of failure, his lack of concern for the values that destroy Emmerich, were passed on by the picture as the ultimate intelligence.

"I was not working against myself in order to conform to the censorship standards of the day," reminisced Huston in *The Cinema of John Huston*, and this romantic pessimism that Huston would pursue beyond the call of the Code—even in such a recent failed-caper story as *The Man Who Would Be King* (1975)—must have convinced James Agee and other critics that here, at last, was an authentic humanist working within the crass commercial system; a claim that, even in Agee's time, seemed worth disputing simply by comparing Huston with other directors who had found a comfortable berth in the *film noir*, such as Jacques Tourneur (who directed *Out of the Past*), Joseph H. Lewis (*Gun Crazy*), and Abraham Polonsky (*Force of Evil*). A genuine human dimension existed in their films, somewhere between Code restrictions and genre conventions, and their heroes never complied with failure as passively as had Huston's losers.

Like *Criss Cross*, *The Asphalt Jungle* opened with views of Los Angeles and its one recognizable landmark, the City Hall Tower, which then har-

Planning and executing the perfect heist. Mastermind Sam Jaffe breaks down the job into individual assignments for hooligan Sterling Hayden, boxman Anthony Caruso, and driver James Whitmore. Later, the job goes without a hitch, or almost. *The Asphalt Jungle*, 1950, a man's crime picture. *Metro-Goldwyn-Mayer*

TWENTIETH CENTURY-FOX
PRESENTS

CRY OF THE CITY

TWENTIETH CENTURY-FOX
PRESENTS

DANA ANDREWS

GENE TIERNEY

in

WHERE
THE SIDEWALK
ENDS

*Twentieth
Century-Fox
photos*

bored the Homicide Bureau. The standard opening shots of a skyline at dawn or dusk, the credits unfolding over brick walls or the sidewalk, the Gershwin-like musical theme *—all these led the viewer to accept the city as an emblematic presence. The urban scene acquired new power, quite removed from the romantic realism of studio-bound "city symphonies," thirties films like *Street Scene, Dead End,* and *Big City.* The location camera work now gloried in, and glorified, concrete and steel, wet pavements, populist vignettes caught in passing—the photogeny of the real that attracted filmmakers long before studios were built, now backed by the evocative traffic music of the big city. The *film noir* succeeded in synthesizing the travelogue and the manhunt story, and it made the city a darker, more disturbing presence than before. "Have you ever tried playing button-button in a city of eight million people?" intoned Mark Hellinger on the soundtrack of *The Naked City,* fancying himself a latter-day O. Henry while relishing the fact that half the exciting, wonderful tales Manhattan offered had something to do with crime.

Produced by Hellinger shortly before his death, *The Naked City* (1948) stands as his final tribute to the big city. (By the mid-forties, the film industry no longer geared its product to the small-town consumer, since by then its main source of revenue came from big-city audiences.) On a hot summer night, the camera peers at random through an apartment window where a murder is being committed: two men anesthetize a young woman, then drown her in a bathtub. Later that same night, one of the killers rids himself of an accomplice who could prove a risk. In the morning, a tearful housemaid summons the police to the dead girl's apartment, and the investigation is under way. The detectives make an expert, hard-working team, kind to suspects, tolerant of crackpots, and mostly Irish. The team includes a crusty, wise inspector (Barry Fitzgerald) and a callow but earnest lieutenant (Don Taylor), and they are perfectly matched. The process of detection in the film is a flat, unexciting routine, and, except for the extravagant time and attention allotted to what seems a relatively unimportant case—stolen jewels, as it turns out—it is depicted in a fairly realistic manner.

The dominating voice in the film was literally Hellinger's, as he delivered his corny narration ("Ever try to catch a murderer? It has its depressing moments."), but beneath the bracing optimism there was an awareness of a harder Social Darwinism at work. The screenplay was written by Malvin Wald and Albert Maltz, and Maltz must have finished his assignment as the House Un-American Activities Committee closed in on Hollywood—by November 1947, he was among the Hollywood Ten, cited for contempt of Congress and subsequently blacklisted. Although *The Naked City* was not half as subversive as, say, the Ben Hecht scenario for *The Kiss of Death* (which offered an unflattering view of the police establishment), it exhibited occasional spurts of social consciousness. One suspect casually mentions that he spends fifty dollars—a policeman's weekly

* The big-city blues that Alfred Newman composed for *Street Scene* in 1931 was reused in at least four films—*The Dark Corner, The Kiss of Death, Cry of the City, Where the Sidewalk Ends*—and gave these crime dramas the continuity of a suite.

salary—for a night on the town. A small-town couple (Grover Burgess and Adelaide Klein) arrives in Manhattan to claim the body of their murdered daughter: "We don't like it here, this fine city," drones the father, while the mother intones: "Bright lights, the-a-ter, furs.... Good Lord, why wasn't she born ugly?" This desolate scene, set in a waterfront near the city morgue as the sun sets behind the skyscrapers and bridges, carried the force of an indictment.

The other major force at work in *The Naked City* was Jules Dassin, a

The most exciting chase sequence of the decade provides the climax of *The Naked City*, 1948. The murderer Willie Garza (Ted de Corsia) overpowers Detective Halloran (Don Taylor) and flees through Manhattan's Lower East Side. Inspector Muldoon (Barry Fitzgerald) organizes the manhunt. Garza is finally cornered atop the Williamsburg Bridge, the city a backdrop to his last acrobatic performance. *Universal*

director yearning after tragedy and transcendence but who was most successful when most coerced by the Hollywood genre system, as his subsequent work proved (he eventually updated *Phaedra* and *Medea* in Europe). But in this phase of his career, his violent catharses were staged within the esthetic of the *film noir*. They focused on the outcast hero pursued by modern furies, as represented by the law or the underworld. The climactic chase scene of *The Naked City* was the best filmed and edited in a forties thriller. Dassin's empathies were obviously with Willie Garza (Ted de Corsia), the hunted murderer, as he is pursued by the younger detective all over the Lower East Side and up among the girders of the Williamsburg Bridge. It is Garza who introduces a reek of genuine sweaty fear and a sexual tension into the picture—even today, audiences react audibly to Garza's feral energy and tend to laugh off the perfunctory private lives of the detectives.

In his previous film, *Brute Force* (1947), which he also directed for Hellinger, Dassin equated the prison system with the fascist state, overtly siding with the inmates against authority. The prisoners had the same lack of depth as Garza, but they shared his suicidal drive to escape, and that was enough for Dassin: he went to work on a subgenre, one that had hardly evolved since *The Big House*, as if he were making a wartime propaganda movie set in a Nazi concentration camp. The sadistic warden (Hume Cronyn) plays Wagner while working over a prisoner with a rubber truncheon; two informers are barbarously executed; and the climactic bloodbath was the most violent yet to be seen on the American screen.

In 1949, while Dassin was on location in London for *Night and the City*, his name was casually mentioned in the testimony of fellow directors Edward Dmytryk and Frank Tuttle before the HUAC hearings. Although he returned to the United States, Dassin never had a chance to testify. His appearance before the committee was arbitrarily canceled, and Dassin found his Hollywood career terminated. He resettled in Paris, where after four years he directed his first film-in-exile, *Du Rififi chez les Hommes* (1955), a caper story that featured a forty-minute, speechless heist sequence involving such prosaic implements as an umbrella and a whipped-cream dispenser. A surprisingly colloquial movie for an American director in exile (apart from the dialogueless holdup), *Rififi* became an international success and launched a European vogue for such caper pictures. Dassin himself returned to the subgenre, in a comic key, with *Topkapi* (1964), but only after the Italians had demonstrated that the best way to deal with the American obsession with the well-done heist was to satirize it, as in *I Soliti Ignoti*, made in 1958 and titled *Big Deal on Madonna Street* for U.S. distribution.

The blacklist, in retrospect, cast a political implication on Dassin's Hollywood pictures that they did not originally possess. (In critical circles abroad he was lionized as a leftist intellectual.) Nonetheless, *Night and the City* (1950), his last film for an American company before he was blacklisted, summarized his *film noir* period, simply because it pushed the premises and the style to excess. Dassin kept the hero on the run from the first

to the next-to-last shot, when the underworld he had used, defied, or betrayed in various ways to further his hysterical ambitions to break away and become legitimate, caught up with him. Harry Fabian, a Soho nightclub tout trying to break into the wrestling racket, is "an artist without an art" other than wheedling favors out of people, a born loser or, as he is again described in the dialogue, "a hustler who will die a hustler." Harry, played by Richard Widmark at his most thyroidal, never stands a chance against the city that Dassin had fashioned from a dozen real locations—a grotesque, expressionistic London, reminiscent of Villon's Miracle Court or John Gay's nation of beggars, where shadows on a low ceiling form a cagelike pattern and brick walls suggest an inescapable prison of the soul. For all the realism Dassin conveyed, the picture could have been made on the sound stages and back lots of Twentieth Century-Fox in California. Siodmak could have put across some of the most obvious symbolism (as he did in *Cry of the City*), but in Dassin's hands, and away from the restraining influence of Hellinger, all the little-people asides of *The Naked City* decayed into viciously sour, desperate turns. A woman in a night club cowers in sensual enjoyment as Harry gets roughed up; his imposingly fat employer (Francis L. Sullivan, incapable of animating a tired cliché) pronounces Harry's death sentence with a light tap on the cymbals; and an underworld kingpin (Herbert Lom) materializes high on a bridge as Harry, tired of running, is strangled by a wrestler (Mike Mazurki) who doubles as a private executioner.

Location shooting had come full circle in a mere five years—from artificiality, to visuals more or less based on fact, and back to an excessively artificial approach. In retrospect, the directors who profited most from the trend were those who took the added realism in their stride and went after a straightforward statement. One of these was Henry Hathaway, who unselfconsciously went ahead and made the world one big sound stage, so smooth was his use of real sites. After *The House on 92nd Street,* the newsreel look had become semiofficial style at Twentieth Century-Fox, and furthermore, the strike of painters and carpenters justified the added expense of sending a crew on location. There had been *13 Rue Madeleine* (1946), a story of OSS wartime activities which Hathaway directed, mostly in Canada (which doubled for occupied France), and *Boomerang* (also 1946), a murder-trial story filmed in Stamford, Connecticut, by Elia Kazan. In 1947, Hathaway was assigned by Zanuck to direct what turned out to be the first major postwar gangster movie, *Kiss of Death.*

Hathaway's pictures of this period expanded the limits of acceptable violence on the screen, in part to match the realism of fresh locales, but also because it was being admitted at last that Americans had learned to play dirty during the war. *The House on 92nd Street* had pulled its punches in

Ritual execution of a prison informer, in *Brute Force,* 1947. Convicts John Hoyt, Jack Overman, and Howard Duff close in on stoolie James O'Rear and force him back with their blow torches until he falls into a stamping machine. *Universal*

"A hustler who will die a hustler," Harry Fabian (Richard Widmark) the hero of *Night and the City*, 1950, has been sentenced to death by the London underworld. *Twentieth Century-Fox*

this respect, but *13 Rue Madeleine* showed for the first time nice, clean-cut American spies being taught how to kill quietly and efficiently.

The hero of *Kiss of Death* is a stool pigeon who informs on fellow gang members in exchange for parole and a few privileges. Nick Bianco (Victor Mature) rejects the blandishments of the district attorney until he learns, while serving time, that his wife has committed suicide and that his destitute children have been taken to an orphanage. (Nick had taken the rap for a stickup in exchange for the mob's promise to take care of his family.) The script, by Ben Hecht and Charles Lederer (from a story by Eleazar Lipsky), takes a bead on the ruthless tactics employed by the office of the district attorney. Nick is drafted into "squealing" by a persuasive, righteous assistant D.A. (Brian Donlevy); he becomes the invisible cog in an elaborate apparatus of deceit (as was the hero in *The House on 92nd Street*) set in motion to entrap one of his former accomplices:

NICK: Your side of the fence is almost as dirty as mine.
A.D.A.: With one difference: we only hurt bad people.

As it turns out, innocents also get hurt as the law becomes entangled in its own coils. The invalid mother of a hoodlum being set up by the D.A. is pushed down a flight of stairs, wheelchair and all, by a moronic gunman, Tommy Udo (Richard Widmark), given to giggles and gurgling: "Do you know what I do to squealers? I let 'em have it in the belly so that they can move around and think it over." When the D.A. indicts Udo in what appears to be an open-and-shut case, Nick is made to take the stand and provide the vital testimony. The D.A. has gone to these unorthodox lengths to secure a conviction for a known killer, but Udo's shyster lawyer (Taylor Holmes) nonetheless gets his client acquitted, leaving Nick exposed to Udo's revenge. Nick knows there is no place he can run to, that the underworld spreads all over the country, possibly the first time such a realistic admission was made in a postwar movie. "All the guys I knew in jail, they move from town to town. I'm the guy they don't like any more.... He's gonna come sometime."

The law has proved ruthless and, worse still, unreliable and uneffective as a force to combat crime. It cannot help Nick any more than it can touch Udo. The D.A. proposes to put Nick back in prison for his own safety, but Nick knows better: he will offer himself as a sacrificial victim, baiting Udo to shoot him in front of witnesses. A moody, low-key sequence captured the perpetual twilight world of the informer: after sending his family away to safety, Nick sits alone in his modest suburban living room, a gun on the table, smoking and waiting for the inevitable, just as the Swede had in *The Killer*. The predictable tragic ending is skirted at the last moment by one off-screen line of narration to the effect that Nick did in fact survive and that Udo was executed. The images, however, belie this concession.

Victor Mature was an unlikely choice for the role of one of the first postwar antiheroes. He nevertheless played Nick Bianco soberly and with a nice ironic edge, but the most memorable performance in *Kiss of Death* was Widmark's Tommy Udo, his first screen role. It was indeed a gimmicky performance: Udo was originally supposed to be a drug addict, but this fact was elided with a few cuts, so that what remained was, if possible, a less extravagant monster. Udo's abnormality, conveyed by the sputtering, psychotic laughter that Widmark adopted as his dominant trait (and reinforced with makeup and wardrobe touches, such as shaving his eyebrows and affecting a certain dandyism) was required to counteract the public's traditional repugnance for informers and turncoats. And fortunately, Hathaway was not a director given to inflating his material.

Before Dassin went symbol-happy in *Night and the City*, the two modes of gangster *film noir*, the realistic and the allegorical, were nobly represented by Hathaway and Siodmak respectively. Like the Italian neorealists very much admired at the time, Hathaway sought to preserve the integrity of natural locations: a street scene was a street scene. On the other hand, Siodmak could not help but project his cultured, visionary imagination on police precincts, subway stations, and tenements: the street scene as a medieval mystery play. Handed similar material and milieu, however, Siodmak made Hathaway seem blunt and unimaginative, qualities that were to become the hallmark of the fifties. No wonder Hathaway's stock rose through the following decade, while Siodmak never again seemed to hit his stride as he had with *film noir*.

The law cannot help the noble stool pigeon (Victor Mature) any more than it can touch the sadistic gunman (Richard Widmark) in *Kiss of Death*, 1947. *Twentieth Century-Fox*

Siodmak directed *Cry of the City* (1948) for Twentieth Century-Fox, with locations in New York and Los Angeles, but most of the wet-night street shots were done at the studio. The film was conceived as a follow-up to *Kiss of Death* and was meant to exploit the rediscovered potential of Victor Mature. The story came from a novel, *The Chair for Martin Rome* by Henry Edward Helseth, adapted by Richard Murphy, who had proven his skill (in *Boomerang*) at placing character and situation in specific locales. *Cry of the City* is related to *Manhattan Melodrama* and *Angels with Dirty Faces* in theme, although Sternberg's *Sergeant Madden* seems closer to its sensibility. Lieutenant Candella (Mature) and Martin Rome (Richard Conte) are both slum-bred Italian-Americans who had the same breaks, yet the former grew up to be a police detective and the latter a hardened killer. The Cain and Abel motif is wittily summarized in an exchange:

MARTIN ROME: How much money do you make a week?
CANDELLA: $94.43.
MARTIN ROME: Did you ever go to Florida a week, bet $200 on a horse?
CANDELLA: No, but I sleep nights.
MARTIN ROME: OK, you played it your way and I played it mine.

In *Cry of the City*, Candella's obsession to put Martin Rome behind bars and keep him there suggests that his commitment to the law cannot be ratified as long as Rome is free to remind him of his other, darker self. Siodmak elaborated on the correspondence between the two characters throughout the film, and, although Conte made Martin Rome the most charismatic gangster of the forties, a worthy successor to Robinson, Cagney, and Bogart, the film never contemplated an uplifting truce or a show of friendly devotion. In the climax, Candella must invoke the power of the law he represents to bring himself to shoot Martin Rome, to whom the dying gesture of flicking open a switchblade appears the most natural of reflexes. Rome is killed as he flees from a church, which seems a pointed reversal of the gangster's death and spiritual redemption in a thirties film like *The Roaring Twenties*.

But *Cry of the City* is rich rather than bleak, with every actor, however minor, illuminating the character and motives of the two heroes (Conte's feat is to keep up the fascination of the deadly, narcissistic Rome.) Siodmak manipulates our sympathies in the same manner that Rome manipulates the feelings of those he comes in contact with: the spinster nurse (Betty Garde) who consents to act as a go-between, the trusty (Walter Baldwin) who regains his self-esteem long enough to help Rome escape from a hospital, the former girlfriend (Shelley Winters) who shelters him, and the illegal refugee doctor (Konstantin Shayne) who tends his wounds. Each is overtaken by the law, in the person of Candella, and each is duly punished. Not everyone is a pushover, however, and Rome has to contend with characters more hellish than himself, like an unctuous shyster (Berry Kroeger) and a giant of a masseuse (Hope Emerson), both of whom seem to gratify Siodmak's weakness for gargoyles.

Perfectly self-sustaining genre films like *Cry of the City* and *Kiss of Death,* which transcended the facts and figures that inspired them, did not allude directly to the realities of postwar crime. It was left to a *March of Time* documentary entitled *The American Cop* (1946) to make the first reference to the booming crime rate of that period. The same year, Hoover made public statements attributing the rise in crime to juvenile delinquency as spawned by the war and the ensuing lack of parental control, particularly in fast-growing industrial cities. In 1948, *The Street with No Name* became the first Hollywood feature to come to grips with the headlines. The script, by Harry Kleiner, was based on cases from the files of the FBI, which extended every courtesy to Twentieth Century-Fox, including permission to photograph scenes at the training academy in Quantico, Virginia, and at Washington headquarters. As he had earlier, in *The House on 92nd Street,* Lloyd Nolan played Hoover's *homme de confiance,* while the great man himself remained off-screen behind the imposing door of his inner office. *The Street with No Name* was an update of *G-Men*—William Keighley, who had won the bureau's trust with that picture, was borrowed from Warner Brothers to direct again. This time, the film carried Hoover's personal endorsement: "The street in which gangsterism and crime flourish has no name and runs across the nation. . . . An alert and vigilant America will make for a secure America."

The official FBI line was immediately apparent in *The Street with No Name* when Nolan, the official spokesman for the bureau, instructed us: "We know that gangsterism is returning since the war. Juvenile delinquents have grown into criminals more intelligent, more dangerous, than the old-time gangsters." The Stiles gang in the film, however, is fictional, and their methods, described by Nolan as "scientific," do not appear so different from those of the caper planners in *The Killers.* (The implication was that the younger generation of hoodlums who had the benefit of a middle-class education posed a greater threat than the underprivileged gangsters of the thirties.) The film opens with a bank robbery and night-club holdup during which a woman is shot. The FBI then selects and trains a youthful agent (Mark Stevens) to infiltrate the Stiles gang and gain the confidence of its leader (Richard Widmark). This plot device—at least as old as *The Gangsters and the Girl* (1914)—became standard formula for most films produced under the aegis of the various federal and state agencies.

Dramatically, the imposture never fails to work, for a parallel between the procedures of crime and crime detection is established, with daring displays of cunning from each side. What amounted to a dual role was provided for the actor playing the undercover agent. Other departments granted more freedom of characterization—the agent could even be a Mexican working with U.S. Immigration, as in *Border Incident* (1949). But not the FBI which, at the time, preferred to have agents portrayed as one-hundred-percent, simon-pure Americans. (Was it because James Cagney was shown hanging out in a night club that *G-Men* had not attained official status?) The Treasury Department allowed the hero of *T-Men* (1948) to undergo a severe beating while carrying out his mission; the unblemished image of the federal agent made audiences sense a profanation if anyone dared to lay a finger on a G-man. No wonder this rather pallid figure had such a tough time holding his own against a new and complex breed of criminals bearing little resemblance to the crude Barton McLane types of yesteryear.

In *The Street with No Name,* the moment that Richard Widmark made his entrance—a raffish young man munching on an apple—the picture was his: "Here, buy yourself a closetful of clothes," he tells the undercover agent as he passes him a few large bills, "I like my boys to look sharp;" and a flirtatious complicity is established that might not be quite what Hoover had in mind. The Widmark character was a hypochondriac who lived in fear of drafts and who staged slapping, screaming bouts with his girlfriend (Barbara Lawrence). Such quirks never fail to enrich a role, and Widmark was so personable that he got through the picture without giggling once, and he still overshadowed the more modest performance of agent Stevens.

In principle at least, the new police-procedural film attempted to take up where the *Crime Does Not Pay* series had left off a few months earlier. The anticrime semidocumentary had to hold its own against the encroaching darkness of *film noir:* the straightforward style and simplified motives it demanded had barely survived the war. Television, as it happened, was more receptive to its highly moralistic tone, in shows like "Racket Squad," "Highway Patrol," "The Line Up," and especially "Dragnet," which borrowed its approach from *He Walked by Night* (1948) with the same nonchalance with which it pirated Miklos Rosza's ominous four-note leitmotif from *The Killers* for its signature music.

Nonetheless, the moment audiences first squinted through John Alton's camera work in *T-Men* and *He Walked by Night* (1948), they must have realized that verisimilitude was doomed. An establishing montage of documentary scenes opened *T-Men,* while a narrator reeled off figures about the high percentage of felons sent to the pen by U.S. Treasury agents, and the audience was set up to accept what followed as authentic. But most of the scenes in both films were mannered and claustrophobic, framed for tension rather than naturalism, and shot from above- or below-normal eye level. These two films—plus *Raw Deal* (1948) and *Port of New York* (1949)—were produced by Eagle Lion, a short-lived company put on the map by its crime movies. The Eagle Lion house style featured the most flamboyant lighting and camera angles of the period despite, or maybe because of, budget restrictions. This style was the joint creation of an inventive, forcibly fast-working cinematographer, the Hungarian John Alton, and of Anthony Mann, who directed *T-Men, Raw Deal,* and reportedly parts of *He Walked by Night,* and who would become a major American stylist during the fifties. Mann and Alton eventually moved to Metro-Goldwyn-Mayer, where they continued their association in two films along the same lines as the Eagle Lion product.

In most of the titles mentioned above, the viewer was treated to two conflicting films for the price of one. Scenes demonstrating the process of

investigation were evenly lit, orderly, and reassuring; night became the province of the aberrant wrongdoer, a symbolic place suggesting the diseased condition of modern cities and of American life in general. The police-procedural film works with this polarity—seasoned professional lawman versus vicious creep—and each world is so defined by the characters' activities that there is little room for sentiment. In *T-Men,* a well-trained undercover agent (Alfred Ryder), on the trail of a counterfeit gang, dutifully denies his own wife so as not to give himself away. He is found out anyway and murdered; a teammate (Dennis O'Keefe) looks on as he is shot, repressing his anguish but unable to intervene, for the mission comes first.

Obviously, a new and greater urgency was manifest at the end of the forties—the cold war was intensifying with the fall of Czechoslovakia and the Berlin crisis—and a new, official hard line was implicit in the narration that summed up the police-procedural film. Counterfeiters, pushers, and alien smugglers, who gummed up the works in a great democracy, were for all intents and purposes aiding the real public enemies of the postwar period —the Communists. The criminal without politics was only filling the void between Nazis and Reds.

The dehumanizing paranoia of the Red Scare, which saw otherness as a threat, was portended in *He Walked by Night,* in which the fanatical, introverted killer (Richard Basehart) might as well have been a conspirator. An electronics expert without family, friends, or underworld affiliations, he remains as much an enigma to the police as to the viewer—although we, at least, get to intrude on his privacy and even watch him stoically remove a bullet from his torso. It is only through the efforts of the Los Angeles citizenry that the police can assemble a composite portrait—as clear as a passport picture, a *foreign* passport, since the killer's apartness has made him suspect to normal Americans of every ethnic group and social class.

Inevitably, the HUAC hearings also affected film content. Behind Eric Johnston's official assertion that the MPAA was ready to resume the fight for democracy, one senses a gradual suppression of freedom of speech. All the more extraordinary then that films like *Force of Evil* and *Key Largo* were made in 1948, the first year of the blacklist. Both of these films used the crime genre to make a larger statement about the need to preserve or regain one's integrity, a possible paraphrase for the actual situation of liberal and/or left-wing filmmakers.

Ostensibly, *Force of Evil* was an exposé of the numbers racket, an illegal form of lottery thriving on the small bets of millions of people and operating from clandestine "banks" scattered throughout big cities. That the film failed to illuminate how the racket worked was due in part to the

Archetypal situations in the police procedure film. Undercover agent Dennis O'Keefe watches in anguish as his fellow T-man Alfred Ryder is shot by counterfeiter Charles McGraw, so as not to give away his true identity, in *T-Men,* 1948. The inevitable triumph of the authorities: narcotics smuggler Yul Brynner in the hands of the Coast Guard in *Port of New York,* 1949. *Eagle Lion* cutting of some twenty minutes of footage prior to its release (as a Christmas attraction, yet no file is more imbued with anxiety and guilt), but also was possibly due to a looming subtext cluttered with issues, and dialogue so self-consciously lilting and repetitious as to sound like a lost Clifford Odets play. What Abraham Polonsky said about his previous screenplay for *Body and Soul* also applies to *Force of Evil:* it is "a folk tale from the Empire City."

The picture was independently produced by John Garfield and by the director, Polonsky, who also coscripted with Ira Wolfert, author of the novel, *Tucker's People,* which had served as point of departure. The hero is Joe Morse (Garfield), a shrewd, ambitious lawyer who has sold out his legal know-how and principles to a corporate racketeer named Tucker (Roy Roberts). A takeover of New York's numbers banks has been planned as part of Tucker's expansion plan; the most expeditious way to force the smaller banks out of business is to fix the July 4 lottery so that the winning number comes out 776, which is favored by millions of superstitious bettors. A human adding machine, "Two by Two" (Sid Tomack), will see to it that the numbers are juggled beyond probability.

Joe Morse would like to rise in Tucker's empire and take his older brother, Leo (Thomas Gomez), with him. But Leo proves a liability; not only does he always seem to be addressing God with rhetorical questions, but he runs a neighborhood numbers bank and stubbornly refuses to merge. Leo is a bit more honest than Joe—his ambitions go no farther than his block, and he respects the little people who are his customers and employees, while Tucker, from his penthouse and Wall Street office, sees the people only in terms of nickels and dimes adding up to a fortune.

Early in the film, there are shots of Wall Street in the morning sunlight, dark concrete slabs crowding and stifling old, genteel Trinity Church, a metaphor (less obvious then than now) for American big business. And, like all small-time businessmen, Leo is doomed to disappear. Knowing that his bank will be wiped out, Joe tries to get him to sell it before July 4, but Leo refuses, bellowing: "I want to see my own face in the mirror, not yours." Eventually, Joe cannot even save Leo's life, so he turns against Tucker and his silent underworld partner (Paul Fix) and kills them both. Then, as the film ends, he and Leo's devoted secretary (Beatrice Pearson) find Leo's body dumped at the foot of the George Washington Bridge, an early dawn scene allegorized by David Raksin's "regeneration" theme and some of the most colorful phrasing hitherto heard in a soundtrack: "I felt bad there," recites Joe, "I was there to find my brother. I kept going down and down, to the bottom of the world. To find my brother. I found my brother down there."

So far, so florid. According to Polonsky, for the picture to obtain the Code seal it had to make explicit that Joe Morse was going directly from the end credits to the D.A.'s office to pledge his cooperation. Extra lines were added: "If a man has lived his life to end like this, like rubbish, something was horrible, and had to be ended one way or another. I decided to

The numbers racket feeds on the nickels and dimes of the little people. John Garfield visits his brother's illegal "bank" in *Force of Evil,* **1949.** *Metro-Goldwyn-Mayer*

help." These words must have left a bitter taste in Garfield's mouth, and not only because they meant that his personal project had been tampered with. At a time when, as Muriel Rukeyser recalls, "personal and public treachery were in the air," Morse's acquiescence might well have been construed as readiness to testify before HUAC. In 1951, Garfield did appear before the committee as a "friendly witness," an experience that took its toll in health and self-esteem: he died the following year without betraying his friends. As for Polonsky, it was twenty years before he could direct again. "We had the right feelings," said Polonsky, reliving the witch hunts years later.* Like its makers, however, *Force of Evil* appears to have suffered but retained its poetic convictions. It was unusual for a Hollywood movie of 1948 to advertise, if ever so subtly, the politics of its director—there certainly was no reference to them in the reviews of the period.

* Interview by William Pechter: *Film Quarterly,* Spring 1962.

Like the prewar playwrights Polonsky brings to mind—Odets, and Irwin Shaw at the time of *The Gentle People*—he could be verbose but flavorful. On the other hand, Maxwell Anderson was merely verbose, and his 1939 play, *Key Largo*, even shorn of its blank-verse tirades by Richard Brooks and John Huston (who also directed) and updated to the late forties, remains a tired melodrama of ideas, a high-falutin' version of *Casablanca* or *To Have and Have Not*. Bogart starred in the by-then familiar role of a cynic forced to fight for ideals he professes to have renounced. A war veteran without a will to fight, he is ultimately compelled to act against the mobsters who have taken over a remote Florida hotel, "to cleanse the world of ancient evils," as the script portentously asserts.

The gunmen are led by Johnny Rocco, a deported gang leader illegally reentering the country and intent on regaining his former power. "Rocco was supposed to represent a sort of evil flower of reaction," *Time* magazine quoted Huston. "In other words we are headed for the same kind of world we had before, even down to the ganglords." To personify this living relic of the thirties, Huston cast Edward G. Robinson in a reprise of his infamous role in *Little Caesar*. Not even mobsters, however, can go home again. The character had lost its childlike innocence and reached the stage of aggressive sexuality. Huston provided Rocco with an alcoholic mistress (Claire Trevor) to slap around and a wistful-widow heroine (Lauren Bacall) to lust after. Rocco whispers obscenities in the widow's ear—Rico Bandello, one imagines, was above such things—and we are expected to recoil, as if this lack of respect for womanhood were the definitive outrage.

Elsewhere, the tactics that Rocco would employ to bring back the old days sound as hopelessly *passé* as Bogart's decision to take up arms seems ill-timed for such a confused, hysterical period as the cold war. One of Rocco's lines must have tickled Robinson's sense of irony: Rocco tells of his humiliation—he had been kicked out of the country, "as an undesirable alien, like I was a dirty Red or something." *Key Largo* brought Robinson back to Warner Brothers after six years of uneven work for other studios and a brush with the blacklist. But it is never made clear why an anachronistic gangster would make a better symbol of fascist resurgence than would a World War II veteran's reconversion to the militaristic line. (Some of Bogart's concern for the aimlessness and political corruption of postwar America sounds suspiciously close to John Birch.) Although Robinson's snarl was a welcome sight in 1948, his returning crime czar seems never to have heard of corporate rackets, or people like Tucker (in *Force of Evil*) who could afford paneled offices and employ the best legal minds. Any anti-Hoover liberal could have told him that the FBI was massing forces against the Red Menace, leaving only a fraction of manpower to keep an eye on the Syndicate.

A year after *Key Largo*, Cagney followed Robinson's lead and returned to Warner Brothers to play the lead in *White Heat* (1949), his first gangster role since *The Roaring Twenties* a decade before. Whereas Huston paralyzed Robinson with synthetic conversation, Raoul Walsh kept Cagney on the move as they reviewed every development of the crime film since the war. (Walsh, it is rumored, had also directed the climactic gun battle in *Key Largo,* which was mercifully short on words.) Heavy, jowly, and looking every one of his fifty years, Cagney's Cody Jarrett still bore some remnants of the feisty street punk of old, but neither history nor society could now be blamed for his delinquency. Cody was a mother-fixated epileptic, and through Cody's paranoia, Walsh and the screenwriters (Ben Roberts and Ivan Goff) recapitulated the major trends of the forties. The film featured a couple of "scientific" heists, a tight penitentiary sequence, and many location scenes handled with the off-the-cuff skill expected from someone like Walsh, who was filming in the Bowery as early as 1915.

In *White Heat,* the tired cliché of the gangster who breaks his poor old mother's heart is taken for a ride. Cody's Ma (Margaret Wycherly) pampers him, nurses him through epileptic fits, and in everyway fosters her boy's career in crime. It could be a tale of motherly love, as told by Ma Barker to her brood between bank jobs—a mobster's best friend is his mother, certainly not his moll. Cody's wife, a vixen named Verna (Virginia Mayo) takes up with Big Ed (Steve Cochran), another gang member, the moment that Cody goes to jail. On visiting day, Ma Jarrett comes to prison and tells all. When Cody warns her to watch herself, she drawls back in her flinty Yankee voice: "Any time I can't handle someone like Big Ed, I'll know I'm getting old."

Aware of Cody's dependency on the old woman, the Treasury Department plants an undercover man in his cell, so that when Cody suffers his next seizure, Hank Fallon (Edmond O'Brien) will be there to rub his neck. And Ma proves no match for Verna and Big Ed after all: Cody learns of her death at mess time and goes spectacularly berserk. Again, Fallon provides understanding, and a transference begins to take place. When Cody crashes out soon after, he takes Fallon along. Cody is so fond of him that he decides Fallon should get the same take as the late Mrs. Jarrett.

Walsh made a perfectly *noir* Western, *Pursued,* two years before, and would approach *The Enforcer,* a gangster film, from a more somber point of view a year later. The only real darkness in *White Heat,* however, is in the unusually abrasive humor—each one of Cody's outrages travesties a similar situation in *The Public Enemy.* Cody munches on a chicken leg as he pumps bullets into a car trunk, the informer locked therein having complained of a lack of air. A symbolic grapefruit seems to hang over Verna, whose two-timing is rendered obnoxious by the way she spits out her chewing gum before embracing Big Ed. Our expectations are wittily disappointed when Cody, having disposed of Big Ed, gallantly offers Verna his arm, later to dismiss her with: "Go read your comic books. Good girl." Cody's account of the Trojan Horse episode—which inspires him to plan a daring heist—is a vernacular event.

Cagney still had a couple of gangster roles in him, although neither of the same caliber as Cody Jarrett. In *White Heat,* the actor and director seem willing to go the limit, sometimes at the expense of the actor's dignity. In the mess-hall sequence, news of Ma's death travels down the table from a lip-reading convict, who acts as a semaphore, along the row of prisoners until it reaches Cody; and the inaudible whispers seem like sparks from a fuse rapidly approaching its end. As the grief-crazed Cody hurls himself on the table, the previous camera movement is reversed; china and cutlery scattering along his passage, as if a grotesque salmon were swimming up-stream. A cut to an overhead long-shot transforms the dining hall into a playing field in which guards attempt to tackle Cody's blind run. The "fish" motif returns as Cody is carried aloft, kicking, screaming, like some reluctant dinner course.

The apocalyptic fireworks that conclude *White Heat* suit Walsh's penchant for generational disasters—like the Crash in *The Roaring Twenties*—as much as Cody's delusions of grandeur. Betrayed by Fallon—his surrogate mother—Cody is surrounded by the police atop a gas tank in a chemical plant. Wounded by Fallon's long-range rifle fire, he still refuses to drop. "Made it, Ma, top of the world!" he bellows maniacally as he fires into the tank which explodes like the A-bomb on Bikini atoll. The final image is a mushroom cloud, testament to the ultimate madness in history, not just in the forties. When Manny Farber summed up Walsh's cinematic personality in *Artforum* (November 1971), he was more accurately writing Cody's epitaph: "He [Walsh] is like his volatile, instinctual, not-too-smart characters who, when they are at their most genuine, are unreclaimable, terrifying loners, perhaps past their peak and going nowhere."

It was around this time that both Nicholas Ray and Joseph H. Lewis first gained attention—Ray with *They Live by Night* (1948), Lewis with *Gun Crazy* (1950), two *films noirs* that shared a remote inspiration in the Bonnie and Clyde legend, and a more recent one in Fritz Lang's *You Only Live Once*. There are further analogies. The justly celebrated four-minute take of a bank robbery (with the camera in the getaway car) from *Gun Crazy* had a precedent in a similar, if less spectacular, sequence in *They Live by Night*. Both Ray and Lewis became cult directors in France before being recognized back home, and their careers seem to have ended prematurely. Later work, however, indicated that Ray's best and most personal films were outside genre. *In a Lonely Place* (1950), *Rebel Without a Cause* (1955), and *Bigger than Life* (1956) were strikingly original works only marginally related to the psychological thriller, the juvenile-delinquent film, or science-fiction. Lewis, on the other hand, remained the perfect genre stylist, working in Westerns and gangster films until 1958, after which he moved to television, which was by then more receptive to genre than was commercial film-production.

Ray's early pictures, *They Live by Night* and *Knock on Any Door* (1949), took as their hero the persecuted innocent-at-heart whose delinquency and untimely death are preordained by a harsh environment and a vindictive society that demands punishment for a first, youthful offense. Even before the credits appear in *They Live by Night*, hero and heroine (Farley Granger and Cathy O'Donnell) are shown in a gloomy valentine behind a title that reads: "This boy . . . this girl . . . have not been properly introduced to this world of ours." In *Knock on Any Door,* Nick Romano (John Derek) is traced back to a pristine, choir-boy (literally) state of grace. Nick's motto is "Live fast, die young, and have a good-looking corpse." Ray's attitude in these two crime pictures is bracketed by the two statements: the unstable seventh-heaven lyricism perpetually undercut by fleeting hints of doom just round the corner. Trains whistle in the night, messengers of gloom appear (in *They Live by Night*), like the seedy justice of the peace (Ian Wolfe) who marries the fugitive couple in "a class-B wedding," and the embittered housewife (Helen Craig) who informs on them. A bad-omen scene in *Knock on Any Door* focuses on the making of *crêpes flambées* at a wedding party, with the newlyweds' hopes going up symbolically in smoke.

The source of *They Live by Night,* a Depression novel by Edward Anderson published as *Thieves Like Us* in 1937, was much funnier and tougher than Ray's version. (A 1974 remake by Robert Altman retained the original title and period, and was closer to the spirit of the book.) For instance, Ray's film took pains to exonerate Bowie, the rustic bank robber, from any heartfelt participation in crime; Anderson (and Altman) accepted him as a convicted murderer with a certain enthusiasm about his chosen way of life. Ray's whitewash—dictated in part by the censor—removed any notion of an individual flaw in Bowie's character, turning him and his girl into Romeo and Juliet of the sticks, assailed on one side by grotesque ex-fellow convicts and by the invisible yet inescapable network of the law on the other.

Everything that was implicit in Ray's direction of *They Live by Night* was dogmatically, tiresomely articulated in *Knock on Any Door,* by Humphrey Bogart in the role of a liberal lawyer defending a Chicago slum tough charged with killing a policeman. A slam-bank robbery sequence in and around an elevated-subway station opens the film; thereon, every stock situation of the they-made-me-a-criminal type is revisited in a series of flashbacks narrated by Bogart. (The film is no Bogart vehicle: his role is secondary to John Derek's.) The stages of social decay are predictable: poolrooms and bad company; a stint in reform school, which brutalizes and hardens him; a pathetic marriage that ends with the gentle wife (Allene Roberts) putting her head in the oven. Romano is too aware of his sociological implications to be an effective character—like James T. Farrell's Studs Lonigan, who shared with Romano the Chicago slum experience—and social significance is too laggard a notion for the late forties. The *film noir* approach was more subtle and also more effective, and Ray would waste no time in delivering a prime example in *In a Lonely Place* one year later. At the beginning of his career, his direction was already far ahead of his subject.

By contrast, the crime films of Joseph H. Lewis—especially *Gun Crazy* and the later *The Big Combo* (1955)—stamp him as a legitimate, if personal, choice as the genre director par excellence. Lewis's potential was already apparent in *The Undercover Man* (1949), the only film to slip under the line when the Capone clause was appended to the Code. Purportedly based on the revelations of one Frank J. Wilson, a retired Secret Service agent and presumably a member of the Eliot Ness group that garnered evidence against Capone and made his indictment possible, the film complied with the new Thirteenth Section by failing to establish period and locale, and by showing only the back of the neck and hat of a ganglord referred to as the Big Fellow. There is a strong suspicion that *The Undercover Man* passed the censor (at the script stage) because it contained an unabashed eulogy for the American way of life—which was put in the mouth of an Italian-immigrant mother—at a time when the industry was being told, in no uncertain terms, to toe the patriotic line.*

The producer, Robert Rossen, brought Lewis to the project and assigned Sidney Boehm, a former crime reporter, as screenwriter. Together, Lewis and Boehm staked out a territory that the fifties would thoroughly explore, most successfully in Fritz Lang's *The Big Heat,* also scripted by Boehm. In *The Undercover Man,* crime was an almost abstract evil which, left unchecked, would reach out and pollute the American family, and the message was that involvement in the fight against crime (or any other form of anti-Americanism) must begin at home. At another level, the apathetic taxpayer was encouraged to take a stand, run a risk, and deliver information to the law-enforcement bodies—an appeal to stir the public to civic responsibility which echoed that of *The Star Witness* at another moment of national crisis.

Fortunately there was no trace of didacticism in the picture. It was the sort of genre exercise that a studio like Columbia turned out regularly on a restricted budget, in black and white, and with a contract star heading a modest supporting cast. In *The Undercover Man*—a misleading title, as it turns out—Glenn Ford, as a federal investigator, quietly plods through reams of paperwork, after incriminating proof that would enable the Treasury Department to prosecute the Big Fellow. When Warren (Ford) makes a rendezvous with a stool pigeon, the man is gunned down in broad daylight, and witnesses to the killing are intimidated into silence. A "front man" for the gang is shot before he can testify. The suicide of a crooked cop further discourages Warren, so that when the gang's mouthpiece hints at reprisals against Warren's wife, he is almost ready to resign his job. Then, the old-world mother and all-American daughter of the slain "front man" teach him a lesson in courage by producing a ledger containing the necessary evidence to crack the case wide open.

The action sequences revealed Lewis in perfect control, and later, more prestigious, films, from *On the Waterfront* to *The French Connection,* would find inspiration in the trim, violent scenes in *The Undercover Man.* In one, Warren and the suave, corpulent shyster (Barry Kelley) are threatened by

---

* Addressing the Screen Writers Guild in 1948, Eric Johnston laid down the law: "We'll have no more *Grapes of Wrath.* We'll have no more *Tobacco Roads.* We'll have no more films that show the seamy side of American life. We'll have no more pictures that deal with labor strikes. We'll have no more pictures that show a banker as a villain." Johnston later recanted in part by allowing *The Grapes of Wrath* to be exported worldwide.

an oncoming car in an alley, and, without being unduly explicit, Lewis makes the viewer cringe with the awareness that the shyster is doomed by his vulnerable bulk. In another, a street chase appears to take flight via a marvelous tracking shot of the hunted man (Anthony Caruso) dodging pushcarts and unconcerned passers-by, and the chase fades out on a shot of his little girl (Joan Lazer) staring in horror at his body sprawled among the trash cans. During this breathless pursuit, Burnett Guffey's camera made the familiar Columbia backlot teem with the bustle and breath of a slum on a summer day.

Lewis's audacity and total commitment were much more evident in his next film, *Gun Crazy*, which was produced by the King brothers in the hope of scoring another *Dillinger*. Those connected with the making of *Gun Crazy* disclaim any conscious intent to revive the exploits of Bonnie and Clyde on the screen, but there were a number of covert suggestions—such as the heroine's bonnet, which recalls a famous snapshot, and a peculiar equivalence between the names of hero and heroine, Barton Tare and Annie Laurie Starr, and those of Parker and Barrow. The screenplay was the work of Dalton Trumbo, then blacklisted; the credits on the film mention Millard Kaufman, a sympathetic "cover" for Trumbo, and MacKinlay Kantor, who wrote the original story. Although written in anonymity as a not-too-profitable commission, the script was one of Trumbo's best—pithy, well constructed, and, for once, truly dissentient. From Trumbo's script, Lewis made a definitive statement on the American myth of the gun.

In an impressionistic sequence, Bart Tare is introduced as a young kid obsessed with firearms who grows up to become a superb marksman totally lacking the killer instinct. After a stint as an army instructor, Bart (John Dall) returns to his California town and meets Annie Laurie Starr (Peggy Cummins) at a local carnival, where she is the star sharpshooter. Laurie and Bart marry and attempt to lead a normal life; when their money runs out, however, Laurie convinces Bart that their unique talent should be exploited. Bart's scruples are overcome by his infatuation, and together they commit a series of robberies and holdups. Inevitably, Laurie shoots and kills two people at the scene of a payroll robbery that was to have been their last. Now the object of an interstate manhunt, the two return to Bart's hometown and hide in the nearby marshes, where they are besieged by the local police. Rather than allow Laurie to shoot his boyhood friends, Bart turns killer for the first and last time. With Laurie lying dead at his side, he offers himself as a willing target.

Lewis turned the rich, pervasive gun imagery into the currency of passion for Laurie and Bart. During their carnival marksmanship contest, gunplay substitutes for foreplay as Laurie shoots aflame a crown of matches on Bart's head. "Almost killed a man once," she says flirtatiously, taking aim. "Shot a little low." She misses once and loses the match to Bart, whose score is perfect. Recruited for the act, Bart is made to wear a faintly ridiculous buckskin outfit that matches Laurie's Annie Oakley costume. They become sideshow attractions, freaks enacting an erotic ritual in which guns are like physical extensions. As they take aim, someone remarks that "they look at each other like a couple of wild animals." Target and object of desire have become indivisible.

Intimate moments in drab hotel rooms are fraught with sexual tension, as Laurie wheedles acquiescence from Bart. Later, when they agree to separate in order to avoid arrest, an overhead shot frames the two cars as they start off in opposite directions then reenter the shot as the camera cranes down on the two figures reaching to embrace in the middle of the highway, their cars stalled by the wayside, themselves incapable of breaking away even for the sake of safety. As the law closes in at the end, Bart sums up a world of erotic obsession which is *film noir* at its most genuine: "Laurie, no matter what happens, I wouldn't have it any other way."

In the early fifties, *film noir* declined and was replaced by a harsher, more pragmatic sensibility that found esthetic expression in the technical assertiveness of color, wide screen, and stereophonic sound rather than in a rich gradation of blacks and whites. There were a few late examples: films like *Black Widow* (1954) and *Slightly Scarlet* (1956) even proved that the *noir* vision could survive CinemaScope and color. But it was Joseph H. Lewis

The most lyrical and erotic of the films based on the career of Bonnie and Clyde: John Dall and Peggy Cummins in *Gun Crazy*, 1950, young, in love, and killing people. As time runs out, they are confronted with a domestic tableau, presided over by Anabel Shaw. *United Artists*

who delivered, in 1955, a last valentine from the forties, *The Big Combo*, from an original screenplay by Philip Yordan. Reviewers and the public, however, were disoriented by the film's blunt iconography and by John Alton's baroque camera work, dismissing it as an old-fashioned genre picture; some were offended by its brutality when, in retrospect, it is precisely the manner in which Lewis elided the violence that today seems remarkable.

The Big Combo is a tangle of personal obsessions in which the fate of the characters is resolved in terms of their individual motivations and foibles. The rivalry between Lieutenant Diamond (Cornel Wilde) and Mr. Brown (Richard Conte) is conducted as a private feud, not in the impersonal terms of the law versus crime. Diamond tries to break Brown's hold on the city as money-man in the Combination, a euphemism for the eastern branch of the Syndicate; but, aside from this civic crusade, he would break Brown's hold on Susan Lowell (Jean Wallace), whose enslavement is based on the mobster's charisma, as Brown wastes no time in reminding Diamond: "You think it's money. It's not. It's personality."

Brown looks and acts like a successful executive, communicating with Diamond through an abject yes-man, McClure (Brian Donlevy), a former big shot in the Combination who has failed to adapt to the changing times. Brown has effaced his shady past along with his Italian origins: he represents the new breed of mobster who resorts to violence only when every other form of persuasion fails. "I'm trying to run an impersonal business," he ad-

Lee Van Cleef and Earl Holliman as homosexual gangsters in *The Big Combo,* 1955, which carried the ambiguities and obsessions of the *film noir* into the fifties. *Allied Artists*

monishes the old-fashioned McClure, "killing is very personal." It follows, through true *noir* poetic justice, that Brown must be undone by personal motives and not through the impersonal process of the law.

The theme of jealousy was central to *The Big Combo,* and Yordan illustrated it with sexual allusions that played on the opposition of power and frustration. Diamond's affair with a stripper (Helene Stanton) who works across the street from his hotel seems nothing more than a passionless, convenient arrangement. In contrast, a seduction scene between Susan and Brown—a one-take track forward to frame her face in close-up as Brown disappears below the frame—went as far as the Code would allow in 1955. It is Susan's jealousy of Brown's wife that sets in motion the events that ultimately destroy the gangster's power. But the most ironic character twist is reserved for Brown's bodyguard-executioners, Fante (Lee Van Cleef) and Mingo (Earl Holliman), who are devoted to each other, work in tandem, share the same bedroom, and in general behave like a well-adjusted homosexual couple.

In *Gun Crazy,* Lewis had based his complex *mise-en-scène* on the visual correspondence of marksman to target, switching viewpoints at key moments. (One such cut, from Laurie about to fire to a terrified woman supervisor about to be shot, jolted the viewer with the realization that Laurie, unlike Bart, was a born killer.) The shifts of perspective in *The Big Combo* were aural rather than visual. Throughout the story, McClure's hearing aid establishes his impotence in relation to Brown: inserted in Diamond's ear and plugged to a radio, it creates a novel form of torture that leaves no physical mark on the victim. Diamond twists in pain, but we only hear dialogue at a normal voice level. Delivering the treacherous McClure to Fante and Mingo for execution, Brown disconnects the hearing aid in a mock-generous gesture: "You won't have to hear the bullets." Cut to the submachine guns blazing away in dead silence.

In every successful film, the individual contributions of director, writer, and cameraman must join without a trace. *The Big Combo* was so secure within the gangster-film tradition that it could enjoy the luxury of abstraction. Alton could dispense with décor and define space with a pool of light, as in the scenes set in a fog-bound airfield. Yordan gave free rein to his invention, knowing that by then gangland was psychological terrain. Lewis could charge two-shots with such tension that he could dispense with the usual violence. Such chances paid off because the filmmakers were aware that genre could fill in the empty spaces.

8. The Syndicate

Everybody had different theories as to why the FBI really had to be brought
into organized crime kicking and screaming. Some of the ex-agents felt that
Hoover didn't, first of all, want to get into it because his statistics would go
down. . . . Some of them said that he didn't want to put his agents into a
position where they could be corrupted, have them dealing with gamblers and
hoods. . . . Others said that he got in a big pissing match with Harry Anslinger
over at Narcotics . . . and Anslinger had the Mafia coming out of the sewers
the same way Hoover had the Communists coming out of the sewers. So
Hoover got himself locked in saying there was no Mafia.

— William Hundley, quoted by Ovid Demaris in *The Director*
(New York: Harper's Magazine Press, 1975)

ALTHOUGH the revelations of Abe Reles in 1940 left no doubt about the existence of a national crime syndicate, history and politics were to intervene in favor of the underworld; and the notion of such a network, with an executive arm in every major city, its own killer force, its own undertakers, cemeteries, and technical jargon, would have to wait a decade to be clarified for, and assimilated by, the public. Reles had served Murder, Inc., for years, and the deposition he delivered nonstop for twelve grueling days, and which filled twenty-one stenographer's notebooks, accounted in full for some eighty murders and furnished evidence on another thousand. And Reles reeled out a new roster of names that included Albert Anastasia, Joe Adonis, and Bugsy Siegel and implicated most prominently Lepke Buchalter, the man responsible for the original concept and smooth functioning of the murder-by-contract racket.

Lepke was then serving a sentence in Sing Sing, but it was still possible for him to mobilize Murder, Inc., from his cell, and he had many potential witnesses liquidated in the months that elapsed between Reles's confession and the trial—a period referred to by crime reporters with underworld connections as the Big Heat. Buchalter also put out a fifty-thousand-dollar "contract" on Reles, who had been offered immunity by Assistant District Attorney Burton B. Turkus. A year earlier, when the heat had become too intense for the Syndicate to continue operations, Lepke had been offered as a scapegoat in a strategy that recalled the underworld's 1935 purge of Dutch Schultz. Like Schultz, Buchalter had become a top risk and was deemed expendable. It was a measure of the times and the new policies that, instead of being executed, he was compelled to surrender to Hoover, with Walter Winchell acting as intermediary.

Lepke was a prize catch, but Turkus lined up Anastasia and Siegel for indictment, preparing his case around the Reles testimony. Reles, however, never appeared in court. He was found dead beneath the window of his top-security sixth-floor bedroom at the Half-Moon Hotel in Coney Island.

And three weeks after Reles fell (or was he pushed?), the Japanese bombed Pearl Harbor and the country went to war. During the rush to mobilization, the FBI took the heat off the underworld. For the next seven years, Hoover continued to assert that the Syndicate had been put out of commission by the 1944 execution of Buchalter and two of his men (Mendy Weiss and Louis Capone), even when the gambling racket in New Jersey alone was netting more than thirteen million dollars a year. In Don Whitehead's *The FBI Story*, there is no index entry for Mafia, Syndicate, Murder, Inc., or Reles. And Buchalter makes the index merely as the operator of a protection racket.

In 1950, the Senate Crime Investigating Committee chaired by Senator Estes Kefauver reawakened public interest in organized crime. It was another brief moment of exposure for the Syndicate—Frank Costello could be seen on nationwide television, wringing his hands in close-up—yet once again a national convulsion (in this case, the aftermath of McCarthy's charges of Communist infiltration in the State Department) diverted the attention of the media.

The publicity surrounding the Kefauver hearings had moved Warner Brothers to action, however, and *The Enforcer* (1951) became the first major Hollywood release to deal in some depth with the Syndicate. Ironically, although the Martin Rackin screenplay was largely based on the Turkus investigation of a decade earlier, it was Kefauver and not Turkus who delivered the film's spoken prologue. Considering that neither Reles nor Buchalter, nor for that matter Turkus, was mentioned by name, *The Enforcer* was nonetheless a remarkable *film à clef* in which organized crime was not simply a metaphor for some other type of conspiracy, as it was in many subsequent crime pictures.

Two-thirds of *The Enforcer* consists of flashbacks: the testimony of various killers, informers, and minor hoods interrogated by District Attorney Ferguson (Humphrey Bogart) as he assembles the pieces of an ugly, violent gangland puzzle. In the process, the lay public was acquainted with the secret argot of Murder, Inc., which has since passed into common usage: a "hit" is a victim marked for murder, a "finger" points out the "hit" to the executioner, usually an out-of-town gunman impersonally carrying out a "contract." Thus, an almost perfect, because motiveless, crime.

The first flashback concerns Malloy (Michael Tolan), a young but seasoned gunman who goes soft on his intended "hit," a girl who once witnessed a gangland slaying. Malloy carries out his "contract," gives himself up to the police, then hangs himself in his cell; but not before mentioning enough names in his delirium to start Ferguson on the trail of an underworld leader named Mendoza. At the outset of a brilliant career, Mendoza (Everett Sloane) was a small-time hood who did his own dirty work. Caught by a cabdriver and his daughter in the act of murdering a restaurant owner, Mendoza had his lieutenant, Rico (Ted de Corsia), liquidate the cabbie. Years later, Malloy was assigned the contract of Angela Vetto (Pat Joiner), the now-grown-up girl. In exchange for protection, Rico becomes

Ferguson's key witness against Mendoza, but, driven by an irrational fear that there is no possible escape from the organization, he falls to his death from a ledge. Mendoza stands to be acquitted. The night before the trial opening, Ferguson visits him in his cell, confronting Mendoza with the photos of his victims. Both men realize, almost simultaneously, that Malloy did not kill Angela after all, but instead he had mistakenly murdered her roommate. Angela Vetto's big blue eyes had haunted Rico for years: the dead girl's eyes were brown. Through a phone call to his attorney, Mendoza puts out a new contract on Angela Vetto, but Ferguson saves her in the nick of time. "I want to see Mendoza smile when he sees those big blue eyes again," announces Ferguson as he escorts his witness to the courthouse.

The above synopsis hardly conveys the Chinese-box structure of the film, but it shows that Rackin did his homework in fictionalizing the salient features of the Turkus-Reles case. *The Enforcer* was possibly meant to be more explicit than it appeared upon release. The original title, *Murder, Inc.*, was discarded (except in England), and the dread name was never heard in the soundtrack. Originally completed by a Warner contract director, Bretaigne Windust, it was largely remade by Raoul Walsh in another of his salvage missions. Walsh staged the climactic shoot-out between Ferguson and a gunman in the lobby of a building, and he wrapped it up excitingly with the mortally wounded killer (Bob Steele) caught in a revolving door.

Obviously, Mendoza and Rico were not the old-fashioned gangsters that Walsh had celebrated from *Regeneration* to *White Heat;* in a way, the same lack of glamour extended to the D.A. hero. Walsh's personal contribution was the atmosphere of fear that pervaded the film and went beyond the limits of the genre—the dark atavistic terror of breaking tribal vows. Nor will the conviction of Mendoza wrap up the case as neatly and naïvely as in the Hollywood of yore. When anonymous marksmen take their positions on rooftops around City Hall to draw a bead on Rico, an invisible, omniscient empire of crime is conjured up. Piles of shoes are marked as evidence of killings on an astonishing scale. The banality of professional murder is captured in a brief exchange between Rico and the Syndicate undertaker:

UNDERTAKER:—Two of them? A busy night.
RICO:—Are you keeping score?

For all the new ground it broke, any hint that the Syndicate could hold sway over local authorities in major cities was glossed over. Reles's death while under close surveillance revealed the extent of corruption in the New York City police department, but Rackin had carefully avoided this issue in the screenplay. *The Enforcer,* for all its good intentions, had to pull its punches, as the time was not right, or Right enough. However, as the fifties progressed and a general mood of distrust spread in the wake of the McCarthy hearings, a political conservatism settled on the film industry, the primary effects of which were the blacklist and the banning of social themes. Another, more aberrant, effect was the appearance of the civic-minded hero, turning his back on corrupt or lax institutions to face up to the un-American enemy, be he a Syndicate member, a Communist, or one of the various Invaders from Outer Space—all of whom fell under the intergeneric denomination of *aliens*.

As hero figures, district attorneys and federal agents were handicapped by the dignity of office or the image of the bureau. No district attorney ever captured the popular imagination, not even when impersonated on screen by Bogart. As for the G-man, his exclusive mission in the Cold War was to fight the Communist conspiracy: in films like *I Was a Communist for the F.B.I.* (1951) and *Walk East on Beacon* (1952), the Communists were depicted as hard, intellectual villains, hardly a threat to inspire a trend. But taking up where *film noir* left off, a number of brutal, alienated, but basically honest loners began to crop up in crime films like *Where the Sidewalk Ends* (1950), *Detective Story* (1951), *On Dangerous Ground* (1951), and *Rogue Cop* (1954). In two of these films, the conflict between hero and the law was internalized by making the rogue cop the son of a criminal and himself something of a criminal in uniform.

The most epochal of these rogue-cop films, *The Big Heat* (1953), opens with a gunshot that sounds like trouble and reverberates through a city pseudonymously identified as Kenport. A corrupt police official has committed suicide and his widow, Mrs. Duncan (Jeanette Nolan), takes possession of a farewell letter linking the city administration with Mike Lagana (Alexander Scourby), the Syndicate executive who runs things from his posh suburban mansion. Mrs. Duncan withholds the note from the police in order to blackmail Lagana. A police detective, Sergeant Bannion (Glenn Ford), refuses to drop the investigation even when pressured from above. His wife (Jocelyn Brando) receives an obscene phone call, and since Bannion is no correct copper but "a corn-stepper by instinct," as his low rank makes clear, he pays an undiplomatic visit to Lagana. As a result, a bomb is planted in Bannion's car, and the bomb accidentally kills his wife. To pursue his private war against Lagana, Bannion resigns from the force. Asked to turn in his badge and gun, he complies halfway: "That [gun] doesn't belong to the department. I bought it."

The crack screenplay of *The Big Heat* was adapted by Sidney Boehm from a novel by William P. McGivern. It retained most of the original plot, adding incidents from Boehm's previous screenplay for *The Undercover Man*. Boehm obviously knew his stuff, and his knack for providing a convincing family background for his characters resulted in some telling detail. Lagana, for instance, is portrayed as a first-generation immigrant whose kids will grow up to be upper-class Americans with only a faint notion of the underworld. A self-made man, Lagana surveys the city from a penthouse terrace as if he owned it, but his old-world origins tend to surface occasionally: "I don't want to land in the same ditch with the Lucky Lucianos."

By accepting the genre constraints dictated by Boehm's script, Fritz Lang created what is arguably his best American film, one that never overshot the subject but matched the rawest of emotions to the most rigorous visuals. Lang's almost musical control of violence deferred both apprehension and catharsis. Quiet, intimate moments were invested with characteristic threat through the intrusion in the frame of a lampshade or a potted plant; empty rooms seemed to lie in wait for people. The tension was so expertly set up that when the picture finally let go with the violence, the viewer was ready—indeed rooting—for it.

As Bannion turns his back on the law to seek his private revenge, *The Big Heat* skirts perilously close to a vigilante fantasy. Bannion, an average man, is being pushed by the events to the limits of his capacity for violence. His sense of loss is conveyed in the scene in which he takes one last look at his former home, now as empty of furnishings as of life, as bare and bleak as the future that awaits him. There is a certain fulfillment in violence to be sure—when he works over a hired gunman (Adam Williams) the body hold suggests a sensuousness that travesties the conventional love scenes between Bannion and his wife. But Bannion's outrage stops short of murder. For all his hate, he cannot bring himself to strangle the devious Mrs. Duncan, whose death would automatically result in the publication of the letter and Lagana's downfall.

It is left to Debbie (Gloria Grahame), a glib, frivolous moll, to shoot the widow in cold blood. Debbie stands for the new fifties heroine, no longer a *femme fatale* or a sex object, but a combination dumb blond, *dea ex*

Bannion's wife is killed when the Syndicate plants a bomb on his car. Glenn Ford and Jocelyn Brando in *The Big Heat*, 1953. *Columbia*

machina, and victim. What was lost in sexual appeal was gained in humor and social consciousness. In the mysterious ways in which Hollywood genres cross-pollinate, Debbie is a straight-drama version of the good-time girl who develops a civic spirit in the comedy *Born Yesterday*—a positive counterpart to the materialistic middle-class embodied by Mrs. Duncan, who drove her husband to cooperate with Lagana and, eventually, to suicide. Debbie's lines are delivered by Gloria Grahame as so many choice moments of truth. "Listen, I've been rich and I've been poor. Believe me, rich is better," she states as her personal philosophy on a first visit to Bannion's hotel room. After her sadistic boyfriend (Lee Marvin) scalds one side of her face with a pot of boiling coffee, she returns to pour out her pain and her panic, wryly concluding that "I'll have to go through life sideways." Confronting Mrs. Duncan in a matching fur coat, she observes that "We're sisters under the mink," before letting the widow have it.

Most of the violence in *The Big Heat* was directed toward women, as if to contradict the Bugsy Siegel adage that "We only kill each other." Thus, at its most pragmatic, the picture warned that if the man in the street did not actively fight crime, neither home nor family would be safe for long. Movies hammered out this message with such vigor that, in mid-1955, Kefauver instigated a Senate investigation of Hollywood violence and its effect on youth. On the agenda were mostly crime pictures like *New York Confidential, Chicago Syndicate, Black Tuesday, Big House U.S.A.,* and *The Big Combo* (all 1955), with a private-eye thriller, *Kiss Me Deadly* (also 1955) coming up for special censure.

Nothing could be more pointless than to take *Kiss Me Deadly* as a debased portrayal of the Chandler shamus and his almost sacred quest for truth. Even in its time, the violence in the film was too unrestrained for its satirical intent to go unnoticed. The more violent moments cannot compare with the gloating sadism of Mickey Spillane's original first-person narration (which does not exist in the film). A more legitimate writer, A. I. Bezzerides, altered character and motivation to build a system of mazes for the detective to run through like a compulsive rat. Instead of humanizing Mike Hammer, it raised his search for the Great Whatsit to a new level of absurdity by having the mysterious metal box that everybody is after contain not a shipment of drugs, as in the original, but an atomic isotope that destroys whatever comes in contact with it. The desperate efforts and mindless savagery of the characters seem petty and old-fashioned when they are confronted with instant annihilation.

At the core of the picture is an anxiety that Robert Aldrich, who directed it, attributed to McCarthyism but that, more likely, seems to be a case of genre running wild. Most of *Kiss Me Deadly* is impossible to describe, but its sheer recklessness is liberating. It is all style—exacerbated, bizarre, as

Last of the private eyes: Ralph Meeker as Mike Hammer in *Kiss Me Deadly,* 1955, and the birdbrained Pandora (Gaby Rodgers) who almost brings about the destruction of Southern California. *United Artists*

visually sophisticated as the early work of Orson Welles, to which it pays tribute more than once—most noticeably, when a reticent singer (Fortunio Bonanova delivering a variation of his role in *Citizen Kane*) remembers a telling detail as Hammer (Ralph Meeker) crumbles a priceless Caruso seventy-eight.

As in the novel, Hammer gives a lift to the mysterious Christina (Cloris Leachman) when she flags him down on the highway; to all appearances a fugitive from an asylum, she turns out to be naked under her trenchcoat, and scared to death. The topsy-turvy world we are about to enter is quickly established during their nocturnal drive, with the opening credits rolling downward on the screen and Nat King Cole getting us in the mood by singing "I'd rather have the blues than what I've got." Shortly, Christina and Hammer are set upon by hired thugs who torture her to death and force him over a cliff in his car. He survives and sets out to find the answers—out of pique, curiosity, and greed.

Wherever Hammer goes, he finds fear and silence; death is not far behind. He has to bully and beat information out of terrified oddballs who shortly afterward are found slain. Behind all this, it would appear, is the California Mafia in the person of Avello (Paul Stewart) and his goons. Avello, however, turns out to be a mere tool of Dr. Soberlin (Albert Dekker), last of the cultivated, soft-spoken villains of the forties, a scientific sadist with a taste for mythology which the climax fulfills—a harebrained murderess (Gaby Rodgers) cannot refrain from playing Pandora to the Great Whatsit. The last we see of Hammer, he is waist-deep in the Pacific Ocean, staring in awe as a familiar mushroom cloud hovers over Malibu.

The film industry had timidly avoided labor themes for years, but union racketeers began making periodic appearances in *The Mob* (1951), *On the Waterfront* (1954), *Slaughter on Tenth Avenue* (1957), and *Garment Jungle* (1957). The cause of unionism was hardly advanced by portraying the unions in the grip of the Syndicate; yet, in retrospect, the making of these pictures smacks more of Hollywood opportunism than of reactionary politics. *The Mob,* a B-picture completed as *Remember that Face,* had its title changed to profit from the sudden interest in organized crime that followed the Kefauver hearings. This film is the familiar tale of the undercover agent who infiltrates a protection racket, only now the racketeers were shown trying to gain control of a dockers' union in a major city. Its most notable feature was the presence of a crooked police sergeant named Bennion, two years before *The Big Heat.*

Such a takeover had been the subject of a series of articles for the *New York Sun* that won a Pulitzer Prize for journalist Malcolm Johnson in 1949. In 1954, the Johnson pieces were adapted by Budd Schulberg as the screenplay of *On the Waterfront,* directed by Elia Kazan and filmed mostly in Hoboken, across the Hudson from Manhattan. (Schulberg later fashioned a more pessimistic novel from the same material.) The presence of Marlon Brando as Terry Malloy in the lead accounted for a good part of the critical and popular success of the picture. Most of those involved—Brando, Kazan,

Schulberg, the cinematographer Boris Kaufman—won Academy Awards, as did the picture, the first time that such an honor was bestowed on a crime film.

The more socially aware critics, especially abroad, detected signs and situations which, in the context of longshoremen's union problems, betrayed reactionary intentions. In the Spring 1955 issue of *Sight and Sound,* Lindsay Anderson attacked *On the Waterfront* as fascistic on the strength of its final sequence, in which the hero, bloodied but unbowed, leads the dockers back to work past the corrupt union leader, an affirmation of the individual over collective action. Wrote Anderson: "One might say that the potency of Marlon Brando—physical, emotional, dramatic—is effectively employed to palm off a number of political assertions, all of them spurious and many of them pernicious."

Kazan and Schulberg replied to these charges with the familiar claims to authenticity that filmmakers have employed, since Griffith and *The Birth of a Nation,* to justify their viewpoint: *On the Waterfront,* Kazan said, had drawn its inspiration from actual working conditions in Hoboken, and many characters—notably the hero and a waterfront priest—were based on real-life people. (Later on, Anthony De Vincenzo, who served as model for the Brando role, successfully sued for invasion of privacy.) A prologue refers to conditions that had once existed—and indeed there had been a union cleanup since Malcolm Johnson revealed the involvement of union officials and racketeers with politicians and shipowners. However, as the film shaped up, Hoboken and the longshoremen's union receded into the background, and the qualities of exposé became negligible. *On the Waterfront* copped out with trite clichés, like the obvious bigwig who is seen from behind, sitting in his luxurious apartment and watching the televised appearance of the union boss before the crime commission. Terry Malloy's gradual awareness of the civic and moral necessity of testifying against the union leader, Johnny Friendly, his former friend and employer, became central to the conflict. At the time, Kazan found himself accused of delivering an apology for his appearance before the HUAC as a friendly witness; years later, Kazan admitted to some truth in the charge. Other films of the mid-fifties, and even before (like *Kiss of Death*), shared a preoccupation with taking the stand, which unconsciously amalgamated the Kefauver crime investigation and the HUAC hearings.

On the Waterfront was further hampered by Kazan's tendency to overstate the obvious. The symbolism of the pigeons was too insistently poetic. Many scenes were borrowed from more modest crime pictures and blown out of proportion—Terry and his girl pursued by a truck down a dark alley brought back memories of *The Undercover Man.* The closing shot of an iron door being lowered threw the picture off-balance; it was a negative image that opened up areas studiously avoided until then. (Were we to conclude that eventually Terry would become another Johnny Friendly and that there is no real hope for a clean union?) The overload extends to the acting, some of which marked the heyday of the Method: Brando and Rod Steiger, who played Terry's older brother and who ended up hanging from a docker's

hook, were in control of their shrugs and hesitations; but Lee J. Cobb and
Karl Malden mugged beyond the call of duty.

One can imagine a different film about the union racket that would have
for a hero the character of Johnny Friendly—the blustery self-made leader
who has worked his way up from the hatch, bearing the scares of labor wars, to
earn his cut of "the fattest piers in the fattest harbor in the world." Such a
picture was eventually made in 1978: although *F.I.S.T.* was no match for
On the Waterfront—the role demanding a Brando and settling for Sylvester
Stallone—its tale of unfair working conditions in the thirties, of ideals compromised, and of the inevitable corruption of power, seemed a more valid
commentary on unionism than did Kazan's misguided attempt.

In *On the Waterfront*, Kazan's esthetic soul-searching complicated a
crime story already cluttered with documentary facts and Actors' Studio in-
terpretations. Kazan, like Sidney Lumet after him, could not resist trans-
forming B-film situations into Something More Meaningful; but working
within the B format and perfectly conscious of budget, running time, studio
supervision, and the Breen Office, Phil Karlson and Don Siegel made the
best, most lucid crime movies of the fifties. In a period of displaced anxiety,
Karlson made crystalline films about the encroaching power of the underworld, such as *Tight Spot* and *The Phenix City Story* (both 1955), and *The
Brothers Rico* (1957). Siegel's early experience as a film editor paid off in
the spare, muscular style of *Baby Face Nelson* (1957) and *The Lineup*
(1958), both pictures that probed criminal behavior and dispensed with
moral judgment.

After years of directing well-crafted B-pictures, Karlson first received
critical attention with *The Phenix City Story*, paradoxically neither his best
nor most typical work; only this time, journalistic fact imparted credibility to
Karlson's brand of genre fiction. The film was a rough, black-and-white
exposé, filmed on location in Alabama only a few months after the smashing
of the gambling, vice, and dope ring that had earned Phenix City the title
of "America's Wickedest City" in national magazines like *Look, Time,* and
The Saturday Evening Post. The clientele that supported the brothels and
honky-tonk casinos along notorious Fourteenth Street were, for the most
part, soldiers from nearby Fort Benning. There had been several murders,
and the townspeople had organized action groups to keep crime from
spreading beyond the red zone. The final outrage was the killing of State
Attorney-elect Albert A. Patterson: within days, the Alabama National
Guard descended on Phenix City. The debris had just begun to settle when
Karlson and his crew arrived.

The Phenix City Story opens with a prologue in which reporter Clete
Roberts conducts on-the-spot interviews with local witnesses in order to
stress the authenticity of what is to follow; these scenes could be cut by

Labor boss Lee J. Cobb works his wiles on a hero (Marlon Brando) who must yet learn
that there is honor in informing. Charley the Gent (Rod Steiger) pays for his brother's
awakening conscience. *On the Waterfront,* 1954. *Columbia*

exhibitors in the South, and often were. Karlson's film did not really need them, except possibly to get some of the violence past the censor, for the original facts had been effectively dramatized by Crane Wilbur and Daniel Mainwaring to fit within the Last-Just-Man trend; it just barely avoids the pro-vigilante flavor inherent in the story by counteracting it with a subtle liberal slant. The town boss, for example, is a hearty, neighborly redneck (Edward Andrews) who echoes the southerner's resentment of civil-rights enforcement when he reminds the hero that "half the trouble with the people in the world today is they just don't want to let things the way they are." Later, when the body of a wantonly murdered black child is dumped on the hero's front lawn as a warning, he is moved to take a stand even though it means endangering his own family.

Karlson dealt obsessively with the theme of corruption on such a vast scale that, in his crime pictures, the world became a huge organization, with the criminals virtually indistinguishable from the rest of the citizenry, and the final commitment of the hero (or heroine, in the case of *Tight Spot*) is rendered all but futile by the sheer range and power of the opposition. In *Tight Spot*, a more relaxed program picture made prior to *The Phenix City Story*, a mid-Manhattan hotel suite is turned into a besieged outpost facing the onslaught of a Mafia warlord. Originally an unsuccessful play (*Dead Pigeon*) by Lenard Cantor, the basic one-set situation was retained through most of the film. The opening sequence, however, made exciting use of New York locations to suggest the almost limitless resources of the organization. A stool pigeon is led, in great secrecy, from Staten Island to Lower Manhattan to testify against his former boss; as he climbs the courthouse steps, a shot rings out from nowhere and the man falls dead; the guards turn to face myriads of Wall Street windows. From here on, *Tight Spot* concentrates single-mindedly on the strategies involved in getting a wisecracking moll (Ginger Rogers) to give evidence and on the odds against keeping her alive.

Karlson's best picture of the fifties, arguably the decade's final statement—with Don Siegel's *Invasion of the Body Snatchers* (1956)—on the takeover paranoia, was *The Brothers Rico*, from a novel by Georges Simenon. The film was practically devoid of violence, relying for its punch on the suggestion of an awesomely efficient organization so well integrated into the straight world as to be invisible. In *Invasion of the Body Snatchers*, the peculiar behavior of seemingly normal people was accounted for by the fact that they were extraterrestrials: in *The Brothers Rico*, the explanation was that they were mobsters. It was a premise that, in the sixties, would inevitably swell into turgid metaphors, like Arthur Penn's *Mickey One* (1965,) in which the organization becomes a vengeful god preying on the hero's primal guilt; or John Boorman's *Point Blank* (1967), in which a Kafkaesque twist reveals the ultimate underworld power to be an ubiquitous Man in the Street.

In *The Brothers Rico*, Eddie Rico (Richard Conte's last effective gangster role) is a retired mobster assigned by the Syndicate to locate his younger brother Johnny, in hiding since taking part in a gangland slaying, and persuade him to leave the country until the investigation is over. Eddie complies out of respect for Sid Kubic (Larry Gates), a Syndicate executive who professes great affection for the Ricos and whose life was once saved by Eddie's mother (Argentina Brunetti). Too late, Eddie realizes that he has been duped into leading Kubic's henchmen to his brother (James Darren), a potential witness who must be silenced.

Like Eddie, the film is suspended between anguish and disbelief. Every accidental meeting turns out to be "planted," mobsters come out of the woodwork, and even the telephone company begins to look shady, judging from the dire results of every phone call. In what must certainly be one of the most claustrophobic scenes in the genre, Eddie is lectured in his hotel room by a kindly but firm older gunman (Harry Bellaver), as plans are laid to have Johnny killed. "We're all brothers," explains the hood. "Did that ever stop anything? Johnny's already spoken for, he doesn't count anymore, but you're alive." Karlson cuts to a long shot of two cars arriving in the night at Johnny's hideout; then cuts back to the hotel as a brief phone call informs Eddie that the terrible job has been done.

In Simenon's novel, Eddie swallowed his grief and accepted Kubic's decision as the superior wisdom of an elder statesman of crime—perhaps more realistic compromise than Karlson was ready to grant or the Breen office to sanction. Instead, *The Brothers Rico* goes into full throttle as Eddie, bent on revenge and on exposing the organization, evades an underworld dragnet that seems to surpass any police dragnet in spread and thoroughness. Traveling in cattle cars and hitching rides with strangers, he succeeds in reaching his mother's home in Little Italy—where he finds Kubic waiting in the kitchen. The ensuing gunfight, staged within these cramped, homely quarters, is Karlson's way of restoring the conflict to a human dimension.

In 1957, Don Siegel directed *Baby Face Nelson,* an independent, low-budget movie, shot in nineteen days, that was in release before anyone could realize that the interdiction laid down by the Thirteenth Section against showing historical gangsters on the screen had been broken. In 1955, United Artists had defied the MPAA, to the point of resigning from the Association, on the issue of *The Man with the Golden Arm,* which dealt with the forbidden subject of drug addiction. Obviously, many of the Code restrictions had outlived their usefulness, and members of the MPAA were chafing at the competition provided by television. In December 1956, the bans on the representation of drug addiction, prostitution, abortion, and miscegenation were lifted. These revisions were publicly lauded by Senator Kefauver, who, a mere two years before, had been a severe critic of Hollywood violence. Hoover, faithful to himself, scored *Baby Face Nelson* as the glorification of a criminal in a letter to the MPAA that was widely circulated among the major studios but drew no comment from the censor's office.

Hoover's claims were unfounded, for how could Siegel have glorified a manic, off-the-wall character like Nelson? Historically, Nelson (born Lester Gillis) was renowned for his small size and boundless ferocity, traits on

which Daniel Mainwaring based the character which Mickey Rooney played as a bantam psychotic, a country cousin to Cagney's Cody. Since in the sticks it was not easy to tell a hood from a hick unless he had a catchy name, Gillis fabricated an identity for himself—he adopted his moll's last name because, as the script puts it, "any name is better than my old man's," and Dillinger completed the job by dubbing him "Baby Face." Nelson remained throughout his crime career (which was mercifully short) the sulky kid trying to prove himself to the older boys, and this made him more interesting to Siegel than Dillinger and Capone put together.

Much of this is conveyed in the scene in which Nelson joins the Dillinger gang in a playground, grown men sitting on swings, waiting for the boss to arrive. "So that's the big man, uh?" mutters Nelson, impressed despite himself; and a fellow gunman taunts back: "Big enough for you?" Siegel's Dillinger (Leo Gordon) is a taciturn father figure whose experience and control make him a restraining influence in Nelson's life. After Dillinger is killed, Nelson attempts to measure up to his new title of Public Enemy Number One through reckless violence. Although alienated to the point of betraying his own gang, he still cannot bring himself to murder an abducted bank manager (George E. Stone) because he, too, is a runt.

Siegel admits to such an involvement with his desperate characters that he was not aware, while filming *The Killers* in 1964, that he was in effect remaking his own *The Lineup* rather than Siodmak's classic *film noir*. Loosely derived from the TV series about a pair of police detectives, *The Lineup* concentrated on two hired gunmen assigned to recover a heroin drop. In Siegel's version of *The Killers*, the professionalism of the killers stamped them as members of an elite corps, men who have taken special vows. The films were basically a dialogue on violence conducted by two expert practitioners, one older and more experienced, the other an uncouth, ruthless acolyte. In the earlier film, Julian (Robert Keith), clearly fascinated by his young partner, Dancer (Eli Wallach), queries him about their victims' dying words, which Julian dutifully jots down:

JULIAN: Did he say anything?
DANCER: He said, "Why be greedy?" Last words.
JULIAN: That would make a swell epitaph.

As we progress from the pioneer generation to the corporate underworld, the vestigial normality of Baby Face gives way to almost inhuman specialization. The latter-day gunman lives in hotel rooms and moves across the country like a salesman in his Ivy League suit, carring his rod in a briefcase. Women are notably absent from his life. In *The Lineup*, Julian informs a female hostage: "Women are weak. They have no place in society. You don't understand the criminal's need for violence." After *film noir* granted

The mob-infiltrated family unit: Argentina Brunetti fights for her son's life, as the avuncular Larry Gates takes a bead on Richard Conte, in *The Brothers Rico*, 1957. *Columbia*

women the exalted/dubious status of treacherous muse, a passionless misogyny settled on the genre. In his version of *The Killers*, originally made for TV but given a theatrical release because of its violence, Siegel was much more brutal to his admittedly vicious heroine than Siodmak ever was to any of his; and the picture itself, with its slabs of color and its hard finish, was a diurnal nightmare from which eroticism was largely absent.[*]

The basic conflict in Siegel's films was not between the law and the criminal, but within the criminal himself. The criminal hero, as long as he functioned without involvement, was an invulnerable, depersonalized cog in the machinery of a large criminal system: the way to the hero's destruction lay in his curiosity to know where the power comes from. As long as Dancer is known only to Julian (and to a driver, assigned to them by the organization), he can preserve his anonymity and keep his distance. But Dancer wonders about the Man, the unseen executive who hires him, refusing to report through the usual channels. As he confronts the Man himself, he realizes that he has renounced the isolation that made their working relationship possible. Likewise with Charlie and Lee (Lee Marvin and Clu Gulager) in *The Killers*.

After *Baby Face Nelson* there came a search for the roots of the new underworld in a string of pseudohistorical biographies that left no major hoodlum unsung. In 1958, there were *Machine Gun Kelly* and *The Bonnie Parker Story*. In 1959, *The Purple Gang* revived the Detroit bootleg war. In 1960, *Pretty Boy Floyd*, *Ma Barker's Killer Brood*, and *The Rise and Fall of Legs Diamond*. In 1961, Vincent Coll, Dutch Schultz and Arnold Rothstein lived and died again in *Mad Dog Coll*, *Portrait of a Mobster*, and *King of the Roaring Twenties*. *Party Girl* (1958) pitted a composite ganglord—equal parts of Capone and "Longie" Zwillman—against a fictional attorney inspired by Thomas Fallon. The cycle came full circle with a reasonably factual *Murder, Inc.* (1960) and a detailed reconstruction of *The St. Valentine's Day Massacre* (1967).

Once the unmentionable bogey of the MPAA, Al Capone had his own screen biography in 1959, besides making guest appearances in *The George Raft Story* (1961), and a two-part television special (which began the long-running series "The Untouchables") released in 1962 as a feature, *The Scarface Mob*. Capone's convulsive rise and nonviolent downfall were difficult to fit into a conventional structure—tax evasion and syphilis being a poor substitute for a hail of bullets in some photogenic gutter. To make up for lack of dramatic progression, Richard Wilson, director of *Al Capone*, and his writers, Malvin Wald and Henry Greenberg, approached Capone as a Shakespearan character: Capone plays Iago to the vacillating Johnny Torrio, his mentor in the Chicago underworld, and he plays Macbeth to his liege,

[*] Misogyny found a utilitarian basis in Irving Lerner's *Murder by Contract* (1958), in which a hired killer (Ben Edwards) renegotiates a "contract" when his "mark" turns out to be a woman: "Don't like to kill women. It's hard to kill someone who's not dependable."

The gangster movie that outraged Hoover and indirectly caused the lifting of the Dillinger ban: Mickey Rooney and Carolyn Jones in *Baby Face Nelson*, 1957. *United Artists*

Big Jim Colosimo; like Richard the Third, he woos and wins the widow of one of his victims, and as befits a mighty gangland Caesar, he is set upon by his peers on an Alcatraz rockpile. (Is it a coincidence that Wilson was once an associate of Orson Welles, a fact that brings to mind such Welles productions as an all-black *Macbeth* and *Julius Caesar* laid in fascist Rome?) As Capone, Rod Steiger is loud, operatic, belligerent—but never provides the flash of latent viciousness, the wicked humor and peasant innocence of Muni's *parvenu* Camonte.*

Like *Al Capone,* most of the biographies were conventional, black-and-white, medium- to low-budget efforts, but not without some distinctive work done by directors trying to fit personal subjects within the revisionist trend. The need to supply a companion piece to *The Bonnie Parker Story* prompted Roger Corman to make *Machine Gun Kelly,* a black comedy about the most inept and exploited gangster of the thirties. Corman selected Kelly because he was a moll-dominated simpleton with a morbid fear of death—the public enemy as henpecked mate. Any relation to the facts of the Urschel kidnap case was coincidental: Kelly (Charles Bronson) plays patty-cake with an abducted child while his girlfriend (Susan Cabot) reviles him "I gave you a machine gun, a name, everything!" Even for the comparatively bloodless fifties, *Machine Gun Kelly* was noticeably shy about violence: a television series like "Gangbusters" or "T-Men in Action" spilled more imitation gore in half an hour.

A different sort of demystification was at work in *The Rise and Fall of Legs Diamond,* a joyless film about one of the most colorful personalities of the twenties, whittled down to an unsympathetic, opportunistic Don Juan who uses women to advance in the underworld and is, inevitably, undone by one such discarded mistress (Arnold Rothstein's moll, no less). As directed by Budd Boetticher, a specialist in taut, minimal Westerns, everything pertaining to bootlegging and Prohibition was made to seem as remote as the Old West: whatever social forces molded Legs Diamond appeared as distant in 1960 as those that motivated, say, the opening of the Oklahoma territory. The familiar standing sets in the Warner backlot seemed eerie, deprived of the salty characters that once inhabited them.

As Diamond, Ray Danton was more Vegas than Broadway, his early *chutzpah* and later moaning intonations being peculiarly inappropriate for the wild Irishman that Diamond is reputed to have been. But even more frustrating was the misuse of the real Diamond story, as varied and violent as any gangster's. A crack shot who dominated New York nightlife for a decade, he survived enough shootings to earn the nickname of the Clay Pigeon, supported a loving wife and a string of mistresses, and was finally killed—presumably on orders from Dutch Schultz, a rival for the rich Manhattan bootleg territory. In an improbable, downbeat ending, the film makes Legs a victim of the newly formed Syndicate, which regards him as an outmoded embarrassment.

---

* The Capone family filed a complaint of invasion of privacy against Desilu, the producers of "The Untouchables," in which Capone was impersonated by Neville Brand. The appeal was rejected by the Supreme Court in 1965, ratifying the notion that Capone belonged to the ages as well as to the public domain.

The historical trend was exhausted by Roger Corman's *The St. Valentine's Day Massacre,* which resembled a map of the city of Chicago overrun with colored flags to denote positions, areas of occupation, raids, and retaliations. Corman, for once in the genre, named names—there were almost no fictional characters in the film. Capone, Bugs Moran, Dion O'Bannion, Hymie Weiss, and other bigwigs of the gang wars led us to the big event— the machine-gunning of seven of Moran's men by a Capone hit squad on February 14, 1929. The Howard Browne screenplay went to the extreme of having a newspaper file on each participant read by a noncommittal, off-screen narrator, to take the survivors beyond the time span of the action—a combination oracle and obituary, a device that neither moralized nor editorialized but simply clarified the various allegiances and operations.

The factions are Moran's predominantly Irish North Side gang and Capone's South Side Italians, and in the film their feud was traced back to immigrant basics and territorial claims through an uninhibited use of racial slurs rare in a post-1933 film. Every skirmish was placed in chronological context, advancing or retarding Capone's takeover. The only major factual lapse was Capone's personal (and wholly fictional) execution of Joseph Aiello (Alex D'Arcy), boss of the Unione Siciliane, which was posited as a nearly Oedipal act—a break with the old-world criminal system, which had become an obstacle to Capone's policy of waging war on the competition "just as modern nations and corporations do."

The massacre itself was perceived as a major historical event, suspended in time between Lindbergh's triumphant flight and the stock-market crash. The precredit sequence is already set on the fateful morning: we discover the mass killing through the horrified reaction of an inquisitive neighbor. The film then flashes back to build up to a replay of the massacre—for the viewer knowing beforehand which characters are marked for death, the conventional suspense is replaced by ironical detachment. The bloodbath is an exercise on temporal delay in the montage style of the silent cinema— staccato crosscutting between twisting bodies, contorted faces, impassive executioners, and crumbling brick; water spouting from a punctured pipe to wash over the gore; the seemingly endless, deafening blast coming to a sudden stop with a shot of the smoldering gun barrels.

Famous scenes from the repertory of gangster films were reclaimed, like the assault on Capone's headquarters at the Hawthorn Hotel, which was given the warlike connotation of a saturation barrage—in contrast to the cosmic demolition in *Scarface.* Tributes were given a comic twist, as when Pete Gusenberg (George Segal), the film's putative hero by reason of his youthful good looks, smacks his mistress across the face with a deli sandwich, like a kosher Cagney. During a lull, a gunsel (Jack Nicholson) explains the quaint custom of dipping bullets in garlic, so that "if the bullet don't kill you, you die of blood poisoning"—a crack that has a factual basis in Johnny Torrio's hysterical concern with having his wounds cauterized after being shot by Weiss and Moran in 1924.

Jason Robards conformed even less than his predecessors to the official Capone image, but he got a lot of mileage from emblematic props: the cigar,

Jason Robards as Capone, holding a war council which results in the most notorious event in gangdom's annals: *The St. Valentine's Day Massacre*, 1967. *Twentieth Century-Fox*

the slashed cheekbone, the hat with the brim turned down. His grimacing
Eyetie turns seem at first the wrong sort of distancing effect—the payoff
comes when Robards jolts the viewer with a sudden vicious outburst. Possibly the most awesome moment in Corman's very bloody chronicle was not
the massacre after all, but a low-angle shot of a frenzied Capone as seen
from the viewpoint of two kneeling hoodlums he is about to execute with
a baseball bat.

Two 1960 films illustrate diverging approaches to the Syndicate theme
of the late fifties and early sixties, demonstrating that fact does not necessarily serve as a better dramatic source than imaginative fiction. *Murder, Inc.*
was a semifactual retelling of the Abe Reles story, based on the book by
Burton Turkus and Sid Feder, with Peter Falk delivering a miscalculated
comic performance as the garrulous stoolie; the power and resonance of *The*

**Police stenographers exhausted by a tale of murder on a massive scale. Peter Falk as
Abe Reles, in *Murder, Inc.*, 1960.** *Twentieth Century-Fox*

Enforcer were missing, chiefly because the facts tyrannized the weak screen-play. Conversely, *Underworld, U.S.A.*, a free and colorful fiction written and directed by Samuel Fuller, packed the visual and dramatic wallop of an atrocity photo in *The National Enquirer.*

For inspiration, Fuller borrowed the revenge plot of Elizabethan and Jacobean drama, then boldly transposed it to the modern underworld. There are close affinities to Cyril Tourneur's *The Revenger's Tragedy* (1607), but the film is set in a milieu so American and so generic that it not only ends, but also begins, with death in the gutter.

One New Year's Eve, Tolly Devlin, teenage hustler, watches four men beat his father to death in an alley and vows revenge. Serving time for safe-cracking, the adult Tolly (Cliff Robertson) learns that one of his father's killers is in the prison infirmary. He approaches Vic Farrar (Peter Brocco) on his deathbed, offering absolution in exchange for the three other names. "I ain't no fink," wheezes Farrar, but as death approaches and Tolly per-severes like a sadistic confessor, Farrar finally weakens. In possession of the names, Tolly slaps Farrar, calls him a fink, and contemptuously watches him die. The thugs who killed his father have risen to occupy positions of power in the underworld corporation run by Connors (Robert Emhardt). Tolly works his way into their confidence to sow distrust among them, contrives to have one legally executed and two liquidated by the company hit man, Gus (Richard Rust). Having accomplished his mission, Tolly envisions marrying Cuddles (Dolores Dorn), a prostitute he rescued from Gus and used to further his scheme. To protect her, Tolly is driven to kill Connors although he bears no grudge against him. Wounded by Gus, he staggers down from the executive penthouse to die in the same back alley as his old man.

As Fuller described himself in a cameo appearance in Jean-Luc Godard's *Pierrot le Fou* (1965), he is a purveyor of "love, hate, action, violence, death: in one word, emotion." As with the Jacobeans, dialogue can often obscure dramatic construction, and Fuller's seemed to call for comic-strip balloons. Furthermore, he overindulged a taste for irony—he could not let Tolly die in peace without having him stumble on a trash can marked KEEP YOUR CITY CLEAN. It is understandable that the structure-conscious New Wave directors would lionize Fuller while most American critics were dismissing him as strictly 42nd Street.

Fuller also shared the Jacobeans' taste for extravagant violence and their gift to place characters in situations that invariably close in on them like a deathly trap. Throughout, Connors, the modern crime potentate, is depicted beside a swimming pool, an obese toad drawing life from the proximity of water: his watery death at the hands of Tolly follows with ruthless logic. Elsewhere, Fuller borrowed well-remembered scenes from other crime films—such as *The Big Sleep* (death awaiting whoever opens a certain door) and *The Big Heat* (the exploding car)—and detonated them for all their cumulative emotional charge.

A hesitant, unfocused picture like Wilson's *Al Capone* seemed to paste on Shakespearean credentials, but in *Underworld U.S.A.* the quotes were perfectly assimilated into the narrative and given a perverse twist. We can still recognize the source of the scene in which Cuddles pleads with Tolly to accept her love, which he rejects to pursue his obsession. Tolly's confrontation with Gela (Paul Dubov), the last of the three murderers, carries an incestuous intimacy. Previously, Gela had offered himself as a substitute father figure; now Tolly forces him to confront his doom in the person of Gus, who is waiting to execute him outside Gela's front door. It was as if Fuller had substituted Claudius for Gertrude in mid-scene.

The portrait that Murray Schumach draws of Fuller in *The Face on the Cutting Room Floor* (William Morrow, 1964), which may be intended as devastating criticism, in fact shows Fuller aware of the available variations within the iconography of the gangster film. Fuller is quoted as saying: "What is quiet brutality? ... We have a professional killer in my picture [Gus in *Underworld U.S.A.*]. He is no psychotic. He is no idiot. No strange chuckle before he kills. No twitch. A normal young man. He's just a professional executioner.... The only thing he does—and this is like the atavistic outcry of the warrior—immediately before the job he puts on dark glasses.... If you are going to buck television you need an original idea." Fuller might have just described the Dancer character in Siegel's *The Lineup*: Siegel himself would later borrow the detail of the glasses for his version of *The Killers*. Such is the continuity of genre.

The options reside in each director's temperament. One senses that Siegel would have centered *Underworld, U.S.A.* on Gus, the killer with the Presley good looks, who moonlights as a lifeguard for underprivileged kids invited to the executive pool; yet when the situation calls for it, he dons the famous dark glasses and runs his car over the child of a bothersome witness. Karlson would undoubtedly have exploited the paranoia attending the underworld's marketing techniques, which Fuller sums up with characteristic bluntness by having Connors advise Gela, his executive in charge of narcotics, to "put more men in the field, to work on schools."

Yet who but Fuller would be as bold or perceptive as to select a large American conglomerate as the sole autocracy with power over the life and death of its subjects, the perfect modern counterpart of the Italianate courts in Tourneur, Webster, and Ford? In the ten years between *The Enforcer* and *Underworld, U.S.A.*, the genre reevaluated the threatening image of the Syndicate. Attuned to the successive fears of the decade—the Communist conspiracy, the brainwashing techniques exposed during the Korean war, the subliminal control of the consumer public as expounded by Vance Packard—the genre concluded that the acquisition of a businesslike facade was the most disturbing aspect of the Syndicate, because it blunted the line between the legal and the illegal. Fuller's film was fiercely iconographic in its opposition of disparate entities, the second-rate, free-lance street hoodlum and the corporate crime board. Inevitably, as the crime film abandoned back alleys and gutters for the dehumanized modernism of the skyscraper, money disappeared as a commodity, to be replaced by the new coin of the realm, unlimited power, an abstraction. *Underworld U.S.A.* was a cut-off point in the genre—just beyond lay the psychedelic absurdities of John Boorman's *Point Blank*. The next time an unspoiled, naïve gunman (Lee Marvin) would bulldoze his way into the Syndicate's sanctum to collect his dues, he would be told by the top man himself (Carroll O'Connor) that the cash reserve in the entire building is less than thirty dollars.

9. Bonnie, Clyde, and the Kids

Clyde was the leader. Bonnie wrote poetry. C.W. was a Myrna Loy fan who had a bluebird tattooed on his chest. Buck told corny jokes and carried a Kodak. Blanche was a preacher's daughter who kept her fingers in her ears during the gunfights. They played checkers and photographed each other incessantly. On Sunday nights they listened to Eddie Cantor on the radio. All in all, they killed 18 people. They were the strangest damned gang you ever heard of.

— British poster for *Bonnie and Clyde*

APPROPRIATELY ENOUGH—although the fact seemed to outrage conservatives, who worried about America's image abroad—*Bonnie and Clyde* received its world premiere on opening night of the Montreal International Film Festival, part of the 1967 World's Fair, at the height of a summer when half the youth of North America seemed to have assembled there while the other half was dispersed on the road to Haight-Ashbury. With a few exceptions, such as Pauline Kael's defense in *The New Yorker* (which made her reputation as a pugnacious, offbeat critic), most establishment critics took the film to be immoral, irresponsible, and as provoking as a puff of marijuana smoke blown in their faces. In a few weeks it progressed from the dubious status of a summer release bankrolled by Warner Brothers at the impassioned persuasion of Warren Beatty, its producer and star, to that of a runaway hit with a million runaway kids. In its first year, *Bonnie and Clyde* grossed more than $20 million. The nameless *Time* reviewer who carelessly dismissed it in a few harsh words as just another inauthentic, violent gangster movie was summarily replaced and, belatedly, *Bonnie and Clyde* made the magazine's cover, no longer as a mere motion picture but as a cult phenomenon that had pop sociologists all over the country reaching for their rationales.

If nothing else, *Bonnie and Clyde* confirmed the old Chaplin aphorism that if comedy is a matter of long shots, then tragedy is a matter of close-ups. The ratio of emotional commitment to visual distance was never so graphically demonstrated as in the various long shots of vintage cars bouncing like bugs all over dusty country roads and grassy knolls to the strains of some exhilarating banjo picking (by Nashville's own Flatt and Scruggs); this placed the viewer in a context as safe as that of a Keystone Kops comedy only to jolt him into a different world altogether with a quick cut to a man's face being blown away by a gunshot, his blood spattering the windshield of one such jaunty jalopy. One of the great stylistic conventions in commercial movie-making is that dramatic forms must never change in mid-movie; yet here was a full-blooded gangster film alternating burlesque slapstick with shocking violence and finally settling into its own fake folk-ballad style. The slow-motion effect used to suggest the impact of a bullet had been used before (notably by Don Siegel in *The Killers*) to convey time suspended between life and death. Now it was a gust of bullets that swept Bonnie and Clyde into the realm of legend, a "ballet of death" that incorporated deliberate provocation in its esthetic violence.

The same abrupt transitions in mood, the same critical awareness in approaching basic genre material, was found in the films of New Wave directors Jean-Luc Godard and François Truffaut, who had both influenced the writing of the script and were at various times expected to direct. The final choice was Arthur Penn, a New York director, albeit no stranger to Hollywood, who pulled together the various contributions so that *Bonnie and Clyde* was balanced between its Hollywood graphics (camera work and leading players) and its New York sensibilities (writers, editor).

After seeing Penn's version, Godard reportedly said to Robert Benton and David Newman, who originally conceived the project: "Now, let's make *Bonnie and Clyde!*" Obviously, the subject was far from exhausted, even if this was the third picture directly based on their exploits (not counting the distant inspiration they provided for Lang, Ray, and Lewis). What made these trigger-happy hicks so fascinating to filmmakers? They were little more than a footnote in John Toland's *The Dillinger Days* when Benton and Newman first read about them. The squalid facts of their career in crime—their biggest haul netted them a mere $1,500, and they killed twelve people in four years—matter less than the few snapshots, poems, and letters they placed in local newspapers, acting as their own press agents. The image of fugitive lovers-in-crime was disputed even in their lifetime, mostly because Clyde was supposed to be homosexual and also because of the lesser known fact that Roy Thornton, another gang member, was Bonnie's husband. At the time of their death, however, the headlines made them a couple for keeps.

Previous film versions were perforce less glamorous, but they never quite demystified the two. Even with Hoover calling the shots, the 1939 version, *Persons in Hiding*, generated sympathy for the heroine—the scene in which she visits her toil-worn mother can only be construed as an apology for an ambitious girl unresigned to the drudgery of farm life. A parallel reunion scene in Penn's picture became a sun-hazy love-in, and this last and most famous version would also have a rough time matching the perversely comic moment in *The Bonnie Parker Story* when Bonnie (Dorothy Provine) scatters thumbtacks around her bed to keep both Clyde and her husband away. Nor could Penn, for that matter, come close to the casual poetic touch of the ending—with Bonnie herself, not with the official narrator, speaking from the grave and having the final say. These were the rewards of the B-film, sneaked in while the censor was napping.

Bonnie and Clyde enter the pantheon of the counterculture in a slow-motion "ballet of death" that carried an esthetic provocation. *Warner Brothers*

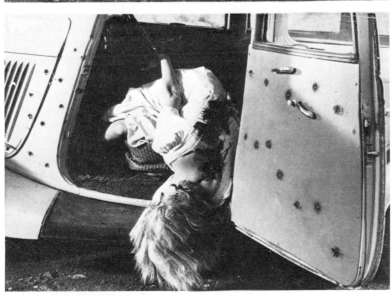

The new Bonnie and Clyde reeked of the nonconformism of the sixties rather than of the hard-up survival spirit of the thirties. Warren Beatty and Faye Dunaway portrayed them as endearing, irresponsible amateurs who never quite learn the ropes of bank robbing and must reassure themselves of their criminal standing by adding a folksy "We rob banks" to their self-introduction. This touch of improvisation was perhaps the must cunning of Penn's strategies: as soon as their holdup technique is polished, we never see them pull a robbery again; just as, after their first murder, there are few reminders that these beautiful, dapper, corny people are killers as well.

One of Penn's initial concerns when he took over the project was to situate the Barrow gang in a historical reality. To this effect, scenes were added to the script: in one, Clyde lends his gun to a farmer being evicted by the local bank so that he can shoot out the windows of his lost homestead; in the other, the gang, decimated and pursued, is given shelter in an Okie camp. The first suggested a photograph by Walker Evans, the second an NRA poster—both were cultural quotes that reduced the Depression to fixed, inert images. Due to the stylish designs of Theadora Van Runkle, the film launched the *rétro* look in fashion: the thirties seen through a golden haze of nostalgia. This amounted to a kiss of death to a socially committed vision of the period, and the kiss was made passionate by the Technicolor re-creation of the Dust Bowl by Burnett Guffey, the cameraman of *The Undercover Man, Tight Spot,* and *The Brothers Rico.* Somehow, the authentic Southwest locations added up to a magic heartland where the last American outlaws could lose their pursuers by simply driving their flivvers around a turn of the road.

The message that came through, raising the most eyebrows and selling the most tickets, was that it was better to live fast, die young, and leave good-looking images in the collective mind than to conform to the indignities of growing old and being co-opted by the straight, practical world. Beyond a certain moment, Bonnie and Clyde had to die, not because history decreed their death, but because the film's particular fiction was of the sixties, and death had to rescue them from adulthood, domesticity, and the middle class, fates far worse than death in the age of the dropout. (It was no accident either that the 1968 film of *Romeo and Juliet,* with teenagers in the leading roles, was the most financially rewarding of all adaptations from Shakespeare.) Having at last consummated their love in bed—Clyde's impotence exorcised by Bonnie's doggerel about his being "honest and upright and clean"—they are ambushed and shot, as they return from buying groceries like a married couple, by a posse led by a humorless Texas Ranger (Denver Pyle).

One proof of the film's negative impact on the establishment is the fact that, in spite of being the most written about and successful of the year, it received a mere two Academy Awards—one for Guffey's cinematography, the other for Estelle Parsons in the supporting role of Clyde's sister-in-law. A dozen years later, it is still difficult to assess correctly the ambiguities that made the film's fortune; for instance, the esthetic double standard that was applied to the protagonists and the rest of the characters. Compared to *Badlands* (1974), one of the many films it inspired, *Bonnie and Clyde* lacked artistic cohesion. A bravura editing job by Dede Allen kept things going headlong, relating it somewhat to the fragmentary, cartoonish world of Richard Lester, another director whose films *Hard Day's Night* (1964) and *How I Won the War* (1967) gained form and viewpoint on the editor's bench. As a director of violence, Penn's long-winded rationalizations are, on paper, as apologetic as the actual bloodshed on the screen is visible and

"The strangest damned gang you ever heard of." Michael J. Pollard, Faye Dunaway, and Warren Beatty in *Bonnie and Clyde*, 1967. *Warner Brothers*

realistic. The mood changes may have been French, but the violence was borrowed from Italian Westerns and Japanese swordplay movies.[*]

It was not long before isolated efforts like *Pretty Poison* (1968) and *The Big Bounce* (1969) borrowed the insouciant *Bonnie and Clyde* slogan ("They are young, they are in love, they kill people.") and applied it to their own fictional joyrides. Apart from their individual merits, the interest of these pictures lay in their feeble, not quite articulate attempts to endow gratuitous violence with a political bias. Whether candid or disingenuous, they seemed to nurture the conservative view of the radical movement as

---

[*] A rhetorical question: Would *Bonnie and Clyde* have been as successful had it ended as in the original script, with off-screen shots over a still photograph of the bank robbers, the ending used by the equally successful *Butch Cassidy and the Sundance Kid* two years later?

perpetrator of irrational violence as much as they played on the fantasy of
an adult society visiting retribution on the nonconformist young.

The most direct descendant of *Bonnie and Clyde* was Roger Corman's
Bloody Mama (1970), based on the insane, murderous Barker gang. A regular contributor to the repertory of crime films, Corman availed himself of
the locale and background music of Penn's picture, but returned to the
Freudian outlook of *Machine Gun Kelly*, as if *The St. Valentine's Day Massacre* had never been made. In the prologue of *Bloody Mama*, the child who
will grow up to become Ma Barker is raped by her brothers in the backwoods. "Don't know why you ain't hospitable, Kate," admonishes her father,
"blood's thicker than water." The blood-water counterpoint dominates the
film visually as well as metaphorically.

Untouched by metaphysical or moral concerns, the Barker clan con-
stitutes a tribal community that admits drugs, incest, and homosexuality. Ma
Barker (a performance of ruthless carnality by Shelley Winters) bathes her
grown-up sons and beds with them occasionally. She also allows them to
bring an occasional mistress or male lover into the family she rules as absolute but benign matriarch—having disposed of her meek, improvident husband before launching into a series of noisy, bloody, but finally not too productive bank robberies.

Corman was obviously fashioning a grotesque amalgam of Dogpatch
and the Manson gang while keeping his distance from the facts. The
obligatory Oedipal references are all over the place: Ma Barker finally loses
control of the family upon the intrusion of an equally strong father image, a
kidnap victim (Pat Hingle) who is kept blindfolded because the Barker boys
cannot hold his unflinching stare. The boys are ultimately unable to force
themselves to kill him.

Less a rip-off than a riposte, *Bloody Mama* exposes some of the more
cautious, calculated tactics in *Bonnie and Clyde*, Corman rushing in where
Penn feared to tread. In *Bonnie and Clyde*, any character trait, any action
that could truly alienate the audience's affection, was discarded. The original
Benton and Neman scenario retained Clyde's homosexuality, making his
relationship with Bonnie and their driver (Michael J. Pollard in the finished
film) a *ménage à trois:* steering away from major risks, Penn prevailed to
make Clyde the victim of temporary impotence, induced, one assumes, by
his anomie. In contrast, Corman's bank robbers are depicted as irredeemable
taboo breakers, their ferocious mixture of libertarian violence and primitive
religion posing a threat to established order at a deeper level than the merely
criminal.

The family as an incestuous, murderous unit was a notion that would
gain sudden currency, after August 1969, with the Manson murders. (*Bloody
Mama* was halfway through production then, and the publicity attending
the Manson case may have damaged the film's chances rather than improved
them: the Corman film was far from profitable, especially considering its
moderate budget.) The tribal concept was already present in *Bonnie and
Clyde*, where it received cursory treatment, Penn stressing the normality

of the family members (they listen to the radio, watch Busby Berkeley movies, feel guilt, have normal reflexes). Corman, who was equally active in the horror-film genre, reminded the viewer of the more unsavory, almost cannibalistic, aspects of the clan. A communal sacrifice is suggested in the drowning of a young woman (Pamela Dunlap) who poses a security problem as well as a threat to Ma Barker's dominance. Emotional identification with such a sympathetic, "normal" character leads the viewer to expect the Barker boys to come to her aid, at which point Corman violates our expectations (even in a realistic sense) by switching to an "impossible viewpoint"— from the bottom of the bathtub, the camera looks up at the girl's head, which is being held underwater by the implacable Ma, her brood standing around the tub in passive attendance.

When the FBI finally moves against the Barkers, the family has started to disintegrate from within, the agent of its destruction being the hostage who reminds the sons of patriarchal order and, by extension, of society's norms and prejudices. Around the besieged hideout, crowds gather to picnic and watch the horrible Barkers be destroyed, not just because they robbed and murdered, but because their presocial innocence broke all social interdictions. If anything, Corman politicized the message of Bonnie and Clyde, but by refusing to make the Barkers "just folks" and beautiful, he implicated the spectator in their destruction in a way that Penn never would have dared.

For a time, American movies relived the thirties. The fashion for vintage cars and thrift-shop finery was launched. Crisis was again in the air, and so was divisiveness. Not since that era had there been as many fads, or differences so strongly emphasized. In fact, one could revisit a 1929 movie like Woman Trap and substitute the word pusher for bootlegger without loss of reality. History seemed to repeat itself as the studios opened up to the boy wonders of the music industry, just as it had earlier received the sophisticates from Broadway. This time, the most vocal and free-spending of the consumer groups, the young, was expected to pull the industry out of the slump.

Yet dissident, youth-oriented, counterculture pictures never became the rage. The films with the best liberal credentials of 1969, Haskell Wexler's Medium Cool and Arthur Penn's Alice's Restaurant, were overshadowed by the year's big hit, Easy Rider, which grafted the road-action trend to the rock-and-drug sensibility of the moment—no mean feat in itself, it remains one of few films to grasp and exploit the polarization that had split the country in the wake of the Democratic Convention the year before. By the time Zabriskie Point (1970) and The Strawberry Statement (1971) were being disowned by the very student groups the films portrayed and pandered to, the radicalization of the American film had failed.

The most obvious knowledge to be gleaned from the various efforts to enlist the criminal into the program of this or that political party is that the genre itself is politically neutral but highly susceptible (more so than

the Western) to taking on any ideological coloration. The peculiar reversals in the gangster pictures that followed *The Godfather* (1972)—biographies like *Lepke* and the new *Capone* (both 1975) in which the mobster was made to be as sober and conservative as a city father on issues like drugs and sex—were meant to even the score against the youthful cult of Bonnie, Clyde, and the kids. These reversals balanced the liberal slant of films like *Boxcar Bertha* (1972) which literally conferred martyrdom on young criminals, in this case union organizers who turn to bank robbery to further their cause. Produced by Corman and directed by Martin Scorsese, *Boxcar Bertha* was freely adapted from the memoirs of Bertha Thompson, and it reached its climax with the crucifixion of Bertha's lover to the side of a freight car by railroad agents.

In 1974 alone, there were *The Sugarland Express, Dirty Mary Crazy Larry,* and *Macon County Line* to rearrange fact and fiction in behalf of their young criminal heroes. Unique among the rural-crime and car-chase pictures was *Badlands,* the first feature of Terrence Malick, a young Texas screenwriter who seem perfectly attuned to the peculiarly hermetic mentality bred by the empty spaces of the plains states. (Malick's second feature, *Days of Heaven,* 1978, was all spectacular vistas and opaque characterizations.) In *Badlands,* he denied himself and the viewer any facile explanation for the murder spree of a young couple, obviously based on Charlie Starkweather and Caril Ann Fugate, who had killed ten people in Nebraska and Wyoming during the winter of 1957–58. Starkweather was executed; Fugate, whose complicity was never clearly established, served twenty years. Teenagers gathered at the gate of the Nebraska State Prison, a morbid little fan club, the day that Starkweather went to the chair.

This kind of erratic violence could not be adequately accounted for, although Truman Capote, in *In Cold Blood,* attempted to draw up a list of real and imagined grievances that might have engendered a similar case, the slaughter of the Clutter family in Holcomb, Kansas, in 1959. In the film version (1967) of Capote's journalistic fiction, Richard Brooks lingered tendentiously on the execution of the two killers yet spared the viewer the

Warner Brothers

even more shocking sight of the Clutters being butchered, the one scene that could possibly have given the film its moral balance. On the other hand, *Badlands* showed the killings perpetrated by the hero as the excruciatingly gratuitous acts they were, as if making the point that these unpredictable, almost accidental decisions could not be traced to any well-defined cause; and there was no complacency, for once, in the way they were filmed, quickly and bloodlessly.

Had the murders been committed for material gain, class hate, or even passion, we could safely have ranged them within the limits of our common experience. Daringly, Malick suggested instead that cruelty and callousness are part of childhood as much as innocence, and that awesome acts may be committed in a state bordering on grace. The fact that, since its unsuccessful original release, *Badlands* has found a large youthful audience is added proof that Malick's withholding of moral outrage, coupled with the missing sense of transgression in his characters, registers perfectly with a generation that grew up in the sixties, when senseless murder suddenly became a theme of popular culture, unexposed to the images of a well-ordered society.

Kit Carruthers (Martin Sheen) is a garbage collector in a South Dakota town when he first meets Holly (Sissy Spacek), a wraithlike schoolgirl whose notion of life, love, and death are highly colored by teenage magazine fiction. To her, Kit looks just like James Dean, the original rebel without a cause. There is unforced irony in the fact that whereas Dean's revolt paid dues to a number of valid causes of the fifties—it was a gesture against conformity, shaky role models provided by parents, and sexual repression—Kit has accepted, at least on the surface, the values and goals of the Eisenhower era, signally an inchoate need for renown which fails to correspond to any realistic achievement.

The romance of Kit and Holly has at first a relaxed, humorous quality to it, only slightly marred by rhetorical rumblings from Holly on the soundtrack. ("Little did I realize that what began in the back alleys of our little town would end in the badlands of Montana.") When they finally make love by a stream, Kit takes home a rock as a memento of the occasion, although it certainly did not live up to Holly's movie-fan expectations. When Holly's sign-painter father (Warren Oates) discovers the truth, he shoots her pet dog in retribution. Kit does not really plan to kill him—he just happens to carry a gun in his back pocket when he comes calling against the father's orders, and, after firing a shot at the floor to impress the man (who is duly impressed), he cannot refrain from putting two bullets in him. Even to Kit, the murder has no sense. Trying to cut a record in a penny arcade that evening, to explain to the world how it happened, the allotted sixty seconds prove too long for his confession. He leaves with Holly the next day, after setting her home on fire, a sequence scored to the piping choirboys of Carl Orff's *Musica Poetica*—a child's holocaust.

On their way through the badlands to the Canadian border, Kit kills three bounty hunters on their trail, his friend and fellow garbage collector Cato (Ramon Bieri), and a young couple who turn up at the worst possible moments (this last killing is elided, so we are never sure they have been killed). Except for the bounty hunters, whom Kit figures did not deserve a chance, the other killings are done almost half-heartedly: after shooting Cato, Kit holds the door open for him. "I got him in the stomach," he explains to Holly. "Is he upset?" she asks. "He didn't say anything to me about it," replies Kit. Waiting for Cato to die, Holly keeps him company and makes polite enquiries about his pet spider.

Awed by the manners and aura of the upper classes, Kit spares a rich old man whose mansion provides temporary shelter and a few useless mementos. On the rich man's Dictaphone, Kit leaves a message addressed to American youth that, for its vacuous advice, could have been worded by any high-school counselor—but is, in fact, edited from Starkweather's testament on a tape. Along their flight, they bury a time capsule meant to outlast even atomic attack: "He said that if the Communists ever dropped the bomb, he wished they'd drop in the middle of Rapid City," comments Holly. To preserve some of the absurd romanticism Holly reads about in her magazines, they dance at night by the headlights of their car to Nat King Cole's "A Blossom Fell." The next morning, Holly decides she has had enough and refuses to leave.

Without a willing audience—a girl "to scream my name when I die"— Kit allows himself to be captured, but first builds a cairn to mark the site. "Hell, he ain't no bigger than I am," says a surprised deputy sheriff. To the world at large, Kit and Holly have become improbable monsters: he turns out to be no different from any of his escorts, all of whom treat him with a deference usually accorded to celebrities. Kit will not die an obscure death after all, and Holly will carry the story beyond his death, telling how she got probation and "a lot of nasty looks." To the end, Kit and Holly remain scaled within their own innocent banality: they performed their senseless rituals in a futile longing for transcendence, unaware that the bodies of Kit's victims already guaranteed them a measure of immortality.

10. All in the Family

I always wanted to use the Mafia as a metaphor for America. Both . . . have roots in Europe. Basically, both . . . feel they are benevolent organizations. Both . . . have their hands stained with blood from what it's necessary to do to protect their power and interests. Both are totally capitalistic phenomena and basically have a profit motive. Of course it's a romantic conception of the Mafia.

— Interview with Francis Ford Coppola by Stephen Farber
in *Sight and Sound,* Winter 1972–73

Crime isn't a disease, it's a symptom. . . . We're a big rough rich people and crime is the price we pay for it, and organized crime is the price we pay for organization. We'll have it with us for a long time. Organized crime is just the dirty side of the sharp dollar.

— Raymond Chandler: *The Long Goodbye,* Houghton Mifflin, 1954

LET US REMEMBER that any sign of ethnic criminality was expected to disappear from American films after the new Production Code went into effect in 1933, specifying in Section 10 ("National Feelings") that "no picture shall be produced that tends to incite bigotry or hatred among people of differing races, religions or national origins." Only a year before, Capone, who could not be called by his rightful name, had become Gorio in *Bad Company* and Camonte in *Scarface*—pseudonyms that left no doubt about his Italian origin. The active campaign to dissociate minorities from gangsterism dates back to this period: consequently, the mid- and late thirties were a period in which the melting pot on the screen lost much of its pre-Code flavor—the Irish faring best of all minorities, because less than admirable traits of rowdiness and a high tolerance for alcohol were just as lovingly retained by token-Irish directors like Ford or Walsh.

The power of anti-defamation leagues over the movies was a reflection of the pressure they exerted in city politics. In 1942, the Turkus investigation of organized crime had been undermined by a gradual realization on the part of William O'Dwyer, then New York district attorney and Turkus's superior, that it was in effect alienating Italian voters indispensable to O'Dwyer's political future. The war had a role in restoring a measure of racial prejudice: unlike the Jews, who emerged from the conflict with added dignity, Italians happened to be on the enemy (and losing) side, and they were subject to ridicule and stereotyping for the duration. After the war, pains were taken to sprinkle Italian names on both sides of the law—as in *The Kiss of Death* and *Cry of the City*—rather than to renounce the use of colorful, mouth-filling names in crime pictures. Nonetheless, the pressure became so intense in the postwar period that Joseph Breen was rumored to moan: "Movie villains should be unemployed white Americans, without religious, professional, labor union, or other affiliations."

One could still detect minute acts of outspokenness in half a dozen films throughout the fifties: for instance, the word *Mafia* being casually bandied about in Karlson's *Tight Spot*, a picture which rather eccentrically made its gangland czar a WASP-ish character, played by Lorne Greene, answering to the name of Benjamin Costain. In 1961, a lowly B-picture like *The Most Dangerous Man Alive* could still toss in a reference to the Apalachin gangland convention of November 1957. It was right after Apalachin, as a matter of fact, that the Sons of Italy intensified their campaign to remove any hint of the existence of the Mafia from Hollywood films.

The Godfather was a spectacular success, first as a novel in 1969 and then as a two-part film in 1972 and 1974, because it reversed some of the prevailing clichéd attitudes toward minorities, especially where crime was concerned, and restored to the American gangster the mystique and dynastic prestige of his European criminal forefathers. In forty years, sporadic attempts at portraying the Mafia on screen had yielded *The Black Hand* in 1950, *Pay or Die* in 1960, and *The Brotherhood* in 1968. The first two covered roughly the same historical territory: the assassination in Palermo in 1909 of Joseph Petrosino, a lieutenant in the New York Police Department on duty abroad to collect evidence against mafiosi at home. The third, a sort of first draft of *The Godfather* (but produced before the publication of Mario Puzo's novel), seemed so flavorless in character, so lacking in resolve, that it created only a ripple of protest from the coalition of Italian-American groups. These groups, more than a hundred in number, were demonstrating against the filming of Puzo's *The Godfather* and Peter Maas's *The Valachi Papers* only a year later and threatening to call a boycott against any such film that stigmatized Italians as criminals.

The flood of books and films dealing with the Mafia that ensued, both here and abroad, demonstrated that, dramatically at least, the criminal society was still Sicily's most productive export. There are no equivalents of the Mafia in the rest of Europe. One possible comparison is the Chinese Tongs of the early nineteen hundreds, now reactivated in the United States, London, and non-Communist Asia; another is the Japanese *yakuza*, which has furnished the inspiration for an entire Japanese genre. But to Westerners, the mysticism, secrecy, and bonding spirit of these Oriental societies seem too alien. On the other hand, Luigi Barzini has commented on the exportability and romanticism of mafioso types, placing them on a par with the cultural stereotypes rendered familiar by Italian opera and the commedia dell'arte. (On one occasion at least, grand opera and the Mafia shared the headlines in New York, when a bomb was planted at a Caruso recital at the Met, an episode reenacted in *Pay or Die*.) Such a rich trove of material was kept off-screen by boycott threats from groups such as Joseph Colombo's vocal Italian-American Civil Rights League (later discredited as a Mafia front). But these groups were effective only until Puzo, a non-Sicilian writing about what every Sicilian knows by heart, revealed to the public the most arcane and influential subculture in the country. The entertainment world moved in on the Mafia, returning the call years after the Mafia had muscled in on show business.

Until then, the traditional approach to the Mafia crime film had been

typified by *The Black Hand*, a B-plus Metro picture that starred Gene
Kelly, in a nondancing role, as a fictitious Italian-American fighting the
Mafia's hold on Little Italy circa 1910.* The film covered itself carefully
with a lengthy written prologue that reeked of MGM's patriotic utopianism:

At the turn of the century there were more Italians living in New York than in
Rome. Many had hurried here seeking fortune and freedom. Some of them found
only failure and fear. From these Italian immigrants came no truer American
names than DiMaggio, Pecora, Giannini, La Guardia and Basilone. This story
deals with the hard, angry days when these new citizens began to place their
stake in the American dream—when they purged the Old World terror of the
Black Hand.

The key word in the above statement is *purged,* crime being identified
not as a real social problem but as something foreign that was imported
onto American soil, a disease to be eradicated firmly and efficiently, like
typhoid fever and smallpox. In *The Black Hand*, the story was placed in the
safety of the past so as to impress on the viewer the transience of the events

* The name Black Hand was coined by a Brooklyn police reporter around the turn of the century, and it referred to the crude drawings of a hand that usually accompanied threats from the
Mafia.

A Mafia movie that almost prevented the making of *The Godfather:* Kirk Douglas and
Alex Cord as mobster brothers in *The Brotherhood*, 1968. A Times Square billboard
depicting this "kiss of death" was removed when judged too provocative. *Paramount*

portrayed. Even so, the film worked better at making the Black Hand mythical than at demystifying it as merely a group of racketeers from Sicily
adept at bomb throwing and extortion. The opening, for instance, was quite
effective in suggesting a brotherhood of crime with power enough to infiltrate the new-world authorities, and it was shot like a frightening childhood memory. A distinguished-looking man bids good-bye to his wife, who
weeps and clutches a statue of the Madonna; a young boy (later to grow
into the hero) watches from his bed and makes the sign of the cross. The
husband, we infer, is an upstanding lawyer in the Italian community, and
he is about to supply proof to the local police of the Black Hand activities
in Little Italy. His rendezvous with a policeman is held in a dimly lit tenement room, but the deposition is cut short by the entrance of the very
mafiosi the witness is describing. They proceed to their bloody business,
with the chilling acquiescence of the policeman.

Arguably the one memorable movie in the career of director Richard
Thorpe, *The Black Hand* succeeded simply by concentrating on primitive
emotions—ruthlessness, betrayal, heroism, fear, death. It was much like a
penny dreadful of the period it recreated, but also much like opera. It was
a picture that identified totally with its subject, without any hindsight other
than the wishful thinking of the prologue. Yet there was a courtroom sequence in it which *The Godfather*, for all its sophistication and inside
knowledge, could not improve upon: it showed a key witness faltering on
the stand at the sight of a spectator casually drawing a matchstick across his
throat. A similar moment in *The Godfather: Part Two* worked overtime to
suggest the primeval bonding of the race, the tradition of *omertà* being
stronger than death and uniting mafiosi against the outside world. (*Part
Two* even established a parallel with Imperial Rome, where an enemy of
the state could make his children Caesar's wards if he committed suicide.)
In *The Black Hand*, the threat of violence to oneself and one's family was
enough to reduce a witness to silence. Mafiosi were exposed as criminals
who preyed on immigrants and were bound together by nothing more profound than profit.

In the late forties, the film industry went into one of its periodic surges
of civic consciousness, dealing with discrimination against blacks and Jews
in pictures like *Lost Boundaries* and *Gentleman's Agreement*. In the courtroom scene mentioned above, *The Black Hand* delivers its plea for tolerance, a rather belated and gratuitous plea, but it is delivered with grace
and fervor by J. Carrol Naish, an Irish actor specializing in dialect roles,
who played Lorelli, the fictional counterpart of Petrosino, as a shrewd,
philosophical Maigret of the tenements. "No dagos, no wops, no guineas
allowed. They don't think we're good. All they read in the papers is about
murder. Are we an inferior race as they say?" It was a speech clearly destined to soothe any feelings bruised by Hollywood's rummaging through the
past.

Naish gave *The Black Hand* its historical weight. The historical Petrosino refused to admit the mystique of the Mafia; unfortunately, he also ap-

pears to have underrated its powers of organization. Convinced that the
Black Hand was made up of expatriate *camorristi* and mafiosi, most of
whom were subject to deportation because of criminal records in Italy, he
set out to gather the evidence in Sicily. Marked for death by the Mafia, he
was ultimately ambushed and shot in a dark square. His findings, however,
had been either communicated to the Italian police or mailed to New York,
and they were responsible for a renewed anti-Mafia campaign in Little
Italy, where Petrosino was hailed as a martyr. The case was a cause célèbre
in Mafia annals and still features prominently in any work dealing with the
history of the society, most recently in Gaia Servadio's *Mafioso: A History
of the Mafia from its Origins to the Present Day.*

But Petrosino was not enough of a hero for Metro. The film relied
mostly on the fictional heroics of Johnny Columbo (Kelly), the son of the
murdered lawyer who returns years later from abroad to seek out the
killers. Fear and *omertà* prevailing among the immigrants, he is driven to
extract names at knife point like a born *guappo*. The more picturesque
action in *The Black Hand* was deeply embedded in the genre itself: the
legal process took too much time and had to be rushed on (and somewhat
diminished) by individual, justifiable violence. After blowing up the Black
Hand's headquarters—a butcher's shop where dynamite is stored next to
the meat—Columbo successfully goes after the oily, pockmarked Mafia
chieftain (Marc Lawrence). The fireworks proved to be cathartic in a
simple-minded sort of way, and the viewer was left reassured that from the
smoldering wreck of the butcher shop a crime-free, perfectly integrated
generation of Italian-Americans would come forth to take its place in baseball's Hall of Fame, the Bank of America, and even in city hall.

In 1950, such optimism could be justified; the Syndicate was maintain-
ing a reasonably low profile. In 1960, three years after Apalachin, the illu-
sion could no longer be supported. A second film based on the Petrosino
case, *Pay or Die,* was much less conclusive about the lasting effects of Petrosino's posthumous triumph. "Yes, lieutenant, you got [pause] me," murmurs
the banker Zarillo (Franco Corsaro) as he is exposed as the head of the
New York Mafia at the close of *Pay or Die*—so implying a more realistic
view of the permanence of crime in the modern world, even an added hint
that the Mafia and big business were hardly strangers to each other at this
early date. Directed by Richard Wilson in a punchy, corner-cutting B-picture
style, *Pay or Die* was a follow-up to his *Al Capone* of the previous year.
While less patronizing than *The Black Hand*— at least Petrosino was allowed to retain his own name and central role in the story—*Pay or Die* was
just as cautious in its casting. In retrospect, Richard Conte might have been
the one Hollywood Italian capable of projecting an ethos without resorting
to the inflections or mannerisms of a Henry Armetta. But Petrosino was

From the ruins of Little Italy will rise a perfectly integrated generation of Italian
Americans. Gene Kelly going for Marc Lawrence in traditional Old World style, in *The
Black Hand,* 1950. *Metro-Goldwyn-Mayer*

New York police lieutenant Joseph Petrosino (Ernest Borgnine), shot and killed in a
dark Palermo alley as he gathered evidence against mafiosi back home, in *Pay Or Die*,
1960. *Allied Artists*

played instead by Ernest Borgnine, who had won an Oscar for his performance as a sensitive, lovesick Bronx Italian butcher in *Marty*, and Borgnine
made the detective a shade too sensitive and lovesick, just to be on the
safe side.

An ironic resurgence of Italian pride followed the release of *The Godfather* and *The Godfather: Part Two*, and an equally ironic stardom was
bestowed on Al Pacino and Robert De Niro for playing mafiosi in a saga
over six hours long during which the disputed word *Mafia* was mentioned
only once (by the dopey chairman of a crime commission who is obviously
no match for a mafioso worth his name). Since words like *Mafia*, *mafioso*,
and *Cosa Nostra* never appeared in the original screenplays, their absence
in the final version was hardly a symbolic victory for the Italian civil-rights
groups; the film industry had been adept at sacrificing minor points since
the days of the by-now defunct Hays office. However, the shrewdness of the
euphemisms the films employed should not be underestimated; after all, the
Justice Department had been persuaded to drop the offending words from
their communiqués on organized crime, and *syndicate* is a functional word
that lacks any ethnic resonance. *The Godfather*, not only for the sake of
authenticity, substituted the word *family* to denote each of the various
gangs comprising the Mafia, and the two component films, stretching over

almost fifty years, became a family saga that juggled both senses of the word.

For all the curiosity the Mafia arouses in the layman, *The Black Hand* and *Pay or Die* adopted an external, legalistic viewpoint and an attitude tinged with outrage. *The Godfather* reversed the viewpoint, looking from inside the underworld out into a hopelessly corrupt society from which tradition, loyalty, honor, and respect for one's elders had almost totally vanished. This daring dramatic device would ruinously have failed had the outside, straight world been allowed to intrude. Two of the most debatable propositions about the criminal world were carried to a claustrophobic extreme; namely, that there is a code of honor among thieves, and that this perfectly self-contained (and self-sustaining) world rarely touches the man in the street. There was a frightening, memorable scene in Walsh's *The Roaring Twenties* in which an elderly couple was caught in the crossfire between rival gangs at a restaurant. There were virtually no bystanders in *The Godfather,* and none of those who were included retained any innocence.

The Godfather might be reviewing the Renaissance through the eyes of the Medici, a perspective similar to that adopted by the Italian director Luchino Visconti in *The Damned* (1969), wherein he showed the rise of Nazism through the eyes of the (fictionalized) Krupp family. In fact, there is more of Visconti in *The Godfather* than of any of the above-mentioned directors. Coppola's Don Corleone appeared at times as a kindred soul to Visconti's Sicilian prince in *The Leopard;* both icons of an order about to pass. Visconti's original choice for his princely hero was Laurence Olivier; so was Coppola's for the godfather. For a role demanding a charisma beyond that of most actors, George C. Scott was also considered, but Marlon Brando, Puzo's first choice, was the final choice. Olivier would have undoubtedly brought to the part his own thin-lipped, ascetic alertness as well as some of the papal authority that is apparent in photos of a genuine godfather such as Carlo Gambino; he would have been chilling in the role. Brando, affecting a wheezy delivery and using more makeup than any major star since Paul Muni, mellowed the Don into a patriarch in autumn.

For visual style, Coppola and his cameraman, Gordon Willis, relied mostly on one lingering, controlling image, that of hushed ceremonials among men in darkened rooms. The lowered Venetian blinds that established the mood in *films noirs* by casting stripes of psychological guilt across the screen now suffused interiors with amber, old-masterly light. In the opening shot, the mood was already confessional and the godlike character of Don Vito Corleone was boldly established. Holding audience and granting favors on his daughter's wedding day, Don Corleone listens to an outraged father demand death for the attackers of his daughter who have been set free because of family influence or the sheer laxity of the law. "That would not be fair, my friend, your daughter is alive," is the sober reply, as if the godfather were restoring a rapport between deed and retribution long lost in the byways and intricacies of the legal system, and dispensing an

Hushed ceremonials in darkened rooms: Michael Corleone (Al Pacino) is sworn fealty
by Clemenza (Richard Castellano), as Neri (Richard Bright) looks on. *The Godfather,*
1972. *Paramount*

eye-for-an-eye justice in direct contact with the plaintiff.

In *The Godfather,* when Don Corleone took on his main adversary from
the straight world, a Hollywood producer patently inspired by Harry Cohn,
and when his younger son and heir, Michael (Al Pacino), clashed with a
U.S. senator in *Part Two,* these opponents were depicted as racist, uncouth,
venal, and, more significant, as sexual perverts. (*"Infamia!"* mutters Don
Corleone upon learning that Jack Woltz, the producer [John Marley], keeps
a child star in his palatial home for sexual purposes; the WASP senator plays
heavy sado-masochistic games with prostitutes.) Their proclivities clearly
offend the Corleones, abstemious family men, more than does their pride.
The producer and the senator appear guilty of crimes against nature, next
to which the Corleones merely granting justice without resorting to
the law, or at worst transacting business in an unorthodox way. The manner
in which the guilty are humbled, in blood-soaked beds, seems somewhat
scriptural, as if the godfather were omniscient as well as all-powerful. This
power and its resultant status are to be passed on from father to son, if
the son proves worthy.

The Godfather is also about the transition from the archaic, relatively
honor-bound order of Don Corleone to the more pragmatic and less scrupu-
lous regime of his younger son, who would develop the family business into
an impersonal national corporation. When first introduced, Michael is an

unlikely candidate to head a prominent Mafia family in the eastern United States; a college student and a war veteran, Michael seems on his return to civilian life uncommitted to the family business. Soon enough, an attempt is made on Don Corleone's life, and Michael is claimed by the imperatives of honor and of his own Sicilian blood to take revenge on his father's enemies. When Michael kills for the first time, the act takes on an aspect of ritual blood-spilling: the training and planning, the breathtaking gravity with which Michael dispatches the two men at a restaurant table, the deadly calm that follows the shooting as Michael unhurriedly leaves the scene, abandoning his gun (which cannot be traced: an enchanted weapon)—each step has its own initiatory justification.

As the new Don, Michael expands the family's sphere of influence to the gambling casinos of the West. *The Godfather* concludes with the death of Don Corleone and the ensuing bloodbath, a fictional counterpart of the Banana War of the late forties, that will consolidate Michael's power within the Mafia. The old Don's death, of a heart attack while playing with Michael's son in a sun-drenched orchard, serves for an effective improvisation: Don Corleone has fashioned a grotesque denture from an orange peel in order to play the bogeyman for his grandchild, and the little boy struggles with the same ambivalence experienced by the audience—the scary suggestion that a monster lurks after all behind the benign grandfather figure.

Part Two provided the addenda and corrigenda to a subject treated a bit too hurriedly in *The Godfather*. The making of the first film was marked by dissension between the producer, Al Ruddy, and Coppola, who went on to produce the sequel himself, combining leftover material from Puzo's novel with an updating of the plot that took the Corleone family into the late fifties. By then, Michael had moved the seat of power to Lake Tahoe in California and had planned an alliance with the Jewish branch of the mob, as represented by Hyman Roth (Lee Strasberg), that would result in profits undreamed of by Don Corleone. Patterned after the notorious Meyer Lansky, best publicized of the Jewish gangsters in the Syndicate, Roth delivers Lansky's by now legendary boast: "We're bigger than U.S. Steel." The wily, avuncular Roth lacks the warmer traits of his Italian contemporary, and, compared to Don Corleone's, Roth's family life is drab and there is no visible issue, only a few hulking bodyguards prowling around his modest Miami house. Munching a sandwich in front of his TV set, Roth reminisces: "I've loved baseball since Arnold Rothstein fixed the World Series in 1919." Poor Rothstein, dead for more than forty years, was the only real gangster mentioned by name in all of *The Godfather*.

Part Two pursued the parallel between crime and big business into the imperialistic fifties, transporting Michael and Roth to Havana and seating them at the table of dictator Fulgencio Batista, next to the ITT representatives, to take part in the despoiling of the island. Although it is obvious that Michael, deep inside, finds the operation distasteful—he is equally ill at ease at the live sex shows patronized by American tourists—he backs out of the deal, not because of any moral qualm, but because his Harvard Business

School instinct tells him that the Batista regime is about to collapse; his mafioso flair scoops even *The New York Times*. Stateside, another climactic purge is launched to liquidate Roth and his supporters, among them Michael's weak, older brother. The success of the purge leaves Michael alone at the top, sharing the desolate fate of those who gain the world but lose their immortal souls—or so Coppola would have us believe.

Mario Puzo's novel was on *The New York Times* best-seller list for sixty-seven weeks. Paramount picked up the film rights for a paltry $50,000 before publication—the recent failure of *The Brotherhood* seemed to have soured any prospects for a successful Mafia movie. *The Godfather* surprised even its makers by becoming the most profitable film up to its time: in December 1977, *Variety* listed rentals of $86 million. The sequel came up to $29 million. Both pictures were later combined with one hour of discarded footage to make a nine-hour television film aired on four successive evenings

Don Vito Corleone (Marlon Brando) dispensing an-eye-for-an-eye justice in direct contact with the plaintiff, Bonasera (Salvatore Corsitto). *The Godfather. Paramount*

Michael is claimed by the imperatives of family honor and his own Sicilian blood: Richard Castellano and Al Pacino in *The Godfather. Paramount*

in November 1977, for which rights the National Broadcasting Corporation paid $12 million. Billed as "the complete novel for television" and preceding each chapter with the most absurd disclaimer ever—"does not represent any ethnic group . . . fictional account of a small group of criminals"—the series failed to capture the vast, nation-wide audience that had made *Roots* a television event earlier that year. Along with the millions of viewers who had flocked to the theaters only a few years before, something had been lost in transition.

Back then, apart from the film's intrinsic quality, a chain of events had conditioned audiences to accept *The Godfather* as the long-awaited, final word on organized crime. Paramount had carefully orchestrated press releases during production. There had been warnings and threats from Italian civil-rights groups and, reputedly, from the Mafia as well. *Time* reported that the producer's car had been riddled with machine-gun fire, although the fact was never authenticated. It did prove, however, that publicity agents still functioned the same old way, like lower-echelon mafiosi—the filmed-under-threat routine had worked wonders back in the days of *Doorway to Hell.* Interviews during production and at the time of release stressed authenticity above all. Robert Evans, then a top Paramount executive and a Coppola supporter, justified his director in a *Time* interview: "He knew the way these men ate their food, kissed each other, talked. He knew the grit." Anyone with a family connection, however remote or fictional, seems to have

The mafioso as statesman: Michael's instinct tells him to back out of an alliance with the Jewish branch of the Syndicate, as represented by Hyman Roth (Lee Strasberg). Michael must therefore have Roth and his supporters, including his own brother Fredo (John Cazale), liquidated. *The Godfather: Part II,* 1974. *Paramount*

"A fictional account of a small group of criminals." Luca Brasi (Lenny Montana) gar-
roted in a bar. *The Godfather. Paramount*

been consulted, or appeased, or in some cases hired. Despite opposition from
the production staff, a Las Vegas master of ceremonies, Carlo Russo, landed
a meaty minor role as Carlo Rizzi, Don Corleone's treacherous son-in-law.
He got the part on the strength of his friendship with Anthony Colombo,
who was Joseph Colombo's son and vice-president of the Italian-American
Civil Rights League.

The elder Colombo contributed his share of headlines during the production, some of them in tragic opposition to his platform. In June 1971, at
an Italian-American Unity Day rally in New York, he was shot in the head
by a black gunman named Jerome A. Johnson, who had allegedly been hired
by a rival New York family headed by Joseph Gallo. Johnson was killed on
the spot by Colombo's bodyguards. (At first, it seemed unlikely that a black
assassin would do the job for a Mafia family; but that one indeed had only
proved that eligibility rules had been relaxed in the sixties in order to admit
blacks and Puerto Ricans.) Colombo died in 1978 without ever recovering
from the wounds inflicted by Johnson. In April 1972, when *The Godfather*
had been playing for only a few weeks, Gallo was shot dead while celebrat-
ing his forty-third birthday at Umberto's Clam House in Little Italy. It was
soon afterwards made public that an underground war had been raging be-
between the Colombo and Gallo families.

The Mafia was very much alive, despite Colombo's campaign to pronounce it dead and gone with a generation of Italian and Sicilian immigrants. *The Godfather* could be read as a *roman à clef,* and it was considered hip to detect the fictionalized portraits of Harry Cohn, Frank Sinatra, Meyer Lansky, and Bugsy Siegel. Puzo had done his homework thoroughly. The Corleones were made up of a composite of various Mafia families, and set into a historical context. Puzo used some real names, including Maranzano and Lucchese. As he candidly admitted later in *The Godfather Papers,* he had done a job that even met with the approval and respect of those concerned; a fact corroborated by Gay Talese in *Honor Thy Father,* a detailed chronicle of the Bonanno family.

Puzo supplied the Corleones with fairly mythological dimensions, but Coppola was to go even farther in the same direction. The director adopted as key scenes in both films that classic moment in mythological fiction in which the hero, under the influence of the past, confronts his fate and accepts it, as if the future had suddenly been revealed to him. Michael's first kill in *The Godfather,* Vito's in *Part Two,* did not carry the same significance in Puzo's novel, where they were presented as stages in the development of the characters.

NBC's high hopes for a second *Roots* were not so absurd, for in its way *The Godfather* undertook a similar exploration in time, striving to set up a continuity between the old and the new world. In the spring of 1978, the four-part television film *Holocaust* almost matched the success of *Roots.* Both series dealt with the trials and tragedies of racial persecution, concluding with statements of achievement and hope. But *The Godfather* traced a downward graph within a mere two generations. The final effect was far from elating; as the romance of immigration hardened into a power play behind closed shutters, the mystic freemasonry of crime deteriorated into utilitarian carnage. The films contrasted a romantic past—bucolic, primitive Sicily; Little Italy through a patina of affection—to the harsh and somber present. Rearranging the events in chronological order, the TV version exposed this strategy a little too starkly, gambling on the cumulative effect of the dynastic novel, an effect, that, in this case, turned out to be depressingly negative.

The Godfather, especially *Part Two,* has undergone close scrutiny (in *Jump-Cut* magazine, for one) along critical lines that constitute a politicization of Robert Warshow's famous dictum that the gangster embodies a denial of capitalist society. And Coppola, at least ex post facto, encouraged this reading of *The Godfather* by admitting to a metaphorical critique of the American system. It was a metaphor, however, that Coppola could only activate at the expense of genre, that could only function by leaving narrative gaps which, were they filled, would compromise the dominant premise of the Mafia as a self-supporting, self-regulating, alternative society.

Where does the Corleone family income come from? There was some talk of power and influence, of the family "owning" judges and politicians, but not one word about such bread-and-butter activities as prostitution,

Key scenes in *The Godfather* and *The Godfather: Part II:* the heroes (Al Pacino, Robert
De Niro) commit their first, sacramental murders. *Paramount*

hijacking, loan sharking, or the numbers racket. At times Coppola went soft on his characters in a way Puzo never did. The godfather refused to get involved in the drug racket because of vague moral principle—"Drugs will destroy us" was the Don's one failed prophecy—while Puzo simply presented the deal as a shaky investment that the shrewd Don turned down. Sonny Corleone (James Caan) was not portrayed as the feared family executioner he was in the novel but as a lusty, boyish ladykiller.

The almost total suppression of the godfather's criminal dimension removed his main social characteristic from the film. The murders, extortion, and exploitation of others which originally inscribed the character in the underworld were transmuted into retaliatory action, correction of power abuse, business transactions of a more ethical nature than seemed customary among mobsters. The intimidation of potential victims—the godfather's famous offer that cannot be refused—was carried out on behalf of the deserving and the deprived, whether to obtain a Hollywood contract for a favorite godson of certified talent or to obtain a stay of eviction from a miserly slum landlord.

Another sleight of hand concerned the role of Kay (Diane Keaton), Michael Corleone's girlfriend, later his second wife. A Yankee princess, Kay might have functioned (as she did in the novel) as a representative of the non-Italian, noncriminal world she left behind to marry into the Corleone family. But her role gave Coppola the worst trouble, since to admit the honest outside world would have imperiled his airtight universe. Consequently, Kay was made to act unduly stupid, asking questions that no sensible mafioso wife had the right to ask her man (the answers being more than obvious); and once this tiresome tactic made her presence expendable, there was the unexpected revelation that she has willingly aborted Michael's third child. This was truly the unkindest blow to the character, since abortion, in the eyes of the Catholic Church, is sin, and Kay thus joined the "unnatural" company of the pedophile producer and the sadistic senator. When Michael slammed the door in her face, his action had all the force of justifiable rejection, and audiences were bound to accept and even applaud it. Kay had no place in the cinematic saga of the Corleones.

At the height of the war between the families, Don Corleone delivers a short but precise line, "This war stops now." During the period in which *The Godfather* was made and released—that of the Vietnam war—this sort of pacifist slogan in the mouth of a ruthless and powerful man had the force of an exorcism and henceforth identified him as the righteous man whose moral superiority transcended all legality. In the final analysis, Don Corleone is the upholder of natural law, God's law, separating good from evil. By intent, religious ceremony was used repeatedly to counterpoint some of the most violent deeds of the Corleones: the preparations for a massacre are intercut with the christening of Michael's firstborn; a procession is in progress as the young Vito stalks his first victim across the roofs of Little Italy. Rather than implicating the Church in the underworld, as the Marxist observer might have it, these parallels serve to turn the violence into a sacra-

"This war stops now!" A pacifist slogan stamps Don Vito as the Righteous Man whose moral superiority transcends legality. Marlon Brando in *The Godfather*. *Paramount*

ment. To reinforce the impression of justified, sacramental violence, some vaguely Biblical references were scattered throughout: the hand kissing, the "kiss of death" with which Michael casts off his treacherous brother Fredo (John Cazale), and some visionary lines, such as "Whoever comes to you at the Barzini meeting, he's a traitor," or "Before I get to my hotel, I'll be assassinated," which sounded like parodies of parables.

Toward the end of *Part Two*, fiction became historically certifiable, and the film was thereby led into implications it could not handle. Following the Cuban revolution and his falling-out with Hyman Roth, Michael says: "If history has taught us anything it's that you can kill anyone." Considering the failed attempts on the life of Roosevelt, Churchill, Hitler, and, closer to the film's own *milieu*, Frank Costello, all of these evidence to the contrary, the line can only strike the viewer as an intimation of things to come: the suspected underworld participation in the Kennedy assassination or the documented involvement of the Syndicate in the CIA plots against Fidel Castro, in which John Rosselli, once of Hollywood and Bioff and Browne notoriety, acted as middleman. The line worked on the viewer all right— Michael proved his point by having Roth assassinated in full view of the FBI by a Kamikaze gunman—but by then it was too late for the film to avail itself of a fresh set of implications. Having spent close to seven hours of screen time to establish a seemingly valid parallel between criminal and corporate behavior, *The Godfather* still could not sound the alarm on crime.

"We had been sure of the square audience," wrote Mario Puzo with a certain surprise at what Coppola had wrought from his novel, "and now it looked as if we were going to get the hip avant-garde too." To *Rolling Stone,* the godfather seemed an omniscient figure capable of taking on Con Edison single-handed, a displacement of authority away from the establishment. What if the films also endorsed a paternalistic, repressive, sexist subsociety that conservatives all over would recognize, identify with, and tip their hard-hats to? Later in the seventies, the godfather seems more castrating than charismatic—a figure of the Nixonian era rather than a man for all political seasons—because ensuing events have left the film's cool, knowledgeable, guiltless stance behind.

Thus, a movie for détente. In 1972, the year of the first *Godfather* and also the year of Watergate and the Republican Convention in Miami (during which Norman Mailer appropriated the title "Godfather" for Richard Nixon), concerns like the perfectability of society and the regeneration of the criminal seemed to belong forever to the twenties and thirties. Over such issues the film extended the soothing acquiescence that, left to themselves, criminals would leave society unmolested except to dispute the powerful for a slice of the power. Rarely has there been a film so much of a piece with its discourse, so untempered by distance or irony. Could *The Godfather* have pleaded less openly for peaceful coexistence with the underworld or seemed less accepting of things-as-they-are and still have become in its time the most successful film ever?

In the year following its release, *The Godfather* won Oscars for Best Picture, and for Brando as Best Actor, while the sequel received in turn the awards for Best Picture, Best Director, and for Robert De Niro as Best Supporting Actor. Aside from their financial success, the pictures generated a "godfather syndrome" to be reckoned with whenever the subject of the Mafia was seriously discussed, as in the *Time* cover story of May 19, 1977, which deplored the public's tolerance and its new infatuation with the more romantic aspects of organized crime. Imitations and rebuttals began to crop up. Films like *The Don is Dead* (1973) and *Black Godfather* (1974) seem inevitable rip-offs destined to cash in on the then current craze, but a number of other works, like Menahem Golan's *Lepke* and Steve Carver's *Capone* (which was produced by Roger Corman), appear as typical of a new conservatism in gangster films that had replaced the disturbing effrontery of *Bonnie and Clyde.*

Now that ethnic groups were less touchy about the screen representation of their criminal forefathers, *Lepke* and *Capone* found their heroes in history and draped them in the rich golds and browns from Coppola's films, dropping more real gangland names in the process than did Walter Winchell in his day. In some respects, *Lepke* tried to be a Semitic *Godfather.* Buchalter, however, lacked the charisma of his Italian contemporaries, real or fictional. As played by Tony Curtis, he was the bad Jewish boy who made good in the rackets and who was done in by the combined efforts of the Mafia, Hoover, and Dewey: offered leniency if he surrendered to the FBI, he became nonetheless the only major gangland figure to be legally executed.

Is atonement such an inherent part of the Jewish ethos that the three major Jewish gangsters ever to merit film biographies had to be made scapegoats? Arnold Rothstein in *King of the Roaring Twenties* and Bugsy Siegel in the television movie *The Virginia Hill Story* (1974) were portrayed as victims of the machinations of civic and underworld bargainers. *Lepke,* made in Hollywood by an Israeli filmmaker, becomes solemn to the point of ritual once Lepke is delivered into the hands of his executioners. The gangster's death is possibly the most graphically detailed in an American crime picture. Lepke eats heartily, bathes, dresses in white hospital clothes, is tonsured, walks the last mile, sits on the chair. The camera pulls back as he is strapped in, there are close-ups of his feet, of the mask and the electrodes being applied. Then the lever is pulled three times, Lepke's body twists, and Walter Winchell's voice (actually imitated by satirist Vaughn Meader) delivers a factual epitaph as if he were reciting a lay version of the Prayer for the Dead.

The latest reincarnation of Al Capone in the person of Ben Gazzara, in the picture simply titled *Capone,* is another figure for the staid, retrenched seventies. Although there is plenty of violence in *Capone* (lifted from *The St. Valentine's Day Massacre*), it seems doubtful that it would disturb or outrage the viewer, considerations of familiarity apart. The new Capone, for instance, disapproves of young girls who drink bathtub gin, loves opera and his family, and acts like a father to a young mistress (he even recites an Our Father over her dead body when she is machine-gunned by Moran's gang). As the film ends, Capone, a deposed crime czar, sits forgotten in his Miami winter palace, his reason destroyed by paresis, ranting against the Communists as the true enemies of the nation.

The more serious rebuttals to *The Godfather* were all Italian productions, for all the American names on the credits and the use of actual New York locations, and so are outside the scope of this book. They are worth mentioning, however, since they aspired to present documented fact and to serve as a sort of salutary demystification of Coppola's films. Released in November 1972, *The Valachi Papers* was based on the testimony of a minor mafioso, Joseph Valachi, as recorded by Peter Maas in a best-seller that antedated Puzo's novel. Back in 1963, the McClelland Committee regarded Valachi as a somewhat unreliable, self-aggrandizing witness, a pawn the FBI used to corroborate, amplify, or simply mouth the testimony of previous informers. Valachi had died of a heart attack in a Texas prison by the time the film went into production in 1971; and Vito Genovese, the man Valachi dreaded most, the Mafia leader whose undeserved persecution had triggered all the informing, had died in Leavenworth two years before, also of heart failure. Valachi's tale could thus be sold as gospel truth. Since Valachi had rendered the term *Cosa Nostra* a household word, it was difficult for the producer, Dino de Laurentiis, to keep the offending name off the soundtrack. The film was primarily shot in Roman studios, ostensibly to escape harassment from the Italian-American Civil Rights League. In fact, *The*

Valachi Papers played in Italy under the more lurid title of *Joe Valachi: I Segreti di Cosa Nostra,* and it did fair business abroad. It received uniformly bad reviews in America, where the critical consensus was that its British director, Terence Young, just didn't know the grit. Judging from its commercial career in this country, the last thing Americans wanted to see in the wake of *The Godfather* was a clinical, clumsy roll call of thirty years of gangland murders.

De Laurentiis followed *The Valachi Papers* with *Crazy Joe* (1974), another Mafia chronicle that flashed all sorts of historical dates on the screen, as if to lend credence to, in this case, a cast of pseudonymous mobsters. The film's hero, Crazy Joe (Peter Boyle) is "street meat," a Mafia enforcer trying to make a name for himself, an insurmountable problem when one considers that the screenplay (by Lewis John Carlino, who also scripted *The Brotherhood*) never dares to breathe Joe's family name, which is Gallo. By some accounts, the late Joe Gallo deserved a better tribute than this irresolute film. Acquainted with the writings of Sartre and Camus, Gallo was a popular character in "gangster chic" circles, and he was trying to promote his own memoir, *A-block,* when he was killed. *Crazy Joe* had a tough time making a case for Gallo against Colombo; finally, both are shown as pawns sacrificed by the Kissinger-like Don Vincenzo (Carlo Gambino as played by Eli Wallach) to the needs of the Honored Society. Most damaging of all, Carlo Lizzani is an Italian director who, alas, cannot direct action scenes, which in a project like *Crazy Joe* is the true kiss of death.

Much more ambitious was *Lucky Luciano* (1973), directed by Francesco Rosi in his typical semijournalistic style, which openly solicited sympathy for a fallen ganglord manipulated by a system even more ruthless than his own. In order to dispose of some clichés clustered through the years around Luciano, the Night of the Sicilian Vespers, the historical purge in which Luciano wrested control of the New York underworld from the higher-ranking Maranzano and Masseria in 1931, was shown as an opening montage with a Neapolitan aria throbbing on the soundtrack. There was little violence in the remainder of the film, and the youthful splurge at the outset was made to seem a romantically crude stage of crime that Luciano would endeavor to outgrow for the rest of his career.

Rosi opened the film with Luciano being deported to Italy in 1946, after serving nine years in prison. From his cell in Dannemora, he had waged his still considerable power over the New York waterfront to prevent wartime sabotage and his agents abroad had acted as liaisons to the American Army in the Sicilian campaign; for such services, he was granted a pardon by Governor Dewey, his erstwhile nemesis. The director follows the exiled Luciano—a dapper, aloof businessman harassed by the United Nations Drug Commission and by the Italian police, who suspect an involvement with the international narcotics trade. Ultimately, Rosi shows Luciano as a scapegoat, a wasted old man shouldering the corruption of two continents.

Neither Rosi, nor Gian Maria Volonté, an all-purpose "progressive" actor of the early seventies, supplied an emotional pipeline to the character;

and for all the overlay of information, Rosi's inquest yielded few revelations
(even though Charles Siragusa, the narcotics agent who kept close watch
on Luciano during his late years, played himself and acted as technical con-
sultant). In fact, the best that Rosi could come up with was an epitaph
reminiscent of the *film noir:* "Everybody runs around and in the end they
find themselves right where they started." Born in Lescara Freddi, Sicily,
Luciano was buried in St. John's Cathedral cemetery in Queens, New York,
some hundred feet away from Vito Genovese. Between the two sites there
lies the American criminal experience that seems to evade European filmmakers and that Coppola, for all his omissions, captured so eloquently.

11. The Techniques of Violence

America is becoming less and less a stable country, one that can be relied on. It is returning to its old demons.
— Charles De Gaulle, quoted by Jean-Raymond Tournoux,
in *La Tragédie du Général*, Plon, 1967

FROM THE VANTAGE POINT of the late seventies, the richest period of the American film is generally acknowledge to have followed the arrival of sound and to have come to an end with the dissolution of the Hollywood studio system. This was the golden age that managed to span the Depression, the Second World War, the Cold War, the Korean War, the decline of Western imperialism, and so many other events that made the second stage of the Age of Uncertainty all the more uncertain. During these years, the film industry was admonished to stay away from the subject of politics and to accept the regulations of the MPAA in matters concerning sex, violence, and language. The strictures were often absurd, the concessions often miserly and pathetic, but the films nonetheless managed to deal covertly with all the forbidden subjects, and in the process their visual language was refined.

In 1966, the film industry was faced with the loss of a sizable percentage of its previous audience to television and to the growing pop-music industry. It was decided, as a desperate measure, to do away with the Code and permit the treatment of "controversial, shocking subjects," to liberalize acceptable screen language so that it could include profanity, and to allow nudity when justified by the demands of the plot. This was a brazen attempt to lure the adult audience back into the theaters. Speaking for the producers who felt the urgency to draw the line between films and television at a time when studios were embarking on the production of TV movies, MPAA president Jack Valenti proposed to channel the old Code authority into the creation of a rating system for various age groups. The assumption that the American public had a certain maturity of judgment was given as the major reason for a move that was definitely not abrupt but nevertheless constituted a policy reversal.

Valenti's move was a shrewd one, since television was at the time, and still is, regulated by the 1934 Communications Act, which also applies to radio, and which states that broadcasting must be "in the public interest, convenience and necessity." Besides, the networks had adopted a code of ethics on a voluntary basis as the film industry had in the early thirties (and, in the opinion of some critics, the networks were condemned to repeat the film industry's mistakes). American films would henceforth separate the men from the boys, figuratively and literally. "Mature" audiences would be allowed to watch the Hollywood equivalents of foreign films like *I Am Curious: Yellow* and *Night Games,* which had trailed behind them court warrants and sold-out art houses. Producers were no longer afraid to have their films banned by the National Catholic Office, and in certain cases an NCO ban was even wished for. When *Hurry Sundown* and *Reflections in a Golden Eye* (both 1967) were rated "C" (for Condemned), their chances for success were marginally improved.

The new classification went into effect in November 1968, and Hollywood poised itself for the leap to maturity. Yet filmmakers seemed unable to benefit from the long awaited and much discussed freedom to deal with the realities of the period. Frontal nudity—mostly female, intercourse—all soft core, and profanity—self-conscious and overabused, did not noticeably enlarge the repertory of dramatic situation or contribute to any real maturation of attitudes. Nudity and profanity escalated so rapidly and indiscriminately that they soon went largely unnoticed, and nowadays obscenities are mainly noticed when the films play on television to an obligato of bleeps. The new films prescribed the same mixture as before, but they administered it in overdoses, and genuine aberrations, like the virtual exclusion of women in the "buddy film," quickly followed.

The public may have grown tired of cinematic sex, but its tolerance for violence seemed undiminished. No clear disposition in the revised code concerned the depiction of crime in films, but it was tacitly understood that violence should be dramatically justified, and these films rated accordingly. Explicit sex may have been intimidating, but Hollywood had enjoyed long decades of practice in depicting violence. What is undoubtedly the most violent era in American films began in 1968 and today seems far from abating. During the years in which the Hays and Johnson offices had functioned as the power of repression, an explanation for movie violence was that if you could not titillate an audience, you had to brutalize it—an extension of the oversimplified theory that sexual repression usually finds release in brutality. This explanation is still echoed occasionally, as in 1976 issue of *New York Magazine* in which the screenwriter Steven Shagan was quoted as saying, "The only sensuality in our movies is in violence." Such a view fails to take notice that violence also reaches the audience as an all-purpose metaphor. Hollywood could hardly make a political statement that would be acceptable to all factions of the audience, but violence proved extremely useful to put across views from either the right or the left in the past decade.

New styles of violence demand new types of criminal, and the only obvious delinquent hero to emerge from the sixties was the pusher. The character, however never really took hold of the public's consciousness as had his predecessor, the bootlegger. Like alcohol, addictive drugs and marijuana were legal in the early years of the century, then declared illegal when they seemed to become a threat to social order. The issue has subsequently been falsified in one way or another. Whether the use of drugs amounts to criminal behavior was a point argued by scientists like Thomas Szasz, and along more evangelical lines by Timothy Leary, Alan Watts, and the counterculture. The inescapable outcome was that in the dramatic scenario of the sixties the pusher was assigned a shadowy role and a moral ambiguity that he seemed unable to shake off. The new image also had to contend with lurid memories from popular culture—the corrupter who stalks the playground, the leech who preys on the lower classes, and the more recent breed of solicitous sadists who serviced the hero in fifties films like *The Man with the Golden Arm* and *A Hatful of Rain.*

It was not until *Cisco Pike* (1971) that the pusher was elevated to the role of hero and dealing drugs was portrayed as a valid way of life. Written and directed by B. W. L. Norton, the film turned the standard roles of pusher and cop on their heads. It followed Cisco (Kris Kristofferson) in his travels through the Los Angeles area as he attempted to dispose of a carload of marijuana dropped into his hands by an aging, embittered police detective (Gene Hackman). The sale of the drugs would supposedly result in a clean record for the pusher and a comfortable pension for the cop. Already a familiar singer and composer, Kristofferson brought to his first dramatic role the relaxed weariness of the nonstraight trying to make ends meet and gradually, almost against his will, being accepted into straight society. People from the various levels of society were shown, unhysterically, as partaking of drugs very much as sophisticates were often depicted as drinkers in the early thirties.

The dealer had hitherto been a supporting character who supplied the requisite contemporary cool, especially in the black films that Hollywood began turning out after the breakthrough success of *Cotton Comes to Harlem*—which grossed $5.2 million in 1970—and *Shaft*—$6.1 million in 1971, obviously more than the black market alone could provide. Black films soon reached absurd levels of wish fulfillment and hero-mongering in *Super Fly* (1972) and *The Mack* (1973). Overcompensating for years of black dehumanization on the white screen, the latter two pictures glorified the pusher as the supreme cool operator who, unlike the more realistic Cisco Pike, could retire with impunity after one final deal and a million-dollar profit; and they portrayed the pimp as a superstud whom all whores fight for. Both represented a defiant attempt to flaunt characters that, to the white world, represented the scourges of drugs and prostitution afflicting the black world; but at least they were a departure from Hollywood formulas that obviously derived from the white experience.

For the most part, black movies were limited by a misguided attempt to recast white experience in black terms, and many black movies were actually remakes of white successes in the crime and horror genres. *Cool Breeze* (1972) adapted *The Asphalt Jungle* with a timely twist that might have amused W. R. Burnett: the motivation for the high-precision diamond heist was the founding of a black people's bank—the caper perhaps ennobled by such altruistic intentions, but also somewhat reduced to a simple transfer of funds. The inspiration for *Black Gunn* (1972) and *Black God-father* was evident from their titles. *Hit Man* (1972) was a black version of a British gangster picture, *Get Carter; Bucktown* (1975), a black version of *Walking Tall*. In due time, there was a black spin-off of *The Exorcist* titled *Abby* (1975).

The Black Artists Alliance of Hollywood was ready to concede that black pictures were hardly advancing the cause of a new black image, echoing the statements made by writers such as LeRoi Jones and James Baldwin. The hustler, the pimp, and the pusher, despite the alarm of the NAACP, must have struck black audiences as a more integral part of ghetto living than private eyes like Shaft or night-club owners like Gunn, who were in fact carried over from white crime thrillers. "Harlem gave its full support to *Super Fly*," boasted the film's white producer, Sig Shore. "It was a movie with whose sentiments and viewpoints blacks could identify." At a time when the ghetto exercised a morbid fascination for most audiences, the impact of Priest, the pusher hero in *Super Fly*, snorting cocaine from a huge cross around his neck, was to be preferred to a depiction of more meaningful social rituals. It was a shrewd touch to place a Black Panther beret on Priest's head; the hint of militancy further exorcised the "good nigger" image that had vestigially survived in more positive family dramas like *Sounder*, a film that "square" white reviewers had praised as dependably as they had deplored the others.

The composite image jointly projected by Richard Roundtree in *Shaft*, by Ron O'Neal in *Super Fly*, and by Jim Brown in *Slaughter*, as well as in their sequels, was that of a militant macho with a taste for the right consumer goods, like playboy pads and European cars, running afoul of the honkies as he led a black action force against the white Syndicate.

Sexuality and violence were made the true emblem of blackness, and the films were openly racist and inflammatory. Words of reason or concern were regarded as shots fired unnecessarily. A tangible resentment of the Man operated behind the token justification of making the white man a criminal. Villains were not always the comic-book characters that Dr. No and Goldfinger had been in the James Bond thrillers of the previous decade. Instead, they were recognizable images of oppression: white mafiosi, hopelessly square, who looked and acted like executives or landlords and wore expensive suits, or wasted, effete playboys behaving like the unlikely offspring of Vincent Price. Even at the height of the cycle, the action retained the flamboyant choreographic effect of the Bond pictures, which was a fortunate distancing device, and the films themselves were never taken that seriously by the black audience, despite white reviewers' reports to the contrary.

As abruptly as it began, the cycle of black crime pictures waned in 1974, and, being so dependent upon that moment of crisis, they are not often revived. The reason for their decline relates in part to the fluctuations of urban tension. Decisions within the film industry itself, such as a more effective integration of black performers in racially mixed films or the assimilation of a more exacerbated type of violence by high-budget productions were more responsible. Although a black style in films never evolved comparable to that in music—the scores by Isaac Hayes for *Shaft*, Curtis Mayfield for *Super Fly*, and James Brown for *Black Caesar* had a genuine hard-hitting energy that the films themselves either lacked or faked—a more recent effort like *Car Wash* (1976), directed by Michael Schultz, a black, seems to open up a new direction for the black film, channeling abrasiveness into a comedy of interracial manners in everyday situations.

How to handle freedom is a test of character, nowhere more than in the motion picture, and for black filmmakers of the 1971–74 period the problem was compounded by the fact that the only turf common to both races was the violent urban thriller, of which a white model, perhaps the model *par excellence*, already existed. Most black directors, scenarists, and actors who suddenly became active had no option but to imitate, adapt mostly second-hand notions, or try to abide by conflicting theories on the political uses of film. And so their rage and their energy were channeled into the crime picture, which seemed, at least superficially, to estrange them from white culture while their own black culture was being created.

Except for *The Godfather*, which practically preempted the genre, the gangster disappeared as an important screen character in the seventies.

Ron O'Neal in *Super Fly*, 1972: the pusher as the supreme cool operator. *Warner Brothers*

He was replaced by his mirror double, the cop. Hoover's prestige was at an all-time low after the assassinations of Martin Luther King, Jr., and Robert Kennedy—Hoover was to die in 1972 and remain as controversial in death as in life—and television had taken over the job of glorifying the FBI. The most often heard epithet during those days, aside from *whitey* and *nigger,* was *pig.* In his novel *The Little Sister,* Raymond Chandler summed up the plight of the cop in short, hard words: "It's like this with us, baby. We're coppers and everybody hates our guts. . . . Nothing we do is right, not ever. Not once. If we get a confession, we beat it out of the guy, they say, and some shyster calls us Gestapo . . ." Whether rogue, maverick, vigilante, or working-class hero, cops were far removed from the idealized presence of Hoover's G-men. They allegorized the moral issues of the period—allegiance to the system, individual choice, the uses and misuses of violence—that previous cop pictures usually ignored or dealt with in scoutish terms. A seventies paradox, the cop embodied the traumas and tensions of the decade better than the criminal.

The cop as emblematic figure was born out of Vietnam, or to be more exact, out of Hollywood's failure to deal with a conflict so controversial at home and so unpopular abroad that, for the first time in its history, the film industry hesitated to exploit it for fear of alienating hawks, doves, and foreign audiences.

Vietnam, Hollywood decided, belonged on television (where it had been consigned, pessimistically, by McLuhan), but the war could be paraphrased in films about metropolitan crime. Thus, violence could be made active while ideological assumptions would be repressed—a total *volte face* from a situation that prevailed during World War Two. In American films of the Vietnam era, when war was dealt with at all, in films like *Patton* or *Tora! Tora! Tora!* or *M*A*S*H*,* it was in the protective guise of tales from the Second World War or Korea. These films paid homage to heroism on both sides. The most successful, *Patton* (1968) was no mere eulogy for a four-star general but a shrewd portrait of a bastard who won battles, shortened the war, and saved countless lives, the sort of bastard that is a necessity in wartime.

Heirs to the Patton mystique, the cop pictures favored swift, unorthodox action over humanistic values, and, more often than not, they reduced the majesty of the law to tatters and flaunted an impatient contempt for the maddening byways of the democratic process. At their most idealistic, cop pictures portrayed the metropolitan force as the thin blue line standing between the inner barbarians and a society that clearly betrayed its death wish through such Supreme Court rulings as the *Escobedo* and *Miranda* decisions (1964 and 1966 respectively). These rulings guaranteed a suspect the right to counsel before and during interrogation, and it has been contended in some quarters that they extend protection to the criminal that rightly belongs to the victim. There was a clear reference to the decline and fall of lax civilizations in *The New Centurions* (1972), based on a novel by Joseph Wambaugh, an ex-member of the Los Angeles police force who has since mined his experience for the screen in *The Choirboys* (1977) and *The Onion Field* (1979), and for television in the "Police Story" series.

The heroes of *Bullitt* and *Madigan* (both 1968) were law officers who were recognizably decent citizens with domestic problems, deserving of our allegiance and sympathy, and professionally at odds with superiors depicted as venal, hostile, or uncomprehending. They were still identifiable as cops of the Kennedy era, the rear guard of the humane lawman tradition that goes back to *The Naked City* and TV's "Dragnet." Bullitt's mission—to protect the life of a state witness at the expense of a decoy or two—is complicated by the political ambitions of the district attorney, a smooth executive whose limousine bears a sticker reading, "Support Your Local Police." Madigan was the more memorable of the two because his story was more tragic. Madigan (Richard Widmark) and his partner are Manhattan police detectives penalized for losing their guns to a psychotic killer, Barney

Steve McQueen as *Bullitt*, 1968, still identifiable as a cop of the Kennedy era, the rearguard of a humane tradition dating back to *The Naked City*. *Warner Brothers*

Benesch (Steve Inhat), as they were decoyed by his nude bedmate in an off-guard moment. Madigan, especially, is put on the spot by the commissioner (Henry Fonda), an ex-cop so strict that he once returned a gift Christmas turkey so that he could not be accused of taking a bribe. The commissioner's strictness has become legendary in the precincts, and he looks down on Madigan as a cop who uses his badge to finagle side benefits. When Benesch shoots two policemen, killing one of them with Madigan's stolen gun, and holes up in East Harlem with a hostage, the pressure is on Madigan to bring him in at all costs, which means Madigan must die a sacrificial death, attracting Benesch's fire to spare the hostage. His last words, breathed in pain and anguish, are: "I killed him, didn't I, Rocky?"

A heroic policeman who lays down his life in the line of duty is an inspiring sentiment straight from Hoover's file. *Madigan,* however, leaves the viewer with the bitter aftertaste of doubt: was this death necessary? Was it all worth it? The answer is to be found in the works of Don Siegel, who directed *Madigan, Coogan's Bluff* (1968), and *Dirty Harry* (1971), a lawman trilogy which significantly balances the unholy triptych of *Baby Face Nelson, The Lineup,* and *The Killers,* all of which featured the psychotic professional gunman as hero. The reason Siegel, in mid-career, shifted his attention from the criminal to the policeman may be locked deep in his psyche, although it also corresponds to the shifts in Hollywood policy, which is to say, to the temper of the times.

Madigan's world is deftly established as a society of deceit and compromise which somehow manages to function on a live-and-let-live basis. Mrs. Madigan (Inger Stevens) has social aspirations unwarranted by her husband's record; she almost capitulates to the advances of a fellow officer, while Madigan is drawn to an occasional mistress for sympathetic support. The police commissioner himself is above bribery but not above adultery, and his chief of police, a boyhood friend, is playing ball with the Syndicate to cover up for his son's delinquency, a bit of information casually gleaned through wiretapping. A black albino suspect is relentlessly grilled at the the police station, and a Harlem preacher fears he may not be able to stall the next riot. All this is offered by the scenarists, Howard Rodman and Abraham Polonsky, as evidence of the system's fallibility.

Siegel, however, is much too concerned with helping the characters through a particularly tough weekend to wonder whether the system works. (In fact, the one direct result of Madigan's death is that the chief of police gets a second chance from the commissioner.) Knowing from experience that time spent on any one character rather than on another determines the viewer's adherence, Siegel stays close to Madigan and his partner, follows their investigation in detail, making us conscious of their skill, instincts, and capacity for failure. The same scrutiny worked in favor of the psychotic gunmen in *The Lineup* and *The Killers.*

Siegel is more interested in the operations of crime and detection than in passing moral judgment. It is therefore necessary that Benesch be reduced to a rough sketch of a myopic hypersexed freak, in appearance a

The pressure is on Madigan (Richard Widmark) to bring in Benesch (Steve Ihnat) at all costs, which means he must attract Benesch's fire to spare the hostage. *Madigan,* 1968. *Universal*

shipping clerk who has gone berserk, if our sympathy is to remain with the cops. Benesch, in fact, is repudiated as crazy and unreliable by the underworld (shades of *M!*), which is pictured as a fruity, well-adjusted subsociety, no more decayed than the establishment. There is a Coney Island dwarf (Michael Dunn) who can afford a perfect specimen of a bodyguard; the punchy ex-prizefighter (Harry Bellaver) who will inform for a bit of attention; a handsome pimp (Don Stroud) afraid to lose his looks to the fist of an unappreciative cop.

Madigan is still recognizable as a humane, harassed, well-intentioned policeman. His imperfections are ingrained in his character, not exploited for easy laughs and sympathy as, for instance, in *The Super Cops,* (1974) where black undercover agents went unrecognized by the white heroes and were beaten up. But Madigan is almost the last of the line. In *Coogan's Bluff,* Siegel had Clint Eastwood playing an Arizona deputy sheriff who travels to New York to collect a fugitive and bring him back for trial. Coogan behaves like a hick in the big city, a sort of Mr. Deeds going to town against crime. Much to its credit, the picture implies that Coogan will return to the Southwest a changed man, touched however lightly by the liberal good sense of a social worker (Susan Clark) who befriends him and patches him up after his periodic brawls. Coogan takes on a gang of toughs in a poolroom fight, but surprisingly, this is a film without any serious violence or casualties. Eastwood's wide-brimmed hat and cowboy boots can be deemed a tribute to Gary Cooper, whom he resembles in size and grace.

One of the best, possibly the key scene in *Coogan's Bluff* is also quite disturbing, because it heralds a drift in the politics of the cop picture. Searching for his man, who has escaped him in the big city, Coogan enters a discotheque and is instantly surrounded by a mass of painted faces and bodies heaving and twisting to rock 'n' roll. As he towers above the hippie nation, Eastwood seems the ascetic ideal of the still uncorrupted West, the last just man walking unscathed through the fires of hell, and here the film loses its picaresque quality: gradually, Gary Cooper fades out and Dirty Harry fades in. The ideology of the frontier is being invoked in a moment of crisis.

The figure of the mad-dog killer who must be destroyed for the sake of society returns as the sniper-sadist of *Dirty Harry.* His is a villain so abhorrent that he compensates for the excesses of the vigilante hero, Harry Callahan, a San Francisco homicide lieutenant who does not always go by the book (hence the nickname), a dead shot with a .44 magnum who is usually dead right about whom he shoots. (*Dead Right,* a more ironic and politically alert title than *Dirty Harry,* was dropped after the leading role was refused by Paul Newman and Frank Sinatra; perhaps it gave too much away.)

"Harry is a fantasy character," Clint Eastwood told *The New York Times* in 1976, when he had just reprised the role for the second time. It was easily the most congenial role Eastwood ever had, the one that best suited his heroic physique. "Nobody does what Harry does. He cuts right through the bull, tells his boss to shove it, does all the things people would like to do in real life but can't." So far, so good, and innocent enough, but then the actor fell into the trap of identifying with the character beyond the shooting schedule of the three pictures. "Harry believed in a higher morality, people who conducted themselves according to the climate of the time." It was also the climate of the time—Vietnam, activism, the civil-rights movement, which Eastwood dismissed when he talked of people "coming off that big sixties concern with the rights of the accused"—which accounted for the film's violent reception as much as for Eastwood's belated, misguided defense of its hero.

Siegel, who knows the crime genre better than any other director of his generation, must have been mystified by the reaction to his film. *Dirty Harry* was reviewed in *The New York Times* and *The New Yorker* as a violation of civil rights; it was defended in *Rolling Stone* as a superior genre piece and attacked as excessively violent by practically everybody, and it still grossed $16 million in its first year. As a role model, *Dirty Harry* surpassed the record of *Little Caesar:* two real-life murders were traced directly to the film—the Padilla case in Brooklyn (1974) and the Thompson case in

Coogan in the netherworld: Clint Eastwood as an Arizona deputy sheriff visits a New York discotheque. From *Coogan's Bluff*, 1968. *Universal*

Columbus, Ohio (1977). Because of its violence, *Dirty Harry* was refused telecasting by Philadelphia's KYW-TV station as recently as 1976. There is no doubt that the picture was taken up by a large section of the public in much the same way they adopted a tongue-in-cheek ditty like Merle Haggard's "Okie from Muskogee" and inflated it into a rousing roughneck anthem. ("We don't smoke marijuana in Muskogee / Like the hippies in San Francisco do / 'cause we like livin' right and bein' free.")

The screenplay—by Harry Fink and R. M. Fink, a husband-and-wife writing team—was tailored to Siegel's and Eastwood's specifications by one of their regular scriptwriters, Dean Riesner, and some additional dialogue was written by John Milius. The script has two major roles, Harry and Scorpio, both larger than life; the rest are victims, or just plain static. The Scorpio character is an amalgam of the major criminals of the sixties, from Charles Manson to Charles Whitman (the Austin sniper who killed eighteen people in 1966), and from San Francisco's own Zodiac Killer to the kidnappers who buried alive a Florida heiress, Barbara Jane Mackle, in 1968. Scorpio's credentials must be that monstrous to justify Harry's outrage when told that he has violated the suspect's rights by breaking into his home without a search warrant and beating him up. "Well, I'm all broken up about that man's rights." What further works on the viewer to make the wrong connections is not exactly what Scorpio does, but what he looks

An amalgam of the major criminals of the sixties, from Manson to Whitman: Andy Robinson as Scorpio the Sniper, in *Dirty Harry*, 1971. *Warner Brothers*

like. Played by Andy Robinson, he is a longhair who wears boots, jeans, and a crooked peace symbol on his belt buckle. He is the all-too-common phantasm of the post-1969 period, the hippie as fiend, tragically embodied in Manson and his followers.

Siegel dissociated himself from any extremist politics to be read into his film. If well-reasoned works of art like Wagner's operas can be claimed by opposing factions, as was the case under Nazism and in recent Bayreuth productions, what chance does a genre film like *Dirty Harry* have? Admittedly, Siegel took the film to a new "wall-to-wall" level of violence, yet the picture was more stylized than usual, demanding less personal involvement than *Madigan*, in which the death of one single policeman was felt as a tragic loss. Siegel was keeping watch on two opposite, yet strangely similar, operational methods: that of a cop who breaks the law in the interest of justice, and that of a hate-ridden citizen (a Vietnam veteran? a drug-crazed peacenik?) on a destructive rampage. The implications, and the Siegel oeuvre bears him out, should have been existential rather than political.

The film made it clear that, had Scorpio not existed, Harry would have invented him, so completely do they fulfill each other's fantasies of order and chaos. San Francisco is the location of *Dirty Harry*. No longer the impersonal background of a cops-and-robbers anecdote, as it was in Siegel's *The Lineup*, it has become a city of political resonances. And San Francisco adds a needed symbolic landscape to the confrontation which New York, for instance, could not provide. In the American collective mind, New York represents the East, the city of beginnings, the melting pot where all cultures coalesce, while San Francisco is the end of the empire, the last outpost of frontier values. Coogan could bring a fresh whiff of rawhide to the relative effeteness of Manhattan, and this made *Coogan's Bluff* a near-comedy. Dirty Harry is cornered between the devil of a complex legal system and the deep blue sea where the American dream of expansion ends in the bottomless pit of the San Andreas fault, and this makes him a character on the verge of extinction.

The opening shot, a dedication to the San Francisco police dead in the line of duty, and a dissolve from a badge to a young girl in a rooftop pool being sighted by a sniper is an ambiguous replay of the old *Crime Does Not Pay* logo. The new policeman is hardly your *Sergeant Madden* kind of a cop—rather, he is a tough misanthrope so alienated that he is at a loss when asked why he chooses to remain in the force. Harry informs us that his wife was killed by a drunken driver; he remains celibate, sublimating with his magnum. At the sight of Harry's gun, Scorpio, himself prone to caressing his rifle discreetly, gurgles, "My, that's a big one." Both men take an awful lot of punishment from each other, and there's an almost postcoital quiet after the surges of violence.

The key scene is the long anticipated face-to-face encounter between Harry and Scorpio. (Previously, Scorpio wore a grotesque ski mask, but they have already left marks of violence and recognition on each other.) Harry traces Scorpio to his lair under Kezar Stadium, chases him into the field, shoots him, stomps on him, and, in a majestic helicopter shot, the two of them are swallowed by night and fog, as if to conceal the consummation of this hate from the spectator, very much in the same manner reserved by the classic Hollywood cinema to suggest the unshowable (that is, sex).

After Scorpio, released on legal technicalities, finds himself stalked by Harry, who is acting against orders, there is the feeling that both men could disappear into the city, locked in a near-Dostoyevskian dependency of hunter and quarry. Is it for Eastwood's sake that the story is made to gather momentum once again, with Scorpio going on another of his rampages— so that Harry will fulfill his commitment to kill Scorpio and be proven right? The concluding scene shows Harry flinging his badge on Scorpio's body, both his mission and his raison d'être ended. This finale is reminiscent of Gary Cooper's desolate gesture in *High Noon*, the popular 1952 Western that castigated a community for not coming to the aid of a just and besieged sheriff. Except that *Dirty Harry* makes no claims about the consecrated aspect of its lawman hero. Try to picture Cooper playing Harry's own game of Russian roulette, offering his opponent a last chance to better him: "Did I fire five shots, or six?" Neither reconciled to society nor excluded, it is difficult to imagine what Harry's life will be without Scorpio.

All the more unlikely then that Harry Callahan would return in two

Harry Callahan (Clint Eastwood) tracks Scorpio to his lair under Kezar Stadium, his .44 Magnum at the ready. *Dirty Harry. Warner Brothers*

sequels. *Dirty Harry* was Siegel's fourth film in a row with Eastwood, after which they parted company amicably. The first sequel, *Magnum Force* (1974), was directed by Ted Post; the second, *The Enforcer* (1976), by James Fargo; both were produced by Eastwood's own company, Malpaso. It is possible that Eastwood, who was surely responsible for the success of *Dirty Harry* and was the number-one box-office star of the period, may also have thrown Siegel's original concept out of kilter. It is known that Eastwood resisted the final scene (in which he cast off the badge), and there are many low-angle shots of Harry to emphasize a mythical stature, scenes that seem foreign to Siegel's style. Since *Dirty Harry,* it has become clear that Eastwood's Christ complex permeates his own work as director and that of others less willful than Siegel; it manifests itself in lingering scenes in which the hero suffers savage beatings (and various forms of rejection), followed by equally mandatory scenes of repair work performed on the Eastwood physique: passion, stigmata, and resurrection. This is never more visible than when Eastwood directs himself, as in *The Gauntlet* (1977), which was at heart a paranoiac fantasy carried to sadomasochistic extravagance. Harry Callahan could have been conceivably less disturbing if the role had been played by an actor like Richard Widmark (who was Siegel's Madigan), who can summon resources of doubt, anguish, and fallibility that Eastwood's superhuman stoicism knows nothing of.

A much less controversial Harry reappeared in the sequels. Not only did he have his badge back, but Harry the Racist was paired with a black policeman in the first, and Harry the Sexist was provided with a woman assistant in the second. Unlikeliest of all, Harry the Right-winger was forced left-center by a band of rookie patrolmen who had organized their own version of the Brazilian Death Squads, and by fake radicals who kidnapped the mayor of San Francisco and entrenched themselves in the now-abandoned Alcatraz. John Milius wrote the original story for *Magnum Force** (which he subsequently adapted with Michael Cimino) at a time when he was marketed by the media as the latest *enfant terrible* of the film industry. Milius was then voicing a hard-line conservatism and a fascination with firearms too calculated to convince any but the most dedicated flower-child and too outrageous to alarm any but the most liberal film critics.

Milius had directed his first picture, *Dillinger,* in 1973. In spite of the new permissiveness, *Dillinger* was not quite the bloodiest film ever made, as everyone had a right to expect. In fact it was considerably more romantic than the austere Max Nosseck version: in the context of 1945, a shot of a jagged beer mug being thrust at the camera was more shocking to the viewer than all of Milius's carefully rigged bullet wounds and spurting blood.

Milius's hangup with weaponry, however, did sustain *Magnum Force.* To match its fetischistic vision we must go underground to Kenneth Anger's pioneering *Scorpio Rising* (1963), which first explored the motorcycle mystique in terms of its regalia and was rife with the homoerotic implica-

* Milius also did some uncredited writing for *Dirty Harry.* One of his famous lines—"This being a .44 magnum, the most powerful handgun in the world, that will blow your head clean off, you gotta asks yourself a question. Do I feel lucky?"—turned up as the epigraph of *Magnum Force.*

tions of male bonding. *Magnum Force*'s death squad swarms about San Francisco on motorbikes, dispensing summary execution to pimps, pushers, and labor racketeers whom the law cannot touch for lack of evidence. The death-squad members are closer to Jean Cocteau's motorcycle angels than to the Hell's Angels; the ace killer was played by David Soul, later a costar of the "Starsky and Hutch" television series (a diluted version of the vigilante films which still gets away with some startling attitudes). And Soul was so ambiguously attractive in goggles, white helmet, and black leather, his Aryan looks were so perfect, that the scriptwriters could not refrain from injecting a few gay asides in the dialogue. The phallic symbolism, for once, was out front. When the impregnable esprit de corps displayed by the killer rookies is made the butt of a homosexual crack, Harry replies sourly: "If the rest of you could shoot like them, I wouldn't care if the whole damned department was queer." When Soul betters Eastwood at target practice, Harry is moved to prove his virility with an Oriental neighbor.

As far as Harry is concerned, a man who can shoot straight is to be allowed a few kinks in his private life. He refuses, though, to be enlisted into this massive cleanup of the Bay Area. The secret leader of the vigilantes is revealed as mild-mannered Lieutenant Briggs (Hal Holbrook), a typical CIA bureau chief who makes a perfect scapegoat / villain. "When

The death squad in *Magnum Force*, 1973, swarms about San Francisco dispensing summary execution to those the law cannot touch. Squad member David Soul could pass for a Jean Cocteau angel of death. *Warner Brothers*

the police start becoming their own executioners, where is it going to end?"
Harry asks Briggs. "Pretty soon you start executing people for jaywalking,
and executing people for traffic violations, and then you end up executing
your neighbor 'cause his dog pisses on your lawn." Harry has become the
voice of reason; not that he likes the system that much, it's just that there
is nothing else to set up limits. The sequels were clearly intended as counter-
irritants to Harry's original politics. Now equipped with a social conscience, Harry can shoot the bad guys on his own side, more in self-defense
than in anger at the mayhem they perpetrate. In a gesture equivalent to his

Now equipped with a social conscience, Harry Callahan (Clint Eastwood) can shoot
the bad guys on his own side, but more in self-defense than in anger. *Magnum Force.*
Warner Brothers

discarding the badge in *Dirty Harry,* Harry kicks the white helmet of one of
his opponents into San Francisco Bay at the conclusion of *Magnum Force,*
as he mutters to himself: "You guys didn't have enough experience." The
young rookie vigilantes had prided themselves on being "the first generation that's learned to fight." But Harry has proven them wrong. They are
much too ambiguous to prevail. Throughout *Magnum Force,* Eastwood is
photographed from the hip up: he is the original first-generation lawman,
and, significantly, he is never seen in uniform.

STREET CRIME CLIPS SHOW BIZ—*Variety* summed up 1971 as a disastrous
experience for both exhibitors and residents in America's large cities. The

body count seems staggering both off- and on-screen through the dark period of 1968–76, when a rise in crime begat an equally alarming increase in crime films, driving a final nail into the coffin of the escapism theory of movie attendance. Granted a gestation period of one or two years—the wheels of production grinding slower than in the thirties and forties, when pictures like *The Finger Points, Foreign Correspondent,* and *Casablanca* benefited from up-to-the-minute revisions—what Hollywood delivered was a late and mostly inadequate compensation for a very real fear—according to a Gallup poll, 50 percent of Americans were wary of walking in their neighborhoods after dark. The crime rate accelerated steadily, fueled by unemployment, recession, the fiscal troubles of New York City, and the migration of poor minorities into the major cities.

A comparable economic situation in the thirties failed to produce an alarming rise in crime, but class differences were less blatant then than in the era of glass houses that television and consumerism built. Rather than prevent crime, which seems inconceivably utopian, films rode the crest of the crime wave for six years, the trend abating only with the drop in the crime rate in 1977. For the most part, Hollywood ignored the causes of crime in America (again unlike the films of the thirties), preferring to depict symptoms rather than work out an immunity program. But if we are to consider the chilling statement issued by the University of Chicago Center for Studies in Criminal Justice that, rather than any effective curbing action from the police or the government, the major cause in the decline of crime is that "people are doing more to reduce their exposure to risk," then all that shrill, opportunistic violence on the screen was not a total waste after all, and crime pictures find some sort of belated social justification. For, even if they failed to offer a viable solution to the crime problem, Hollywood films at least provided a valuable lesson in survival techniques.

In the police movies of the seventies, the policeman was very much his own man—judge, jury, and executioner—and he had lost his allegiance to the law. The criminal, too, lost human definition and became a mere target. Society lost its authority and was usually portrayed as an ineffectual, often corrupt entity that condoned the excesses of both policeman and criminal. The decade belonged to the street man, at odds with the higher echelons of either crime or order (a legacy, perhaps, from the black pictures). The archetypal film of the period might well be *The French Connection;* it certainly was the most successful and imitated, garnering Oscars for its leading man (Gene Hackman) its director (William Friedkin), its scenarist (Ernest Tidyman), and its editor (Jerry Greenberg), while its producer, Phil D'Antoni (and the film owes its existence as well as its most cherished effects to his vision) accepted the Academy Award for the Best Picture of 1971. It has grossed (up to December 1978) $26.3 million in the United States alone.

The French connection, as the film made known the world over, was the clandestine route for heroin traffic between Marseilles and the United States in the early sixties. It figured highly in the reminiscences of Eddie Egan and Sonny Grosso, two New York City police detectives involved in the case, which the journalist Robin Moore adapted as a book that subsequently inspired the scenario. The film told in detail of an attempt to smuggle a 112-pound shipment of heroin into New York and of its successful interception by the police. Egan and Grosso, who themselves played minor roles in Friedkin's film and were portrayed by Hackman and Roy Scheider, provided the inspiration and / or authenticity for other police stories such as *The Seven-Ups* (1973), *Badge 373* (1973), and *Report to the Commissioner* (1975). Police procedure was never more accurately depicted or, in a bow to realism beyond the call of duty, the letter of the law more consistently violated.

There is a strong suspicion that Friedkin and his team may have moved in on the French connection case long before its conclusion, therefore missing out on some of the more extravagant twists and implications that have kept it far from closed as recently as 1978. For openers, in 1972 the heroin shipment which was held as evidence was found to have been stolen from the property clerk's office, along with other large quantities of narcotics. The very daring of the theft prompted *The New York Times* to consider that "the huge profits to be gained in the narcotic trade have turned some members of the police into agents who actively foster crime as well as fight it." The Knapp Commission's investigation of corruption in the New York City Police Department corroborated the fact that New York's finest were indeed also its most corrupt. Another disturbing turn is that the two major figures to be convicted in the case were murdered within months of each other while serving their sentences in the federal penitentiary in Atlanta. Dominique Orsini, who was said to have supplied the heroin in the original case, and Vincent C. Papa, a Mafia narcotics dealer, were slashed to death in 1978 and 1977 respectively; also murdered was another inmate rumored to be an informer for federal authorities.

The factual aftermath of the French connection is really no concern of a film which, for all its realistic detail and location photography, tends to abstraction. The film begins in mid-case, with Frog Two (Marcel Bozzuffi) gunning down a narc in Marseilles; it stops inconclusively when Frog One (Fernando Rey), who has masterminded the operation, disappears, almost by magic, in the wintry desolation of Rikers Island on the East River. Between these two locations, drug runners and police deploy the skill, ingenuity, and sheer energy that, in simpler times, would be exclusive attributes of the right side, and the story ends in an impasse of sorts.

The automobile chase is here elevated to a major stylistic device, one whose obvious forerunner would seem to be *Bullitt*—also produced by D'Antoni, who made a trademark of the choreographed demolition derby, *vide The Seven-Ups*, which he also directed—but in fact the chase can be traced back to Don Siegel's *The Lineup*. Then as now, cutting and the logistics of stunt work collaborate to cancel any but the most visceral commitment, moral issues are left suspended by all that frantic motion.

By comparison with a film of classical manufacture like *The Lineup*,

the characters seem sketchy and are best defined by their means of convey-
ance. In time we come to feel for the car what we normally should feel for
the driver, a perfect film metonymy if there ever was one. There is a sequence, as awesome as an autopsy, in which a confiscated Lincoln suspected
of being "dirty," is taken apart in the police garage while its owner, a
fashion-plate French TV star (Frederic de Pasquale) tries desperately to
have it returned. Time is almost up for the cops when the heroin is found,
hidden in the splash pans, like a treasure or a malignant tumor. Then,
breathlessly, the Lincoln is reassembled and produced for its owner.

Editing can make or break characterization (in *The French Connection*
we would welcome a few long takes on the actors), but it cannot hurt cars.
There are loving close-shots of license plates and bumper lights, dizzying
viewpoint shots from cars in motion, zooms through the windshield, quietly
intense takes of cars stalking other cars through night streets. The best
remembered sequence has the detective commandeering a passing car to
pursue Frog Two on the elevated subway and whizzing below the overhead tracks through a large and mercifully deserted section of Brooklyn.
Bill Hickman is credited for the stunts in *The French Connection:* the
picture rightly belongs to him. Cop pictures can be indexed from here on by
the number of junked cars and cubic mass of demolished hardware.

It is typical of the seventies *cool* film, as opposed to the inflammatory
vigilante film like *Death Wish* or *Walking Tall,* that the heroin in the case
is viewed without undue awe or moral revulsion, but simply as an investment to be protected or a piece of evidence to be obtained; almost a plot
device like Alfred Hitchcock's celebrated "MacGuffin," whose function is to
start the plot rolling and then discreetly self-destruct. The heroin could
just as well be a diamond cache or a secret treaty; all there is to know is
the value. An underworld appraiser, a new, strange breed of chemist and
winetaster, upgrades the stash from "Good Housekeeping Junk-of-the-
Month" through "Gold Star Poison" to "Absolute Pure Junk," worth roughly
$32 million in the streets of New York.

The film was uniquely guiltless in this respect. We share in the joy of
the drug runners when the operation of transferring the heroin from the
French connection to the American dealer is honorably carried out (a fresh
departure in a genre fraught with double-dealing and betrayal), as we do
when Popeye and his teammate, after days of fruitless wiretapping, find
their suspicions confirmed and hug each other like players after a score.
The audience's allegiance to each side is made to switch every so often. A
playful hide-and-seek in Grand Central has Frog One carrying the day by
waving his umbrella as a magic wand to open the shuttle's doors at the
last moment. As a subtle intimation of the cultures that begat such different
vocations, Friedkin cuts from the French criminals enjoying a three-star
luncheon to the dogged detective outside, munching pizza in a drizzle and
spilling a container of coffee all over his shoes.

A cop hero could then go quite far and still fail to qualify as a "pig,"

New York detectives Doyle and Russo (Gene Hackman and Roy Scheider) about to crack open the Marseilles–New York drug pipeline. *The French Connection*, 1971. Frog Two (Marcel Bozzuffi) as the scourge of the subways. *Twentieth Century-Fox*

as long as his antiauthoritarian nature was made clear. "One of the things with *French Connection* that was frightening to me," Gene Hackman told Pete Hamill in a *Film Comment* interview, "was to open the film beating up a black guy, using the words *spick, wop* and *nigger* . . . and then you say to the audience: 'You're gonna stay with this guy for two hours and you finally gotta like him, you gotta respect him, you gotta feel something for him.'" What audiences felt for Hackman's brutal, bigoted, foul-mouthed cop was a profound comradeship with the maverick at odds with his superiors; what they responded to was a fanatic dedication to a dirty job that needed to be done. Doyle never offended liberals as Harry Callahan did: his regulation revolver was small enough to conceal in his sock, and his love life, not quite a Hollywood romance, was plausible enough for a man who keeps irregular hours. What's more, Popeye actually shoots the wrong man, a federal agent assigned to the case, without loss of sympathy, which is again symptomatic of the period. In 1971, government agencies were unpopular and no longer protected by mystique; as such, they were fair game and a safe scapegoat for the cop film.

Seventies cop films have emphasized the humanity of the policeman, sometimes even his eccentricities. Popeye carries a silly Buster Keaton hat in his car. The cops in *The Super Cops* wear sneakers, the better to pursue drug dealers in their own streets. The tolerant, bemused inspector in *The Laughing Policeman* (1973) has to cope with a head cold as he tracks down a mass murderer in San Francisco, while the police detectives in *Report to the Commissioner* and *Hustle* (1975) must contend with inner doubts and personal obsession. Not quite convinced of the sacredness of his mission, the police hero was a perfect home-front surrogate for the other unsung combat fighter in Vietnam.

Often, the facts furnished an ironic footnote to the films, and not only in the case of *The French Connection*. *The Super Cops* was based on the exploits of two real New York police detectives, Dave Greenberg and Bob Hantz, whose unorthodox behavior earned them the nicknames of "Batman and Robin." In June 1978, Greenberg was convicted on charges of extortion and obstruction of justice. Eddie Egan had to appeal to the Supreme Court to obtain his pension after being dismissed on charges of failing to appear in court and turn over impounded narcotics. Frank Serpico, a New York City police detective who, along with David Durk, a sergeant on the force, became the key prosecution witnesses at the Knapp Commission hearings, exiled himself to Switzerland for safety; and Durk (renamed Bob Blair in the film *Serpico*) was reassigned to a minor post in Queens.

Serpico's story had fueled the Knapp Commission and furnished the subject for a book by Peter Maas, *Serpico: The Cop Who Defied the System.* It had actually begun in 1966, when Serpico first reported graft and bribes from organized crime to his superior officers with the hope that his report would launch a discreet investigation; instead, he ran into the organizational code of silence under which a police department member must never inform on another, and, when he persisted, he was threatened by his captain with

After Popeye Doyle, the image of the policeman loses all definition, but there remains a certain consistency in police methods. Ron Leibman in *The Super Cops*, 1973 *United Artists,* and Al Pacino in *Serpico*, 1973. *Paramount*

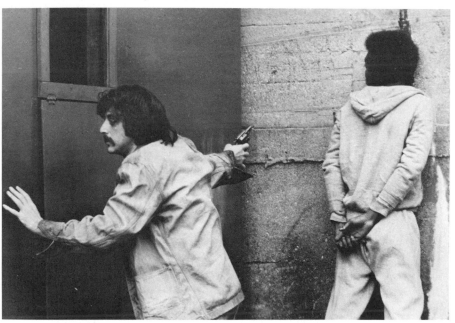

"the East River." Serpico and Durk accompanied a sympathetic superior to *The New York Times* in 1970: the result was New York's most recent purge of its police department, although it was not unduly severe. For openers, the captain who had threatened Serpico with death got off with a fine. Durk went on record as saying that the Knapp Commission had ignored the "ultimate accountability" of city officials like Mayor John V. Lindsay, then a potential presidential candidate. In February 1972, Serpico was left unprotected by his fellow detectives during a raid on a Brooklyn apartment, and he was shot in the head; to this day he carries bullet fragments too close to the brain to be safely removed.

Within a year of the last report of the Knapp Commission in December 1972, the film version, directed by Sidney Lumet, was produced by Dino de Laurentiis with the cooperation of the new administration of Mayor Abraham Beame.

Serpico was a liberal hero cop whose patron saint was Daniel Ellsberg, but Buford Pusser was someone out of a Bible Belt fable, a Tennessee sheriff who fought to rid his home county of vice and gambling, and succeeded after brutal reprisals from the local Syndicate left him a widower with half a face. Pusser's story had been told in a book, *The Twelfth of August,* by W. R. Morris, and his reputation in the South was established by the time Roger Mudd interviewed him for "CBS News" in 1969, which led to a bid for the film rights from the producer Mort Briskin. Pusser was satisfied with the picture Phil Karlson directed from Briskin's screenplay and with the way he was impersonated by Joe Don Baker, a morose, hulking actor equally adept at projecting extreme withdrawal or total commitment. On August 24, 1974, hours after Pusser had accepted the offer to play himself in a sequel (eventually released as *Walking Tall II;* a third part appeared in 1977, *Final Chapter: Walking Tall*), the red Corvette he was driving along Highway 64 near his home town crashed and burned; he was thrown out of the car and killed instantly. According to his mother, who spent part of Pusser's royalties having the death investigated, Pusser died because he had been criminally administered a drug, possibly curare, in order to make him lose control.

Walking Tall bore an uncanny resemblance to Karlson's previous *The Phenix City Story;* as Pusser regarded the film as 80 percent true, it would seem as if facts had molded themselves to preexisting fiction, but more likely the same approach served both films.* *Serpico* may have the same ratio of verisimilitude except that Karlson played by genre rules that Lumet, priding himself in never working in the Hollywood studios, would ignore almost as religiously. *Serpico* and *Walking Tall* may have been cardinally opposed, but not because of the liberal or reactionary ideologies ascribed to them.

Lumet organized the essential facts of the Serpico case to reprise the

---

* Facts that the film ignores or fails to utilize: Pusser's father was an ex-police chief. He never went beyond boot camp but liked to describe himself as an ex-Marine. The most manipulative use of fiction: he is given a small son instead of older children, so that the child can stand guard by his father's bed in the hospital, with a small toy gun.

theme of the rebel son whose defection is intended to bring about the ruin of the parental establishment. It was an intimate family drama of the sort recurring in Lumet's work, and it qualifies him as a director with a personal theme, even though he is officially disowned by *auteur* critics. Lumet's preferred version of dramatic conflict requires highly articulate characters tearing into each other, high flights of rhetoric at close range, and a psychological (not necessarily spatial) claustrophobia that usually adheres to adaptations from the stage. (Were he to remake *Stagecoach,* he would probably confine the action to the coach itself and have the passengers interplay frantically at the expense of the action.)

Inside the factual exposé of police corruption in *Serpico,* there is a family feud struggling to get out, as well as the story of a latter-day Savonarola and the church he would reform at the price of his expulsion and safety. It is suggested in Lumet's film that Serpico is not really a man capable of sustaining a durable relationship with a woman; that his only real attachment is to the police force. His tormented but genuine love affair with the force lasted eleven years before its final, violent breakup. After being critically wounded, the realization of his now utter isolation from the world overwhelms Serpico in the hospital, and, for the first time, he breaks down crying. At the conclusion of the Knapp Commission hearings, Serpico is asked why he went through the ordeal, risking his life and certainly making his position on the force untenable, and he answers that it was not for society, or even for the force which was his childhood ideal, but for his most private self which would not tolerate otherwise. An epilogue informs us that Serpico exiled himself to Europe, a man renouncing his own society.*

Serpico was the product of people conversant with radical issues and also with a prevailing type of intellectual chic, both missing in the more stylized genre works. The paradox is that a film so full of facts would fail, in the long run, to provide the viewer with the necessary information, something with which the good genre film, operating within its set of rules and realities, cannot be faulted. The viewer wonders about a man who served eleven years in an organization such as Lumet describes, what psychological traits are inherent in the vocation to be a cop, and how much more Serpico must have compromised to stay that long instead of resigning and pressing his charges sooner. The film's virtues and absences were embodied in Al Pacino, who played Serpico with a consuming pentecostal fervor. But since Serpico's undercover jobs require him to look as little as possible like a policeman, and more like a hippie or a shaman, the image lacks definition— Pacino could have been replaced by Dustin Hoffman in medium shots—and we must connect through the actor's eyes, which have the soulful, suffering gaze of a saint or a freak. The screenplay, at the expense of less idiosyncratic detail, informs us that Serpico knows Spanish, enjoys Bach, is into meditation, and once took ballet classes; he is without doubt a prince among

---

* The real Serpico returned to America, with a new interest in politics, to nominate the former Attorney General Ramsey Clark for the Senate in 1974. The facts until then were with the film, which would much rather play up Serpico's Pyrrhic victory at the expense of society's gain and confine him to the isolation of the tragic hero.

cops, but, at any rate, Pacino's Serpico is an aberration in the context of a police station.

Buford Pusser, like Serpico, takes arms against the corruption threatening to stifle him, this time literally (there's the rub), by wielding a giant club whittled from a hickory branch, and smashing skulls and gambling tables alike in a one-man raid against the famous "Stateline Bunch" that operates along the Tennessee-Mississippi state line. The film's Pusser returns to his home town with wife and children, having left the wrestling world because he didn't like to be told when he should throw a match. He seeks to recapture a way of life that could only survive in small semirural communities; he finds instead a string of motels, roadhouses, and gambling joints, and he receives a bloody initiation when, after defending a friend in a crooked dice game, he's taken for a ride and dumped for dead on a country road.

He survives, and part of the film's peculiar power resides in the spectacle of Pusser, a Brahma bull of a redneck, taking an awesome amount of punishment; much of the emotional release derives from watching him turn on his tormentors. A good genre film never raises questions it cannot answer. Pusser was a perfect genre hero by dint of his sheer commonplaceness. There was no distinction to the Pusser family, and the landscape was equally undistinctive: modest whitewashed homes, dusty roads, green space. The relatively rough-hewn quality of society was still close enough to the West for some of the more debatable Western mythologies to pass without offense (which was not the case in a city film like *Death Wish*).

And Karlson is hardly the crude manipulator the film's detractors claim. The heritage of the B-film lies in this very concision and drive that obliterate any doubts in the viewer. And there was also an effective use of color and setting underlying the seemingly realistic choice of location, which was totally unobtrusive. For instance, the rural landscape with its whites and greens was contrasted with the unnaturally lit, red-brown interior of the gambling joints and roadhouses, so the latter took on the symbolic coloration of pollution. The lingering color scheme of *Walking Tall* would be that of blood on starchy white material. As Pusser goes on trial for assault and destruction of property, he wears a burgundy shirt and sits against a background of townsfolk in summery pastels. The one man already marked through contact with the Syndicate, he removes his shirt on the stand, baring his torso covered with hideous, fresh scars, a badge of suffering and honor. The citizenry rallies behind Pusser: he is acquitted and elected sheriff.

Was Karlson aware that *Walking Tall* would become even more of a rallying cry of the right-wing backlash than *Dirty Harry?* "I wanted to make a picture for once in which the good guy was the hero. I was tired of pictures which glorified crooks, petty chiselers, and con men. I was horrified by *The Godfather*, which sentimentalized the Mafia, and by *The Getaway*, in which Steve McQueen and Ali MacGraw knock off banks, steal thousands of dollars, and ride off into the sunset to loud applause. I thought, 'Let's do something in which people will learn respect for a decent lawman.'" Ultimately, the cop picture, of which *Walking Tall* was a more politically neuter vehicle than most, betrayed its intentions through the gender, race, or sexual persuasion of its victims and villains rather than through the nominal politics of its heros. There was an exceptionally ugly shooting of a transvestite in *Freebie and the Bean* (1974), for example, and the death rate of women in *Magnum Force* and of Puerto Ricans in *Badge 373* was appallingly high.

The color scheme of *Walking Tall*, 1973, is blood on starchy white material. Joe Don Baker as Tennessee sheriff Buford Pusser, whose wife was murdered by the Stateline Bunch. *Cinerama Releasing*

At least the villains in *Walking Tall* (including a mean, pistol-packing madam) were stock figures of the fifties gangster film and, as such, prepolitical. What is generally construed as a vigilante statement is scarcely more than a statement of the classic conservatism which still defines criminals as harmful and society as worth defending. Abiding by genre rules, Karlson localized the malaise in illegal practices such as moonshining, crooked gambling and prostitution; it went no deeper. *Walking Tall* reaffirmed traditional values in a way that a film of modern persuasion, like *The French Connection*, never could.

The disintegration of society has been the underlying theme of crime pictures in the last decade, from the moment Bonnie and Clyde offered a gun to a sharecropper to blast the foreclosure sign on his land. The new nihilism has been very big on describing symptoms, short on causality, and hopeless in prognosis. To arrest the general decay there is no alternate solution to violence, regardless of whether the balance falls to the left or to the right. A reasonably well-mannered picture like *The Laughing Policeman* (based on one of the popular Swedish thrillers by Maj Sjöwall and Per Wahlöö and featuring a police inspector as a shrewd, amiable hero) filled in the background of an investigation with so much sleazy detail that any vestigial relief at discovering who machine-gunned a busload of passengers in San Francisco was compromised by continuous subliminal appeals to dissociate ourselves from the establishment. "I'm making it a political thing," concludes a brash young inspector, "it's the Panthers or one of the Chinese gangs in this town." It is neither of course, but arms smugglers, prostitutes, and pimps, even nude go-go dancers, are ogled and recorded in passing as added proof of widespread decay.

The excesses of a picture like *Death Wish* were written off as the hysterical imaginings of nonresident New Yorkers—De Laurentiis, the Italian producer; Michael Winner, the British director—but the natives took the film to their hearts through the uneasy summer of 1974, and *The New York Times* thought it worthwhile to conduct a poll among the spectators. Given a little more conscious humor, *Death Wish* might have joined the ranks of *The Out of Towners* (1970) and *Little Murders* (1971) as another black satire on New Yorkers and their misconceived stoicism. The camera doesn't turn a corner where a mugger is not caught in the act, and junkies and weirdos run rampant wielding switchblades in front of apathetic subway riders; they are the same faceless fiends who once wore war paint and feathers to furnish a similar provocation in the Western.

The story of *Death Wish* (from a novel by Brian Garfield, who denounced the film as "a vicious distortion") could in fact be told in the familiar terms of a Western: A peaceable homesteader finds his wife murdered and his daughter raped by a band of marauders, becomes obsessed with vengeance, and takes to roaming the range disposing of desperadoes, without benefit of a marshal's badge. The law finally catches up with him, but, realizing the service he has rendered to the community, it allows him to escape to another state, where presumably the crime rate will drop thereafter. Now substitute a West Side apartment, New York City parks and streets, an engineer who was a conscientious objector at the time of the Korean War, some contemporary muggers and rapists, and you have the makings of a perfect vigilante fantasy, complete with the by-now obligatory plug for Gun Power.

Some of the film's more obvious effects were blamed on Charles Bronson, who played the leading role and who, to put it mildly, is not exactly Joan Baez's idea of a pacifist, however lapsed. A behavioral actor in the line of the great Hollywood personality stars, Bronson's specialty was that of the cunning, inarticulate, basically violent hero; his limitations paid off handsomely, for by this time Bronson was reputedly the best paid actor in the business, and there is no doubt that, like Clint Eastwood in *Dirty Harry,* he was the prime factor responsible for the success of *Death Wish*. Bronson slipped into his role of deadly avenger with such a natural ease that it made shambles of any moral qualms that may have existed on paper. As Bronson plays the urban vigilante, violence seems to be man's natural state, a release from a long period of self-denial. If he vomits after shooting his first mugger, this is an attendant reaction to the warrior's initiation, and soon after— without the saving grace of irony or distance, for there is quite an important subject here—he is thriving in his new state. He redecorates the old apartment to obliterate memories of a dead wife and a catatonic daughter and finds a new lease on life by keeping bachelor hours, most of which are spent not at the local singles bar but cruising parks and streets where men go after each other with sex or murder on their minds. Bronson offers himself as bait, luring those he is about to kill at the first sign of aggression but, curiously, no one ever makes a pass at him, for that would take the film into the uncharted territory of the Great Unspoken.

Beyond Bronson, *Death Wish* catalogued every reactionary viewpoint, almost as if to allay any liberal hopes raised by the same producer's *Serpico:* an attitude toward women that would rather see them dead than defiled (though possibly both); the concept of the urban criminal as a parasocial being, a creature of the welfare state, coddled by society into wanton acts of violence; the notion that any deprecation of the great American institutions—home, church, country—should be answered by massive overkill. This is all topical overlay. One remembers nostalgically how a conceptually similar role was played by Fredric March in William Wyler's *The Desperate Hours* (1956) and how strenuously, (to the film's credit) the screenplay justified his taking arms against the three escaped convicts who invade his home and terrorize his family. Both March and Humphrey Bogart, who was the gang leader, played their roles as men of equal strength fighting to retain authority over their group. The climax left March in possession of the only gun in the house, keeping the sardonic Bogart at bay:

BOGART: You don't have it in you, Pop.
MARCH: You put it there.

Still, no amount of outrage or provocation will get March to pull the trigger. Know thy enemy and you'll find it impossible to hate blindly, but it's easy to shoot at an impersonal target. *Death Wish* dehumanized its muggers and junkies very much like war propaganda made gooks out of the Vietnamese, and the film pleaded shamelessly for the viewer's complicity in the carnage.

Death Wish was a vigilante picture, but *Taxi Driver* (1976) was a pic-

A wanton act of violence triggers the vigilante in Charles Bronson: after wife and daughter are raped, he becomes the night avenger of Riverside Park. *Death Wish*, 1974. *Paramount*

ture about a vigilante; a matter of distance, not wordplay. By his own admission, Paul Schrader based his original scenario on a 1961 French film, Robert Bresson's *Pickpocket,* about an unexceptional, petty criminal cursed, or blessed, with the metaphysical anguish of a saint. This seems like an unnecessary alibi for a picture very much in the domestic tradition of *The Sniper* (1952), *Without Warning* (1952), and *Targets* (1968), all of which focused on young men drifting into psychosis, human bombs going undetected until they explode. Schrader chose as his hero a Vietnam vet, Travis Bickle (Robert De Niro), who drives a taxicab in Manhattan, and we view the world through a windshield darkly: New York at night, neon-colored fumes rising from the manholes, cars in slow motion, latent violence everywhere.

Inevitably, the city and its twisted creatures, who sometimes leave traces of blood and sperm on the back seat of Travis's cab, begin to corrode his psyche. If he really were the good-natured rube he appears to be, Travis would take the city madness in his stride, like his fellow cabbies, who even get a few laughs out of the crazies. But Travis is different, so much so in fact that it looks as if the screenplay never intended to give him a sporting chance. He could be suffering from a war-induced trauma, from sexual inadequacy, from terminal anomie. He cannot cope with the most natural situation: he rather charmingly courts a high-class girl, an almost unattainable ideal, then takes her to a porno flick on their first date. The one person that Travis seems capable of communicating with is a twelve-year-old prostitute (Jodie Foster) who, in his mind, represents an innocent like himself, ensnared by the big city. Except that the girl would rather not be rescued by Travis; she loves her pimp (Harvey Keitel), and on a rare occasion when we are allowed to glimpse the world on our own and not through Travis, the child-whore and the pimp dance together, and no other two people ever come this close in the film.

The world darkens; it is summer and Travis hopes for an apocalyptic rain "to come and wash away all the scum off the streets." He retreats to his dingy rented room to build up his physique and sets himself cruel tests of endurance, like holding his hand over an open flame. He assembles a small arsenal, making ready for a one-man punitive expedition against the corrupt city. But what embodies that corruption best? One evening he happens to be in a grocery store when a holdup man pulls a gun, and Travis blasts him before disappearing into the night with the grocer's grateful connivance. (The scene ends on an even more violent note, as the grocer finishes off the wounded robber with a bat.)

There is a political candidate, a suave demagogue who once rode in Travis's taxi and would make an acceptable target—a George Wallace to Travis's frustrated Arthur Bremer—but by now Travis's madness is beginning to tell, he has cut his hair in the style of a Mohawk brave, and the security guards chase him away. So Travis falls back on his fantasies of rescuing the prostitute from the pimp and his cohorts, and the operation becomes a massacre. The self-conscious O. Henry ending throws a few twists at the viewer. Travis not only survives his wounds but is praised for his civic deed; he's back at the wheel, demons exorcised . . . at least for a while.

Technically speaking, Travis's split personality could be the result of Robert De Niro's ingratiating improvs shattering the iron-clad determinism of Schrader's scenario. But the film's hyperrealism, its baroque approach to some urgent topical issues (like hand-painted combat photographs), is the doing of the director, Martin Scorsese, himself a New Yorker and the sole author of *Mean Streets* (1974), a previous and truly original contemplation of the contemporary criminal scene. Where most filmmakers would pull back and pass judgment on the characters, Scorsese gets high on their funky lyricism. A traveling gun salesman (Steven Prince), also dealing in cars and dope, displays his wares on a hotel bed and discourses on the lethal properties of this or that model, conjuring for Travis, the prospective buyer, a vision of the damage they could wreak, for instance, on a woman's sex or a woman's face. The sexual analogue of the scene is the spiel of the street pimp sales-talking Travis, the potential john, on how to get maximum value out of ten dollars or ten minutes. Both speeches soar on wings of profanity and take the viewer along.

Some important comments were made in *Taxi Driver:* that there must be some people left in the country who cannot handle the new sexual permissiveness, that violence has come a long way in being accepted as a form of self-expression—*Taxi Driver* should have had a punk-rock score to live up to its premises and its period, instead of Bernard Herrman's "city" score with its forties sax redolent of more romantic times. But Scorsese was too wrapped up in style—his own and that of Hitchcock, of Godard, of Chabrol, of lesser directors who earned their spurs in the B-film—to sacrifice any of the surface brilliance for an instant of real seriousness.

Scorsese took greater risks in *Mean Streets*, in which a ragged, loose structure accommodated improvisation and a wealth of incident, and was finally perceived as the ideal form to convey the theme that crime has lost so much definition of late that it is virtually impossible to filter it out of everyday experience. The young Italian-Americans in *Mean Streets* would hardly think of themselves as criminals, although at one level or another they are all connected with crime. They are stunted adolescents bound together by endless wheeling and dealing, boozing and whoring, and the boundaries of a turf they defend jealously against outsiders. What eventually pulls them apart is a fumbling for self-respect that must be expressed in violence.

Charlie (Harvey Keitel) is the nominal hero, being more sensitive than the others, something of a lapsed choirboy suffering from residual devotion and pangs of guilt. He works for his uncle (Cesare Danova), an aristocratic mafioso of the old school who holds court on Essex Street and fills Charlie's ears with memories of Lucky Luciano and sound advice on how to get on in the world. Most of the uncle's advice concerns Johnny Boy (Robert De Niro), Charlie's boyhood friend, who is a bit touched in the head and as such a bad risk, and Teresa (Amy Robinson), who is Charlie's girl and an epileptic, which makes her unacceptably sick to uncle. Charlie tries to preserve his relationship with both, even at the cost of humiliating himself, but Johnny Boy proves to be a definite problem.

In Charlie's crowd, the worst insult a man can hurl at another is *scumbag*, and the second worst is *mook* (for moocher, he who shirks paying his dues). And Johnny Boy piles insult on injury when he pulls a gun on Michael (Richard Romanus), who is a collector for a loan-shark operation run by his uncle, and calls him a "jerk-off." In consequence, Michael must preserve his standing in the community, which means that Johnny Boy is

Honor raises its head among the punks: the final sequence in *Mean Streets*, 1974, when Richard Romanus and Martin Scorsese (who also directed) drive alongside Harvey Keitel's car to pump Robert De Niro full of lead. *Warner Brothers*

doomed. Suddenly, lifelong buddies who would gang up against outsiders stand back embarrassed, for this is *cosa nostra* and regards only two people. At last honor has raised its head among the punks; what matters if it is a pitiful distortion of manliness and self-respect? With Teresa at their side, Charlie smuggles Johnny Boy out of Little Italy. They get as far as Brooklyn; then a car sidles along, Michael at the wheel, and, from the back seat, a quiet little guy (played by Scorsese) we have noticed around the group pumps Johnny Boy's head full of lead. Charlie crashes his car into a hydrant. Johnny Boy stumbles out and takes a terribly long time to die. Teresa has nearly gone through the windshield, but she and the dazed Charlie will live.

At this moment, Scorsese takes leave of his characters, crosscutting between the various characters caught in late-night waiting or watching television. Charlie's mafioso uncle is watching Fritz Lang's *The Big Heat*, the scene in which Glenn Ford extricates his dying wife from the bomb-wrecked car. Scorsese's film was the antithesis of the classical genre film with its well-differentiated trinity of criminal, law, and society, and Scorsese was here paying his respects to the tradition he was about to bury. But *Mean Streets* was genuine in its demystification, from the title's ironic use of Chandler's line about men of a certain nobility trapped into ignoble pursuits, to the concept of the godfather as a family fixture, not an icon to be revered. Much in genre films depends on the choice of stylized motifs, and Scorsese rushed so much behavioral detail at the viewer—his people were constantly slap-

Classic scenes from the gangster film deteriorate when shot with a hand-held camera: a long-haired amateur (Robert Carradine) makes a mess of the killing of a drunken mark (David Carradine). *Mean Streets*. *Warner Brothers*

ping each other on the face or the back, play-acting other characters, or erasing the lines between dramatic moments—that the inevitable quotes from classic crime pictures stood out as formal set pieces that immediately deteriorate in contact with hand-held camera movements. A shooting in a men's room attempts something like a ritual staging: A long-haired youth (Robert Carradine) removes his hat to let his hair fall loosely over his shoulders before blasting a drunken mark (David Carradine) with three or four shots, yet the victim refuses to die in the neat genre style; he stumbles out trailing blood, knocking over bar stools, and making a mess of things.

The mid-seventies produced strange mutations of the crime film, such as *Bugsy Siegel* (1976), an English-made parody of gangster films in which hoods and molls are all played by children, and machine guns shoot custard instead of lead, and *The Driver* (1978), a Hollywood repossession of the French gangster picture, long on form and short on genuine energy, something like ragtime adapted by Darius Milhaud—perfect for the Salle Pleyel, but they'll never recognize it on Basin Street.

Possibly the final development of the crime genre is the conspiracy film, which took a good decade to incubate and then exhausted itself in the brief spell between the Warren Commission Report and Watergate—a left-wing paranoia of autocracy to balance the fifties right-wing paranoia of a Communist conspiracy. This subgenre boasts such paranoid thrillers as *Executive Action* (1973), *The Parallax View* (1974), *Three Days of the Condor* and *The Killer Elite* (both 1975), and *The Domino Principle* (1976), and it peaks with *All the President's Men* (1976). Until the Kennedy assassination, the conspiracy subgenre had subsisted on the level of the apolitical thriller as far back as *Suddenly* (1954) and *The Manchurian Candidate* (1962) which left everybody off the hook, except for a lone fictional gunman (played by Frank Sinatra in *Suddenly*) or the much-fantasized NKVD (preying on Sinatra in *The Manchurian Candidate*). The movies have an unlimited potential for ironic coincidence: the secret-service agent who (temporarily) saves Abraham Lincoln's life in *The Tall Target* (1950) is named John Kennedy in the totally fictional scenario; it is said that John F. Kennedy enjoyed the wild melodrama of *The Manchurian Candidate*, which availed itself of brainwashed snipers activated by right-wing domestic control agents.

It took history to provide a happy ending for Woodward and Bernstein, but until then the standard conspiracy film sacrificed its hero (and its doubts) to a vast, vague, faceless corporation which reunited the phantasm of depersonalization, of big-business efficiency techniques, and of Texan autocrats and splinter groups from the various government agencies, not to mention an alliance between Cuban expatriates and the Mafia that seemed less unlikely as Watergate progressed. The conspiracy film's problem was to process all of these possibilities in the interest of some abstract American ideology.

The Warren Commission theory of the lone assassin came again under attack, at the time of the Nixon tapes, in *Executive Action,* which was financed by Herbert Magidson, a Los Angeles businessman with an interest in liberal causes, and coauthored (in the first version of the screenplay) by Mark Lane, the number-one conspiracy buff in the country and the author of the nonfictional *Rush to Judgment.* The film was meant as a reappraisal of evidence on the tenth anniversary of Kennedy's death, and it was produced under conditions of relative secrecy, and despite reported threats from the CIA. When released, it failed with both critics and audience. The final screenplay, by the veteran Dalton Trumbo, bore no other hero than President Kennedy, who was seen in newsreel shots and in others that were expertly simulated. The conspirators were presented as a group of reactionary patriots that included a disenfranchised CIA official (Burt Lancaster), a couple of Texas oil men (Robert Ryan and Will Geer), and other high-placed executives who had various reasons to remove Kennedy from power. Curiously there is no reasonable alternative to the president-elect, no four-star war hero or four-general junta; there is only a liberal leader who must be destroyed. In fact, Kennedy is supposed to be on the brink of signing a test-ban treaty with the Kremlin, handing the government over to Black Power, and pulling out of Vietnam. This is a target picture, no doubt about it: the only memorable scenes concern a trio of expert snipers target-shooting dummies in a moving car, and the hideously familiar drama in Dealey Plaza.

The film was released through National General rather than a major Hollywood company. There are signs of tentativeness to compromise a claim to something more than exploiting paranoia. The London *Sunday Times* had conducted a study in 1967, tabulating the odds against the deaths of eighteen material witnesses of the Kennedy assassination who died within three and a half years of the event, coming up with a figure of one hundred thousand trillion to one, and this alone could have fueled interest in having this film made, a superfreak show backed by probabilities. Judging from the liability of simulating newsreel film of the actual shooting, it is easy to deduce that the filmmakers meant to leave details and speculation where they found them, and to have the film feed the popular notion that deadly and sinister forces are at work beneath the surface of American society and politics. (Neither is there mention of the controversial 8 mm. footage shot by a non-professional witness, Abraham Zapruder, the closest to admissible evidence which could shatter the theory of the lone gunman.)

Executive Action, with its low-key, intelligent, well-defined conspirators (who would question the motives of a character played by Lancaster or Ryan? They are icons of integrity and, who knows, political murder may serve a higher reason of state that we cannot grasp at first sight) was little more than a narrative statistic—something like a Pete Smith short film on who killed Lincoln, *The Man in the Barn* (1937), that teases historical knowledge into what-if speculation. But, treading the same fictional ground, *The Parallax View* was a more rewarding reversal of the hallowed tradition of an inquisitive hero setting out to unravel an enigma of national dimensions, *North by Northwest* as imagined by Kafka, a slow drop into a bottomless pit of possibilities. This was Alan J. Pakula's second installment in a trilogy of crime pictures. In *Klute* (1973) crime was a most individual expression, the act of a deranged mind. In *The Parallax View* and *All the President's Men*, crime was the expression of a deranged nation. *Parallax*, in fact, was a fictional rehearsal for the infinitely more melodramatic, if veridical, *President's Men*, and coming in 1974, it was hopelessly mistimed.

But *The Parallax View* was a fascinating movie, formally superior to Pakula's other two films, which were more successful. It administered a *coup de grâce* to the Hollywood hero as paragon of intuition, resourcefulness, and courage; in this case a small-time reporter named Joe Frady (Warren Beatty), who has all the good qualities of the real-life Woodward and Bernstein but none of the luck. (In the seventies, fiction tends to be more pessimistic than fact: Vietnam ends up as a landscape of the mind.) Frady is cued to look into the assassination of a senator by a hysterical colleague (Paula Prentiss), who brandishes the statistics the London *Sunday Times* made so popular; the space of a cut and she is lying on a slab, dead from barbiturates, alcohol, and reckless driving. Frady finds, eventually, that the solution to this and other murders-to-be lies with the giant Parallax Corporation, which recruits not only murderers but also unsuspecting scapegoats destined to throw the new batch of "conspiracy peddlers" off the scent. Frady, in fact, belongs to the latter, and the film's agoraphobic style is the formal visualization of its theme. Much of the visual tension in Pakula's picture seems to be upward, directed toward roofs or rafters that span immense enclosures. This metaphorically locates the conspiracy in "high places" while following an expanding pattern from the vortex position of the hero; concentric circles of involvement that become more and more diffuse; the paranoid syndrome of universal malevolence encroaching on the individual.

This outward dispersion could be read as the final stages in a breakdown of the codes that first made the crime film possible, the notion that one could whittle away at evidence to end up with an unchallenged truth. It is the systematic dissolution of binary values like good / evil, right / wrong, true / false, inside society / outside society. Except for Beatty, the cast in *Parallax* is conceived as a series of bland obstacles to the hero's search for truth, nowhere as defined as villains. Even in the later works of Don Siegel, who was the outstanding practitioner of the crime genre in the fifties and early sixties, there was a comparable lack of definition between characters nominally associated with worthy or unworthy causes. In *Charlie Varrick* (1973), the Syndicate replaced the law as antagonist to the modest, likable bank robber, "the last of the independents." In *Telefon* (1977) there were two agents from the merging intelligence services of the U.S and the Soviet Union hunting a defecting third—two are ruthless, one is crazy—and the film was almost an interoffice-memo exchange of technical experts.

There is the same diluting of moral conflict, the same downgrading of cause and exaggeration of effect, in a recent spectacular variation like the doomsday-plot movie, which hinges on a great catastrophe averted at the very last minute, as in *Black Sunday* (1976). A pseudopolitical elaboration on the diagrammatic tactics of *The French Connection,* the factions are now Palestinian and Jewish (instead of Popeye *versus* Frog One), and the stake is a Miami stadium full of football fans about to be sprayed with a deadly charge of shrapnel from the old, familiar Goodyear dirigible hovering above a big game. Because political sympathies would only stand in the way of enjoying this or that splendid feat of daring, the Black September terrorist (Marthe Keller) and the Israeli intelligence officer (Robert Shaw) must be furnished with an interchangeable alibi that will justify their hatred of the other's cause, a few brief expository lines about families sacrificed in military operations; but they themselves must be shown capable of humane decisions as well as of ruthless fanaticism. Similarly, a made-for-television film like *Raid on Entebbe* (1977) called forth as much political controversy as a commercial for American Express.

There have been doomsday-plot films within the realm of historical possibility, like *The Day of the Jackal* (1973), which was about a thwarted attempt on the life of Charles De Gaulle during the Algerian War. But most of the others, like *The Parallax View* (two senators assassinated), *The Domino Principle* (the target is either Nixon or Kissinger), even *The Day of the Dolphin* (1973, a foundation supports a research project that may serve to murder the president), have been extravagant fantasies. The image that haunts Americans the most nowadays, if we judge from the films of this decade, is no longer that of the Syndicate operative—who has been metamorphosed into an avuncular businessman concerned with enlarging operations without rocking the boat—but that of his two most recently acknowledged partners in crime: the giant corporation and the government agency. New sources of threat are now found right within the establishment. The shadowiest role in the whole sinister tragicomedy of the CIA plots to assassinate Fidel Castro belongs not to Sam Giancana nor John Rosselli—who were simply expected to use their Cuban connections from Batista's day—but to Robert Maheu, once of the FBI and later an associate of Howard Hughes. Maheu is the stuff that paranoic fantasies are made of.

After the official consecration of *The Godfather,* organized crime has virtually vanished from film. Any assassination attempt, successful or not, any play truly foul, can be safely placed now at the door of the CIA, the FBI, or some giant corporation functioning as a law unto itself, or with the slightest nod of approval from higher up. When CIA Director William Colby opened up secret files to the Pike and Church committees, he not only demoralized the entire intelligence apparatus but provided crime pictures and fiction with a most serviceable villain. In *Three Days of the Condor* (1975), the hero, in charge of computerizing fiction and periodicals for the CIA, sud-

The Doomsday Plot movie is all motivation and no morals: Robert Shaw and Marthe Keller on opposite sides of the Jewish-Palestinian conflict are both justified in their hate. *Black Sunday,* 1977. *Paramount*

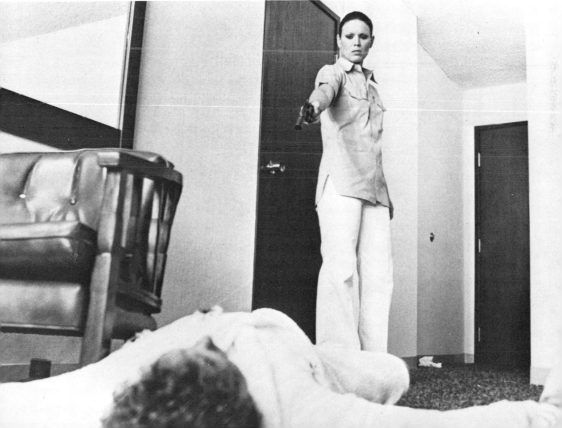

denly and inexplicably finds himself the lone survivor after his entire section is massacred by paid assassins, that is, paid by someone within the CIA. The agency would like to clean house, including compromising witnesses of interdepartmental strife, and the hero has nothing to turn to but that haven of the beleaguered seventies liberal, *The New York Times*. It won't do to call the Marines.

It is the next-to-last-minute intervention of a federal aide that provides Sidney Lumet's *Dog Day Afternoon* (1975) with a desperately needed villain to rescue the picture from wallowing in its own humanism. The screenplay (by Frank Pierson) derives from fact: on August 22, 1972, two young nonprofessionals fumbled the holdup of a Brooklyn branch of the Chase Manhattan Bank; one of them, Sal Naturile, was killed that evening by the FBI at Kennedy Airport, where the two had been lured with the promise of safe conduct to another country. The other, John Wojtowicz, was a self-admitted homosexual, estranged from his wife and kids, and a Vietnam veteran to boot. He had conceived the holdup as a way to obtain money to finance a sex-change operation for his male lover. The facts received as much coverage in *The Village Voice* as in *The Daily News*, and public reaction was sympathetic to Wojtowicz; it was simple, just a case of an average strung-out New Yorker who had cracked sooner than most. The picture that resulted proved how difficult it is these days to keep politics, especially sexual politics, out of the crime film.

Warner Brothers paid Wojtowicz, named Sonny in the film, $7,500 for his story, plus a percentage of the profits. (He was then serving a twenty-year sentence.) Lumet and Pierson tread softly until the climax, when, after reels of coddling the viewer with hysterical comedy—mostly at the expense of a typical New York media circus—an FBI agent (Lance Henriksen) cold-bloodedly refocuses the film as a crime story. Having bungled the heist, Sonny (Al Pacino) and Sal (John Cazale) hold the staff as hostages while the police lay siege to the bank. Escalation ensues, mostly instigated by Sonny, who knows the importance of the "Six O'Clock News" and how to make the sensation seekers roar on cue at the mere holler of "Attica!" As details dribble out, the Gay Liberation Front forms picket lines, and a well-meaning cop (Charles Durning) vies with a federal agent (James Broderick) for the attention of the fake desperadoes. Inside, hostages and captors are absurdly drawn to each other.

Lumet, who made his film debut in 1956 with *Twelve Angry Men* and who served his novitiate on television, is really between generations of directors, and he hardly ever employs violence, in *Dog Day Afternoon* or in *Serpico,* except to intensify highly charged confrontations. His method in *Dog Day*—which the film's success vindicates, at least for its unstable period—is to assign a sort of natural morality to an unreliable hero like Sonny and thereby appeal to the latent liberal in every spectator. He is not a director, however, who is on top of his ironies or sure of his audience. Would anyone be offended by a homosexual hero? Pacino's unrestrained bravura lacks the slightest gay mannerism. A rare moment of gravity has

Sonny on the phone to his lover (Chris Sarandon): dare anyone giggle? To make sure no one does, the women in Sonny's life are portrayed as castrating caricatures. Can *Dog Day Afternoon* be the last caper movie to win favor with a large audience? It is a story of failure as much as *Criss Cross* and *The Asphalt Jungle* were, but its hero is now the loser as criminal, which is incidental, instead of the criminal as loser, which made the existential beauty of the genre.

In the past years we have reached the age of the fragmented audience that literary critics, like Alex Comfort, prognosticated in relation to the novel thirty years ago. Filmmakers are no longer certain what kind of an audience is out there in the dark, which was not the case with old Hollywood, when a perfect symbiosis seemed to be operating. Seen today, a film by Fuller or Walsh strikes us for its absence of any hesitation; it seems to charge into the audience in a perfect rapport of creation and consensus (another possible definition of the classic American cinema). The values and certainties that were intrinsic to the form are no longer there for the filmmaker to use. This aspect of communication, between a system of conventions and an audience capable of interpreting them (even at a subconscious level), inevitably brought the movies to the attention of semiology in the past dozen years. Not by accident either, the more convincing semiological analyses deal with classic Hollywood pictures like *Young Mr. Lincoln, Morocco,* and *Sylvia Scarlett.*

It is understandable that a new generation of directors, say from the mid-sixties on, would attempt to approach filmic material from an angle other than genre, which after all presupposes values that no longer apply, and which the director must now create from scratch, or run the risk of appearing old-fashioned, sentimental, or melodramatic.

Genre is clearly in crisis. For there to be transgression, the norm must be apparent; but since the norm has been devalued, since the consensus on crime, law, and society was altered profoundly by the sixties, it can no longer effectively support a genre that thrived precisely on concepts of morality and guilt.

The crisis that affects all genres today made itself felt first in relation to the Western, the first genre to evolve in the American cinema, the best defined and most popular through Hollywood history, and, since the rehabilitation launched by the *auteur* theory, the most dissected and praised. The Western did not depend directly on topical inspiration, since its locale and chronology were drawn from a historical period already in the past when the genre began to take form, but it could be reinterpreted in the light of current developments: there was a psychological Western, an Indian Western, a McCarthy Western, and so forth.

Still, the Western declined in the early seventies, and at the moment seems to be altogether missing from production schedules, which means it has reputedly lost favor with the mass audience. The last significant Westerns, Arthur Penn's *Little Big Man* and Robert Altman's *McCabe and Mrs.*

Miller, were made at the beginning of the seventies, and they begat few others that were either widely seen or creditably detected; there are no Western series on television either. The audience seems to have no more use for the myth so long embodied in the Western. It is too fraught with distortion, although it is absurd to claim that this or that genre is inherently reactionary.

If anything, genre proposes a set of rules of conduct that present themselves as fiction but have relevance to contemporary reality. As society keeps evolving, rules change and even cease to apply. The Western surrendered its primacy to the crime film in the last decade, and at present the horror film seems to have taken the lead. The horror film alone, the most subversive of genres, continues to thrive, for it works at a nonhistorical level and attacks the basic tenets of straight society (monogamy, the sanctity of the home, sexual normality) in a way that does not depend on topical feedback, as is the case with the crime film.

But genres never disappear completely. How can they, when the problems they deal with, the modes of conduct they prescribe, the solutions they so naïvely propose are the sometimes beautiful, sometimes clumsy expressions of a period trying to define itself.

ACKNOWLEDGMENTS

I KNOW NOTHING OF STRUCTURALISM," the French filmmaker Eric Rohmer once told me in an interview, "and the best way to educate myself would be to make a documentary film about it." Likewise, the best way to learn about crime films is to write a book about them. Most of the films discussed here were already familiar to me when I undertook to write this book, but I had to watch them again from the viewpoint that the genre imposed and with particular attention to aspects that had escaped me before or failed to impress themselves on my memory. Therefore, the book proved to be a revision of a lifetime of moviegoing. Unless otherwise stated, every film discussed here was screened during the three years in which I wrote the book.

Luckily there was television, which for the sheer detachment it induces in the viewer—at least on a viewer of my generation, accustomed to losing himself in surroundings darker and less familiar than a private home—can compare with studying films on a Moviola. Also, with the help and guidance of Charles Silver, Emily Sieger, and Ron Magliozzi, dozens of films were screened for me at the Film Study Center of the Museum of Modern Art. I was lucky to live in Manhattan at the time when Roger McNiven and Howard Mandelbaum operated their exceptional CineClub—I've never seen films in more satisfying circumstances. From the library of Films Incorporated, Douglas Lemza supplied a generous selection of titles; not everyone in his position is an enlightened or concerned with film scholarship.

Bill Everson provided a number of prints, as did Bill Kenly. John Belton, Robert Ducharme, Michael Geragotelis, George Morris, Alan Rostoker, Steve Ross, Robert Smith, Eric Spilker, Ken Vose, and Jeff Wise came up with rarities at one time or another. And still it was necessary to seek out additional titles in a dozen closets and cellars, here and abroad, whose owners prefer to remain unacknowledged.

John Kobal of London supplied rare stills. Mary Corliss and Carole Carey, from the Film Stills Department of the Museum of Modern Art, came to a last-minute rescue with some more. The libraries of the Museum of Modern Art and of the Theater Collection at Lincoln Center supplied most of the cut-and-paste information inevitable in books like these: Daniel Pearl at the former, Paul Myers, Max Silverman, David Bartholomew, and Monte Arnold at the latter, were patient and trusting beyond the call of duty. Kathy Slobogin arranged for me to examine the files of *The New York*

Times. Eileen and Bill Bowser provided esoteric information not likely to be found elsewhere, as did Leonard Maltin.

The following were interviewed, sometimes between planes or during meals, and not necessarily on the subject of crime films. They all nevertheless offered useful insights or facts: Roger Corman, Henry Hathaway, John Huston, Phil Karlson, Mervyn LeRoy, David Newman, and Don Siegel.

Francis Coppola, Robert Florey, Arnold Gillespie, Howard Hawks, Charles Higham, William Keighley, Genevieve Tobin Keighley, Fritz Lang, Boris Leven, Jack Nicholson, Nicholas Ray, and Fred Roos gave of their time and memories, and were indispensable to the book.

I am most grateful to Howard Mandelbaum, for clarifying details and refreshing my memory, especially about films discussed in chapters six and seven. Don Miller's perfect recall and sense of humor also came in handy.

A number of friends provided a roof over my head at various times: Laurie Frank, Tom Gallagher, Clay Jones, Darius Kondjhi, Ricki Levenson, Michael McKee, Peter de Rome, Olivier Thual, Joel Weinberg, and William Wright.

My agent, Maxine Groffsky, made it all possible. My dedicated editor, Margaret Wolf, made the book possible to read. Ed Barber, at W. W. Norton, supervised the various phases of editing and production. Caroline Shookhoff typed the manuscript and contributed criticism and suggestions. Veronica Windholz copyedited a portion of the manuscript. Marjorie Flock designed.

To them all, my gratitude.

BIBLIOGRAPHY

Alloway, Lawrence. *Violent America: The Movies 1946–1964*. New York: The Museum of Modern Art, 1971.
Bogdanovich, Peter. *Fritz Lang in America*. London: Studio Vista, 1967.
Borde, Raymond, and Chaumeton, Etienne. *Panorama du Film Noir Américain*. Paris: Editions de Minuit, 1955.
Burch, Noel. *Theory of Film Practice*. New York: Praeger, 1973.
Coffey, Thomas M. *The Long Thirst*. New York: W. W. Norton, 1975.
Cooke, Fred J. *The FBI Nobody Knows*. New York: Macmillan, 1964.
Corliss, Richard. *Talking Pictures*. New York: The Overlook Press, 1974.
Demaris, Ovid. *The Director*. New York: Harper's Magazine Press, 1975.
Farber, Manny. *Negative Space*. New York: Praeger, 1971.
Fraser, John. *Violence in the Arts*. Cambridge, England: Cambridge University Press, 1974.
Hardy, Phil. *Samuel Fuller*. New York: Praeger, 1970.
Hays, Will H. *Memoirs*. New York: Doubleday, 1955.
Kaminsky, Stuart M. *Don Siegel: Director*. New York: Curtis Books, 1974.
Kass, Judith M. *Don Siegel*. London: The Tantivy Press, 1976.
Lawson, John Howard. *Film in the Battle of Ideas*. New York: Masses and Mainstream, 1953.
MacShane, Frank. *The Life of Raymond Chandler*. New York: Penguin, 1976.
McArthur, Colin. *Underworld USA*. London: Secker & Warburg, 1972.
McCarthy, Todd, and Flynn, Charles. *King of the Bs*. New York: E. P. Dutton, 1975.
Messick, Hank, and Goldblatt, Burt. *The Mobs and the Mafia*. New York: Ballantine, 1972.
Nash, Jay Robert. *Bloodletters and Badmen*. New York: Warner, 1973.
Nichols, Bill, ed. *Movies and Methods*. Berkeley: University of California Press, 1976.
Orwell, George. *Collected Essays, Journalism and Letters*. London: Secker & Warburg, 1968.
Pratley, Gerald. *The Cinema of John Huston*. London: A. S. Barnes, 1977.
Robinson, Edward G., and Spigelglass, Leonard. *All My Yesterdays*. New York: Hawthorn, 1973.
Schumach, Murray. *The Face on the Cutting Room Floor*. New York: William Morrow, 1964.
Todorov, Tzvetan. *Introduction à la Littérature Fantastique*. Paris: Editions du Seuil, 1970.
Warshow, Robert. *The Immediate Experience*. New York: Doubleday, 1962.
Whitehead, Don. *The FBI Story*. New York: Random House, 1956.
Wright, Will. *Sixguns and Society*. Berkeley: University of California Press, 1975.

THE FOLLOWING PERIODICALS WERE USED EXTENSIVELY: *Bright Lights, Cahiers du Cinéma, Film Comment, Films and Filming, Films in Review, Focus on Film, Movie, The New York Times, The New Yorker, Photoplay, Positif, Screen, Sequence, Sight and Sound, Take One, Time, Variety, The Velvet Light Trap.*

INDEX

Page numbers in **boldface** *refer to illustrations.*